Models of
Group Therapy
and
Sensitivity Training

Prentice-Hall Series in Personal, Clinical, and Social Psychology

Richard S. Lazarus, *Editor*

Models of
Group Therapy
and
Sensitivity Training

JOHN B. P. SHAFFER
Queens College of the City University of New York

M. DAVID GALINSKY
The University of North Carolina at Chapel Hill

Prentice-Hall, Inc., Englewood Cliffs, New Jersey

Library of Congress Cataloging in Publication Data

Shaffer, John B.P.   1934–
    Models of group therapy and sensitivity training.

    (Prentice-Hall series in personal, clinical, and
social psychology)
    Includes bibliographies.
    1. Group psychotherapy.   2. Group relations train-
ing.   I. Galinsky, M. David, joint author.   II. Title.
[DNLM: 1. Models, Psychological.   2. Sensitivity
training groups.   WM430 S525m 1974]
RC488.S45   616.8'915   74-861
ISBN 0-13-586081-4

© 1974 by Prentice-Hall, Inc.
Englewood Cliffs, New Jersey

Printed in the United States of America

20 19 18 17 16 15 14 13 12

Prentice-Hall International, Inc., *London*
Prentice-Hall of Australia, Pty. Ltd., *Sydney*
Prentice-Hall of Canada, Ltd., *Toronto*
Prentice-Hall of India Private Limited, *New Delhi*
Prentice-Hall of Japan, Inc., *Tokyo*

To Judy

and

To Dana, Michael, and Adam

Contents

Foreword

Although group dynamics, group work, and group psychotherapy are not of recent origin, this country has witnessed within the past decade a striking increase in the number of small-group experiences offered to members of the mental health professions, to counselors and educators, and to the public at large. These experiences may be labeled as "T-group," "Marathon," "Sensitivity-training," or "Encounter," and may vary from a half-day to a one- or two-week laboratory in residence; in some settings, such as a school or clinic, they are offered on a continuous, often weekly, basis over a period of months. This burgeoning of interest in the educational and therapeutic value of small-group experiences is both a measure of, and a response to, the increasing strength of what is loosely referred to as "the human potential movement." One index of the popularity of this movement is the number of growth centers that, like Esalen in California and Oasis in Chicago, have mushroomed across the nation during this period. At present over one hundred such centers exist within the United States.

Whatever the formal name given to a particular type of group interaction may be, all of the small-group structures or "models" included in this book have several elements in common: (1) they require a finite number of participants, with fairly specific limits as to minimum and maximum numbers, (2) they have clearly designated leaders or co-leaders, who in turn have definite ideas as to their role in promoting the desired group interaction, and some rationale as to what the primary content of the group interaction will be, and (3) they are designed to create for the participant an important experience, usually involving both emotional and cognitive components, that will prove instrumental in helping him toward some sort of new learning or change. Hence it is our conviction that the eleven models of group interaction surveyed here have sufficient commonality to appear together within a single volume, whether they formally fall within the fields of psychotherapy, education, or social work.

Such a survey, emphasizing the varying historical and theoretical contexts out of which each model developed, seems especially important now, when an undisciplined eclecticism on the part of some professionals and many relatively untrained leaders, in addition to an understandable confusion on the part of the general public, have resulted in a general lumping together of all small-group experience that is not psychotherapy under such umbrella terms as "encounter groups" or "sensitivity-training." A similarly eclectic trend is discernible in the fact that the National Training Laboratory, under whose aegis the T-group was born in the 1940s, now offers laboratory experiences that incorporate certain innovations found in the Encounter model as it was later developed by William Schutz at Esalen, such as an emphasis on body movement and on emotional catharsis. A likely result is that within the next few years the T-group and Encounter models may be virtually indistinguishable.

Part of our wish to clearly conceptualize each model as it existed in its pristine form is academic. We assume that the reader, having an intellectual interest in small-group practice, is curious about the *Zeitgeist* out of which a model developed and about the people who were involved in its creation. Part of our wish is practical. It seems to us that it is important for a group leader to have a clear idea of the conceptual model that he is employing and for what purpose it is to be used. Indeed, there is no reason why the skilled leader cannot be conversant with several group-models; certainly one would hope that a group leader would conduct a one-day community session to discuss the problem of drug abuse and drug control differently from the way in which he conducts his weekly, considerably smaller, psychotherapy group.

This kind of conceptual clarity would seem to be especially important in the case of the novice. One often hears statements to the effect that the well-trained group leader (let's call him John Jones) does "his particular thing" no matter what may be the formal designation of the kind of group he is leading, and that the participants in the group are being given an experience in, and demonstration of, John Jones as much as they are a demonstration of what a "T-" or "Encounter," or "Gestalt" group is like. This may be true of the skilled leader, who gradually develops a coherent, albeit idiosyncratic and intuitively employed, framework that feels "right" to him, just as it is often true of the trained psychotherapist, who may also arrive at a form of disciplined eclecticism that is uniquely his own. But where would this leader or therapist have been at the beginning of his training without any systematic model to study, introject, and assimilate? While reality and models of reality are not the same thing, a model can provide an important guide to concrete practice. It is our belief that external models, however much they may be revised, reordered, and partially discarded as a result of experience and evaluation, are still an important feature in the socialization process of the professional leader and therapist. A thorough understanding of a single, clearly conceptualized model of group interaction is still probably the best basis from which to depart in a search for one's own unique style of group-leading.

Moreover, since each model represents a specific attempt to meet a hopefully specific goal, the intelligently eclectic group leader might want to consciously incorporate features of more than one model in leading a group. For example, while the Encounter group model makes available some ingenious techniques for helping people to contact their inner feelings and fantasies, the T-group model is a powerful tool for emphasizing group cohesion and group dynamics, since its single task is to observe and process the group interaction as it occurs. The Encounter leader who is familiar with only the Encounter model will tend to neglect the powerful forces for cohesion and for autonomy that exist within any group; on the other hand, a familiarity with the T-group model would enable him to mobilize cohesive forces within the group, perhaps by his intentionally making fewer interventions early in the group, by his allowing members to take therapeutic responsibility for each other, and by his encouraging the group to examine those norms, like dependency on the leader, that might tend to minimize genuine cohesion.

One of the most formidable problems that confronted us involved a decision as to which models to include and how best to organize them. At the time that we began to write there was a bewildering variety of groups on the scene, including couples, counseling, primal-scream, transactional, rational-emotive, marathon, and bio-energetics groups. Essentially, then, our overall breakdown of group methods into eleven distinct models in itself constituted a model of sorts — our conception of how the diverse strands of current group practice could best be ordered and classified. All models are arbitrary in the sense of emphasizing certain data-clusters and neglecting others; we have no doubt that different authors would have produced a somewhat different organization of groups models. Ours emerged after considerable reflection, discussion, and revision. We believe it is the one that best fits the group scene as it existed during the preparation of the book.

Several of our group therapy models represent the extension of what was initially a model of individual psychotherapy to a group context; these are the Psychoanalytic, Existential-experiential, Gestalt therapy, and Behavior modification groups. We included them because of their historical and theoretical importance, their widespread usage, and their influence on the development of later group models, particularly the Encounter group. However, were we to have included all groups models emanating from a theory of personality or of individual treatment, we would have had to present such a bewildering array of models that the book would have lost much of its instructional value. Therefore, group models based on Adler's interpersonal therapy, Berne's transactional analysis, Ellis' rational-emotive therapy, and so on, were rejected. Family therapy was excluded because it seemed at once too specific an application of psychotherapy and too broad and complex an area to treat in a single chapter; rather it would seem to warrant a separate book in its own right.

Finally, there was a broad area of groups that seemed to fall somewhere between the Encounter and theme-centered models in that they involved a particular leader's doing "his thing" in relation to a specialized interest or focus. Such groups included Satir's communication groups, Bach's fight and pairing groups, Lowen's bio-energetics groups, etc. Here the group is centered on a particular theme, but without a conscious use of Cohn's Theme-centered model, and Encounter techniques of one kind or another are sometimes added. Yet the themes were too specific and the leader's style too idiosyncratic for such groups to fit into the Encounter model as we conceptualized it. Therefore, like many other groups currently extant, these seemed to us to constitute "hybrid" types falling into positions that are either in-between or oblique to our basic eleven models. Since we could not even begin to catalogue all such groups, it will be left to the discerning and interested reader to decide for himself where any particular leader's model falls in relation to our fundamental conceptual scheme. Consciousness-raising groups, which have constituted a prominent aspect of the Women's Liberation movement, most closely resemble Theme-centered workshops in that they have a delimited content focus and some fairly clear guidelines, or ground rules, for how the discussion should proceed. However, their procedures typically are somewhat different from that of Cohn's theme-centered model, the most noteworthy difference being the absence of a clearly designated leader.

When it came to the format for each chapter, we chose a somewhat flexible course wherein our schematic organization was specifically geared to the particular model presented. All model presentations involve a "Key Concepts" section and another section called "The Role of the Leader." Where it seems appropriate we present theoretical concepts and methodological concepts separately. Some of the chapters include an illustration of a typical group session. Others do not, especially if the model's theoretical presentation has embedded within it examples of the kinds of group interaction that it encourages, or if the model is too complex in that it comprises several sub-models and therefore is too complicated for an extended illustration to really clarify or instruct.

We have tried to present each model in an impartial and nonevaluative fashion. Our aim is for the reader to understand the rationale of a model from the point of view of its creators and to appreciate what the creators perceive the model's unique assets to be. It is only in the final chapter that we attempt to compare the various models to each other and to point out some of their relative strengths and weaknesses.

A final cautionary note: this book is not designed to stand on its own as a training manual for group leaders. Because it concerns models of group interaction and because the kind of interaction that occurs in a group is strongly affected by its leadership, we have included some discussion of leadership techniques and interventions. We consider it extremely irresponsible for any professional who has not had supervised experience in leading such groups to think that on the basis of the information presented in this book or in others he could attempt to lead groups. Our position on this matter is subscribed to by the proponents of all the models included in this book, with the single exception of the Encounter model, where there is some vagueness as to what constitutes adequate training for leadership and where some proponents actively encourage "lay" leadership. Our misgivings about this stance are stated in the concluding chapter.

The book, then, is addressed to professionals and students who would use it as a part of structured learning in the area, as well as to those lay readers who have an intellectual interest in learning about the various group models presented.

ACKNOWLEDGMENTS

Several people and organizations have been of invaluable help in the inspiration and preparation of this book. Ruth Cohn's abiding interest in a comparative approach to group-leading concepts, along with the Workshop Institute for Living-Learning's seminar in Models of Group Interaction, helped to set the stage for the conceptualization and organization of our material. At the point where we had outlined what an adequate survey of the major group-leading approaches would look like, Ed Lugenbeel of Prentice-Hall, and Dick Greenbaum, gave encouragement and active support. Once we got down to the hard writing, Dave Singer, Larry Gould, and Jay Seeman helped us to find out what we had not yet learned about the Tavistock approach to groups. And when it came to rendering frequently revised chapters into a coherent manuscript, we received crucial service from Shirley Talley, Jenny Rominger, Jean McCoy Roberts, and Joan Daniel. We also want to express gratitude to Blanche Critcher for assisting in our work in many ways.

Lastly, we want to express very special appreciation to our wives, Maeda Galinsky and Judith Shaffer, for critical review of portions of the manuscript, editing, proofreading, and continued support throughout the project.

John B. P. Shaffer
M. David Galinsky

Models of
Group Therapy
and
Sensitivity Training

1

Historical Introduction and Overview

Modern group methods can be divided into two broad areas: group psychotherapy and human relations training. The human relations area involves groups whose purpose we view as personal growth and development, such as the T-group and the Encounter group, which we treat in separate chapters. We also include within our Human Relations—or "Growth and Development"—category two lesser known models, the Tavistock Small Study Group and the Theme-centered Interactional Method.

THE DEVELOPMENT OF GROUP PSYCHOTHERAPY

The first model that we present is the social work group. While having a more community-based and reality-oriented purpose than the typical therapy group, the earliest social work group, bringing together as it did people having common social, economic, and personal problems, was an historic forerunner of modern group psychotherapy. Probably its earliest and most dramatic milestone was the opening of Jane Adams' Hull House in 1889. On the basis of the model set by Hull House, the early phase of group work developed primarily as a means of providing help for the increasingly large number of people served by settlement houses in the late nineteenth and early twentieth centuries. With social reform as a guiding ideal and overall emphasis, self-help groups were organized to agitate for better housing, recreation, and working conditions. Later other kinds of social agencies, including religiously supported private organizations like Catholic Charities and Jewish Family Service, became integrally involved with the development of group work. Slowly the field began to include groups that were concerned with the immediate personal needs of its members, as well as with the amelioration of adverse

1

social conditions within the surrounding community, thereby moving somewhat closer to the more individually oriented focus that characterizes most
psychotherapy groups. However, social group work has never abandoned its
fundamental interest in the larger social community in which group members
have common origins which in turn provide them a basis for shared needs and
goals. In this sense the group work models bear some likeness to those of the
later therapy and Growth and Development groups that emphasize the group
participants' membership in a common social system or organization—for
example, the Group Dynamic Therapy, the T-, and the Theme-centered
models.

As if to bear out the fine line existing between social group work and
group psychotherapy, the group that is traditionally credited with constituting
the first therapy group proper was one in which members clearly shared both
a common problem or symptom—tuberculosis—and a similar, somewhat im-
poverished, environment. Yet, while having some resemblance to the group
worker's group, this assemblage of tubercular patients, because it was created
under the aegis of medicine and conducted by a physician, formally fell under
the heading of "treatment." It began in 1905, when Joseph Hersey Pratt, a
Boston Internist, developed the "home sanatorium treatment" of consumption
at the Massachusetts General Hospital Outpatient Clinic; virtually all histories
of group therapy now credit Pratt with being the first practitioner of modern
group therapy. Designed for poor patients who were unable to afford
in-patient treatment, Pratt's program organized out-patients into groups, or
"classes," of roughly twenty people. Realizing that these disheartened people
needed encouragement and supervision, Pratt directed his initial efforts at the
kind of psychological approach that is often described as inspirational,
persuasive, and supportive. He checked on the patients' progress and made
precise specifications with regard to matters concerning diet, rest, and sleep;
he was at pains to show them that even in a slum environment they could
approximate some of the elements of outdoor living emphasized in the
sanatorium treatment of tuberculosis.

As time went on Pratt became more sophisticated about the psychological aspects of the group interaction. He appreciated the importance of an
atmosphere of mutual support created by patients having a "common bond in
a common disease" (Spotnitz, 1961, p. 29), a factor that all forms of group
psychotherapy emphasize as therapeutic, and he stressed the beneficial influence that one patient, especially if he were improving in health, could have
upon another. When in 1918 another physician, a psychiatrist named
Edward W. Lazell, used a lecture approach to war veterans diagnosed as
schizophrenic, medical group therapy was extended to patients suffering from
psychological disorders, and soon these patients' overall life adjustment, rather
than their specific psychiatric symptom, was to be defined as a legitimate
focus of the group's attention.

Up until this point, methodology had taken precedence over formal theory in the development of therapy groups, and theoretical rationales tended to be subsumed under a common-sense framework emphasizing the usefulness of instruction, advice, support, and mutual identification among members. Gradually, under the impetus of such figures as Trignant Burrows, Louis Wender, and Paul Schilder, the therapy group was viewed more and more within the conceptual framework of psychoanalysis, which had already had great influence as a theory of individual personality and individual treatment. Burrows referred to his procedures as "group analysis," Wender observed that transference phenomena developed within groups just as in individual analysis, and Schilder, in an attempt to incorporate the Freudian technique of free association, encouraged his group-patients to discuss whatever came to their minds.

The consolidation of the psychoanalytic group model was left to the work of Samuel Slavson, Alexander Wolf, and Emanuel Schwartz. Slavson's initial experiments with groups had begun in his work with children and adolescents at the Jewish Board of Guardians during the 1930s. His orientation was a product of his personal experience as a psychoanalytic patient and his earlier employment in progressive education and recreational group work. He eventually came to call his approach Activity Group Therapy, since it emphasized the importance of expression of the child's conflicts and pent-up feelings through sports, games, arts and crafts, and other recreational activities. Subsequent outgrowths of Activity Group Therapy involved play group therapy for preschool children, "activity-interview" therapy for older children, and finally "interview group therapy," which—since it emphasized communication via words rather than action or play—was essentially a form of analytic group therapy (Slavson, 1950).

Alexander Wolf, a psychiatrist and psychoanalyst, had become interested in group therapy during the early 1930s. Although no formal training in groups was available at that time, he read whatever was available, mainly the work of figures already mentioned—Burrow, Schilder, and Wender. In 1938 he decided to experiment; he approached five men and five women who were patients of his and suggested that they enter a psychotherapy group. Within a year he was running four such groups. By 1947 Wolf had started to hold seminars in psychoanalytic group therapy at the New York Medical College. World War II had played an important role in stimulating an awareness of group therapy among younger psychotherapists in the armed services, since it enabled them to treat more patients than they would have been able to treat on an individual basis. After the war many of these men were themselves becoming patients in therapy groups in order to intensify their training. In 1948 Wolf began a similar training workshop at the Postgraduate Center for Mental Health, then called the Postgraduate Center for Psychotherapy. One of his early students was Emanuel Schwartz, who was also to join the staff of the Postgraduate Center and who coauthored with Wolf two books on what they prefer to call "psychoanalysis in groups" (Wolf and Schwartz, 1962 and Wolf et al. 1970). By 1954 the Postgraduate Center had introduced a certification program in group therapy; psychoanalytic group therapy, now regarded as a specialization requiring formal training, had come of age.

More than any other writers in the field, Slavson, Wolf, and Schwartz stood for a systematic application of psychoanalytic concepts, particularly resistance, transference, and interpretation, to the group context. Although acknowledging that the presence of other patients added an extremely important variable to the treatment process, these analysts insisted that the ever more diverse and complex data of the group setting could still be subsumed and accounted for by orthodox analytic concepts or principles. The therapeutic task remained that of interpreting to the patient how his current attitudes toward the therapist and other people reflected both a defensive resistance to awareness and insight, and an inappropriate carrying-over from the past, or transference, of his earlier, often fearful, ways of relating to his parents. Now that there were other people present in therapy these interpersonal attitudes could be more dramatically evidenced in a number of different interactions. As in individual psychoanalytic treatment, the most penetrating and effective interpretations were believed to be those that connected an ongoing emotional reaction in the treatment situation itself to a remembered, emotionally significant interaction pattern with important figures of the past. The closest the group psychoanalysts came to a revision of their concepts was in the introduction of the term "multiple transference," which was designed to take into account the fact that in the group setting a patient's "transference" now manifested itself not only in relationship to the analyst but to the other group members as well. In other words, these analysts were claiming that in psychoanalytic group therapy the single most important unit of conceptual analysis was to remain that of the individual personality, even though this personality was now being treated in a multi-person, as opposed to two-person, setting. Their remarks were specifically directed against advocates of a group-dynamics approach to psychotherapy, namely Foulkes, Bion, and Ezriel in Great Britain, who emphasized the importance of viewing the group as a coherent entity with its own inherent laws. The psychoanalytic approach insisted that the latters' concentration on group phenomena, while perhaps appropriate for training groups designed for the teaching of group dynamics, constituted an inappropriate conceptual emphasis in the case of therapy groups, where the individual patient and his psycho-dynamics must always remain the primary focus of conceptualization.

Needless to say, Foulkes, Bion, and Ezriel disagreed, along with two American group therapists, Whitaker and Lieberman, who developed their own model of a group-dynamics approach to group psychotherapy. Interestingly enough, these theorists viewed themselves as never really departing from a psychoanalytic orientation, since they had been trained within it, subscribed to many of its conceptions of personality structure and personality development, and viewed psychological symptoms as a compromise between the expression of an impulse and the defense against it. Nevertheless they insisted that group psychotherapy must develop theoretical concepts that were germane to groups in their own right and not borrowed from the psychology of individuals, and they suggested that an appreciation of social psychology, wherein the group as a whole is regarded as a discrete entity, be added to the group therapist's background in clinical psychology or psychiatry.

The concept of the group as a genuine, organized, and dynamic organism in its own right, comparable to the integrity of the individual personality, was and probably still is difficult for many people to accept and for some even smacked, however subtly, of fascistic and totalitarian connotations (Denes-Radomisli, 1971). This difficulty is probably in part due to current psychological and ideological conceptions of man that place high value on his individualism and personal autonomy, and in part due to the fact that the single personality, as a function and property of a biologically distinct human being, is more easily envisaged as a separate force in its own right than is the more physically diffuse group. Yet the concept of an organized and coherent "personality," like that of "the group-as-a-whole," is still a hypothetical construct, and like other such constructs—e.g., the "ego" or the "self"—has no essential correspondence to physical reality. Hence, just as personality could be seen by some theorists as a constellation of "introjects" or "selves," the group could be similarly viewed as a constellation of individual selves or persons. The behavior of any one person in the group could not then be viewed as independent from the behavior of any other person or from the group interaction in general. Such a view has gained wider credence in psychiatry in recent years as the notions of "general systems theory" have become more familiar in clinical circles (Durkin, 1972). The single clinical area that has received the most direct application of systems concepts has been family therapy, wherein the family is seen within the framework of a transactional communication network in which a child's behavior is in part a function of his parents' marital interaction, their interaction in part a function of his behavior, and so on.

General systems theory, however, was just beginning to be developed at the time that Foulkes and Bion were applying their experience with British Army therapy groups to civilian groups in the immediate post-World War II era. Instead these men found Lewin's field theory, which may be viewed as an earlier prototype of general systems theory, to be the most suitable conceptual framework for their purpose and they proceeded to combine psychoanalytic and field theory principles into the various combinations that constitute the three group-dynamic therapy models to be presented in Chapter Four. The practical effect of this theoretical focus was that the group therapist now carefully attended to the group interaction with an eye not so much toward what it revealed about the pathology or characteristic behaviors of each individual patient, but to the overall theme or group-tension that it revealed to be common to all the patients. This "group process," carefully nurtured and guided by the therapist, was seen to be the significant curative factor in treatment, rather than insightful interpretations directed toward a single patient's psychodynamics; hence the therapist's task was to attend to group process variables as much as to the content of individual members' concerns. Only by doing the former successfully could he make interventions that would keep group tensions and group avoidances in a state of optimum balance wherein members would feel encouraged to express themselves, but not at the cost of overwhelming anxiety or threat.

The next major group therapy model that was a clear departure from the psychoanalytic group was the existential-experiential model. It was largely an outgrowth of an existential approach to psychiatry and psychopathology that had originated in Europe, particularly in the work of Ludwig Binswanger and Medard Boss, and that subsequently became better known in the United States through the publication of *Existence,* edited by May, Angel, and Ellenberger (1958). This model's development was also stimulated by the contributions of certain American psychotherapists, among them Rogers (1967) and Whitaker and Malone (1953), who had already been experimenting with a more experiential approach to psychotherapy wherein the therapist permitted himself a greater openness and a more emotionally intense way of relating to his patient.

Like the group-dynamic therapy model, the existential-experiential model is psychoanalytic in its basic conceptual roots because of its fundamental grounding in the concept of unconscious motivation. What was new in its approach was a strongly humanistic dimension that emphasized ontological concepts involving the patient's "being" and the fundamental irreducibility of his psychological experience. While acknowledging that there were unconscious ramifications in what a patient verbalized, the existential analyst rejected a simplistic reductionism wherein a person's conscious experience was viewed as a mere surface "screen" for invisible, unfathomable forces. According to these analysts, a readiness to "interpret" and "analyze" a patient's inner life tended to make the therapist a greater expert on what the patient was "really" experiencing than he himself was, thereby reducing the patient to an object. Instead, any investigation of the unconscious had to have as its starting point a deep, abiding interest in and respect for the patient's view of himself and his world; this was always the primary datum and in this sense the existential-experiential approach was strongly phenomenological.

The experientialism of this approach had a reciprocal aspect in that the therapist's feeling reactions to the patient were to be as open and shared a part of the therapeutic transaction as was the patient's experience of him. The experientialists, while not denying elements of transference and fantasy within the therapist-patient relationship, also wanted to acknowledge the profoundly real aspects of this relationship; their emphasis was on the mutuality of an authentic "I-thou" encounter between two living, experiencing—and therefore inherently equal—human beings. Hence for them the "blank screen" emphasis of the Freudians, wherein the therapist attempted to de-emphasize his reality as a person, was a myth that could not succeed in hiding the fact that everything he did (or neglected to do), including his nonverbal behavior, revealed his fundamental being to the patient; it was this essential quality of his "being"—the person who the therapist was in the most fundamental sense—that was the crucial ingredient in therapy, rather than the specific characteristics of his technique. Such a conception helped the therapist to feel freer to relate in spontaneous and intuitive ways, to share with the patient his fantasies about him, and to perhaps even admit his irritation with some of the patient's resistances. A greater give-and-take between patient and therapist in individual therapy naturally extended to group treatment, where the therapist could now from time to time assume the role of another patient in the group, in the sense of acknowledging some of his own personal concerns, and each member could become more fluid in his expression of his feelings, in his ability to move from fantasy to reality and back again, and in his opportunity to now react to the feelings and fantasies about himself revealed by the therapist.

As had been the case with the psychoanalytic model, the existential-experiential model moved from its origins in individual therapy to an application to groups without its proponents feeling the need for any fundamental theoretical reorientation. They did not see any particular usefulness in a specifically group-dynamics focus in their groups, and in fact did not address themselves to this issue. In general, the overt methodology of experiential groups did not differ markedly from that of the psychoanalytic group; unlike the Psychodrama and Gestalt therapy models, which we are about to discuss, communication was primarily verbal and spontaneous, the analyst was nondirective, and patients continued to feel free to narrate in a conventional fashion "there-and-then" problems from their outside living. The difference in outlook between an analytic and an experiential approach related more to fairly subtle aspects of the therapist's basic attitude toward the patient and toward his therapeutic task. This shift, however, was eventually to lead to more and more behavioral freedom on the part of both therapist and patient, and thereby to become one of the several factors influencing the subsequent development of the Encounter model.

The next model to be considered is Psychodrama. In a strict historical sense it is the oldest model extant, since it had been given some systematic formulation by its founder, Jacob Moreno, as early as 1910. As a pre-medical student, he spent time walking in the gardens of Vienna where he observed the seemingly therapeutic effect on children of their own spontaneous fantasy play, which often involved symbolic re-enactment of difficult family situations. Indeed, Psychodrama had taken on the properties of a formal model or system by 1921, when Moreno opened his Theatre of Spontaneity in Vienna, and it was Moreno who in 1932 first coined the term "group psychotherapy." However, the influence of Psychodrama on the development of group therapy as a whole has been diffuse, and certainly less pronounced than that of the psychoanalytic and experiential models. The method's greatest impact has been on the creation of a specific technique, usually referred to as "role-playing," that is frequently employed by group leaders in conjunction with a variety of other procedures; this technique is employed most often by leaders of growth and development groups, but it is also used by eclectic group therapists, social group workers, behaviorally oriented group leaders, and innovative classroom teachers. Because this influence is usually not acknowledged, Moreno's feeling that his contributions have been slighted and underestimated by most official histories of group methods seems quite justified. Somewhat less prominent on the contemporary scene is the pure Psychodrama group, in which role-enactment techniques are used exclusively. Most of the therapists who practice in this manner have been trained either directly by Moreno or at the Moreno Institute in New York. Even here it is our impression that many of these therapists are beginning to combine Psychodrama techniques with some of the methods introduced by other group models, particularly Gestalt and Encounter.

Probably the most significant emphases introduced by Moreno involved those of action, emphathic identification, and catharsis. While almost all approaches of group psychotherapy from Pratt onward had assumed that opportunities for mutual support and identification among members were therapeutically useful, it remained to Moreno's theoretical framework to take into most systematic account the specific relationship between the patient whose problems were being highlighted at any particular time (the "protagonist") and the rest of the group (the "audience"). The processes whereby audience members, through empathic identification with the protagonist, gain help from him and, through their assumption of "auxiliary ego" roles, also give help to him, received careful attention in this model. Such a conceptualization was bound to bear on the processes involved in most therapy and training groups, for although Psychodrama made the protagonist's role more formal, almost all models of group interaction, from Psychoanalytic through Encounter, involve a scenario in which one particular member, for however brief a period, assumes "stage center" while the remainder of the group focuses on him.

Moreno's basic concern was to help a patient translate his specific psychological problems into a here-and-now, dramatic recapitulation of an important aspect of his life situation, so that both he and others could experience it in concrete, vivid, and visual terms, much as a sleeper's concerns are translated into dramatic, tangible form via his dreams. He chose the method of dramatic action, whereas both the analytic and experiential models encouraged patients to talk *about* their problem in discursive, narrative, "there-and-then" ways, just as one might recount the plot of a play rather than enact it. Moreno's action technique was to have a very important influence on how Perls, in his founding of Gestalt technology, and Schutz, in his formulation of Encounter technique, were eventually to attempt to help group participants communicate their deepest feelings and conflicts. Central to this entire action method was the notion of catharsis—the belief that the protagonist, through a more masterful and effective living-through of past events in a dramatic form, could achieve the therapeutic release of hitherto unexpressed feelings. According to Moreno, Freud and Breuer—the two earliest psychoanalysts—had too quickly abandoned the hypnotic method through which several of their patients had succeeded in achieving crucially therapeutic catharses.

As we suggested above, a strong methodological connection exists between Moreno's Psychodrama and Perls' Gestalt therapy, one that is greater than Perls seemed willing to admit. Indeed, the Gestalt format might be described as an essentially psychodramatic technique in which the same participant enacts all the major "roles" in his life, although in order to have an apt analogy we need to re-define roles in such a way that they include not only the patient himself and the other significant people in his life, but also aspects of himself, such as particular feelings, body-parts, and introjects. However, while both Moreno and Perls consciously introduced a highly theatrical metaphor into their therapies, it should be pointed out that there are some fundamental philosophical differences between their respective approaches.

Perls' approach differed from Moreno's not only in its conceptual heritage (which was more rooted in formal psychological theory than was Psychodrama), but also in its essential aim, for Gestalt was consistently and solely directed toward effecting changes in the patient's awareness and not in encouraging specific means by which he could approach life situations differently. It is true that Psychodrama also attempted to concern itself with intrapsychic change, especially in its emphasis on catharsis; yet its encourage-ment of rehearsals, particularly of pressing present and future events, bordered on an attempt to help the patient "solve" some of his interpersonal problems via different or more adaptive behavior, and actually foreshadowed the behavioral group therapy model (Chapter 8), which was to place even more emphasis on the "practicing" of specific behaviors. This kind of concrete prescription for change—or what Perls called a "program"—was something that he eschewed. Instead the focus in Gestalt therapy was always to be on what *is*, the moment-to-moment flow of awareness, and not on the "should be's" or "might have been's" of a patient's life.

The therapist's task was to help the patient get in greater contact with his awareness continuum, through a variety of techniques that often involved an exaggeration of certain mannerisms and behaviors, including nonverbal ones, and his skill lay in his ability to circumvent the patient's typical employment of various avoidances, including interpersonal "games," as a way of avoiding emotionally painful areas. One means by which he facilitated the patient's awareness task was to minimize the amount of stimulation or group pressure impinging on the latter's phenomenological experience; in order to accomplish this the group was discouraged from interacting with the patient while he and the therapist were working together. In this respect, the Gestalt model goes further than does any other model in isolating the patient "protagonist" from his "audience." Despite the fact that the overt action of the group was now confined to a therapist-patient dialogue, Perls found the group format to be highly advantageous, first because the presence of other people gave the therapist an opportunity to explore some of the patient's typical interpersonal distortions and fantasy "projections" in a direct and immediate way, and second because the other group members, as a kind of empathic "Greek chorus," could learn from and resonate with the patient's highly emotional experience (Denes-Radomisli, 1971). It was only a matter of time before group models that did encourage spontaneous member-to-member interaction began to incorporate specific Gestalt techniques into their methodology—e.g., Schutz's Open Encounter (Schutz, 1971).

In turning our attention to the final group therapy model that we present—the Behavioral approach—we introduce a school of psychology that, like psychoanalysis, has had an enormous influence on the social sciences in general, particularly as they have developed in the United States. Unlike psychoanalysis, however, behaviorism was to have its initial primary impact outside the fields of psychotherapy and of clinical psychology altogether. Founded by an American Psychologist, John Watson, during the 1920s and building on Pavlov's historic discovery of conditioning phenomena in both animals and humans, behaviorism saw one's entire personality as a complex constellation of specific stimulus-response connections that had been sequentially learned over the long period of individual development. Because of its fundamental foundation in animal learning, which could be studied under precise and controlled laboratory conditions, behaviorism developed as a part of experimental psychology and its initial thrust was in the area of basic research. However its emphasis on man as responding stably and differentially to the various stimulus properties of his environment was bound to have important applications to both education and psychotherapy. If a troubled individual could be reconditioned through a reordering of the stimuli to which he was exposed, new, more adaptive, "response hierarchies" could be established. Consequently, the emergence of "Behavior modification" as an alternative approach to psychotherapy was one of the most significant developments within the field of clinical psychology during the late fifties and early sixties.

Although Behavior modification, like most approaches to psychotherapy, initially had individual therapy as its main area of application, it was inevitable that it gradually become extended to a group context. Groups were seen as especially appropriate in handling more complex social behaviors involving shyness, assertiveness, and excessive anxiety around anger. In encouraging the patient to try out new behavior in repetitive and unsatisfying life situations, a behavioral approach has an obvious likeness to Psychodrama, as we briefly indicated above. In both Psychodrama and the Behavioral Practice group, role-playing has a prominent part, and a naive observer watching selected segments from both group approaches might well find them indistinguishable. Indeed, some practitioners of Behavioral Practice groups have acknowledged an indebtedness to the earlier model. In actuality, though, there are distinct differences between these two approaches, and these contrasts are not surprising in view of the fact that philosophically these models have quite divergent views of man. For example, Psychodrama emphasizes spontaneity, free expression, and a loosely organized format, whereas structured and clearly articulated goals for specific behavior change are central to the behaviorally-oriented group. Moreoever, Psychodrama, although concerned with behavior in specific life situations, also aims for intrapsychic changes, particularly those that result from catharsis, with the hope that these inner changes will subsequently and spontaneously, via unconscious processes, lead to different, not-to-be-prescribed behavior in the future, whereas the behavioral group therapist, through the practice of prescribed behavior, attempts to add concrete new responses to the patient's behavior repertoire.

GROWTH AND DEVELOPMENT GROUPS

The final four models to be considered — Tavistock, T-, Encounter, and Theme-centered — are best classified as Human Relations, or Growth and Development, groups. By this we mean groups that are not specifically designed for the rehabilitation of people suffering from specific psychological or psychiatric symptoms, but instead for relatively normal people who are looking for an experience that will enhance their personal living, particularly as it involves relating to others. Both the Psychodrama and Gestalt models, though formally therapy groups, form a useful bridge to a consideration of growth and development models, for both of them began to introduce essentially normal nonpatients into their membership as a way of demonstrating, particularly to professional therapists and counselors, the therapeutic value of their methods. Indeed, in many instances Gestalt and Psychodrama groups have been run as relatively brief training institutes, lasting anywhere from a day to a week, rather than as ongoing therapy groups.

The two earliest growth and development models were the Tavistock "small study" group and the T-group. They differ in both national and conceptual heritage, Tavistock having originated in Great Britain within a psychoanalytic framework, and the T-group in the United States within the scope of behavioral-science theory. Yet both owed something to the seminal work of Kurt Lewin, and they had much in common: both were directed toward helping people to become more knowledgeable about group-dynamics; both saw the learning group's task as that of studying its own behavior; both attempted to keep this learning group as unstructured as possible, claiming that the elimination of the hierarchies, fixed agendas, and quasi-parliamentary procedures found in most traditional working groups would force to the surface those latent group issues and tensions that such routinization normally suppresses; and both embedded this small group as a kind of basic foundation, or core learning experience, within a larger institute-structure—called a "conference" by Tavistock, and a "laboratory" by T- —in which other formal groupings also took place, including didactic sessions, large group events, and meetings between two or more smaller groups.

The Tavistock small study group was actually an outgrowth of the group-dynamic psychotherapy mentioned earlier. The author of the Tavistock method, Wilfred Bion, had adopted—along with his compatriots, Foulkes and Ezriel—an approach to psychoanalytic group therapy that encouraged the analyst to pay careful attention to those forces in the group that made for either greater or less cohesion. Bion, however, who was essentially a theorist, found himself becoming more and more interested in the ways in which all groups, whether large or small, therapy or nontherapy, went about their respective tasks, whatever their nature. The theory that he eventually arrived at attempted to establish universal laws of group behavior and group development and viewed all groups as characterized by a delicate balance between progressive and regressive forces (Bion, 1959). The small study group would be no exception; however, unlike other groups, its only function would be to scrutinize the data of its own behavior in order to formulate the principles that best accounted for them. True to its psychoanalytic tradition, the Tavistock model was essentially making a "patient" out of the group, since the patient in psychoanalysis is similarly encouraged to carefully examine his own feelings and his own behavior during the session in order to better understand his underlying transference. And indeed, the group was treated very much like a single person or entity in this model, since the leader's interpretations were always pitched to the group as a whole, rather than to any of its individual members.

The T-group was also concerned with group processes and with encouraging a group to become aware of its own dynamics as a group. However, unlike the Tavistock model, the T-group also attended to how individual participants differentiated themselves from one another in terms of particular roles taken within the group structure; for example, some members were quick to emerge as leaders whereas others seemed destined to follow, and according to this model these personality differences constituted important data that were to be looked at and talked about by the group. The initial conceptualization and development of the T-group—or "laboratory method," as it is sometimes called—can be attributed to four men: Kurt Lewin and Ronald Lippitt, both social psychologists, and Leland Bradford and Kenneth Benne, both educators. Since Lewin was not only one of the original founders of the model, but also father of the group-dynamics movement in which T-group methodology was initially grounded, it is he to whom primary credit for the model's authorship is usually given. It was Lewin who had first made the study of small-group processes academically respectable and who, through his emphasis on "action research" (Marrow, 1969, p. 158), had encouraged researchers to become actively involved and enmeshed in the very social forces they were bent on studying; in a sense, this approach constituted an application to the social sphere of what, in the area of individual behavior and individual therapy, Sullivan had called "participant-observation" (1953, pp. 13-14). While Lewin's group-dynamics approach had already had an impact on the group-dynamics school of group therapy, this had occurred primarily through the dissemination of his writings, and thus had been an indirect influence. The T-group constituted the one model or group interaction with which he was to become personally involved, although he was to die shortly after its initial planning.

Just as the settlement house constituted the applied setting for the development of social group work, and the psychiatric hospital and clinic the background setting for group therapy, business and industry constituted the backdrop for the creation of T-groups. The idea of the model grew out of a conference held in Connecticut in 1946 that had been designed to help business and community leaders implement the Fair Employment Practices Act. At this conference task groups composed of these leaders had been formed for the purpose of discussing the improvement of intergroup relations, and the use of groups in developing closer relations among communities. The research arm of the conference was led by Lewin and Lippitt, who held discussions with research personnel in the evening about what could be learned from their observations of the task groups that had met during the day.

Soon it became apparent that the most exciting group discussions were those of the evening research meetings, particularly when participants from the afternoon groups began to attend and to register some dissent, not only as to the accuracy of the observations that had been made of their behavior in the afternoon groups but also as to the interpretations offered to explain this behavior. As these discussions became more heated, Lewin and his coworkers started to see in them the germs of a related, but more dynamic group—i.e., a "training group" (soon to be shortened to "T-group"). Members would have the dual purpose of participating in a group at the same time that they studied their participation and would thus be able to better understand both group process in general and their own individual styles of relating to groups. Such a group would bring into simultaneous operation the processes of participation and observation that the Connecticut conference had separated into two distinct phases, the afternoon group for participation, and the evening group for observation. The sole task of the group would be to understand and to learn from the data of its own behavior. No other agenda would be placed before it, and it would be up to the group to decide how best to proceed with its not too well defined task. The group leader, or "trainer," would not fulfill the group's probable expectations of how a leader should behave, and would instead, in a more indirect and Socratic fashion, ask the kinds of questions and make the kinds of comments that would help the group *learn how to learn* from its experience. Because the group would thus be placed in as pure a culture as possible, the covert group dynamics normally obscured by the pressures, agenda, and structures of ongoing business and bureaucratic groups would be thrown into bolder relief. As a result the participant would hopefully return to his back-home organization with an increased understanding of the processes that can impede a group's performance of its task, and more specifically of how he himself often unwittingly contributes to these impediments. In this sense the changing of systems was as much a goal of the model as was the changing of individuals, although the latter had to be an essential focus if the former was to be achieved. And so the T-group was born.

The path from the T-group to the Encounter group is a complex one. Yet, despite the fact that several other developments also influenced the evolution of the Encounter group, there can be no doubt that the T-group was its most direct precursor. Indeed, many of the men who were subsequently to become strongly involved in the Encounter movement, like William Schutz and Jack Gibb, had initially been trained as T-group leaders by the National Training Laboratory (NTL), the official organization of T-group theorists and trainers. Probably the first significant step taken by NTL toward the direction of Encounter was the introduction into its curriculum of T-groups "with a personal-interpersonal focus"; these groups were to be distinguished from the original form of the model described above, which was now identified by NTL as a T-group having "a group relations and organizational emphasis." Also related was the development of the NTL "Microlab" (Schutz and Seashore, 1972, pp. 191-193), in which a series of verbal and

nonverbal exercises were employed to create intensive interpersonal interactions in a much briefer period of time than was required by the less
structured conditions of the T-group. Still another step was the growing
interest of Carl Rogers in what he called the "intensive group experience"
(Rogers, 1967). Rogers had become interested in using groups as a vehicle for
training graduate students in counseling procedures as early as 1946; although
not directly involved in NTL training he began to develop groups that
resembled T-groups in the sense of being geared toward relatively healthy
people who did not have to be in the helping professions in order to
participate. The intensive group experience, however, was directed more
toward helping a person find genuine authenticity in his manner of relating to
others, and to himself, than it was toward helping him develop either
interpersonal "skill" or an increased understanding of group dynamics. The
slowly evolving Encounter group gradually carried this increasingly personalized dimension to its ultimate extent, with the result that there was an
eventual dropping away of any attempt to teach the participant about group
dynamics or to help him relate his group experience to his outside work
situation. Instead, through rather direct confrontation and through a variety
of specific techniques including Psychodrama, Gestalt therapy exercises, and
guided fantasy, he would be encouraged to encounter the "true" feeling self
that lay hidden beneath his social and professional facades. No wonder, then,
that by the late 1960s industry had begun to find that for every executive
who returned from sensitivity-training (now having an Encounter focus) as a
more competent functionary, there was one who, on the basis of his
small-group experience, had decided to leave the company (Calame, 1969).

Given the temper of the times, it was probably inevitable that the
T-group experience would increasingly be used as a means of self-expression
and of a self-discovery that went beyond the issue of one's on-the-job
functioning to the question of what kind of work one most wanted to do, or
of whether one wanted to work at all! Since most people attending T-groups,
however "normal" and however wary lest they reveal too much, were
sufficiently alienated by society-at-large to experience considerable gratification from the emotional intensity that group sessions typically provided and
to find themselves fascinated by the opportunity to learn more about
themselves, only the most concerted discipline on the part of T-group
developers and trainers could have prevented the model's group-process and
organizational focus from becoming diffused. Several other strains within the
society, all of which were interrelated, also hastened the shift to an Encounter
focus in growth and development groups: an increasing interest in humanistic
psychology, which rejected both the conditioning emphasis of behaviorism and
the deterministic attitude of psychoanalysis, and instead developed an existential thrust emphasizing man's freedom to choose; an emphasis on
mysticism and Eastern religions, particularly Zen Buddhism, wherein some of

the traditional dichotomizations of Western thought were seriously questioned—e.g., subject vs. object, man vs. nature, inner (psychological) reality vs.
outer (real) reality, sick vs. well, and life vs. death; and the evolution of a
counter-culture that challenged the validity of rational-bureaucratic values and
roles, championing instead the expansion of consciousness through a variety of
means, including Yoga, meditation, and drugs. By the early 1960s Carl Rogers
was referring to the intensive group experience that he led as the "Basic
Encounter group" (Rogers, 1967), and William Schutz was soon to arrive at
Esalen Institute, where he eventually would develop his "Open Encounter"
variant of the small-group experience (Schutz, 1971).

The Encounter group, unlike its T-predecessor, did not take pains to
make a careful distinction between its purposes and those of therapy groups.
Indeed, Encounter eschewed the medical model of disease and treatment
altogether, and insisted instead that all of twentieth-century man was in
desperate need for revitalization and renewed contact with himself. As such, it
cannot be divorced from earlier therapy models, and we therefore view it as a
logical, almost inevitable, extension of the innovations in group techniques
that preceded it. Once the leader became freer to express himself (Existential-
experiential), once participants could dramatize their problems as well as state
them (Psychodrama), once group therapy methods were defined as applicable
to normal people (Gestalt), once nonverbal models of expression became more
accentuated (Gestalt), and once a humanistically oriented counter-culture
began to question all traditional structures, including the need for fixed roles
and clear-cut goals or procedures, the free-wheeling and relatively loose
Encounter group was a perhaps inevitable result.

The Theme-centered Interactional method, the final model to be
presented, also shows the influence of several of its predecessors. It was
founded by Ruth C. Cohn, a psychoanalyst and group therapist who wanted
to find some way of bridging the apparent gap between the effectiveness of
psychotherapeutic methods with individuals and their relative ineffectiveness
when applied to the social malaise of the larger community or culture.
Starting with a "countertransference workshop" that was designed for the
group supervision of psychotherapists (Cohn, 1969, pp. 260-261), she
gradually began to develop a model that could apply to many different types
of groups involving members who convened together for a common purpose
or task, including classrooms, discussion groups, and committees. The model's
psychotherapeutic heritage was reflected in its consistent emphasis on the
validity of feelings and in its encouragement of each participant to feel free in
stating his here-and-now experience. Yet it made a clear-cut distinction
between a group designed for therapy and one designed for theme-focused
discussion, to the point of formulating specific leadership techniques designed
to bring back to the theme those participants who were veering off into
overly personalized discussion. In its concern with helping a group of people

come to terms with a common task or agenda, often imposed from the outside, the Theme-centered method also bore an obvious relationship to the T-group, which had had a similar concern with helping team members to deal more constructively with their organizational obligations. But whereas the T-group leader tended to be relatively inactive for long periods of time, the Theme-centered leader was encouraged to actively intervene in the group's discussion, and whereas the T-group historically dealt with a relatively fixed theme involving interpersonal and group processes, the Theme-centered method was designed for an almost limitless variety of themes, including Freedom and Control in the Psychotherapy Relationship (for therapists), Live Learning vs. Dead Learning (for teachers), Overcoming the Generation Gap (for parents and teen-agers), and Freeing Creativity (for writers).

Several characteristics of the Theme-centered model make it somewhat antithetical to both the method and the spirit of Encounter groups; these include an emphasis on the occasional need for some fairly intellectual discussion in the group, adapting the group format to the theme-related and outside-life needs that brought the group into existence, and the leader's obligation to protect a member from a deeper emotional experience than the latter had implicitly contracted for. Indeed, the Theme-centered concern with the common goals and the expectations of the group constitutes a strong parallel with the social work group, the first model that we introduced. Other characteristics that the Theme-centered method shares with its social work ancestor is a concern with the larger social and community context in which the group is embedded (called the "globe" in Theme-centered terminology) and an emphasis on some careful planning of a group session ahead of time (what Theme-centered leaders refer to as "theme-setting" and "theme-introduction").

Indeed, it is our impression that of all the models presented in the book, it is the theme-centered one that bears the closest resemblance to the group work model. It seems pleasantly fortuitous that this similarity provides a focus for integration and for helping the book "to come full circle." However, the fact that our last chapter forms a bridge to the first may not be purely coincidental. It may be that after the group-methods movement had experienced its "full head" and ultimate freedom in the form of the relatively unstructured Encounter group, there began to be felt, at least by some, a need for a return to structure, conceptualization, and goal-relevance. We shall return to this issue in our concluding chapter.

References

Bion, W. R. 1959. *Experiences in groups.* New York: Basic Books.
Calame, B. E. 1969. The truth hurts. *The Wall Street Journal,* July 14.

Cohn, R. C. 1969. From couch to circle to community: beginnings of the theme-centered interactional method. In H. M. Ruitenbeek, ed., *Group therapy today.* New York: Atherton Press.

Denes-Radomisli, M. 1971. Gestalt group therapy: sense in sensitivity, 1971. Unpublished Paper delivered at a conference on Group Process Today, Adelphi University Postdoctoral Program in Psychotherapy.

Durkin, H. E. 1964. *The group in depth.* New York: International Universities Press.

———. 1972. Analytic group therapy and general systems theory. In C. J. Sager and H. S. Kaplan, eds., *Progress in group and family therapy.* New York: Brunner-Mazel.

Marrow, A. J. 1969. *The practical theorist: the life and work of Kurt Lewin.* New York: Basic Books.

May, R., Angel, E., and Ellenberger, H. F., eds. 1958. *Existence.* New York: Basic Books.

Rogers, C. 1967. The process of the basic encounter group. In J. Bugenthal, ed., *Challenges of humanistic psychology.* New York: McGraw-Hill.

Schutz, W. C. 1971. *Here comes everybody.* New York: Harper & Row.

———, and Seashore, C. 1972. Promoting growth with nonverbal exercises. In L. N. Solomon and B. Berzon, *New perspectives on encounter groups.* San Francisco: Jossey-Bass.

Slavson, S. R. 1950. *Analytic group psychotherapy.* New York: Columbia University Press.

Spotnitz, H. 1961. *The couch and the circle.* New York: Knopf.

Sullivan, H. S. 1953. *The interpersonal theory of psychiatry.* New York: W. W. Norton.

Whitaker, C. A. and Malone, T. P. 1953. *The roots of psychotherapy.* New York: Blakiston.

Wolf, A. and Schwartz, E. K. 1962. *Psychoanalysis in groups.* New York: Grune and Stratton.

———, McCarty, G. J., and Goldberg, I. A. 1970. *Beyond the couch: dialogues in teaching and learning psychoanalysis in groups.* New York: Science House.

2

The Social Work Group

Maeda J. Galinsky and Janice H. Schopler
School of Social Work
University of North Carolina at Chapel Hill

Social workers are confronted with a broad range of problems, needs, and demands as they meet with clients in groups. A sampling of social group work in the present day might include streetcorner meetings focused on ways for defiant gang members to gain access to legitimate careers; group counseling with parents in a mental health clinic as part of an effort to facilitate their children's treatment; "rap" sessions with ghetto residents at a neighborhood center to share concerns and to plan possible changes in city services; and, club meetings with elderly men at a boarding home to help them to socialize and to pursue their interest. One situation is as "typical" as another, and together these vignettes reflect the diversity of social group work. At various times, the goals of social group work have been geared to social reform, to socialization, to growth and development of normal individuals, to training for participatory democracy, and to treatment of individual problems. Presently, all of these goals are regarded as appropriate but they have been emphasized differentially in the various phases of social group work's development.

The history of social group work has, since the latter part of the nineteenth century, been closely linked to the evolution of the social agencies which have developed to handle the needs of people. Beginning as a "cause" devoted to improving the quality of human life in areas such as labor, housing, and recreation, social group work has moved to the status of a professional method with an identified body of social work knowledge and skills. Group work emerged in the settlement houses that were built in the late nineteenth and early twentieth centuries in response to the mammoth social problems of the poor, and often immigrant, slum dwellers. Jane Addams, who founded Hull House in Chicago in 1889, served as an inspiration to settlement workers in this era of progressive reform and groups were organized to fight for improved housing, better working conditions, and increased recreational opportunities. Education for citizenship and for leisure-time activities was also provided in settlement groups as the workers emphasized the values of social participation, democratic process, learning and growth, and cross-cultural contact.

The zeal for reform faded in the atmosphere following World War I as leisure-time and youth-service agencies developed in response to the needs of a growing middle class concerned with preserving the dominant social values and enhancing the human resources of society. Educational and recreational activities were offered through agencies such as the Young Men's and Young Women's Christian Associations, Scouting Organizations, 4-H Clubs, and Community Centers. The emphasis was on learning skills and values through the group. The group workers of this period were largely untrained and directed their efforts toward providing socialization experiences for the average, normal citizen. The idea of "treating" people in groups had not yet been developed. Although there was little systematic writing about the extensive work with groups during this period, the practice of group work was greatly influenced by the writing of Mary P. Follett, a political scientist who advocated participatory democracy, and the philosophy of John Dewey, who spearheaded the progressive education movement. Dewey's work, in particular, provided a basis for working with small, leisure-time groups and group workers began to develop a methodology as they stressed principles such as "learning by doing," "individualization," and "starting where the group is."

In the late 1930s and early 1940s, the focus of social group work shifted noticeably. Apparently, closer association with the psychoanalytically oriented caseworkers of this period, as well as a desire for acceptance by the social work profession, led to a movement to the use of groups for treatment purposes. Social group workers began to move into a variety of settings, such as mental hospitals, child guidance clinics, prisons, children's institutions, public assistance agencies and schools; and, the broad, ambitious aims of improving society through group participation were exchanged for a concern with treating individuals, albeit in groups. The writings of Redl and Wineman, Coyle, and Konopka in the 1940s and 1950s contributed greatly to the development of the treatment approach and reflected an increasing integration of social science materials in the growing group work methodology. It was also during this period, in 1946, that the American Association of Group Workers formally united with other segments of the social work profession to become a part of the organization that is currently known as the National Association of Social Workers. Prior to this time, most group workers had practiced in social agencies, but their identification with the social work profession was a loose one.

By the 1950s, social group workers had become established members of the social work profession. In formulating social work's approaches to groups, they drew heavily on the rapidly developing social sciences—particularly small group theories, sociological theories of deviance, and systems theory. Most schools of social work provided training in this method of working with people and the social group work method was viewed as an appropriate therapeutic alternative for people with individually based problems as opposed to the earlier group work focus on external conditions. Although some group workers tried to rally support for social reform activities of an earlier era, the methodology associated with using the group for environmental change has been more fully developed within the social work speciality of community organization. Social group workers, while still concerned with the impact of the environment on their clients' lives, now most commonly seek recreational, socialization, and treatment goals.

In the past two decades, social group workers have been involved in building their theoretical and practical knowledge through the incorporation of both social science theory and actual field experience. Numerous formulations of social group work are available, but the writings of Konopka, Klein, Phillips, Northen, Bernstein, Vinter, Tropp, Shulman, and Schwartz have been among the most prominent. Although there are a number of distinctions that may be made among the works of these authors, it is possible to classify them into two major categories: (1) the "remedial" model, perhaps best represented by the writings of Robert D. Vinter and his associates at the University of Michigan; and (2) the "reciprocal" model, most clearly explicated by the writings of William Schwartz who is currently at Columbia University. Vinter developed the "remedial" model of social group work which has been elaborated by his colleagues and more recently referred to as the "preventive and rehabilitative" approach. The emphasis in this model is on treatment of individual problems through the use of small group processes. The worker takes an active and directive role in planning the group and the group meetings. In Schwartz's conception of group work, designated originally as the "reciprocal" model and now as the "interactionist" approach, group processes are used for many ends, including treatment, socialization, and social goals. The worker with this orientation tends to be less directive and would view his role as that of mediator and enabler of group processes.

The theoretical, philosophical, and operational concepts developed in the Vinter and Schwartz models encourage the worker to analyze and act on different facets of individual and group behavior. Although both models have their roots in the history of group work, these two authors draw on different aspects of group work tradition and different social science orientations. Both of these authors have contributed so greatly to the development of current social work theory and practice that it is important to consider their models separately. For each model, we will present the major philosophical and theoretical concepts, the key operational concepts, and the typical course of a group. Recognizing that social workers use a combination of approaches in actual practice, modifying and adapting concepts in line with their own personal styles, we will compare the Vinter and Schwartz models and consider the appropriate use of their concepts in a final section discussing the role of the social group worker as group leader. The following account of a group meeting provides a basis for considering the Vinter and Schwartz models. While we will continue to emphasize the differences between the models, this sample meeting provides some feel for the way a social group worker familiar with a range of models interacts with group members. Its content represents an eclectic use of both models and will be used to illustrate concepts from Vinter and Schwartz as they are presented.

A TYPICAL MEETING

In this account, a group of mental patients at a State Hospital are meeting together for the fifth time. The social worker has contracted to meet with the group eight times to help the members prepare for discharge. The group's members include: Mr. Aaron, an extremely dependent, middle-aged man who plans to return to his parents' home; Mr. Granger, a rather dependent young man who found employment during a weekend pass; Mrs. Lolly, a housewife hospitalized for chronic depression who will be returning to her husband and three teenagers; Miss Millenson, a young schizophrenic who will be provisionally placed at a halfway house; Mr. Smythe, a man in his thirties recovering from an acute anxiety attack who will be returning to a job his former employer "has waiting for him;" and, Mr. Tuttle, a very insecure and paranoid young man who is moving to a halfway house.

> The worker opened the meeting by stating that Mr. Aaron had had a disturbing experience on his weekend home visit and would like the group's help. Mr. Smythe immediately asked Mr. Aaron what happened. Mr. Aaron was visibly upset, rocking in his chair, his voice trembling, as he told the group he had been "interrogated" by a friend of his father during his visit home. With the worker's prompting, Mr. Aaron related the incident. His father's friend started out by asking if Mr. Aaron's thinking was okay yet. He followed this by a series of questions about "shock treatments" and the "crazy people" at the hospital. Although the friend assured Mr. Aaron outright that he didn't think he was "crazy," Mr. Aaron felt as if he were being attacked and became so upset that he retreated to his room for the rest of the weekend. The worker noted that he could see how this must have spoiled Mr. Aaron's whole weekend and wondered if any of the other members had ever had an experience like this. Mrs. Lolly said she knew just how Mr. Aaron felt. When she was at home on the Christmas holiday, her daughter's friends kept looking at her in a funny way; and while shopping, she also ran into a woman from her church who asked her what had been keeping her away from home. Mr. Tuttle shared his feelings of being stared at when outside the hospital. Miss Millenson then stated that

wherever she went, she just told them she was from the State Hospital, whether they asked or not, and, as far as she was concerned "they can stare all they want." The worker intervened, pointing out that it sounded as though most of them had been questioned about their stay at the State Hospital or had felt like people were wondering about them when they were outside the hospital. He stated that Miss Millenson had told the group what she did and indicated it might be helpful to know how some of the other members handled this type of situation. The members gave a variety of responses but most of them shared a dislike of talking to others about their hospital experience and two members had tried to deny their hospitalization: Mrs. Lolly had told the church member she'd been in the hospital with "female trouble" even though she suspected the lady knew where she'd really been; Mr. Granger had told his new employer that he'd been away, looking for work up north. Miss Millenson interjected, with some feeling, that Mr. Granger would be in for big trouble if his employer found out, since following a prior hospitalization she had obtained a job without revealing her convalescent status and lost the job for withholding information.

Following her comments, the members became involved in a debate about whether or not people really could identify them as mental patients and whether or not they should reveal their hospitalization. Mr. Granger continued to maintain that you could only hurt yourself by telling people you'd been a mental patient (they would refuse you jobs, expect you to act crazy, etc.), but other members were uncertain and were afraid of the consequences of trying to "hide the facts."

The worker helped them summarize and they tentatively agreed that it's probably best not to hide hospitalization for mental illness if people are at all likely to find out about it. Mr. Aaron pointed out, however, that even when he feels he ought to tell people or answer their questions about the hospital, he gets very upset and doesn't know what to say or what to do. The worker reminded the group that at the last meeting they had talked about feelings related to being a mental patient. Several members commented positively on the previous meeting and Mrs. Lolly, in particular, said that the discussion had really made her feel better. Mr. Aaron interrupted, saying, "Yes, it was a good session; but I still don't know what to say to people." The worker then commented, "You all seem to be saying that you don't know how to respond; perhaps it would be helpful to try out some different ways of answering people." He suggested that the group do some role-playing and structured the situation.

After reminding the group of Mr. Aaron's problem with his father's friend, Mr. Jenkins, the worker offered to act as Mr. Aaron and asked Mr. Aaron to play the role of Mr. Jenkins. Mr. Aaron reviewed the behavior of Mr. Jenkins with the group. The worker then asked the group for help in planning his role as Mr. Aaron. Several members offered suggestions about how he should act when questioned by Mr. Jenkins. First, Mr. Granger said he would turn and walk away from such stupid questions. Mrs. Lolly quickly pointed out, "But that's what Mr. Aaron did, and it didn't work at all. Shouldn't he give an honest answer?" Miss Millenson agreed, saying, "Yes, just tell them you're in the loony bin but you're not like the rest of the crazy people." Mrs.

Lolly objected: "That doesn't sound right. What you could say is that the patients just have health problems and aren't really crazy like you hear." Mr. Smythe said, "Yes, say it's for mental health and the social workers and doctors help you see your problems and get better." At this point, the worker stated, "This is going to be difficult but perhaps we'd better go ahead and see how it works." Mr. Aaron and the worker then role-played the situation with the rest of the group observing.

After the role-play, the worker helped the group to evaluate the responses to the questioning by Mr. Aaron and to explore Mr. Aaron's feelings. Mr. Aaron said that playing Mr. Jenkins' role helped him understand a little why Mr. Jenkins asked the questions. Then, with some support from the worker, and other members, Mr. Aaron agreed to play himself using the members' suggestions. In this role-play, Mr. Aaron was able to face up to Mr. Jenkins' questions. He admitted he had some problems but said he was getting help for them at the hospital. His performance was enthusiastically rewarded by group members who also made some additional suggestions for handling the situation. During the discussion, Mr. Granger said, "These ideas are just fine for answering the questions of friends and relatives, but they wouldn't be much use when you're out looking for a job." With the worker's guidance the group members considered when and how they would tell a prospective employer about their hospitalization. Then, the group role-played several situations concerning conversation with both employers and fellow employees, and all members participated in at least one role-play. In the last few minutes of the meeting, the worker reviewed the various ways that group members had recommended for telling others about their hospitalization. Although some members were still unsure about their ability to handle the situation, at the worker's instigation all of the members agreed to try explaining their hospitalization to someone outside the hospital during their weekend passes and to report back to the group at the next meeting.

The Vinter Model

The Vinter model is a problem-solving approach that presents a framework for the planful application of social science theory to work with individuals in groups. Although the model has been extended to include prevention as well as treatment of individual dysfunctioning, Vinter's basic formulation is problem focused — recognizing the contributions of both the individual and the environment in the generation and maintenance of problematic conditions. The strong ego psychology base developed by social caseworkers in the 1940s and group workers' initial treatment efforts in the late 1940s and early 1950s are reflected in Vinter's recognition of individual characteristics which contribute to the creation of problems. His appreciation for the impact of the environment on the individual relates to the efforts of early social group workers championing social change. His understanding of this interaction is refined through the incorporation of sociological theory related to social deviancy. His interactional conception of problems provides the basis for assessment and group treatment of individual problems.

Vinter's "scientific orientation" is apparent in the treatment strategy he proposes. The worker is expected to apply his knowledge of individual and group functioning in an orderly, skillful way following sequential steps of assessment, goal setting, planning, intervention, and evaluation as he directs the process of change. This kind of activity can be seen in the illustrative group meeting where the worker helped the members express their problems of explaining hospitalization, maintained this as a focus of the meeting, and guided the group in dealing with this issue through role-playing and discussion. Although the importance of spontaneity and creativity can be assumed, it is the potential of planned activity that is emphasized. This model concentrates on the worker or group leader and provides a guide for his actions.

The individual is the target of intervention and the worker uses a variety of means to help achieve the individual goals of group members. The group, the individual, and the community or environment are all viewed as potentially viable sources of influence. It is to the group, however, that the worker's major efforts are directed. Within the group, the worker structures individual change through his relationship to individuals and his direction of group conditions, drawing upon his knowledge of personality and learning theory, role theory, and small group theory. In keeping with the strong social science base, the most recent elaborations of the model are behaviorally oriented (Sundel and Radin, in press; Lawrence and Sundel, 1972; Rose, 1972). Since the group is regarded as a primary vehicle for change, the worker attempts to build a group whose members will actively strive toward helping each other achieve individual goals and which will have the greatest influence on members. In Vinter's model, discussion is only one program tool among many. The recreational activities which were so characteristic of group work in an earlier era assume a new importance in the model. Activities are carefully structured to contribute to therapeutic individual change and to enhance the potential of the group. The worker in the Vinter model is clearly an influencer, providing an impetus to individual change through intervention with the individual, the community, and most importantly, the group.

KEY CONCEPTS: PHILOSOPHICAL AND THEORETICAL

Interactional View of Deviancy. The sources of behavior are considered to be not only within the individual but also within his social environment; and, behavior becomes defined as deviant or problematic only in terms of an individual's interactions with other persons or with institutions (Vinter, 1967a). In some situations, the expectations and responses of others may be conducive to acting appropriately. In other situations, deviant behavior is expected, evoked, reinforced, and, like a self-fulfilling prophecy of doom, becomes inevitable. Mr. Aaron's behavior aptly illustrates this point. Faced with his father's aggressive friend who apparently expected mental patients to act "crazy," Mr. Aaron was speechless when questioned. Later, in the supportive context of the group, Mr. Aaron was able to respond with some confidence to questions about his hospitalization. The worker and other members then rewarded Mr. Aaron for his performance, increasing the probability that he would successfully handle similar situations in the future. Of course, because of Mr. Aaron's limited ability to respond to hostility, additional negative experiences might well override the benefits of one practice session and further intervention would be required.

Thus, both the individual's characteristics, including his ability to respond in a satisfactory way, and the characteristics of the social context which generates, maintains, and defines behavior, will determine whether the behavior that is evoked will be judged to be suitable. This interactional view of behavior makes it imperative for the social worker to examine the individual's behavior in its social context when assessing a problem. Such assessment may well indicate that the social context, the group, and the individual should all be considered as potential targets for intervention.

Group as Means and Context for Change. In all group approaches, the group is a context for change, a place where changes occur through the relationships that motivate and influence each individual. These relationships among members and between the worker and individual members are similar to the helping relationships formed in individual therapy. They differ, however, because the presence of other people may alter their direction or impact.

The Vinter model provides a useful conception of the group as a means for individual change (Vinter, 1967a). According to this model, the worker builds and directs forces within the small group to create a structured influence system. In the group of mental patients, for example, the worker deliberately created a situation which provided members with an opportunity to model and to be reinforced for appropriate behaviors when he initiated the role-playing.

The individual treatment goals of members determine the requirements for group operation. For this reason, the worker's decisions about how to influence various aspects of group functioning will vary from group to group, depending upon the nature of the specific group. The worker for the group of mental patients might try to help Mr. Smythe exercise leadership since he has exhibited confidence and ability in making his discharge plans; if Mr. Smythe gained leadership status, the other members would be more likely to imitate his successful behavior. In contrast, the worker's efforts in a prison group might be directed toward reducing the power of a deviant inmate who is thwarting rehabilitative aims. The worker might do this through encouraging and rewarding the efforts of more cooperative members, by working individually with the deviant member, or in extreme cases by expelling the deviant from the group. Although maximum group pressure might be created to help members of a prison therapy group with their efforts to achieve basic behavioral changes, in the mental hospital discharge group moderate cohesiveness would be sufficient. The worker needs only enough "group spirit" so that members will utilize peer pressures in facilitating discharge plans. Since members must leave the hospital soon, and should not become overly dependent on the group, the worker would avoid high cohesiveness in this group. He might also limit the number of group rules so as to provide dependent members with decision-making opportunities. In this way, the worker acts on the group to achieve individual goals. With this "bifocal view" of the group as both means and context, the group is not just an arena in which change takes place; it is a living, moving force that contributes to change.

KEY CONCEPTS: OPERATIONAL

Contract. The contract is an agreement between the worker and the clients about the goals they will pursue, the treatment means they will use, and the respective roles they will play (Rose, 1967; Croxton, in press). If the client is to become a partner in the therapeutic process, he must be fully involved as a vital, forceful actor in negotiating the treatment contract. The client and worker must share their expectations and plans, and together, they must come to a mutually satisfactory agreement. In the group of mental patients, the worker and members committed themselves to preparing for the members' impending discharge from the hospital. Although this aim was obviously dictated by hospital policy, the worker had to negotiate with patients and make this proposition attractive to members before the group would engage in meaningful activity. Clients may often feel constrained in voicing their desires because of their status as supplicants; in cases where the agency position is overbearing, as in prisons, this is especially true. Thus, it is the worker's responsibility to elicit client expectations and to ensure clarity about available options.

Contract formation begins when the worker meets with the client individually and explains what services the agency could offer and what behavior would be expected of the client. Contract development later involves the whole group and continues well into the group formation stage. While the contract will always remain open to renegotiation, initial agreement on the terms of the contract should be reached very early in the group treatment sequence.

Since goals established in the treatment contract constitute such an important element in this model, guidelines are provided for facilitating the goal-setting process. Goal-setting is conceptualized as involving first an exploration, and then a bargaining phase (Schopler and Galinsky, in press). During the exploration phase, the group members and the worker share their common and conflicting perspectives on the various alternative ends. The aim in this phase is to provide a basis for mutual understanding of the various interests and goals. In the bargaining phase, typically characterized by some competition and conflict, the group system arrives at a working consensus on the group and individual goals that members will pursue. While these phases may occur simultaneously, they are separated theoretically to emphasize the factors the worker needs to consider in goal formulation. It is the worker's responsibility to ensure that individual treatment goals are stated as clearly and specifically as possible and that they refer to changes in the client's life outside the group. Of course, the nature of group members' involvement in this goal-setting process is geared to the clients' level of understanding and the nature of the problems they bring. For instance, a worker could probably elicit much more active participation from a group of parents having problems with their pre-schoolers than from a group of withdrawn mental patients who have been institutionalized five years or more. Although the worker may take the major responsibility for selecting techniques and planning treatment, the client's consent to the means of treatment should be obtained. Either verbally or experientially, the worker should provide members with some sense of the ways in which they will approach problems and their solutions in the group. This approach advocates the client's right to know as much as possible about what is involved as he enters group treatment.

In addition to reaching agreement on purposes and means, the worker and members must come to some mutual understanding of their respective roles. Explicit discussion of the rights and responsibilities of the clients and the worker is required. Questions of confidentiality, attendance, and honesty should be raised. In addition, members must understand that eventually they will be asked to commit themselves to helping each other. This "secondary treatment contract" is reached well after treatment has begun and is essential if the group is to engage effectively in problem-solving efforts.

The Strategy of Intervention. Within the framework provided by his diagnosis of group members and the initial agreements with members in the treatment contract, the worker plans a strategy of intervention. Although the Vinter approach recognizes the importance of spontaneous interactions and intuitive reactions, it stresses the necessity of planful intervention, based on the worker's current understanding of clients, for effective service. In formulating the plan of action that will provide the most benefit to his clients, the worker must consider several points of entry. He can act to influence clients directly, either in the presence of the group members or alone; he can move to affect small group processes; or, he can intervene in the social environment of the individual clients. This concept of intervention at three system levels – the individual, the group, and the social system – is termed "means of influence" (Vinter, 1967b; Vinter and Galinsky, 1967).

Direct means of influence are worker activities which immediately influence individual clients. These direct interventions are offered within the scope of the relationship that the worker develops with each client. This model acknowledges that these relationships are affected by the worker's personal resources (including his skills, his interests, and his personality characteristics), by his expertise in relation to client problems, by his position in the agency, and by the material resources he can offer. Further, the worker is provided with a basis for planning how he will vary the presentation of himself, depending on the needs of his clients. With a group of juvenile offenders on probation, he may convey the image of an understanding but very strong adult who can help them with their problems and who will also monitor their behavior. With a group of married couples, he may present himself as a mediator and facilitator who can help members find areas of mutual interest and concern, despite their differences. Thus, consciously and purposefully, the worker relates to clients to help them move toward their goals.

There are four categories of direct means that the worker uses to influence individual members. As "central person – object of identification and drives," the worker acts as a model, responds to client feelings, and supports goal-directed activity. In the account of the meeting with the discharge group, there are several examples of the worker relating to members' feelings about being mental patients and encouraging members in their attempts to respond more appropriately. In his role as "symbol and spokesman – agent of legitimate norms and values," the worker is continually involved in clarifying policy, setting limits, creating group rules and pointing out the consequences of behavior. He might, for example, request that all members come to meetings on time or reward a hyperactive youngster for sitting through a brief discussion. Acting as "motivator and stimulator–definer of individual goals and tasks," the worker helps individuals find new ways of handling problems by giving advice, structuring new opportunities, or providing interpretations. In the discharge group, the worker asked members to practice certain behaviors before their next meeting; in a parents' group, he might suggest new ways of responding to a child's temper tantrum. Finally, as the "executive–controller of membership roles," the worker assigns responsibilities and alters relationships within the group. The role-playing activity in the discharge group would provide the worker with an opportunity to assign roles planfully. By helping a member such as Miss Millenson play her role more effectively and practice more appropriate behavior, he might change the group's view of her and influence some aspect of her self-perception. In these and other ways, the worker directly intervenes to effect individual change, recognizing, of course, that these actions usually have some secondary impact on the group process.

Using *indirect means of influence,* the worker's focus is on creating and modifying conditions within the group system. With this means of influence, Vinter provides the worker with a framework for applying the theory and research findings related to small groups. While attention is focused on the potential of direct interventions with the individual in direct means of influence and on the importance of environmental interventions in extragroup means of influence, the use of group conditions allows the group itself to become a primary means for change. Since the utilization of small group theory to create group conditions conducive to individual change is the crux of the Vinter model, Vinter and his associates have written in detail on the application and elaboration of various concepts related to group conditions. These are generally categorized as composition, goals, and structure and processes. A few examples of each of these categories will suffice to illustrate the range and diversity of interventions possible using indirect means of influence.

In deciding about group composition, the worker has an opportunity to use information about the effects of group size and individual attributes in structuring an experience that will optimally benefit the clients. Ideally, he chooses members from a pool of clients using carefully determined criteria. The specific attributes which the worker considers important in selecting members varies according to the purpose the group will have; and, the compatibility and complementarity of potential members must be evaluated in terms of these attributes. In order for the group to be an effective problem-solving unit, the worker must particularly consider the ability of potential members to perform required group functions as well as their ability to serve as models for each other. The group's potential for influencing its members toward achievement of treatment goals is the crucial consideration. The worker's decisions about size are related to the group's purpose and the members' attributes. Using the Vinter model as a framework, Bertcher and Maple (1971) provide a series of guidelines and give illustrations of group composition using knowledge of individual attributes and group-related variables. Of course, in many instances the worker has little or no control over the initial formation of the group and outside circumstances may continually alter the membership of the group. In groups like the mental patients planning for discharge, the "pool of available clients" may be limited to the six members selected. Nevertheless, principles related to size and member selection provide the worker with some basis for understanding the effect of composition on group interaction and some guidelines for adding or excluding members. When his influence on group composition is limited, the worker must rely solely on other indirect means for affecting group conditions.

The formulation of a group goal or purpose from the common concerns and needs of members, discussed under contract formation, is a necessary condition for the achievement of individual goals. In the group of mental hospital patients, the members' recognition of their common concerns about leaving the hospital and their mutual need to make discharge plans provided them with a common focus. Once they had reached agreement on this group goal of planning for discharge, there was a basis for involving the total group in the discharge plans of each member and for motivating members to work on common discharge problems. Goals also served as a guide for choosing group activities and selecting worker interventions. Knowing that all members faced questions and remarks from neighbors, relatives and employers, the discharge group was ready and eager to role-play as the worker suggested and to discuss their mutual and unique fears and responses.

Group structures, or patterns of relationship in the group, constitute another set of group conditions which can either facilitate or hinder individual change. Various structures, such as leadership, communication, and power, are considered by the worker in using indirect means of influence. For example, in the discharge group the worker encouraged an open communication structure which is reflected in the members' participation in the illustrative meeting. In another situation, a worker might need to modify a communication pattern which appeared detrimental to group purposes. For instance, a member of a parents' group who has professional training might monopolize discussion and other members might feel intimidated by her apparent "expertise." To limit this member's domination of the group, the worker would intervene early to broaden the communication pattern before it solidifies.

Group processes refer to sequences of behavior or interaction which may encompass a broad range of events. Processes may span a few minutes during a meeting, as a quick decision is made, or cover the lifetime of a group, as in the case of group development. Areas covered under group process consist of such phenomena as conflict and conflict resolution, norms, group cohesion, problem-solving, decision-making, and changes in group structure. The worker in the Vinter model draws upon his knowledge of group processes as he intervenes in the group situation to keep the group actively involved in its pursuit of individual and group goals and to maintain it as a viable instrument for change. In the meeting of the discharge group, the worker guided the group through a problem-solving process as the group members discussed how to handle comments about their hospitalization. The worker elicited the necessary information about this problem during the orientation phase, helped the group express opinions and suggestions for handling the problem during the evaluation phase, and during the control phase, led the group in role-playing potential solutions (Bales, 1951). In another group, the worker might be concerned about normative processes maintaining delinquent behavior. Over a period of several months, he might work with the group around changing its norms by helping members find rewards for socially approved behavior (Sarri and Galinsky, 1967).

It should be noted that there is not always a clear distinction between direct and indirect means of influence. When the worker relates to an individual member in the group session, other members are present and will be influenced by this interaction. Then, too, when the worker intervenes to modify group conditions, his actions will also immediately affect various individual members. The value of the scheme is that it alerts the worker to the possibilities for intervention at both the individual and group levels and requires him to evaluate the intent behind his interventions.

A third level of intervention, *extragroup means of influence,* can be clearly distinguished. This means of influence focuses the worker's attention on the social systems outside the group and consists of interventions with persons, groups, or institutions on behalf of one or more group members. The worker may seek environmental changes in order to bring about new or modified client behavior or to support and help maintain changes achieved in the group. Using extragroup means, he may modify the behavior of a person who is vitally related to the client's problem. A very punishing teacher, for instance, might be encouraged to ignore negative behaviors and to notice and reward the appropriate classroom behaviors a disruptive child is learning and practicing in group meetings. On other occasions, the worker may create environmental support through interventions with other groups or with institutions. The worker could help a group member, such as Mr. Granger, with his adjustment by making arrangements for him to be accepted in an activity group at the local community center following discharge. In a delinquency institution, the worker might obtain changes in the rules so that teenagers would be allowed to keep their own clothes; this action could help decrease group members' dependence on the institution and increase their interest in their appearance.

As the worker seeks changes in the environment, he may either act alone or involve members. For example, in the delinquency institution, he might meet with officials himself or help group members confront the administration with their requests. Although a worker uses extragroup means of influence to facilitate the goals of group members, his activities may have positive consequences for people beyond the group's membership. Changing the clothing rule, for example, would affect all the teenagers at the institution.

Extragroup means of influence are critical to the Vinter approach. Since the sources of behavior are viewed as lying within the environment, as well as within the individual, interventions at the group and individual levels may not be sufficient. Improvements made in the group may end at termination if new behavior does not become stabilized in the environment. In conceptualizing this means of influence, Vinter ensures the worker's focus on planning for necessary changes in the client's environment to support or to facilitate the achievement of those treatment goals that refer to behavior outside the group.

Programming. Programming, the sequential organization of tasks or activities during group meetings, is a unique feature of the Vinter model. Programs, consisting of discussions, role-playing, games or other activities, are designed to help the group in reaching its goals. In contrast to many other group models where the worker guides the group's efforts on the basis of his current observations in the group, the Vinter model directs the worker toward planning the content of each session in advance. Plans may also be made for a sequence of related programs which may extend for several sessions, even for the duration of the group. Plans are changed or modified during meetings if this seems appropriate to the needs of the group. In planning programs, careful consideration is given to the behaviors that the worker wants to evoke and the behaviors that can be expected to result from a given activity or task. A session of jewelry making which requires sharing of tools and materials may, for example, be used to promote cooperative behavior and increase interaction between particular members. In another situation, practicing and evaluating new behavior may be important; and, role-playing, interspersed with discussion, may be planned as in the discharge group.

A framework for the analysis of program activities and their consequences, developed by Vinter (1967c), provides useful guidelines for effective programming. Some of the basic dimensions of activities which he identifies are: the prescriptiveness (i.e., the type and number of rules required); the provision for interaction (i.e., types of participation required or evoked); and, the reward structure (i.e., the type, number and manner of distribution of rewards). During a meeting of a parents' group related to handling their teenagers' dating behavior, for instance, the discussion could proceed in an informal, unstructured way which would promote friendly, noncompetitive interaction. Further, the program would be likely to be rewarding to all discussants, particularly those who were able to develop new approaches for relating to their teenagers' needs and problems and those who were able to offer constructive suggestions. In another group, a game of football would entail following rules which the worker would have to enforce, would bring out aggressive, competitive behaviors, and would reward the winners most heavily.

Programming is one of the tools available to the worker as he plans for changes at all levels of intervention. Although it is more typically identified as an indirect means of influence and is most frequently used to modify group conditions, it can also be used to directly affect client behavior or to exert influence on the environment. The careful planning of sequential, goal-directed activities required in programming is characteristic of the rational approach to problem-solving advocated by the Vinter model.

THE COURSE OF A GROUP: THE TREATMENT SEQUENCE

In the Vinter approach, the worker plans treatment according to a well-defined sequence consisting of five stages (Vinter, 1967b; Sarri, et al., 1967). At *intake,* the potential client comes, or is referred, to the agency. After preliminary assessment, the potential client and the worker decide whether the client's wants and the agency's services are compatible. If there is agreement, *diagnosis and treatment planning* follow. This stage includes assessment, goal-setting, and planning for goal achievement. The client and significant others are involved in diagnosis of the problem that brought the client to the agency. Internal and environmental strengths and resources available for problem-solving, as well as barriers and constraints to change, are assessed. Priorities are also determined after deciding which problems require most immediate attention and which are most amenable to change. Based on this assessment, the worker helps the client set appropriate treatment goals. These individual goals refer to desirable end states the client can realistically achieve by the termination of service. On the basis of these goals, the worker devises a tentative plan, specifying the means that will be used to reach treatment goals. Then, in the *group composition and formation* stage, the worker selects clients who share common problems and who are likely to be helpful to each other. After composing the group, he aids members in forming an effective group, oriented toward reaching their treatment goals. The stage of *group development and treatment* involves all efforts made by the individual client, the group, and the worker to reach treatment goals. This includes individual interviews with group members, group meetings, and intervention in the environment. *Evaluation and termination* constitute the final step in the treatment sequence. Group and individual achievements are evaluated in relation to goals and members are helped to terminate their group relationships. Sarri and Galinsky (1967) have detailed the member behaviors that can be expected in the course of a group's natural development and specify the worker interventions that may be required in each major phase of development to help the group become an effective treatment system.

The treatment sequence is not meant to be a rigid process, but rather, is intended as a guide to the worker in carrying out his tasks. As he follows this sequence, the worker should be involved, at every stage, in assessing the current situation, planning treatment activity, implementing plans, and evaluating outcomes. A variety of factors may influence the progression of treatment. Client distrust may delay assessment and treatment goals may not emerge until after a group has met for several sessions. Diagnoses and plans may change as new information is obtained. Frequently, the worker has no opportunity for preliminaries or for careful composition; he is asked to work with a number of clients who have similar problems and must help them assess their situations and set goals within the context of the group. Particularly when time is limited, as in the discharge group for mental patients, the worker may find it necessary to "collapse" treatment stages and carry out many activities concurrently. In any event, the treatment sequence provides a valuable outline of the major tasks which must be completed if the client is to receive effective group service.

The Schwartz Model

Schwartz, with his systemic conception of the group, has formulated a model of group interaction that provides the social worker with a broad perspective for understanding human interaction in the group and in society. As Vinter's model represents the influence of social science and the "scientific method," Schwartz's model represents the thinking of a philosopher steeped in the interrelationships between man and his society. Schwartz draws heavily on the systems theory of sociology to explain the imbalances which may occur in man's relationship to man and to society as a whole. His work is somewhat reminiscent of John Dewey's philosophy and the move toward building a better society in the 1930s. Schwartz does not, however, denigrate the importance of the individual; rather, he considers the needs of the individual and society to be reciprocal and believes that balance must be maintained. Social work's function is to act as an intermediary between man and his society; the group is presented as a microcosm of the larger society and is, thus, a convenient medium for the social worker as he carries out his mediating task. Although Schwartz's model has been applied mainly to work with groups, his systemic conception provides the basis for any helping situation.

Since Schwartz considers the interaction between man and society as crucial, his emphasis is on the relationships within the group that represent the working of the larger society. His approach is group-oriented, as opposed to Vinter's individual focus, and he describes the group as a social system — a living unit with interrelated parts. The worker focuses on relationships within this group system and between the latter and the agency system as represented by the worker. The agency defines the limits or boundaries of group activity and becomes a very real and vital system to the group members as they negotiate through the worker for the means to achieve their desired ends.

The worker using this model becomes a mediator of conflicting societal and individual demands as well as a facilitator of the kind of group movement that will help group members achieve a satisfactory balance with their society. Schwartz's conception of symbiotic relationships between man and society is epitomized in the worker's efforts to create a system of mutual aid within the group. The worker using this model takes a philosophic stance toward the group. His function is to help the group determine its work together and to intervene to keep the group working. The worker does not plan his interventions; rather, his decision to act is made in the interaction of the immediate situation. The worker is viewed as one of the interdependent parts of the group system but has defined tasks which he can implement to facilitate the work of the group. His is an enabling role, one which enhances but does not direct the work of the members.

KEY CONCEPTS: PHILOSOPHICAL AND THEORETICAL

Symbiosis. Basic to the Schwartz approach is the assumption that the relationship between man and society is symbiotic (Schwartz, 1961). At the earliest stage of human development, the self is formed in interaction with the environment and a "social self" results (Mead, 1934). A common need and a common striving exist between man and society and, thus, it is misleading to view them as independent. There are, however, times when this symbiosis is diffused or interrupted. Men who have lost their jobs, mental patients who have been shut away, or the poor who have been ignored may feel alienated from a society that views them as useless. Whenever man loses sight of his investment in the social order and whenever society fails to recognize the importance of the autonomous individual, a third party is required to help restore the necessary balance. The social group worker is trained to enter such situations in times of crisis or imbalance and to mediate the conflict between man and society; he sides with neither, but helps each to reach out for the other.

The most common setting for the performance of the mediating function of social work is the social agency. In group work, the group and the agency represent a microcosm of the larger individual-society relationship, and one of the worker's primary tasks is to help the members and the agency discover their need for each other. In the discharge group, the interdependence of the members and the hospital becomes apparent in their mutual investment in discharge planning. The interdependency of group members with each other is, of course, paramount; and, as they experience this mutuality, members will come to recognize their need for other individuals and for society.

The Group as a Social System. The group is conceptualized as a social system with a defined boundary and interrelated parts (Schwartz, 1961; Shulman, 1968). The members and worker are parts of the system and their relations are reciprocal. An interaction between two members will not only affect each of them but will reverberate to other parts of the system, affecting other members as well as the worker. Therefore, in order to understand any one part of the system, the totality of interacting parts must be considered. In the discharge group, Mr. Aaron's account of his distressing weekend elicited accounts of similar encounters by other group members and provided the worker with an opportunity to experience with them some of the specific difficulties of their situation; thus, the worker was able to help the group activate their mutual need to resolve their relationships beyond the boundaries of the hospital.

With this perspective, the group is also regarded as a subsystem of the larger agency organization; and, it must be remembered that other parts of that agency system will affect the group's operation even as the group affects the agency. For example, as the group operates it will be constrained by such agency factors as the time the worker has available, the resources the agency provides, and the rules pertaining to group activity. The agency, in like fashion, will feel the impact of the group's activity and may need to consider reallocating resources to meet group requests or reformulating policies that are restricting the work of the group.

Finally, in some cases, the worker will gain a more complete picture of group members as he comprehends their interaction in other social systems. Relationships with family members or with peers, for example, may influence a member's interactions within the group. Thus, the reciprocal roles of the worker and members are defined within the living, organic group, which is but a part of the interacting systems of society.

KEY CONCEPTS: OPERATIONAL

Mutual Aid System. Ideally, any group can establish reciprocal helping relationships among its members and become a system of mutual aid wherein members extend help to each other in working out their common problems (Schwartz, 1961; Schwartz, 1971b). A beginning sense of a mutual aid enterprise was apparent in the discharge group as members pooled ideas for handling questions about their hospitalization. In helping the group reach this state, the worker must affirm the members' need for each other and their ability to help each other. Further, he must be willing to share his authority equally with the other members of the group system, realizing that his relationship with each member is only one among many. Thus, the worker helps members form relationships with each other that are direct, purposeful, and invested with feeling, relationships that are truly humane and intimate. Through the "give and take" of these relationships, each member is able to strengthen himself as he becomes a part of the productive totality that is the group. The tone and boundaries for this mutual aid system are first set as the worker and members consider the contract together.

Contract. The contract, which defines the relationships within the group system and between the group and the agency, perhaps best represents the theme of responsible interdependence which is so characteristic of the Schwartz approach to social group work (Schwartz, 1961). In this approach, the worker serves as a mediator in the development of the contract—an agreement among the agency, worker, and group members about purposes, roles, and procedures. He helps both the group and the agency establish their "terms": the group must reach some consensus about member needs and the agency must provide some statement about its stake in serving this group. Then, the worker helps both systems find some common ground. In the discharge group, the members identified their common interest in preparing for life outside the hospital; the hospital was interested in facilitating the discharge process; and, discharge planning became the mutually rewarding focus. In the Schwartz model, the worker makes clear the types of purposes the agency can support and the resources the agency can make available. As group members go through the process of searching out their mutual needs and objectives and reacting to the agency's statement as presented by the worker, they come to an open understanding of the purpose they can and will pursue within this agency. Thereafter, this purpose serves as the primary guide to their work together.

As the group members and worker strive to define their mutual aims, they also reach agreement on the types of roles and procedures that will be most effective. In these discussions, the worker emphasizes honesty, openness, and responsibility and, through his role as mediator, lays the groundwork for reciprocal relationships. Throughout this experience, members become aware of the way people and society reach out to each other, and they gain some feel for the process in which they will be engaged.

Work. The most important question that can be asked in the group is, "Are we working?" or, its corollary, "What are we working on?" The first work of the group is to establish a contract; thereafter, most questions about work can be answered by reference to the contract. Work is defined as an output of energy directed to certain tasks (Schwartz, 1971a). The tasks are performed to meet the purposes of the group which in turn were developed to express the needs of the members. Thus, the degree to which members' needs are being met is directly related to how well the members are working. In the account of the discharge group's meeting, the worker suggested role-playing as a response to members' despair about "what to say" in relation to their hospitalization and then provided members with some structure for learning and practicing appropriate responses. In this way, the worker very quickly took responsibility away from the members; a worker using the Schwartz approach would be more likely to press the members to define their work together in this situation and would, thus, involve members in determining their needs and in helping them explore alternative means for meeting their needs.

Schwartz, however, does not define work solely in terms of purpose; work is also related to the development of the mutual aid system. Thus, to answer the question, "Are we working?" the group not only must decide whether it is meeting its goals but also must examine the investment that members have in each other, their flow of affect, and their attention to the common cause. This does not imply that every problem, concern, or task that the members address must be a common one; efforts to carry out tasks based on individual needs and within the terms of the contract also meet the criterion of work. In a well developed mutual aid system, in fact, the group is concerned with the needs of its individual members. A group meeting for an extended period around members' common concerns with marital difficulties might decide to consider each member's problems sequentially.

The contract and the definitions of work generated from it, provide the worker and members with a basis for evaluating their activities together: for knowing when their work is in process, when it is being evaded or subverted, and when it is finished. For instance, in a tenants' council that has resolved to deal with problems around integration, members may digress to topics related to other difficulties in the housing project. No unfounded interpretations of resistance or other psychological motivation are needed as the worker brings the group back into focus with a gentle, "What are we working on?". With a group of adolescent girls who are giggling over personal chatter, a brief "Are we working?" may quickly restore order. These questions provide a rationale for the worker's interventions. If the group is not working, or if it is unclear about its efforts, then the worker's tasks are to help members deal with impediments to work. In such instances, the worker must be careful not to impose his own opinion on the group; his task is to remind the group members of the terms of their contract. The worker must also be sensitive to situations when the contract no longer represents a viable purpose for group members and, in such instances, his task is to help members revise their contract. In essence, the worker represents what is termed the "demand for work."

Worker Tasks. Schwartz (1961) describes worker interventions in terms of the five major tasks of the helping process. Techniques or prescriptions are not detailed, for it is only the spontaneous interactions in the present situation that can determine specific worker actions. Through the demand for work, the worker responds on a human, reciprocal, and intuitive basis, using the terms of the contract as his general guide. The five tasks are presented only as broad categories of activity in which the worker and members engage as the need arises.

The first task entails, "searching out the common ground between the client's perception of his own needs and the aspects of social demand, with which he is faced" (Schwartz, 1961, p. 157). This task rests on the assumption of the symbiotic relationship between man and his society. The worker enables members to look beyond themselves, to weigh their obligations to society. He helps them in defining their own needs, in understanding the needs of others, and in negotiating acceptable terms. The need to "search for common ground" is immediately apparent as members and worker seek to discover similarities in their needs and establish a connection with the agency in the initial contract. As the group continues with its work, this "search" will be necessary whenever transactions within the group or other systems are disrupted or whenever new connections need to be established with people or systems. Friction between two members, for example, may be resolved as they more clearly perceive that their mutual needs outweigh their differences. Discussion of job interviews would present another situation when the worker would want members to consider their needs for work in relation to the demands of prospective employers. In the discharge group, the work of the group will constantly involve "searching out the common ground" as members examine potential relationships necessary to re-entering the community. The worker should be continually aware of the many instances in which he can build connections between the group and its society and among the members in their common pursuits.

In the second task, the worker engages members in "detecting and challenging the obstacles which obscure the common ground and frustrate the efforts of people to identify their own self-interest with that of their 'significant others' " (Schwartz, 1961, p. 157). Obstacles to work may appear in various forms, but they always represent a struggle between members and their present tasks. Members may be unwilling to make decisions, they may avoid helping a fellow member examine unpleasant subjects, subgroups may be at war with one another, or, an individual may refuse to cooperate in sharing his concerns. Whenever these obstructions to work exist, the group is not acting in its self-interest and is failing to achieve its tasks. Although the sources of obstacles may be complex and interrelated, the worker does not need to deal with causal factors. He has, rather, three functions to perform: he alerts the group to the present obstacle but does not condemn members for it; he helps members deal with the obstacle through an examination and understanding of it; and, he prevents members' preoccupation with analyzing the obstacle to the exclusion of their other work.

The third task involves the worker in "contributing data—ideas, facts, and value-concepts which are not available to the client and which may prove useful to him in attempting to cope with that part of social reality which is involved in the problems on which he is working" (Schwartz, 1961, p. 157). As members engage in their tasks, they may lack information which the worker, by virtue of his own life experiences, can offer to them. He may provide welfare mothers with suggestions on budgeting, offer harrassed parents tips on handling temper tantrums, or tell unemployed workers some ways to find out about available jobs. In giving this information to members, the worker shares himself—his impressions, his ideas, his knowledge, his feelings, his values. Further, his behavior serves as a model to other members for freely exchanging information and for investing in the work of the group. He must be careful, however, not to impose himself on the group. Whatever he offers should be directly pertinent to the current work of the group and should be offered as one among many possible views of social reality.

The fourth task requires " 'lending a vision' to the client, in which the worker both reveals himself as one whose own hopes and aspirations are strongly invested in the interaction between people and society and projects a deep feeling for that which represents individual well-being and the social good" (Schwartz, 1961, p. 157). In performing this task, which pervades all facets of the group's work, the worker displays his enthusiasm for, his faith in, his encouragement of, and his caring for the members of the group and the tasks and goals they have selected. When the group or its members are experiencing difficulty, this task can be vital. In the discharge group, for instance, the worker responded immediately to Mr. Aaron's distress and through his concern, involved the other members. On other occasions when members report success in their encounters beyond the group, the worker's joy as he shares these triumphs will enhance the meaning of each transaction. By representing his own investment in the group, by demonstrating his capacity for empathy, and by communicating his feelings, the worker creates a basis for human and emotional relationships with members.

Finally, the worker is involved in "defining the requirements and limits of the situation in which the client-worker system is set. These rules and boundaries establish the context for the 'working contract' which binds the client and the agency to each other and which creates the conditions under which both client and worker assume their respective functions" (Schwartz, 1961, p. 158). The group members, the worker, and the agency have reciprocal responsibilities and the specific rules governing these relationships are established in the contract. Thus, the members may agree to abide by certain rules concerning fee payments, attendance and participation; the agency and the worker may accept the responsibility of providing a meeting place and ensuring fair and equal treatment of clients. The worker's function is to make the members aware of these limits and boundaries as they affect group operation. He may, for example, remind members that they have agreed to report the particular problems they have had during the week. At other times, the worker may need to help both the members and the agency restate their requirements in more specific and unambiguous terms. In either case, it must be clear that the worker is operating within the confines of the contract and is not imposing rules and regulations by virtue of personal authority. The worker's task is not to enforce rules for the members, but to reiterate them when they seem forgotten and to help members redefine, modify, amplify or reinterpret requirements as necessary.

Schwartz indicates that the major factor governing the use of these five tasks must be the enhancement of the work of the group. The type and degree of worker activity will vary with the work each group has agreed to complete and the choice of tasks is left to the intuition and skill of the worker. It is only as the worker interacts with members in a particular situation that he can be sensitive to the form and timing the tasks should take.

Within the framework provided by Schwartz, Shulman has elaborated some of the interactional techniques the worker can utilize in carrying out these tasks (Shulman, 1968). He warns that these techniques are not prescriptions for behavior, but, rather, descriptions of more specific worker activities. In refining the concept of mediating behavior, Shulman divides the techniques into three categories: communications, problem-solving, and cognitive. Communications techniques are designed to facilitate the communication process in the worker-client system. Examples of such techniques would include: asking a client with a perplexed expression what was troubling him; asking a client to elaborate his feelings as he described a troublesome situation; asking the group members for help in identifying how they think a particular member might be feeling. Problem-solving techniques are described as worker activities to enhance task-accomplishment. Serving as both a "catalyst" and a "resource" for the problem-solving efforts of the group system, the worker might give information, point out the common ground between conflicting parties, or ask the group as a whole to work on a particular problem. Cognitive techniques refer to reflective activities which the worker might employ as a prelude to interventions which will be beneficial to the group. Such intellectual musings are illustrated through the worker's efforts in identifying repetitious patterns of behavior or in identifying hidden messages through the interpretation of verbal and nonverbal clues.

THE COURSE OF A GROUP: THE PHASES OF WORK

In the Schwartz model the worker's efforts are patterned in response to four major phases of work—preparations, beginnings, the substantive work together, and transitions and endings (Schwartz, 1971a). Generally speaking, these four phases may apply to the work of a single meeting or to the total life of the group. In either case, each phase poses different demands and has different implications for worker tasks.

In the first phase, preparatory to any encounter with the group, the worker must "tune in" to processes already in motion if he is to be an effective participant in the interaction of the group system. For this preparation, or "tuning in," the worker develops a kind of "preliminary empathy" or "set," a feel for the ways that members may act and react as individuals and as a group. He uses information he may have about particular clients and the knowledge he possesses about broader categories of clients, such as "the aged" or the "mentally ill." If he has already begun meeting with a group he will take account of what has occurred in previous meetings. In the discharge group, for instance, the worker might "tune in" to the particular meeting described by reviewing in his own mind the varied impact that can be expected when a mental patient has a visit home, by recalling the process of the previous meeting, and by sensitizing himself to fit into the current mood of the group. Schwartz's emphasis is not on the use of this knowledge for categorizing or diagnosing clients; rather, he stresses the use of information and understanding for building the worker's readiness to involve himself in the current life of the group. He enters the group, not with a preconceived plan, but prepared to "tune in" and relate to the current situation.

During the second phase, the worker helps the members make their beginnings within the agency under clear conditions of work. As the group's life begins, the worker helps members formulate the contract which will set the limits and boundaries of their work together. He is particularly concerned with helping members gain a clear understanding of the way their work will proceed and, thus, must help them partialize their tasks and set specific guidelines as well as determine their common purpose. He presents the agency's position during this interchange and solicits and encourages members' ideas, feelings, and reactions in relation to these issues. As each meeting begins, the worker is also responsible for providing this immediate orientation to work. In the discharge group, the need to respond to Mr. Aaron's experience quickly involved the group. If members cannot so easily find a common beginning or, if they wander off on a tangent, the worker must help them find a focus for work during their time together.

In the third phase, the worker and members address themselves to the main work of the group, using the terms of the contract as their frame of reference, and move toward the development of a mutual aid system. All the members' strivings, their ideas, their feelings, their actions, and their interactions, must be considered in relation to the group's work. As members of the discharge group shared their various experiences in facing questions about their hospitalization, the worker helped them see their commonality; he then directed them to the demands for work in their mutual situation as he solicited suggestions for action. In this way, the worker uses the appropriate tasks of the helping process as he seeks to keep the group working towards its chosen objectives and to develop the reciprocal nature of the interaction.

The final phase of transitions and endings involves the worker and members in moving away from their present relationship in the group toward new experiences. The worker, at the end of each session and at the end of the group's life, must help members terminate and move on to the next encounter. In the "temporary endings" of a single meeting, the worker can ease the disruption by recognizing work accomplished during the meeting and encouraging work between sessions. Then, to complete the cycle and help the group make the transition into interaction together at the next meeting, he can reach for material developed since the members last met. As the worker engages members in preparing for the group's final ending, he asks them to review their past, deal with their feelings, and prepare for the future. He must be aware of the deep feelings that termination may arouse and the difficulties the group may encounter in ending relationships often formed with great struggle. It may be necessary for him to remind them to use their remaining time effectively; and, it may help for him to share his feelings. In the discharge group, for example, the members' major work involved ending their association with the hospital and preparing for new roles in the community within the limit of eight meetings. Thus, the mutual efforts of these group members to end their hospital experience epitomizes the work of termination and ending.

THE ROLE OF THE LEADER

The philosophical and methodological differences in these two group work models might well lead to very disparate definitions of the social group worker's role as group leader. Workers of the Vinter model could be described as directors of planned change who use group methods for the prevention of dysfunctioning and the rehabilitation of people with problems. A contrasting description, based on the Schwartz model, might picture workers as mediators of troubled transactions between individuals and the systems through which they relate to society. In actuality, the roles assumed by social group workers in their practice do not necessarily reflect strict adherence to a single model. At the present time, social group work practice varies widely. Social group workers may utilize concepts and techniques from a range of social work models and may draw ideas from other models of group interaction.

A review of some of the key concepts in the Vinter and Schwartz approaches reveals some similarities in their conception of what social group workers are expected to do. Both approaches emphasize the importance of the world beyond the group and, in particular, the individual's relationship to other systems: the Vinter approach conveys this through its interactional view of deviancy; Schwartz, through his view of the symbiotic relationship of man and his society. With either view, social group workers must recognize the contributions of both the individual and his related systems as they consider the difficulties of their clients in group treatment. Both approaches, too, recognize the impact of the group system on the individual. Vinter describes the group as both means and context and Schwartz discusses the group as a social system and characterizes its ideal state as a mutual aid system. With either conception, the social group worker is directed toward using the potential power which resides in the mutual helping efforts of members. Further, both Vinter and Schwartz insist on the need for clearly established agreements or "contracts" with group members; and, both describe sequential development of activities required for effective group service, referred to as "the treatment sequence" by Vinter and as "the phases of work" by Schwartz. Although the unique contributions of each of these approaches, detailed previously, should not be obscured by oversimplification, there is considerable correspondence between them with regard to the kinds of activity expected from social group workers as they attempt to relate effectively to clients.

The most significant differences appear, not around "what to do," but rather around "how to do it." Clearly, a comparison of Vinter's "strategy of intervention" and "programming" with Schwartz's "worker tasks" and concept of "work" would support the conclusion that very different worker styles will be required for each model. Vinter very specifically defines the various roles the worker may need to take in relating to individual members, to the group, or to external systems. The worker in the Vinter model is planful and directive; his major concern is with individual behavior and its causes and he uses a variety of techniques and programs to achieve desired changes. An important contribution of this approach is its very rational scheme for utilizing knowledge from the social sciences about individual and group behavior in planning worker interventions. Schwartz emphasizes the worker's reciprocal role in an interacting group system that represents a microcosm of society. Although the members assume major responsibility for defining and completing their work together, the worker's continual "demand for work" helps members maintain their agreed upon focus. Worker tasks are described at a very general level since the worker in this approach acts in relation to the immediate situation. Most importantly, Schwartz points to the importance of feelings, emotions, and cognitive processes in helping members with their problematic relationships and provides a sense of the kind of warm, caring, responsible person that a worker needs to be.

Selection of appropriate concepts from one or another of these two approaches is obviously governed by a variety of factors (Schopler and Galinsky, 1972). The needs, problems, and personalities of the clients should be evaluated. Further, social workers typically operate within the context of a social agency and may find that the agency setting and purpose affect their choice of methods. Another determinant will be the worker's own personality, skills, and philosophy of life—in essence, his "style." In the meeting of mental patients referred to throughout this chapter, the worker represents a balanced use of Vinter and Schwartz in his work with the group. His interaction with group members reflects a selection of concepts based on his assessment of all the clients with particular attention to their unique needs in this meeting. The hospital's influence is apparent in the group's task of preparing for discharge and the worker's style is expressed in his somewhat structured approach to helping the members resolve their difficulties. Thus, in a variety of ways, appropriate to their own styles and client needs, social group workers select from the concepts provided by models of group interaction as they serve people in groups. The social work models are flexible, since the social workers who use them must adapt their knowledge, skill and personal style to the needs of an extremely diverse clientele. Social workers offer group services to people of all social classes and cultures whose problems may be related to their personal lives, their work, or their community.

References

Bales, R.F. and Strodtbeck, F.L. 1951. Phases in group problem solving. *The Journal of Abnormal and Social Psychology*, 46. 485-495.

Bernstein, S. ed. 1965. *Explorations in group work.* Boston: Boston University School of Social Work.

———. 1970. *Further explorations in group work.* Boston: Boston University School of Social Work.

Bertcher, H. J. and Maple, F. 1971. Group composition. Ann Arbor: Campus Publishers.

Briar, S. 1971. Social casework and social group work: historical and social science foundations. *Encyclopedia of social work,* Vol. II. New York: National Association of Social Workers, pp. 1237-1245.

Coyle, G. 1948. *Group work with american youth.* New York: Harper & Row.

Croxton, T. The therapeutic contract in social treatment, in P. H. Glasser, R. C. Sarri, and R. D. Vinter, eds. *Individual change through small groups.* In press.

Feldman, R. A. 1967. Determinants and objectives of social group work intervention. *Social work practice, 1967.* New York: Columbia University Press, pp. 34-55.

Galinsky, M. J. and Schopler, J. H. 1971. The effects of consensus and latitude on group goal formulation. *Social Work Practice, 1971.* New York: Columbia University Press.

Garvin, C. D. and Glasser, P. H. 1971. Social group work: the preventive and rehabilitative approach. *Encyclopedia of social work,* Vol. II. New York: National Association of Social Workers, pp. 1263-1273.

Klein, A. F. 1970. *Social work through group process.* New York: School of Social Welfare, State University of New York at Albany.

Konopka, G. 1963. *Social group work: a helping process.* Englewood Cliffs, New Jersey: Prentice-Hall, Inc.

———. 1949. *Therapeutic group work with children.* Minneapolis: The University of Minnesota Press.

Lawrence, H. and Sundel, M. 1972. Behavior modification in adult groups. *Social Work, 17.* 34-43.

Mead, G. H. 1934. *Mind, self, and society.* Chicago: University of Chicago Press.

Northen, H. 1969. *Social work with groups.* New York: Columbia University Press.

Papell, C. P. and Rothman, B. 1966. Social group work models: possession and heritage. *Journal of Education for Social Work, 2.* 66-77.

Phillips, H. U. 1957. *Essentials of social group work skill.* New York: Association Press.

Redl, F. and Wineman, D. 1952. *Controls from within: techniques for the treatment of the aggressive child.* Glencoe, Illinois: Free Press.

Rose, S. D. 1967. Treatment contract, a programmed course of instruction. Unpublished manuscript, University of Michigan, School of Social Work, Ann Arbor, Michigan. December 5, 1967.

———. 1972. *Treating children in groups.* San Francisco: Jossey-Bass.

Rosen, A. 1972. The treatment relationship: a conceptualization. *Journal of Consulting and Clinical Psychology, 38.* 329-337.

Sarri, R. C. and Galinsky, M. J. 1967. A conceptual framework for group development in R. D. Vinter, ed. *Readings in group work practice.* Ann Arbor, Michigan: Campus Publishers, pp. 72-94.

——— Glasser, P. H., Siegel, S., and Vinter, R. D. 1967. Diagnosis in group work. in R. D. Vinter, ed. *Readings in group work practice.* Ann Arbor, Michigan: Campus Publishers, pp. 39-71.

Schopler, J. H. and Galinsky, M. J. 1972. Criteria for model selection in social group work. Paper presented at the Annual Forum of the National Conference on Social Welfare, Chicago, May, 1972.

———. Goals in social group work practice: formulation, implementation, and evaluation. in P. H. Glasser, R. C. Sarri, and R. D. Vinter, eds. *Individual change through small groups.* In press.

Schwartz W. 1961. The social worker in the group. *The social welfare forum, 1961.* New York: Columbia University Press. pp. 146-177.

———. 1962. Toward a strategy of group work practice. *Social Service Review 36.* 268-279.

———. 1971a. On the use of groups in social work practice. in W. Schwartz and S. R. Zalba, eds. *The practice of group work.* New York: Columbia University Press, pp. 3-24.

———. 1971b. Social group work: the interactionist approach. *Encyclopedia of social work,* Vol. II. New York: National Association of Social Workers, pp. 1252-1263.

Shulman, L. 1968. *A Casebook of social work with groups: the mediating model.* New York: Council on Social Work Education.

———. 1969. Social work skill: the anatomy of a helping act. *Social work practice, 1969.* New York: Columbia University Press, pp. 29-48.

Sundel, M. The historical development of the rehabilitation and treatment approaches in services to groups. in P. H. Glasser; R. C. Sarri; and R. D. Vinter, eds. *Individual change through small groups.* In press.

—— and Radin, N. Diagnosis in group work. in P. H. Glasser; R. C. Sarri; and R. D. Vinter, eds. *Individual change through small groups.* In press.

Tropp, E. 1969. *A humanistic foundation for group work practice.* New York: Associated Educational Services Corporation.

——. 1971. Social group work: the developmental approach. *Encyclopedia of social work,* Vol. II. New York: National Association of Social Workers, pp. 1246-1252.

Vinter, R. D. 1967a. An approach to group work practice. in R. D. Vinter, ed. *Readings in group work practice.* Ann Arbor, Michigan: Campus Publishers, pp. 1-17.

——. 1967b. The essential components of group work practice. in R. D. Vinter, ed. *Readings in group work practice.* Ann Arbor, Michigan: Campus Publishers, pp. 17-38.

——. 1967c. Program activities: an analysis of their effects on participant behavior. in R. D. Vinter, ed. *Readings in group work practice.* Ann Arbor, Michigan: Campus Publishers, pp. 95-109.

—— and Galinsky, M. J. 1967. Extra-group relations and approaches, in R. D. Vinter, ed. *Readings in group work practice.* Ann Arbor, Michigan: Campus Publishers, pp. 110-122.

3

The Psychoanalytic
Therapy Group

As we saw in Chapter 2, social group work models are concerned with a wide range of therapeutic, socialization, and developmental goals. In the present chapter we are dealing with the psychoanalytic group, our first model devoted solely to the field of group psychotherapy.

The introduction of psychoanalytic procedures into group psychotherapy represented a fundamental extension of psychoanalysis, which had hitherto exclusively been a method of individual treatment; indeed, Freud and his immediate followers had hardly envisaged the possibility of treating two or more people simultaneously. Moreover, despite some attempts on the part of Freud to consider man's early history within such fundamental social groups as tribes, clans, and "civilized" societies (1913, 1921, 1930, and 1939), psychoanalysis was primarily a theory of individual personality rather than of groups. The closest Freud had come to a small-group psychology was his analysis of family relations; but even here his approach was oriented more toward the effects of the family, and of the parents in particular, on the developing child than toward the family as a dynamic and coherent "system" in its own right. It remained to later psychoanalytically-oriented theorists, like Gregory Bateson (1956) and Jay Haley (1970-71), to formulate this latter kind of approach. Psychoanalysis has in general, despite exceptions that will be noted in later chapters, continued to define itself as more a theory of the individual than of the group. Indeed, many would argue that, as a scientific and an intellectual discipline, albeit able to be integrated within general systems theory (Durkin, 1972), psychoanalysis must always have the individual man, and his unconscious, as the central core of its concern. As a result, practitioners of the present model, like Wolf and Schwartz (1962), claim that they do not treat groups per se, as do group-dynamic psychotherapists (see Chapter 4), but instead treat an individual patient, just as in one-to-one psychotherapy, but this time in the presence of other individual patients each of whom is also being treated by him. Hence the title of Wolf and Schwartz's formal presentation of their model, *Psychoanalysis in Groups* (1962), as opposed to the psychoanalysis *of* groups.

The strongly influential role that psychoanalysis played in the field of individual psychotherapy has been paralled by its role within group therapy: the psychoanalytic group represented the first systematic application of a well-developed body of theory to group treatment, and its influence on the practice of group therapy continues to be pervasive. In Chapter 1 we reviewed contributions of men like Burrows, Wender, and Schiller, who began to systematically apply the concepts of psychoanalysis to their treatment groups and also the work of Slavson, Wolf, and Schwartz, who continued to develop, and gradually codified, the modern approach to analytic group therapy.

ILLUSTRATION OF A TYPICAL SESSION

Before introducing some key concepts, we would like to re-create a typical analytic group session, its setting, atmosphere, and content, and, in addition, to show the kinds of interventions the therapist might make. To do so, we will take a wholly fictitious example. Our group has seven members, four men and three women. While fairly similar in cultural background (they are for the most part urban and middle-class), its composition shows a fair range in terms of age, occupation, and personality characteristics. The youngest member, Marvin (who is silent in the segment below), is a twenty-year-old college student; the oldest is Felicia, a single woman in her early forties. The group has been meeting for two-and-a-half years. Five of the patients have been with the group for all of this time; Mort entered the group ten months previously, and Ralph joined six months ago, both having replaced a member of the original group who terminated therapy.

> The group begins without any structuring from Dr. M., who is silent. Ruth, a "Hippie"-type girl in her early twenties, is talking about the fact that Bob, the man with whom she is living, is probably having an affair with her best friend, Terry. She knows he is attracted to Terry, and each of them has recently, in talking to her about the other, made some ambiguous and erotically-tinged remarks. Ruth doesn't know what to do about this. She is annoyed with herself for being jealous, for she knows that whatever Bob has going with Terry is a purely "physical" thing. He has made it clear to her when they decided to live together that he did not feel sexually bound by conventional notions of a monogamous relationship; yet she feels hurt and betrayed by Terry. Then, at other times, she feels that she is being old-fashioned, that it's obviously just a "sex-thing" for Terry, who is basically interested in another unavailable man.

Mort, a brunette man in his middle thirties, razzes her. He says; That's right, Ruthie; Bob just has too much love in him to share with just one woman; besides, you love both of them so much, this is really an act of generosity on your part—you're giving two people you love to one another!

Ruth reacts with a slight giggle, and continues to discuss the problem. Mort continues to bait her. Felicia interrupts at this point, saying that it makes her uncomfortable to see the way Mort is baiting Ruth and the way she allows him to do it.

Ruth interrupts, saying: But what difference does it make? I'm used to Mort's sarcasm. What I'm worried about is Bob. Felicia says: Yes, but you take the same crap from both of them. Mort joins in, saying: Yes, she's so goddamned dumb with those rose-colored glasses on; doesn't she know what the world is like? Boy, she really asks for it.

Ralph then joins in for a moment: She may ask for it, Mort, but I notice you're always there firstest with the mostest to give it to her.

Felicia says in a quiet voice: Ruth isn't happy until she has something to make her really miserable.

Ruth then says: Would everyone stop taking about me as though I weren't here?

Felicia expresses pleasure at Ruth's ability to speak up. Dr. M. then asks Felicia what Ruth's talking up does for her, i.e., Felicia. Felicia shrugs, saying: I don't know, I always like to see the underdog speak up; and I don't like the way Mort speaks to Ruth; he browbeats her.

The therapist says: I notice that you're often speaking up for others—those who get stepped on, those who cannot stick up for themselves, and so on; you're like a cheerleader rallying them on, but I don't hear you asking for something for yourself. Felicia answers: I don't know how to ask for myself. I'd rather play Ruth's big sister, I guess; in fact, I admire Ruth. She talks up a lot and tries to work on her problems.

Ruth says: But I don't get anywhere with them! I've lost every boyfriend I've ever had, and I'm afraid that if I start nagging Bob about Terry he'll leave me too. Mort then says to her: But you're already starting to lose him, you dumb bitch! He's in the hay with Terry, remember? Ruth looks a bit cornered, smiles uneasily, and says placatingly: I know you think I'm being silly, but that's Bob's style; he loves me, and he doesn't see whatever he does with Terry as infringing on his relationship to me.

Mort turns to the group in mock disgust, saying: Oh, god! She's such a dumb martyred freak-out; she's hopeless! Ruth begins to cry, and says: Well explain it to me, don't yell at me. The therapist asks her what she is feeling at that moment. Ruth answers: I don't know—I try, I really do; but everybody winds up getting angry with me. I know I probably do something wrong, like acting too helpless, or showing my insecurity too much, something—Dr. M. asks: You mean you feel angrier with yourself than with Mort right now? Ruth nods, and sobs louder.

The therapist says: So right now you're feeling about Mort the way you do about Bob—somehow you're at fault and he's in the right. You just have to find some way of appeasing Mort—or Bob? some way of doing the right thing, even though their behavior makes you uncomfortable and unhappy?

Ruth replies: Yes, I suppose that's true. I don't think I ever really get angry at anybody. Dr. M. asks: Was it always like this, Ruth? Ruth answers: Yes, everyone was always mad at *me* when I was young. I was somehow at fault. My mother hadn't expected me so soon after my sister, and then my father was no longer around; I would try to reassure her that things would be OK, to make it better for her. I was always trying to get people to stop being mad at me.

Ralph then interposes: I know this sounds intellectual, but I think your tears are your anger; I know that has been true of me; and you've cried every time you've been here. Mort says to Ralph: And God forbid you should be intellectual instead of having feelings around here; good boy, Ralph, I can see you're learning to play the group therapy game—a few more months and you'll be a pro at it! The therapist intervenes: Mort, what would you say if you spoke really honestly for once, and put aside your banter and cynicism? Mort answers: Gee, I don't know, doc. I guess I'd say I love you truly, because sometimes when I squint my eyes I have to admit to myself that you look just like my Ma!

A few members laugh: Dr. M. is silent; he doesn't smile. Nelson speaks for the first time, saying to Mort: You've made that crack more than once, maybe there *is* something to it! Mort replies: No, he doesn't really look like my mother; his eyes are darker. Alice says: Mort, you really are unbelievable. Why do you come week after week like this? You're determined to let no one get through to you. It makes me really angry! You're wasting my time too, not just yours.

Mort has a smile on his face and doesn't answer. There is a short silence. Then Felicia speaks up and says: You know, Dr. M., I wonder what you're feeling underneath when Mort razzes you, like that. I don't like it when you don't say anything, when you just keep silent.

Dr. M. asks her: What does my silence do to you, Felicia?

Felicia replies: I don't know—it's like what I said earlier about championing the underdog. I feel like my mother took a lot of abuse from my father; I remember watching her and wishing that she'd say something. And I would be wondering when I would be the next to get it—always thinking it was a miracle that I didn't, cause there was no one else around for him to pick on besides her and me, and I knew she wouldn't protect me.

Dr. M.: And you want me to be able to handle myself with Mort, just like you wanted Ruth to?—and just like you wanted your mother to stand up to your father?

Felicia says: I think so. Yeah, I would feel safer if you could—I guess I'm scared of Mort—it's like it was with my father. I'm surprised sometimes that Mort hasn't given me a full dose of his angry sarcasm like he has with the others, and I think that maybe it's because I'm the oldest woman in the group and something about that intimidates him. But I always feel like: My time will come, and I act tough and complain about how he walks over you others, but I make sure not to tangle with him directly.

Mort says to Felicia: You mean you're pretty scared of me: Felicia answers: Yes, I am. You may think I'm kidding, but I'm not—like just now when you said that to me directly I was surprised and I felt my heart begin to race for a second.

Mort answers: But you must get pissed off at me, too, don't you? I don't hear about that. Felicia pauses, then says uncertainly: Well, I don't like it, it makes me uncomfortable, but I'm not sure it really "pisses me off." I guess it's hard for me to get angry. I'm not aware of being *angry* with you; I'm *scared* of you.

Mort answers: That's a lot of crap! Dr. M. says to Mort: I agree that Felicia is much more aware of the anger in you, Mort, than she is of the anger in herself. But I disagree with your saying she's not scared—I think a lot of people in the group are more scared of you than you think. Just like she doesn't know anger, you don't know fear, so you don't believe people can be afraid of your contempt.

Mort answers disgustedly: I don't know what I believe and don't believe anymore!

And so the session continues. Interaction is fairly lively; interruptions are frequent. By the end of the session, which lasts ninety minutes, all members have spoken up spontaneously, although three have been relatively quiet, and none has "held the floor" for more than a few minutes at a time. The analyst continued to intervene from time to time, but there were periods of seven or eight minutes during which he listened and said nothing whatever.

A discussion of some of the things that the therapist was trying to do in this session will appear in a later section (see "Role of the Leader" below).

KEY CONCEPTS: THEORETICAL

A complete understanding of the concepts employed by the present model would entail a presentation of the psychoanalytic theory of personality development and psychopathology. Such a review is beyond the scope of this book. We will assume some acquaintance with psychoanalytic theory on the part of the reader and will confine ourselves to those concepts that bear on psychoanalytic method, especially as it applies to group practice.

Free-Association. This was the method eventually hit upon by Freud when he discarded hypnosis as too unreliable and too encouraging of suggestibility and dependence on the part of the patient. The analyst instructed the patient to free his mind as much as possible from his typically purpose-oriented, and semirational day-to-day thoughts and preoccupations, and to report every thought, association, fancy, memory, and/or revery that came to his mind—however silly, trivial, incongruous or shocking. The minimization of outer stimuli effected by the analysand's lying on a couch, facing away from the analyst, was thought to facilitate this process. Hopefully the free-associations, being less reality-bound than most associational thinking, would give the analyst, and eventually the patient, easier access to the latter's unconscious processes.

Could this most basic of analytic methods be employed within the group context? Seemingly not, since the face-to-face presence of six or seven other strangers would surely turn the patient away from his inner life to the very interpersonal reality from which free-association had been designed to free him. Yet Wolf, Schwartz, Durkin (1964), and others found that although free-association obviously could not be facilitated in precisely the same way as on the analytic couch, something close to it in spirit could be duplicated in the group setting.

Patients are not explicitly directed to free-associate in a group, and it would be a distortion of the term to claim that patient's overt interactions with one another in a group constitute "free associations". However, the therapist can, through encouraging group patients to discuss what is on their minds—even if it does not strike them as immediately relevant or helpful, by being receptive and having a nondirective attitude, by being tolerant of interruptions and distractions, and by informing the group that their fantasies and dreams have a special relevance, help to establish an atmosphere of permissiveness such that the patient's unconscious dynamics can be revealed much more dramatically and more quickly than they could be in more conventional task-oriented discussion groups. Foulkes' (1964) term "free-floating discussion" would seem to most aptly describe the kind of verbal interaction that such an atmosphere facilitates. Moreover, at certain arbitrary points the leader can intervene and specifically ask an individual patient for "free associations," e.g., if a patient has made a slip-of-the-tongue, the therapist might very quickly ask: "Now what is the very first thing that comes to your mind when you hear your own error?"

Wolf (1962, pp. 16-18) developed the "go-around" technique as a way of adapting free-association to a group context. In it, a patient is asked to go around to each person in the group and say the first thing that comes to mind about him or her. While involving a reaction to a specific stimulus, the patient is asked to react spontaneously and along channels that are usually considered inappropriate to more rationally-focused and "purposive" social conversation. This use of the go-around technique probably could be described as a kind of group free-association. As Wolf and Schwartz see it, the patient who is going around is rewarded whenever his associations "hit home" and the recipient acknowledges this fact; this kind of reinforcement can be particularly valuable in the case of inhibited people who tend to mistrust their more intuitive and spontaneous ideas. The go-around was later to be adapted to a variety of group models, including the T-group and the Gestalt-therapy workshop; however, the historical data indicate that credit for its first use belongs to Wolf, who was using it as standard practice by 1940.

Resistance. The concept of resistance is fundamental to the practice and understanding of psychoanalysis. Resistance is defined by Fenichel (1945, p.

27) as "everything that prevents the patient from producing material derived from the unconscious." Freud first became aware of the phenomenon when he observed the difficulties that his patients experienced in attempting to obey the fundamental rule of free association. He discovered that they continuously, although for the most part unintentionally, used various devices to circumvent his request that they candidly report on their spontaneous flow of associations; they asked questions, they challenged the analytic contract and its rationale, they commented on the physical appearance of the room, and soon Freud came to view resistance as an unconscious dynamic in its own right—one that attempts to defend the personality against intolerable anxiety, which would arise should the patient become aware of his repressed impulses and their concomitant emotions.

Resistance, then, operates in the service of the ego as a defense against anxiety. How is it different from a defense? It is a kind of defense, but one that operates specifically in analytic therapy to prevent the analyst and patient from succeeding in their joint task of gaining insight into the dynamics of the patient's unconscious, even though the latter's conscious, healthy self strives to cooperate with the analytic effort. Because resistance refers to any behavior that serves to prevent the therapist and the patient from understanding the latter's unconscious processes, it can take many forms. Perhaps the most basic is a direct evasion of the therapy altogether; e.g. the patient is often absent or late. Another, also relatively direct form, is a conscious lack of cooperation, and an expression of distrust and doubt in relation to the analyst and the validity of his procedures.

Resistance can also occur in much more indirect and complex ways. One such way is the "transference resistance", which will be discussed more fully below. Another involves what Reich (1949) was the first to label as "character resistances". These are deeper resistances that are not only directed toward the person of the analyst (though this is naturally how they are manifested in individual treatment), but are part of the individual's habitual, day-to-day behavioral repertoire in dealing with other people. They are considered characterological because they develop early in life and are basic to a person's character structure and character defenses. Examples would be the cerebral way of life of the detached intellectual, the denying, "everything's coming up roses" attitude of the Pollyanna, and the clinging, overtly adulatory but covertly hostile-demanding, orientation of the passive-dependent person. Examples of character resistances from the illustrative session above would be Ruth's masochism and Felicia's eagerness to be helpful to others. These kinds of resistances are more pervasively defensive and more deeply embedded within the person's life style than are the avoidance-directed resistances described earlier. A general rule for the analyst in both individual and group therapy is first to call the patient's attention to the more readily observable resistances, since he is less likely to consider them integrally related to himself and his whole style of being; for example, it is typically easier for a patient to accept the analyst's observation that he often changes the subject when beginning to discuss his father, than it is for him to acknowledge such character resistances as dependency and pollyannaism. In individual analysis, such attitudes in the patient may not be remarked upon by the analyst for a fair length of time.

The group situation is somewhat different. While the therapist may still, as in individual therapy, prefer to say nothing about the more pathological aspects of a patient's character, the permissiveness of the group encourages the patient's peers to react openly to whatever behavior he manifests. Such characterological attitudes as bravado, covert hostility, and provocative flirtatiousness are bound to stir up feelings of excitement, envy, and irritation in other people. This is an ideal course of events, since the initial reactions of nontherapist peers will be less threatening to the patient than the interventions of the authority-analyst. While the meaning of these defensive styles, particularly with regard to their connections with childhood events, may await eventual exploration at the hands of the analyst, the patient will at least begin to be more aware of them. One distinct advantage of the group context is that particular kinds of characterological resistances, especially those involving apathy and deviousness, can more easily be reacted to in more angry and confronting ways by a patient's peers than by his traditionally somewhat more aloof and more "professional" analyst.

Characterological resistances that are more difficult to identify involve open displays of seemingly genuine emotion, like anger. While anger for many patients is an underlying emotion that they have difficulty in acknowledging, for others it can be used as a resistance to an awareness of other feelings that are even harder to admit to consciousness; for example, a patient might use hostility as a means of forestalling the rejection and hurt that he fears would occur were he to express directly his tender feelings for another group member. Even where anger is not a defense, its repeated expression can serve to avoid an exploration as to its meaning. This type of resistance is frequently encountered in patients for whom emotional expression is easy, but who have difficulty in taking a more detached and reflective attitude toward their own behavior.

A complex form of resistance that is wholly unique to groups involves a collusion among some members. For example, two patients might form a voyeuristic-exhibitionistic combination in which one expresses great interest in the other's sexual promiscuity. Both appear to be playing the "therapy game"—the first complains about his compulsive sexuality and seems to be revealing significant material, and the second reacts with concern. But is the first exploring his need to arouse envy and excited admiration in the other? And is the second aware of how he uses the first's sexuality vicariously?

Another resistance frequently encountered in groups involves one patient's "playing therapist" to another. Member X's interpretations of Y's behavior may be quite astute and quite helpful to Y; yet they may serve as a resistance for X, who in being therapeutic is saved from having to talk about the problems that brought him to the group as a patient. One way in which the therapist could call this to X's attention is to ask, in a neutral and non-challenging way: "I sense that Y is quite receptive to your remarks, and gains something from them. But I wonder what you would say if you were to use the group for your own problems in outside living. What if Y became your therapist and you her patient; what would you want to say to her?"

Thus in any single session the analyst might be faced with a variety of resistances. Member A may have stayed away altogether. B may be very silent and appear dejected. C, D, and E may chat about what they did over the weekend, while F and G say nothing and give no indication of what they are feeling. There is, of course, no clear guidelines to the therapist as to what form his intervention should take in such an instance. He could conceivably focus on B, since the latter is the one whose feelings appear to be most visible, and wonder what he is experiencing. If it is early in the group's history, where the main goal is to stimulate interaction, the leader may simply wonder what's happening. He senses that people are holding back from talking about what's most on their minds. What are they experiencing?

Transference. Like resistance, transference is a classic analytic concept. Indeed, it has been stated by more than one theorist that the analysis of resistance and transference lies at the core of psychoanalytic therapy, and that any therapy offering systematic handling of these two phenomena may properly be described as psychoanalytic.

Transference manifests itself in individual treatment at that point where "unfinished business" from the patient's past life causes him to distort the present, and either misperceive, or behave inappropriately to, the analyst. It is believed that all patients must eventually do this, because their neurosis in itself indicates that attitudes formed in childhood are being inappropriately carried over into adulthood and because the very conditions of analysis—the analyst's neutrality and relative passivity—facilitate transference distortions. Transference is an extremely dynamic force within the analysis. If handled correctly it can play a highly facilitative role for several reasons: (1) it "charges" up the process, since the patient, rather than just *reporting* on his past, begins to *relive* it in the therapy, (2) his "libidinization" of the therapist holds him to the often painful, frustrating, and time-consuming analytic process, and (3) it can be a major source of information for the analyst, who can now learn from the patient's reactions to him a great deal about his internal conflicts, interpersonal problems, and behavior patterns.

Transference is closely related to resistance in that at a particular point in a patient's individual analysis, it can become a form of resistance called "transference resistance" i.e., when the patient's involvement with the analyst becomes so intense that his original purpose for having entered therapy in the first place becomes lost; he becomes so interested in the analyst that he is more concerned about the latter's regard for him than he is about changing. This point of intensity is also referred to at times as the "transference neurosis". Transference resistance is considered to be a very useful form of resistance for the analyst, since it repeats in microcosmic form the way in which the neurosis initially developed. Yet it is one that is very difficult to resolve because the patient has now lost interest in using the analysis to understand himself and his history; instead he wants to exploit it for a quite different and more neurotic purpose, i.e., to gain from the therapist what he wanted but was unable to get from significant people in his past.

Because an examination of the vicissitudes of the therapist-patient relationship was so basic to the analysis, analysts were initially quite concerned about how the introduction of the group parameter would affect transference. Wouldn't the fact that group members continually interrupt one another, and that each of them develops his own particular form of intense transference to the analyst, make it impossible for the latter to systematically follow the subtle evolution of transference in any one patient? After all, one of the reasons why an analyst treating an analysand in individual therapy was able to follow his transference pattern so closely was the sheer amount of time provided for the patient to verbalize without interruption. And wouldn't the presence of so many fellow patients prevent a patient's transference from reaching a point of maximum intensity?

The group context did indeed considerably alter the original psychoanalytic situation. However, initial experiments with the group method reassured these early practitioners of analytic group therapy as to the continued usefulness and applicability of the transference concept. To be sure, keeping track of the vicissitudes of any one transference relationship had become a more complicated business, and the presence of a group made it less likely that these transferences would reach the point of full-blown transference resistances. Yet transference did develop in a recognizeable and meaningful pattern and it proved amenable to systematic analysis. In addition, the avoidance of a strongly entrenched transference resistance was not necessarily disadvantageous, because in individual treatment such resistances, unless expertly and forcibly handled by the analyst, often kept the patient at a point of such intense dependency that further therapeutic progress was undermined. Indeed, according to Wolf and Schwartz, one of the distinct advantages of the group is that the presence of other members renders less likely this kind of regression.

Even more exciting and not quite predicted was the discovery that "multiple transferences" regularly occurred within the group—i.e., distorted perceptions of other group members as well as of the therapist, which could now reveal important material about a patient that would not have been so readily available to the analyst had he continued to work in an individual context only. More specifically, since analysis in the one-to-one situation emphasized what Wolf and Schwartz refer to as the "authority vector," the analyst in individual treatment was mainly related to as a parental figure and would very rarely be viewed as a sibling. The introduction of the group parameter added a "peer vector," with the result that the analyst could now gain insight into how the patient related to his contemporaries, as well as to authority, and these peer relationships within the group frequently reproduced his early relationships with siblings. Therefore triangles might develop wherein one patient competed with another for the therapist's favor, much as he had done in relation to a particular sibling in childhood.

In addition to the peer vector, certain parent-vector transferences emerged in group treatment that were difficult to elicit in individual treatment. For example once a male therapist was experienced as a father by a male patient in individual therapy, it would usually become harder for the patient to then develop toward the therapist the kind of feelings and relationship that he had had with his *other* parent. Yet such a shift would be essential for a more complete analysis in which the analyst gained an understanding of all the developmental vectors. The introduction of other patients, and the opportunity for multiple transferences that they provided could therefore be extremely important. In the example above the male patient might eventually reveal a highly transferential reaction to an older woman in the group that in many ways recapitulated the mother-son relationship.

Some of these developments were not wholly unexpected. More surprising was a phenomenon wherein the introduction of a peer figure could produce a powerful change in the patient's transference relationship to the analyst. An example of such a shift is given by Wolf and Schwartz (pp. 33-34). In an early session of a particular group, the analyst praised George for the latter's rather perceptive reactions to Helen. In individual treatment previous to the group, Helen had shown some mildly erotic feelings, combined with some fearfulness, toward the analyst; this essentially duplicated what she had felt toward her father as a child. Yet on hearing the latter's compliment to George, she sensed George as "preferred"—primarily because of his more powerful intellect—and reacted with both jealousy and hostility. Gradually it became clear that the therapist had become Mother for her at the point where he made his remark to George; the latter stood for the brother whom she perceived as having won out over her in a bitter competition for their mother's esteem. In her mind George had been successful for two reasons: his greater intelligence and his maleness. The analyst now had a deeper insight into Helen's phallic strivings and her excessive admiration for intellectual accomplishment. It would seem that a *triadic* element had to be introduced into the analytic situation for the maternal transference to emerge.

The recognition and clarification of these transference distortions in the moment of their occurence can constitute an important step toward change.

According to Wolf and Schwartz, the insights that develop in the patient can have a dramatic immediacy in the group setting that they lack in individual treatment because the group members, when they are misperceived by a patient or treated by him in pathological ways, are usually much more emotionally reactive than is the analyst when he is similarly related to in one-to-one therapy. For example, if a woman patient reacts with anger or with genuinely hurt feelings at being inappropriately cast in the role of the "bad mother" by a male patient, her sense of injury may prod him into a more intense examination of the validity of his perception than would the more detached reaction of his analyst, whom he cannot get to know in as real a way as he can this other group member. It is when the group's reaction to a transference distortion "hits home" that a patient often *spontaneously* remembers historical events that provide relevant data about the distortion's development. What also becomes especially alive in the group, particularly for the analyst, who in individual sessions gets no living sense of how the patient interacts with his peers, is the extent to which the patient *provokes* the "abuse" that he claims to so often and so undeservedly receive from other people.

Countertransference. Here the focus of concern is the analyst; countertransference usually refers to the feelings occurring in him as a response to the intense transference-projections and fantasies that he stimulates in his patients. It is important that he recognize these feelings and deal with them—particularly those that activate his own unresolved neurotic conflicts. While countertransference is bound to be a potent variable in individual psychoanalysis, group psychoanalysis can only compound it since the analyst is now confronted with many patients; not only does this mean one transference multiplied by seven or eight, but it also means the possibility of alliances whereby normally timid patients use their multiple strength, or the presence of an unusually arrogant patient, to launch collective attacks against the therapist. Is this intensification of countertransference responses an asset or a liability? Certainly it means stronger emotional stress for the therapist. Durkin (1964) sees in it, however, a potential asset: the analyst, confronted by the sheer "weight of numbers" in the group, is forced to confront traits and feelings in himself that he can more easily discard as aspects of the patient's distortions in individual therapy. If he can find a way of relinquishing some of his needs for omnipotence, the valid perceptions of himself that are offered by a group can help him to engage in a more realistic appraisal of his strengths and weaknesses, which will in turn tend to benefit his work with patients.

Acting Out. Acting out is a term that has been broadened beyond its original meaning to a point where it sometimes is equated with engaging in any socially taboo behavior. In its more restricted and technical meaning it refers to sexual and/or aggressive behavior engaged in by a patient as a way of forestalling a more painful confrontation of his problematic feelings and conflicts in the analytic situation. As Wolf and Schwartz point out, acting out always occurs as a response to transference feelings and always constitutes a resistance to insight and change. For example, a patient begins to transfer the castration fears he felt in relation to his father to his analyst; rather than face these fears he becomes sexually promiscuous as a kind of counterphobic defiance, as if to "dare" the analyst to punish him, just as he had done with his father in childhood. The sexual activity, which is tension-relieving—at least for the moment—helps him to avoid the anxiety that would accompany a direct facing of his problem.

It is often pointed out that group psychoanalysis increases the opportunities that the patient has for acting out in the session. As Wolf and Schwartz point out, traditional analysis virtually immobilizes the patient; he is supposed to lie on the couch and put everything into words, with the result that even his getting up from the couch could be labeled acting out. Group members, on the other hand, chew gum, smoke, occasionally touch, etc. Those groups who regularly have an alternate session from which the analyst is absent have an even greater opportunity to act out. How the present model conceptualizes and attempts to handle this problem is presented below (see *Limits*).

Interpretation. Until now we have referred to the analyst's "dealing with" various resistance and transferences; the way he deals with them is mainly through interpretations, which are directed toward "helping something unconscious to become conscious by naming it at the moment it is striving to break through" (Fenichel, 1945, p. 25). The literature has placed great emphasis on the correct timing of interpretations; as Fenichel's definition implies, they should be made at a point where the phenomenon to be interpreted is at the center of the patient's attention and close to his conscious awareness. Analytic theory viewed as most potent those interpretations that connected a dynamic aspect of the present transference relationship to a remembered childhood situation.

Two very general rules that hold for psychoanalysis in any context are (1) Interpret a resistance or defense before interpreting the emotion or conflict underlying the resistance, and (2) Interpret the *derivative* (or displaced aspect) of a feeling before interpreting the more basic feeling—e.g., point to the patient's sense that he received little *attention* from his mother before pointing out his feeling that he received no *love* from her (and a corollary of this, if the memory data and fantasies productions should go back far enough, might be his feeling that he literally received insufficient *food* from her).

These rules do not require any modification in the group setting. One dimension that does arise in the group is that of aiming interpretations at group-dynamic processes or at dynamic process involving either specific individuals or subgroups—e.g., dyads and triads. The present model clearly de-emphasizes interpretations that are aimed at the group as a whole. Even Durkin (1964, p. 201), who rejects the strong antigroup-dynamics stand taken by Wolf and Schwartz, writes: "In my view, making specific, tailor-made interpretations for each person is the surest way to bring about understanding and change."

Working Through. "Working through" refers to the accumulation of interpretations over time and their cumulative effects on the patient, as he has the opportunity to see the manifold ways in which some of his core conflicts and core defenses emerge again and again—in dreams, in remembrances, in day-to-day problems, and in the fluctuations of his transference resistance. It is as if he is seeing old problems in ever-new clothing, and new connections become evident. For example, if the primary psychodynamic focus is on an Oedipal problem, the patient will have a chance to see how this effects his relations to both men and women, superiors and subordinates, and the areas of both competition and affection in his life. No single interpretation dissolves a resistance forever; therefore resistances, despite newly-gained insights, will reappear—in different guises and at different characterological levels. Hence working through requires a fairly long period of time, especially since one of its primary dimensions is a transference relationship that takes a while to build in intensity and further time to dissolve. The application of psychoanalytic method to a group setting does not substantially alter this "working through" process; it does, as indicated above, make the emergence of the transference more complex and more difficult for the analyst to follow.

KEY CONCEPTS: METHODOLOGICAL

Group Composition. The great majority of practicing group therapists prefer hetereogeneous to homogeneous groups. Wolf and Schwartz give several reasons for their having this preference: (1) a heterogeneous group is a microcosm of the real world, and it is adaptation to the world as it is that constitutes the main goal of treatment; the patient must learn to deal in real life with the kind of disagreement and pluralism that he will encounter in such a group, (2) a heterogeneous group is less likely to encourage conformity to a uniform standard, (3) a heterogeneous group offers a much greater opportunity for multiple transferences; one particular patient may identify a youthful man in the group as her younger brother, an older woman as her aunt, and so on.

The Alternate Session. This is not an inherent feature of the analytic group model, though Wolf and Schwartz, along with many other analytically-oriented therapists, strongly endorse it. Regular sessions expose the patient to the simultaneity of authority and peer vectors, alternate sessions to the peer vector alone. Some patients might find themselves more willing to talk up in the alternate sessions, where they need not be inhibited by fear of the therapist's disapproval; other patients might feel safer in the regular session, since they view the therapist as a protector. Without an alternate session, there would be no opportunity for these behavioral contrasts to reveal themselves. Another value of the alternate session is that it can accelerate the manifestation of transference attitudes; e.g., the shy patient may, in the absence of the therapist, express more negative feelings about the therapist than he is able to do in his presence. Whether or not this material is directly reported in the regular session, it is an important first step in alerting the group to what the patient in question is feeling, and group members may encourage him to express his hostility more directly.

The alternate session is essentially viewed as a half-way house between the "inner sanctum" of the regular session and the everyday, real-life world. Patients visit one another's homes, with the result that they become less anonymous for one another, and they have an opportunity to become more adult-like and autonomous as they are forced to take responsibility for the session in the absence of the parent-analyst.

Limits. The Wolf and Schwartz model is reasonably typical of the analytical model in that it emphasizes that limits are necessary in a group, just as they are in life in general. To some degree this is a reflection of psychoanalytic theory, which emphasizes that frustration is inevitable in life and that maturity entails the ability to withstand it. The group does not continue beyond the prescribed hours for closing, does not accept any new members beyond a certain upper limit, and discourages open sexuality and physical aggression in the session. While awareness and verbal expression of feeling is a goal, so is the exploration and understanding of such feelings.

An immediate practical concern for any practicing group therapist involves the extent to which he will specifically prohibit sexual acting out among group members, either in the alternate session or outside the auspices of the group altogether. The position taken by Wolf and Schwartz on this matter is fairly typical. They prefer to take a neutral position than to expressly forbid sexual relationships among group members. If they were to make a specific prohibition, they would duplicate the original position of the parent who forbade incest, thereby transforming what had been a transference illusion into a reality. And, should a prohibition be made and a patient violate it, he would be encouraged to hide his behavior from the group. Since sexual liasons are not likely to have a destructive effect on the group if they are acknowledged and then analyzed, the implicit taboo in Wolf's and Schwartz's groups was not directed against sexual behavior per se but against any collusion between members wherein they agreed to keep secret from the group significant data about their relationship. Wolf and Schwartz also believe that sexual intimacy within the group can, in certain instances, have constructive results for the people involved.

Combined Treatment. Combined treatment refers to a situation in which a group patient is simultaneously seen in individual therapy, either with his group therapist or another therapist. Combined treatment is the typical practice of many analytically-oriented therapists; yet Wolf and Schwartz do not recommend it. They believe that group therapy is a valid and unique treatment in its own right, and that too often the analyst who sees a patient in both individual and group treatment tends to regard one as supplementary to the other, with the group being viewed as supplementary, and the individual sessions as the core of treatment. In such a situation, the patient can evade having to work out his problems with authority in the group since he knows that he will have the individual hour in which to communicate with the therapist privately. He may also use the individual hour to express feelings about group members that properly belong in the group. Limiting the patient's contact with the therapist to group meetings forces him to come to terms with his therapist in the company of his peers.

Wolf and Schwartz can see having individual sessions with a patient on a limited basis—e.g., to support him during moments of crisis, to see him during a time when he feels he cannot attend the group, or to work out an intense transference reaction to the analyst that does not prove amenable to analysis in the group. They also see individual therapy as preparatory for group treatment; indeed, the great majority of their own group patients had had prior individual analysis, some of them for a period of several years.

SPECIAL USES OF THE GROUP

Because psychoanalysis in groups involved the first deliberate extension of a model that had originally been developed for treating a single person, we would like to briefly review what group analysts saw as the unique advantage of introducing the group parameter. The group helps the patient:

1. to see that he is not isolated and alone in having problems, that others have similar difficulties.
2. to discover in himself resources for listening to and understanding others that he had not suspected were there; this can be an important source of increased self-esteem.
3. to re-experience his early family relationships—but this time in a setting that is conducive to a more favorable outcome.
4. to demonstrate to the analyst in a much more vivid way his pattern of interpersonal relating, especially those things that he does to provoke in others reactions that he in turn finds problematic.

5. to experience in a more vivid way his distorted transference perceptions of the therapist, since many of the group members will perceive the therapist quite differently.

6. to experience, via transferences to fellow patients, early significant relationships that cannot be transferred to the therapist because of some of the latter's objective characteristics—e.g., age, sex, physical appearance, personality, etc.

7. to experience the indiscriminateness of his transference distortions, since he will probably project the same image onto several group members, none of whom—from an objective point-of-view—resemble one another.

8. to gain insight into the effects of his character resistances on others more quickly and more dramatically than he can in individual therapy.

9. to see that it is safe and acceptable to express intense anger—especially toward the therapist—since if he is timid in this regard he has the living example of others to spur him on.

10. to wean himself away from the kind of prolonged, excessively self-searching and increasingly dependent relationship to the analyst that can occur in individual therapy—by interposing the reality of other people, who force their way into what might otherwise become a patient-therapist symbiosis.

ROLE OF THE LEADER

First let us look at some fairly general principles describing the functions of the group leader within the present model, and then consider in more detail how some of these are accomplished. The analytic group therapist: (1) sets limits, (2) facilitates the group interaction by helping to establish an atmosphere that is open and accepting, (3) offers support to an individual when the latter is in need of it and not getting it from the group, (4) is alert to manifestations of resistance and transference, (5) points out resistance and transference to the patient when the patient is at a point of sufficient awareness to accept and integrate such interventions, and (6) interprets, at an appropriate time, some of the meanings of these various resistances and transferences, including—if possible—their relationship to childhood events and patterns; since the criterion for timing is the patient's ability to accept and really *understand* the interpretation, considerable exploration must already have occurred before the group analyst is able to make a definitive interpretation and before the patient is able to acknowledge its validity.

One very general aspect of the analyst's style of relating in the group, particularly in its early life, involves his abdication of formal leadership. In other words, in the absence of his willingness to actively direct the group discussion in any way, or to answer specific questions concerning the meaning of particular behaviors or the advisability of certain action, more responsibility for the formation of the group life is left to the members. The group members begin to interact more and more spontaneously, to take an increasing amount of responsibility for what takes place in the session, and finally to become auxiliary therapists as they begin to point out significant motivations and resistances in one another. An example of this in our illustrative session, would be when Mort pointed out to Felicia that she is much more comfortable in describing herself as frightened than as angry. Wolf and Schwartz place considerable emphasis on the specific therapeutic benefit that this kind of behavior has for the patient *offering* the help, since he is able to sense capacities for resourcefulness, sensitivity, and caring within himself that he may not have suspected were there, and begins to appreciate the transferential aspects of his earlier conviction that it was only the leader who could be a source of therapy in the group.

The group's gradual assumption of responsibility for the session enables the leader to be relatively passive, at least for large segments of time, and to direct his attention to subtle aspects of the patients' statements or interactions. Often this is in the form of questioning: what does this mean to you? what about this disturbs you so much? etc. While not able to have the same kind of anonymity in the group that he can in individual treatment, he still is relatively reserved in stating directly his own immediate feelings about what is going on or about particular members. (If strong feelings of this kind develop within the therapist, he typically regards them as constituting "countertransference" and as thereby indicating that some of his own neurotic difficulties are beginning to interfere with his effectiveness at particular points in the group interaction.) Therefore, Dr. M. in the illustration did not directly react to Mort's attempt to bait him, and when Felicia expressed feelings about his remaining silent in the face of Mort's provocations, he kept the focus on Felicia rather than on himself—that is, he refused to become involved in the *reality* of why he was silent or the reality of what he felt, but instead viewed this as a projection of some internal dynamic within herself.

Other characteristic interventions of the analyst in the segment illustration were the following: (1) Early in the session he asks Felicia what pleases her about Ruth's "speaking up"; as in the example cited immediately above, Felicia focuses on the external happenings of the group, but tends to omit the *affects* inside her that have been stimulated by the proceedings. Thus she tends, in a subtle way, to assume the function of an assistant therapist; she comments in a sometimes helpful way on what is happening, but not in a way that reveals her own personal involvement. This can be seen as a type of character resistance, and the leader tries to pinpoint this when he tells Felicia that he rarely hears her ask for something for herself. (2) Later in the session he tries to get Ruth to see the relationship between the way she deals with Mort in the group and with Bob in her personal life; Ruth is focused on the overt problem with Bob, and tends not to see her tolerance of Mort's sadism as but another instance of her character pathology. The therapist tries to clarify Ruth's difficulty in experiencing conscious anger; as he points out, she prefers to blame herself rather than to strike out at Mort. (3) He encourages Ruth to relate her masochistic way of handling anger to her past by asking her how far back this pattern seems to go. (4) He confronts Mort's highly indirect way of expressing his feelings, but when Mort continues to be provocative, he does not reveal whatever irritation or disappointment he might be feeling. (5) At the end of the illustration, he tries to emphasize for Mort how he attempts to mask his anxiety through counterphobic sadism and attack; this would be an instance of a situation where the therapist sees anger as a *resistance* to other, less conscious affects, like fearfulness and despair.

Hence the leader, albeit at times active, is not quite a full-fledged member of the group. He is more aloof than the other participants, and despite his emphasis on the expression of feeling within the group, concentrates—in his own interventions— on a cognitive clarification of the feelings expressed. In actuality, his clarifications and interpretations arrive slowly and bit by bit; with Felicia, Ruth, and Mort he strove to make just one point or connection. Further clarifications, enlarging on the significance of what he has already pointed out and on its possible connections to childhood events, remain for future sessions.

References

Bateson, G., Jackson, D. D., Haley, J., and Weakland, J. H. 1956. Toward a theory of schizophrenia. *Behavioral Science, 1.* 251-264.

Durkin, H. E. 1964. *The group in depth.* New York: International Universities Press.

——. 1972. Analytic group therapy and general systems theory. In C. J. Sager and H. S. Kaplan, eds., *Progress in group and family therapy.* New York: Brunner/Mazel.

Fenichel, O. 1945. *The psychoanalytic theory of neurosis.* New York: W.W. Norton & Company.

Foulkes, S. H. 1965. *Therapeutic group analysis.* New York: International Universities Press.

Freud, S. 1913. Totem and taboo. In A. A. Brill (Ed.), *The basic writings of Sigmund Freud.* New York: Random House, 1938.

——. 1922. *Group psychology and the analysis of the ego.* London: Hogarth Press.

——. 1930. *Civilization and its discontents.* London: Hogarth Press.

——. 1939. *Moses and monotheism.* New York: Alfred A. Knopf.

Haley, J. 1970-71. Family therapy. *International Journal of Psychiatry, 9:* 233-242.

Reich, W. 1949. *Character analysis.* New York: Orgone Institute Press.

Wolf, A. and Schwartz, E. K. 1962. *Psychoanalysis in groups.* New York: Grune and Stratton.

4

The Group-Dynamic
Therapy Group

The group-dynamic approach to group psychotherapy is best envisaged as a cluster of models, since its major proponents—Foulkes and Ezriel (both British), and Whitaker and Lieberman (two Americans collaborating together)—have developed individual versions of it. Despite some variation, these theorists have enough in common to group them within a single chapter. They are primarily psychoanalytic in their approach to the individual personality, emphasizing the role of psychosexual stages and of the unconscious in the development of psychopathology; yet they believe that the psychoanalytic approach to group treatment, in keeping the individual person as its primary focus of conceptualization, becomes seriously limited in its ability to deal with group processes. As Foulkes put it, "group psychology must develop its own concepts in its own rights and not borrow them from individual psychology" (1965, p. 60). According to the group dynamicists, an appreciation of social psychology, wherein the group as a whole is regarded as a discrete entity, should be added to the group therapist's background in clinical psychology or psychiatry.

An English theorist with a similar approach is Bion, whose interest in groups originally developed within the context of psychotherapy. However, his most significant contributions were eventually to be a general theory of small-group processes and the creation of a "small-study," or training, group that was directed toward helping relatively healthy people become more aware of group dynamics and consequently more adept in handling intraorganizational relations. Therefore, we regard Bion's small study group as a Growth and Development group, and treat it separately in a later chapter (see Chapter 9).

The group-dynamicists, including Bion, generally found Kurt Lewin's field-theory to be the most suitable conceptual framework for their purposes and thus proceeded to combine psychoanalytic and field-theory principles into the various combinations that constitute Bion's approach to the small study group and the three models to be outlined below. A brief review of Lewin's field theory, and of its Gestalt psychology background, is therefore in order; this material will also be relevant to an understanding of the Gestalt-therapy and T-group models (Chapters 7 and 10).

The founders of the Gestalt school of psychology, Kohler, Koffka, and Wertheimer, were primarily concerned with developing a theory of fundamental psychological processes, with particular attention to perception. However, their conceptual approach had a strong influence on theoretical developments in the fields of motivation, personality, and social psychology. One such development involved the motivational concepts of Kurt Goldstein, which made a substantial contribution to the "organismic" school of personality theory (Hall and Lindzey, 1970); another was Lewin's field theory, which eventuated in a theory of both personality and group dynamics.

Gestalt psychology originated in Germany in the 1920s and took issue with the points of view embodied in structuralism and associationism, which until that time had been the dominant schools within academic psychology. Both associationism and structuralism emphasized a "molecular," as opposed to "molar," conception of perception in that they viewed the basic perceptual act as occurring in terms of fundamentally discrete units or elements, which the perceiver then combined—via the effects of learning and of higher mental processes—to form recognizable patterns and configurations. For example, according to the school of structuralism, a table was initially seen in terms of a rectangular plane juxtaposed to four cylinders; it was only through past experience and learning that these five distinct "elements" were seen as fundamentally related properties of a single functional whole. Indeed, even the rectangular table top itself was not necessarily seen as a complete unit, but instead was initially perceived as many discrete bits of sensation that, through past associations to one another and to a functional use, began to be organized as a plane.

The Gestalt psychologists, on the other hand, insisted that pattern and organization inhered in perception from the very first, rather than emerging as a secondary or subsequent phenomenon. Stating the well-known principle "the whole is greater than its parts," and designing some ingenious visual patterns to illustrate it, they attempted to show that incomplete configurations tended to be seen as whole by the perceiver, and that the appearance of an individual element (or, in the language of Gestalt psychology, a "figure") could be totally altered by the larger design (or "ground") in which it was embedded. An example of this latter phenomenon would be the popular puzzles often found in children's magazines in which the child is asked to "find" a "hidden" figure or person in a large and complex picture. Hence "relationships among components of a perceptual field rather than the fixed characteristics of the individual components determine perception" (Hall and Lindzey, 1970, p. 210).

Lewin's field theory visualized both personality and group processes as patterned "fields" or configurations wherein each element (e.g., in the personality, a need or drive; in the group, an individual) could not be meaningfully viewed in isolation but instead had to be related to every other element within the field. This involved a rather direct application of Gestalt perceptual psychology to more complex personality and social phenomena. While Lewin's personality theory did not play an especially formative role within modern personality psychology, his approach to groups enjoys, in many respects, a keystone position in group-dynamic theory. In general, the Lewinian approach to groups places less emphasis than does the psychoanalytic model on what a participant's behavior expresses about his own past, and much more emphasis on how it is a function of whatever tensions predominate within the group at any one point in time. These tensions in turn are influenced by all the significant interrelationships within the group.

Of course the psychoanalytic model of group interaction also gave attention to the effects that members have upon one another, primarily via the concept of "multiple transference" (see Chapter 3). What the group-dynamics therapist argued is that the group psychoanalyst too often limited his awareness to dyadic and triadic sub-group formations and to what they indicated about each person's history rather than to what any particular interaction revealed about the immediate emotional dynamics of the entire group. As an example, let us take an interaction between Fran and Arthur, in which Fran accuses Arthur of ignoring her by consistently paying more attention to every other person in the group than to her. The group-dynamics therapist has little doubt that Fran's reaction to Arthur has a transferential aspect in that it is in part a function of her past relationships to her father or her brother, and in this sense he is in agreement with the group psychoanalyst. However, he is convinced that he will gain the most therapeutic leverage if he focuses instead on the group-process meaning of this dyadic interaction. In attempting to do so, he asks himself the following questions: (1) in what way does the interaction between Fran and Arthur reflect the overall balance of forces within the group at this particular moment? and (2) what does the group either gain or avoid by allowing its tensions and themes to be channeled into this specific two-person interchange?

What the group-dynamics therapist is in effect claiming is that if any significant aspect of the group climate in which Fran accused Arthur were different—for instance, if a new member had not been added the week before—the conflict between them would not have the same content or possibly even take place at all since it is primarily a function of unexpressed tensions within the group as a whole. For instance, a look at what has preceded this interaction reveals that group tensions have been accumulating around the theme of ignoring and being ignored. The group has, since the week before, made persistent attempts to approach its new member, Rick, who has sat tense and withdrawn, responding minimally to its questions. The participants appear to be feeling increasingly helpless and paralyzed in their efforts to come to terms with him. While most of their overt affect has been concentrated on how Rick ignores them, a covert theme expresses anger with the leader for abandoning or ignoring the group at a crucial time of need. It is precisely at this point that Fran accuses Arthur of ignoring her, and the two of them are about to commence a dialogue in which they will attempt to ignore the other patients as they go about exploring the justification of Fran's complaint. For the group dynamicist, then, any concentration on the transferential aspects of Fran's reaction will neglect the major issue. As he saw it, the group context of group therapy transformed the basic psychotherapy situation of the individual patient and his analyst more radically than the psychoanalytic model of group therapy provided for. What was needed, therefore, was a shift from a primarily intrapsychic model of the group to a primarily interactional model.

The one group in which psychoanalysis had shown a distinct interest, from its very beginnings, was the family. However, even here the psychoanalytic model's focus was primarily intrapsychic in that it had tended to confine its attention to the influence that one or two significant people—almost always the parents—had on the developing child. Hence it had remained to a later theorist, like Adler (1927), to formulate a psychology of sibling relationships. Freud had come closest to an interactional focus when he highlighted the three-person system of the Oedipal triangle. Yet even here the main emphasis was more on how each dyadic relationship within this triangle (mother-father, mother-child, and father-child) affected the child's psychodynamics than on the way in which each of these relationships was influenced by, and in turn influenced, the total field of forces within the triangle.

A more total picture of the family would have to leave room for the reciprocal influence that the child has on his parents' marriage. In an interactional framework of this nature, the presence of additional siblings complicates the child-mother-father triangle, and by implication the entire family network, still further. In this conceptual approach the family is viewed as a dynamic configuration in which every member and every relationship makes a distinct contribution to whatever degree of equilibrium or disequilibrium characterizes it. This concept has much in common with the theoretical framework of group-dynamics therapy, and it describes the point of view of such "systems" and "communication" theorists as Bateson, Haley, and Jackson (1956). The group-dynamics therapists have chosen to concentrate their major energies on what Foulkes refers to as "stranger groups" in which patients unknown to one another are treated, while Jackson, Bateson, and Haley have chosen to work mostly in the area of family therapy. Both approaches lie squarely within the tradition of what Durkin (1972) refers to as "general systems theory."

In presenting our cluster of group-dynamic therapy models, we shall place major emphasis on the Whitaker and Lieberman model, since it embodies the same respect for the group as a distinct dynamic in its own right as do the other group-process approaches. At the same time it offers a somewhat clearer conceptual structure and more precise guidelines for when and how the leader should intervene than do the other group-dynamics models. Therefore our "Key Concepts" and "Role of the Leader" sections will relate specifically to the Whitaker and Lieberman model. Before presenting the latter, we shall briefly summarize the models developed by Foulkes and by Ezriel, who, along with Bion (see Chapter 9), represent the British school of group-dynamic psychotherapy.

The Foulkes Model. Sigmund H. Foulkes is a British psychoanalyst who has consistently maintained that the group as a whole is the most meaningful context in which to view the data of the group therapy situation. Foulkes repeatedly reminds us that there is no attempt in his conceptual framework to deny or violate the integrity of the single individual. Instead of a political or ethical issue, the group analyst is here faced with a theoretical problem. Should the events of the group be viewed with the total field of group events as the main "figure," and the individual psychodynamics of each person as its background, or should the emergent properties of the group as a coherent social system be seen as a backdrop against which to view the more important theme, or "figure," of each individual's psychopathology? (Foulkes, 1973). As Foulkes points out (1973, p. 216), this problem is not too different from that faced by a photographer who wants to take a single picture of a building and therefore must choose which perspective or vantage point will offer the fullest and "truest" representation of what it looks like.

For Foulkes the group functions as a coherent and interdependent whole. However idiosyncratic and personal the content of particular verbalizations may seem to be on the surface, they express a latent concern that is common to the group at large. As a patient listens to the comments of others, he unconsciously picks up and reacts to this common thread with associations of his own. In this way each person is acting as a "mouthpiece" for a shared group concern. For instance, if the overall group theme centers on narcissistic body preoccupations, each patient will "resonate" with this theme in terms of his idiosyncratic psychosexual orientation: the oral patient will express themes of taking in; the anal person, themes of expulsion and control; and the phallic person, concerns about castration (Foulkes and Anthony, p. 152).

"The T-situation" is a concept that Foulkes uses to identify what is most therapeutic about the group situation and, more specifically, to clarify the particular role that transference plays in group—as opposed to individual—psychoanalysis. He is at pains to differentiate himself from those psychoanalytic group therapists who view the group as a living out of transference relationships. While acknowledging that transference in its classical sense must play some role in group psychotherapy, he points out that group treatment can never hope to reproduce a patient's infantile Oedipus complex in the same fashion that individual psychoanalysis can. This is because the two-person situation of psychoanalysis, with its inherent frustration of the patient's demand for intimate support, inevitably produces an intensely *vertical* and regressive dimension in which the patient is thrown back to earlier reaction modes of dealing with parental authority. On the other hand, a primarily *horizontal* dimension is created by the group therapy setting, wherein the here-and-now claims of seven or eight other people, each with his own symptoms and crises, will invariably intrude upon whatever tendencies a person has to return to his own past. The development of intensive transference is further diluted in the group by the therapist's greater visibility and more active participation.

In Foulkes' view, however, group therapy offers its own unique variant of transference, and it is one that goes beyond the repetition of specific childhood reactions to a particular person. It is more global, and occurs when a patient transfers characteristics of his current network outside the group to the group itself. A patient, let us say, provokes his children, and his wife and children, into fights with one another which he then attempts to arbitrate; he may also have acted this way in his own family when he was a child and may even do this to some degree in the larger community. Before very long, he will develop similar patterns in the therapy group. According to Foulkes, then, those forces that are traditionally viewed as "intrapsychic" in the psychoanalytic model, are actually part and parcel of, and in dynamic equilibrium with, one's larger familial and socal matrix. Just as the patient's psychopathology originated within the context of such a network, it is best rooted out in the presence of such a network.

How does the leader use his understanding of the group matrix to facilitate change? It is not at all certain that an unsophisticated observer watching Foulkes lead a group would find any notable difference between what he does and what a traditional group analyst does, since Foulkes makes some interpretations and occasionally addresses remarks to individual patients as well as to the entire group. However, it is likely that a Foulkes-led group, if watched closely over time, would reveal that the leader makes somewhat fewer interventions than does a group leader using the traditional psychoanalytic model, and of those interventions that he does make a somewhat larger proportion would be addressed to the group at large rather than to a single patient. One of the reasons for this would be Foulkes' desire that the group "carry the ball" itself. According to him, the group interaction, so long as it is reasonably fluid and focused on a meaningful theme, can have a therapeutic effect on each individual, as he resonates with it expressively and idiosyncratically. For therapy to be occurring, the nature of the latent group theme need not be precisely identified, and each member need not become explicitly and consciously aware of the precise emotional significance that the group dialogue has for him. Therefore, the leader need only intervene when he senses the group interaction to be getting stuck or rigidified.

Foulkes' preference for allowing conflicts and preoccupations to be played out at the group, rather than individual, level is apparent in a concrete instance that he cites involving a woman's grief at the anticipated death of her father (Foulkes and Anthony, 1965, pp. 177-180). Although the group had generally been consoling and supportive during her father's illness, their reaction to his actual death seemed inappropriately callous and facetious. Their levity was finally interrupted by her sarcastically thanking them for their attempt to cheer her up. Foulkes viewed this reaction on the part of the group as constituting a manic form of denial having several meanings, including a refusal to accept the fact of death, a punishment of the woman for threatening whatever equilibrium the group had managed to establish for itself, and a denial of the losses that each member had experienced in his own life. However, the group's manic-depressive oscillation did not stop in this session; in subsequent ones the bereaved woman went through periods in which her mourning alternated with periods of manic elation, as did the group, in a counterpuntal relationship to each other wherein the group became depressed as she became elated and vice-versa.

The kind of counterpoint described above very much resembles a musical theme and variations, and this kind of musical metaphor seems appropriate since Foulkes often likens the therapist's role to that of an orchestra conductor; the latter makes no music himself (i.e., just as the therapist does not participate in the sense of sharing his problems with the group), but instead encourages each instrument to "speak for itself" and tries to make sure that they blend into one another in a way that is appropriately dynamic though not always harmonious. In guiding the manic-depressive cycle above, the leader's job lay not so much in specifically interpreting the defensive implications of the various manic phases, as in permitting the latter to ebb and flow in a rhythmic, counter-balancing fashion wherein the group and the grieving woman could serve as effective foils for one another's moment-to-moment experiences. By doing this, the leader gives the group considerable scope for coming to terms with two dialectical themes, each of which is healthy so long as it embraces the other; psychic pain and one's natural defenses for mastering it.

Foulkes emphasizes both a manifest and a latent level in a group's relationship to its therapist. On the manifest level, the therapist relates to the adult part of group-members' personalities; while analyzing motivations to some extent, he also serves as a model and integrater, demonstrating that powerful feelings can be expressed without danger, that differences among people are the essence of human experience, and that some amount of compromise is essential for adequate social living. In this sense Foulkes' conception of the leader shades into that of an educator, and he is enthusiastic about the possibilities of transforming the group into a community-in-microcosm. On the latent level, the group perceives the therapist as omnipotent, much as the very young and dependent child does his parents. The leader does not interpret this infantile dimension directly, but instead exploits it to create a learning experience wherein the patient develops the emotional resources necessary to wean himself from a leader-dependent position. The group's slowly developing ability to discover its own interactional rhythms— i.e., to function autonomously and to find a source of authority within itself—is a crucial intermediate step in this process.

The Ezriel Model. Henry Ezriel's model can be seen as representing a transitional, or halfway, position between the group-dynamic therapy model, as it is epitomized by Foulkes' version of it, and the earlier psychoanalytic group model; although Ezriel emphasizes the need for the therapist to be aware of and to point out the "common group tension," he also encourages him to specifically interpret how each patient's pathology idiosyncratically dovetails with, and embellishes, this tension. Hence the therapist is encouraged to keep each patient's individual psychodynamics in mind in a more clearcut and focused way than in the other variants of the group-dynamic models. Similarly faithful to the spirit of the original psychoanalytic group model is Ezriel's emphasis on the need for a consistent interpretation of each member's transference to the leader. Indeed, were it not for Ezriel's concern with the common group tension (see below), he could as readily be perceived as belonging within the psychoanalytic model as within the present one.

    The concept of transference, while central in any psychoanalytic model, seems to be of especial importance in Ezriel's, since the analyst is encouraged to consistently attend to the transference implications of every piece of material introduced by the patient. As a result, all of the patient's associations, even those involving past emotional trauma, are examined in terms of their significance for the immediate, moment-to-moment situation existing between the patient and the analyst. If understood correctly, such communications help the therapist to know what in the here-and-now patient-therapist relationship the patient is unconsciously threatened by and consequently attempting to avoid. It is to this issue, rather than to what the patient actually experienced in the events he is endeavoring to recall, that the therapist's interpretations are to be addressed.

    In looking at transference behavior, Ezriel talks about "three kinds of object relations" (Ezriel, 1973, p. 191). The first kind, the "required relationship, entails the kind of relationship that the patient tries to have, either with or without conscious intent, with the therapist. The second kind of object relation, the "avoided relationship," involves the relationship with the analyst that the patient most fears and that he uses the required relationship to defend against. The patient prefers to bypass the avoided relationship because he fears that a calamitous relationship–or "calamity"–would result from it, and it is this calamity that constitutes the third kind of object relation. Since both the avoided and the calamitous relationships exist within the patient's unconscious fantasy, they feel very real to him. For example, a man may relate in an overtly submissive way to his male analyst (the required relationship), in order to exclude from awareness the more competitive relationship he unconsciously experiences (the avoided relationship). His fear is that if he should act out his Oedipal strivings in the therapy the analyst would retaliate (the calamity). According to Ezriel, for real therapeutic improvement to take place, the analyst must not only spell out all three relationships in his interpretation, but must also provide the patient with an opportunity to engage in an active reality-testing of their relationship–i.e., the patient must be allowed to experience the avoided relationship with the analyst (competition) and to learn that the expected calamity (castration) does not occur.

In the group situation, the analyst continues to pay careful heed to the vicissitudes of each patient's transference, with much more emphasis being placed on member-analyst transferences than on member-member transferences. He must also pay closer attention to the dynamics of the immediate situation than on a reconstruction of what transpired between the patient and his parents in the past. (This focusing on the here-and-now aspects of the transference has a particular advantage in group therapy, for in emphasizing the immediate situation it accentuates something that the members share in common and it therefore serves to enhance cohesiveness.) As each member goes about creating a balance of required and avoided relationships that is most meaningful, and at the same time most comfortable for him, he influences, and is in turn influenced by, other members, each of whom is attempting to do the same thing. The product of these interdependent, sometimes clashing and sometimes collaborating forces is a group structure wherein members assume reciprocal roles in one another's transference fantasies. Their common tension is best viewed as a kind of precipitate, amalgam, or common denominator of each one's individual transference; hence the common group tension, like a transference, can be conceptualized in terms of the three kinds of object relations.

In order to illustrate the creation of a common group tension, we shall take an illustrative session cited by Ezriel (1973, pp. 199-202), where a group entertained the idea of having an extra-analytic session or party, and subsequently disagreed as to whether the therapist would approve the idea and whether he should be invited. According to Ezriel, this tension or theme had a predominantly Oedipal coloring: while the group was telling the therapist at the manifest level that it innocently looked forward to a relaxed, anxiety-free session (the required relationship), it was saying at a deeper level that it desired an incestuously-tinged meeting at which "wine, women, and song, i.e. sex" (p. 200) could be enjoyed, but feared that the therapist would disapprove these wishes (the avoided relationship). This, then, was the common group tension shared by the members. At the same time, the way in which each member elaborated on and contributed to this theme reflected his idiosyncratic form of the Oedipal struggle. For instance, members who were more focused on the pleasurable aspects of the wish-fear conflict might emphasize the fun to be had at the party, whereas more anxious participants might worry about the negative consequences that could result from a party; even in the latter group, one member might emphasize apprehension about what the leader would think whereas another might focus on the destructive implications of sexual rivalry within the group. Given these idiosyncratic differences within the common group tension, Ezriel stresses that the therapist's interpretations should be both "group-centered" and "individual-centered" (1973, p. 199), that is, they should identify the common group tension, but also specify the way in which each patient contributes to this tension.

Unless his individual transference is explicitly and consistently interpreted, the group patient will be unable to relinquish his transference needs. He may, of course, in the absence of such interpretations, use therapy for support and for symptomatic improvement, but no true characterological change will occur. Wherever possible, the patient should be made consciously aware of the avoided and calamitous relationships lying behind the required relationship that he tries to establish with the therapist. He should also be given ample leeway in which to test the reality of his catastrophic expectations, and such reality-testing is never so effective in extra-analytic settings as it is in the actuality of the therapist-patient relationship.

It is in this sense of stressing the importance of individually-oriented transference interpretations that Ezriel's model moves toward Wolf and Schwartz's psychoanalytic approach. However, his concomitant emphasis on the overall field of forces produced by the interlocking of each patient's here-and-now transference expectations—i.e. the common group tension—has led to his repeated inclusion within the group dynamic school of group therapy (for example, see Durkin, 1964 and Whitaker and Lieberman, 1965).

The Whitaker and Lieberman Model

Dorothy Stock Whitaker and Morton A. Lieberman are psychologists who at one time were both affiliated with the University of Chicago, originally as graduate students and later as teachers. As social scientists, they have been somewhat more interested in a systematic empirical investigation of the group processes on which their theoretical model rests than have been either

Foulkes or Ezriel (see "Methodological Considerations" below). Partly as a result of this, Whitaker and Lieberman offer a carefully articulated framework for conceptualizing group processes, which in their model are analyzed in terms of the specific concepts, "focal conflict," "theme," "group solution," and "group culture." Consequently, the group therapist—especially the beginning one—is given an unusually concrete guideline as to both the content and the timing of his interventions, one that mainly revolves around the axis of "enabling" versus "restrictive solutions" (see below).

Whitaker and Lieberman, the model's authors, (1965, pp. 14-19) describe in some detail how focal concerns and themes become elaborated. When Patient A makes a comment, B can pick up on any one of a number of aspects of it. What he responds to is that aspect of A's statement that in some way resonates with him. C does the same in relation to what A and B have said prior to her. For instance, A may talk about how his father disappointed him by never playing ball with him. B also expresses anger toward his father, but he relates the anger to a different facet of the father-son relationship. C's anger is more with her mother; yet she states this symbolically, by talking about the disappointments she experienced in her relationship to her aunt, and some attempts to defuse her rage are apparent in her statement that she feels sorry for this pathetic woman. Hence, while there are idiosyncratic aspects to each one's angry concerns, A, B, and C find themselves coalescing around a single theme involving hostile feelings toward parent and/or authority figures; they have managed to select out what is of common concern to them.

As such motifs generalize to the larger group, there is movement from a shared subgroup concern to a common concern of the entire group. What is happening is that each member, when faced with both the private, "there-and-then" preoccupations that he brings to the group, and the "here-and-now" of the group atmosphere and current group discussion, unconsciously interweaves these two strands by expressing those idiosyncratic concerns that are in some way evoked by the interaction's predominant leitmotif. Hence, if, in the situation just illustrated above, Patient D had come to the session discouraged about his job, A, B, and C's common focus on resentment of authority might well cause him to select, out of the several features of his work situation that are dissatisfying to him, the difficulties that he is having with his boss.

Group concerns are normally stated in a disguised fashion. For example, in the discussion illustrated above, the group's expressed resentment of authority probably reflects a resentment toward the therapist of which it is not yet aware. Indeed, the patients do not necessarily experience themselves as expressing a shared theme or focus; they may often perceive the group as fragmented, with each participant expressing his own egocentric preoccupations. The group therapist's skill lies in his ability to ferret out the underlying shared theme, much as the psychoanalyst engaged in individual treatment tries to discover an underlying coherence in the analysand's seemingly unrelated free associations.

KEY CONCEPTS

The Focal Conflict. According to this model, all group therapy sessions can be characterized in terms of a single over-riding focus or concern; this focus corresponds loosely to what Foulkes often refers to as a theme or shared concern, and to what Ezriel terms the "common group tension". Whitaker and Lieberman prefer to conceptualize the focus as a conflict between two competing motives, the first termed disturbing and the second, reactive. Both motives reflect shared concerns of the group members; the disturbing motive is usually conceptualized as a wish, and the reactive motive, a fear. An example cited by Whitaker and Lieberman (pp. 24-32) involved the first meeting of a reorganized inpatient group; we shall refer to this group as Group A. A review of Group A's initial session indicated the gradual emergence of a strong wish on the part of several patients to have a unique and gratifying relationship with the two therapists; equally clear was a motif expressing the fear that such a relationship would invite some sort of retaliation from the therapists.

One might wonder why a particular shared wish must of necessity prove "disturbing" enough to create a counter force. While Whitaker and Lieberman do not answer this question directly, one explanation that is in keeping with their overall point of view derives from the fact that each person in the group has his own aspirations, conflicts, and anxieties. Any unconscious wish that is strongly held by two or more group members and therefore shared by them—whether it is to be singled out by the therapist, to talk about taboo material, to compete sexually, etc.—is bound to provoke some degree of anxiety and consequent opposition from one or more other group members. Another factor helping to explain why any strongly shared group-wish sets up a counterbalancing group-fear lies in the psychoanalytic conception of personality, wherein all strong wishes (or "cathexes"), because they originate within the instinctual and most repressed part of the individual, invariably set off some sort of defense (or "countercathexis") that checks or in some way inhibits the wish. Hence, the group member himself is bound to be ambivalent about his strongly felt wishes and for this reason to be almost as ready to abandon or deny them as to gratify them.

The Group Solution. Groups, like individuals, can cope with only certain amounts of tension. Hence a group tries to find some agreed-upon solution for its focal conflict. For example, in the initial group meeting cited above, each patient's effort to establish some sense of uniqueness for himself was consistently blocked, either by challenges from other patients or by what was experienced as the therapists' disapproval. As a result, the members eventually gave up on their attempt to find some partial relief for this disturbing motive, and decided instead that they were all fundamentally "alike" in the sense of being essentially friendly people who had some problems, which they were willing to discuss with one another.

For a group solution to be successful, it must (1) be consensually agreed upon, however implicitly, by all its members, and (2) reduce anxiety. An example of how these two criteria operated in a specific instance is seen in another first session cited by Whitaker and Lieberman (1965, pp. 50-57). This inpatient group—let us call it Group B—began with several patients indicating that they would like to reveal their faults to the group (the disturbing motive); also expressed, however, was some fear of the kind of criticism, particularly from other patients, that might follow such self-exposure (the reactive motive). The group was beginning to hit upon a provisional solution wherein a majority of the group was coalescing around the idea that since no one of them was perfect, they should all agree to tolerate one another's shortcomings. This solution was immediately blocked by one patient's insistence that he indeed *was* perfect. Much energy in the group was then directed toward getting the "deviant" patient to change his mind, but he refused to budge. A solution eventually emerged when one patient commented that each of them was a "perfectionist" in the sense of trying to improve himself and this went unchallenged by the deviant. However sophistic and semantically tortured this resolution might appear to be, it seemed to genuinely work as a group solution in that at this point in the discussion tension began to clearly abate; the patients had reached a tentative consensus to the effect that while they constituted a quite superior group in some ways, they could still each hope to gain some personal benefit from the group experience. This solution therefore left room for a further exploration of what some of their individual difficulties might be.

The kind of solution just referred to furnishes an example of what Whitaker and Lieberman term an "enabling solution," for it helped to relieve the anxiety around the reactive motive—fear of criticism—at the same time that it also paved the way for partial satisfaction of the disturbing motive—the wish to reveal faults. If each patient agreed that he was a perfectionist in the sense of wanting to improve himself in *some* way, a new basis now existed for mentioning those personal areas—however minute or trivial—in which one could conceivably look for change.

Not all solutions are enabling. A "restrictive" solution is one that alleviates the fears involved in a reactive motive without affording any satisfaction of the disturbing motive. It is illustrated by the first session of Group A, in which a wish for each patient to have a unique relationship with the co-therapists (the disturbing motive) was opposed by a fear of retaliation from them (the reactive motive). As we indicated above, any patient's attempt to differentiate himself from the others was successfully countered. For example, a woman who was trying to present herself as an alcoholic was reminded by a second patient that probably each of them had one kind of addiction or another, and to prove his point, he pointed out that Tim—a third patient—obviously had an "addiction" to sleep. And when those patients who had previously been in group treatment showed signs of coalescing as a subgroup around this special status, their stab at claiming uniqueness was inadvertently discouraged by a remark from one of the therapists to the effect that the "new" patients were probably unable to follow their conversation. Therefore the group finally was forced to establish a restrictive solution having the flavor of "We're all basically alike in this group—friendly people with problems that we're willing to discuss"; this constituted a restrictive solution in that the assumption of nonuniqueness altogether thwarted the disturbing motive.

Since groups work best, according to this model, in an atmosphere conducive to enabling solutions—which help members to individualize and reveal themselves—the therapist's intervention just cited (wherein the old members were reminded that they were ignoring the new members) constituted a blunder on his part. Such an error underscores the need for the therapist in this model to always keep in mind the wider implications that each of his remarks will have for the subtle balance between enabling and restrictive solutions (see "The Role of the Leader").

Successful solutions—whether restrictive or enabling—end the life of that particular focal conflict to which they constitute a response, and pave the way for a new focal conflict to emerge.

The Group Theme: A "theme" in the terminology of this model has a rather technical meaning; it refers to a series of focal conflicts that are linked by a similarity in their disturbing motives. For example, if we chart the first four sessions of group B (Whitaker and Lieberman, 1965, pp. 64-75), we find that the disturbing motive shifted from revealing faults in general, to revealing "bad" impulses, and more specifically—in the fourth session—to revealing angry, hostile impulses and feelings; hence, while there are reasonably clearcut shifts in focal conflicts as one session follows another (punctuated by various successful solutions), a single theme—the disturbing motive of a wish for self-revelation—connects them. The fifth session was characterized by a highly transitional, anxious, and diffuse quality—it was difficult to specify the nature of its focal conflict—and by the sixth session there were substantial implications that a new theme involving dependent feelings toward the therapist had emerged.

While successful groups can be characterized by a progression of ever-more enabling solutions which permit successively greater amounts of expression on the part of patients (see "Group Culture" below), the life of even the most successful group is marked by occasional exacerbations of reactive motives, which in turn cause periodic returns to restrictive solutions. Whitaker and Lieberman employ an equilibrium-model for charting these forces; they find that the state of equilibrium at a session's ending has a strongly influential role in what happens in the subsequent session. If a session ends on a note of high anxiety (i.e., with emphasis on the reactive motive), patients are more likely to mobilize their defenses during the interval between sessions, with the result that the following session is characterized by a reduced degree of anxiety and a readiness on the part of the group to institute enabling solutions that successfully cope with the anxiety at the same time that they afford some satisfaction to the disturbing motive. It is as if the group is saying: "O.K., we've suffered enough—let's get down to business so we don't have to keep feeling so afraid." When the session ends emphasizing a disturbing motive—implying that patients have indulged themselves in expressing their dependent, or competitive, or angry, or sexual feelings—they are likely to experience an exacerbation of anxiety between sessions, with a sense of "Should I have gone *that* far?!" In this case, the next session is more likely to stress restrictive solutions in which there is less exposure and more concentration on protection against reactive anxieties.

The Group Culture. Whitaker and Lieberman believe that each therapy group gradually establishes its own unique culture, which generally consists of standards defining what is acceptable and unacceptable behavior within the group. A more specific definition, and one that incorporates the model's key concepts, is the following: "The culture of the therapy group is understood to consist of the successful solutions which a group generates to deal with successive focal conflicts" (Whitaker and Lieberman, 1965, p. 96). At any given time, a group's culture consists of whatever solutions are currently operating; since solutions are always being modified, the culture is in a state of constant evolution throughout a group's life.

Some solutions, however, prove to be surprisingly stable. Group B, for instance, was not able to modify the solution it had arrived at in its initial session—namely that all its members were to be viewed as basically alike—until its seventh session. At this time a consensus began to develop to the effect that although the members were *fundamentally* similar, certain surface distinctions did exist among them. This constituted a more enabling solution than the first, since under the umbrella of supposedly "superficial" differences the patients began to allow themselves increased amounts of self-exploration and differentiation. In accounting for this kind of movement in group forces, Whitaker and Lieberman emphasize differences among members as to their varying susceptibilities to either the disturbing or reactive motives. For example, in Group A (see above), where there was both a strong disturbing wish on the part of individual members to have a gratifyingly unique relationship to the co-therapists and an equally strong reactive fear that such relationships would invite retaliation from the therapists, eventual pressure for enabling solutions permitting more self-expression came from Clifford, who pressed harder than other members in the direction of the disturbing motive, and from Paul, who seemed less affected than others by the reactive motive. Clifford, who found it especially important to claim some sort of uniqueness for himself in the group began to bring out idiosyncratic details about his life, and Paul, who was less afraid of authority figures than some of the other members, indirectly expressed the notion that the punishment that people expect for open self-expression may not always be forthcoming.

Group members typically have to exert much more personal force to influence a solution that has already been established than they do to block an attempted solution before it has been put into effect. For instance, in the example above six sessions had to elapse before the solution that had been initially effected in the group's first session was substantially modified. Hence the model's authors, while cognizant of the role played by personality factors in helping to shape the group's movement, emphasize that the ultimate impact of individual personalities is necessarily influenced, and at times significantly constrained, by the action of specific group-structure variables, particularly the focal-conflict solutions that are in effect at any particular time.

Whitaker and Lieberman (1965, p. 123) cite solutions that typically are encountered early in a group's history: Claim that the friendly feelings that members have about one another don't include sexual ones; Find someone who is willing to acknowledge personal difficulties and then aggressively focus on him; Talk about hostile and envious feelings only in relation to people outside the group. Hence solutions often impose boundaries on what can or cannot be discussed within the group or dictate which members are permitted to bring up particular topics. Some solutions involve putting pressure on the therapist, as when the group urges him to provide more direction. Certain basic solutions are associated with typical disturbing motives. For example, systematic "turn-taking", wherein group members agree to each become a focus for a certain amount of time (thus precluding a more spontaneous interaction), is frequently a way of defending against competition among the members for "the floor" and also against hostility toward the therapist for not providing more direction. Some solutions by their very nature are less stable than others. A displacement in which one member unconsciously agrees to become a vicarious spokesman for the group by focusing on his own problems will probably be much shorter-lived than will turn-taking, since the latter guarantees each person the floor for at least a while, whereas the former will keep almost all members silent and thereby stimulate competition for the floor; once the members begin to compete the displacement solution is undermined and patients will begin to speak for themselves.

According to Whitaker and Lieberman, therapy groups commonly have an initial formative phase involving a series of critical focal conflicts and themes in which a series of tentative solutions are established and modified. The end of this formative phase, and the beginning of an "extended established" phase typically occurs somewhere between the eighth and twelfth sessions. The ushering in of this second phase is characterized by solutions that successfully deal with fears around criticism and punishment and that afford some degree of gratification for the disturbing motives. At this point the group is beginning to develop a viable culture; members are beginning to feel some sense of comfort, commitment, and hope. The established phase then continues until the group's termination. Two important enabling solutions frequently persist throughout this period. The first involves a basic consensus and confidence within the group as to the therapist's ability to afford a certain minimum of psychological safety, and the second, an assumption of basic similarity among members (an assumption that, as we indicated earlier, can include a tremendous number of supposedly "surface" differences). Restrictive solutions that reemerge from time to time during the established phase typically involve digressions to irrelevant topics, scapegoating, and discussions of purely intellectual issues. Restrictive solutions will always reappear, no matter how successful a group, since under the conditions of enabling solutions patients will engage in considerable amounts of self-exploration that will in turn inevitably lead to periods of anxious pulling-back and regression. Hence the therapist should anticipate occasions when the group may require some sort of restrictive solution as a kind of safety measure or "escape hatch." How he attempts to encourage various enabling and restrictive solutions will be discussed below.

METHODOLOGICAL CONSIDERATIONS

Because of their emphasis on an empirical verification of their central hypotheses, Whitaker and Lieberman have a somewhat firmer basis for charting the progression of various focal conflicts and themes than is typical in other group-dynamics approaches to psychotherapy. Rather than leaving the specification of the focal conflict to clinical speculation, they have developed a procedure (1965, pp. 37-38) wherein each of two independent raters, working from a verbatim tape, comes to some sort of conclusion regarding what he believes the focal conflict in any session to be; the tape is accompanied by a written summary (submitted by a therapist or observer) that includes significant situational features and nonverbal events. The rater includes in his final analysis the steps that he went through in arriving at his formulation.

The two raters then compare their findings. While agreement is never complete, the results have been somewhat encouraging. Sometimes the intervening steps that each rater went through are similar to each other, while their respective specifications of the focal-conflicts differ; sometimes it is the other way around. For the purposes of Whitaker and Lieberman's research, the two raters argue their respective positions until they come to a common agreement that satisfies both of them. Because of this amount of empirical analysis, generalizations concerning relationships between successive focal conflicts, themes, and group solutions rest on a more solid empirical foundation than is the case with most group models, where the therapist's or leader's formulations concerning processes, patterns, and stages of group development depend on a largely impressionistic and intuitive procedure.

ROLE OF THE LEADER

Whitaker and Lieberman believe that in order for a therapist to do effective group therapy he must unlearn several of the lessons he has learned in relation to individual therapy. Now his source of therapeutic leverage on the patient no longer lies in the direct therapist-patient interaction, but instead in his ability to influence the group culture. He must be prepared to recognize the fact that he cannot begin to exercise the same degree of control over the therapeutic process in the group that he can in individual treatment, because of the presence of so many other people, and he cannot enjoy the same direct responsiveness to the comments made by an individual patient, whether in the form of questions, clarifications, or interpretations.

However, what he loses in his ability to communicate with patients in the highly individual manner of one-to-one psychotherapy, he makes up for in his ability to guide the forces within the group. According to this model, there are three essential reasons why he is in a uniquely favorable position to alter the subtle balance of group tensions. First, by virtue of the transference attitudes of the group he can relatively quickly, through his reassuring and nonjudgmental manner, reduce some of the more superficial fears of his disapproval, thereby inviting varying degrees of self-revelation. Second, as the leader he has the realistic power to make certain administrative decisions that he knows will increase the group's sense of psychological safety. For example, in a situation cited by Whitaker and Lieberman (1965, pp. 71-73), a therapist in an early session was asked by an inpatient group if it would meet the following week since a World Series baseball game was scheduled for that time. He, knowing that the group was experiencing a high degree of anxiety, informed it that there would be no group session if the game were held. Symbolically he was assuring the participants that he would take their preferences into consideration, and that avenues toward occasional psychological withdrawal would not be blocked. Third, the therapist, although empathic, does not participate at the same level of immediacy as do the patients; the intellectual distance that he gains by being able to view the group process as an outsider enables him to understand the group's dynamics in a way that no patient-member can.

The therapist's understanding of the dynamics of the group's culture is especially crucial when he is provided an opportunity for circumventing the institution of restrictive solutions. For example, if a group seems ready to acquiesce to a member's suggestion that they not inquire directly into one another's sex lives, the leader might ask the participants what they believe will be gained by this procedure. Timing here is important because he is in a much better position to block a restrictive solution before it is established than afterwards. Despite the general desirability of enabling solutions, it is essential for the leader to remember that there are occasionally moments, especially during the formative phase of the group, when anxiety is sufficiently intense for members to need the kind of psychological safety that is afforded by restrictive solutions.

As Whitaker and Lieberman see it, it is the group's unconscious readiness to adjust its level of psychological safety to the combined needs and anxieties of its members that gives it its uniquely curative powers. The patient finds himself increasingly involved in the group as more and more of its focal conflicts, which inevitably involve sexual, angry, and intimate feelings, and their associated dangers, touch on his own unresolved emotions. Although these themes frighten him, some security is provided as consensually arrived at solutions emerge that promise to keep anxiety and conflict within manageable proportions. For example, an adolescent group may implicitly establish that while an exploration of sexual feelings within the group is permitted, discussion of sexual feelings about one's parents is for the time being off-limits. However, without the skilled interventions of the leader, these group forces are not likely to achieve their optimal balance. His expertise lies in knowing when enabling versus restrictive solutions are called for, and how to facilitate the blocking or adoption of particular solutions at hand.

The fact that the primary direction of the therapist's attention is the group rather than the individual need not mean that he never focuses on a particular patient, for Whitaker and Lieberman point out that one can approach the individual via the group and the group via the individual. For instance, if a leader wants to implicitly challenge a tentative (and restrictive) solution wherein a group has decided to minimize competition, he might encourage a patient to report a dream in the hope that this kind of individual attention will stimulate competitive strivings (here he approaches the group via the individual). On the other hand, a therapist who senses that a timid patient wants to talk about sexual matters but feels inhibited about doing so, might ask the group—assuming that it has not established any prohibition on the discussion of sex—why it has so consistently avoided sexual material during the past few sessions. This way he gives permission for the patient to speak without "putting him on the spot" (here he is approaching an individual via the group).

There may be times that the therapist wants to address himself to a particular patient for the latter's sake. This procedure is permissible so long as he keeps in mind the overall group context and is sure that his individual focusing does not threaten an established group standard (unless, of course, he intentionally wishes to do so). On some occasions the psychological needs of a patient may be so acute that the therapist intentionally interferes with a group's solution, even if it is a potentially constructive one, so as to protect the individual concerned. Whitaker and Lieberman cite an instance where a paranoid man who had willingly held the floor during the previous session was pressured by the group to do so again in the following session (1965, pp. 231-232). The patient probably would have complied out of weakness, but was showing signs of considerable disorganization. The therapist asked the group why it preferred to discuss the problem of one particular patient even though he realized that his question would probably forestall a reasonably sound group solution that would have afforded the other members a goodly measure of psychological safety. He was, in a sense, "sacrificing" the interests of the rest of the group in the service of protecting this particular patient, on the grounds that the other members were in a better position than he to deal with their anxiety.

With respect to group composition, Whitaker and Lieberman recommend that group members be reasonably homogeneous in their ability to tolerate anxiety; if not, the group is likely to generate either enabling solutions that stimulate too much anxiety for the highly vulnerable patient or restrictive solutions that do not provide a sufficiently open atmosphere for the intact patient. When it comes to the content of their conflicts and their ways of dealing with tension, group members should not be homogenous; if they are, they will too readily reach an agreement as to what topics are permissible and what procedures desirable, and these restrictive solutions will go unchallenged.

When it comes to rules governing confidentiality and the permissibility of outside contacts, Whitaker and Lieberman think that it is preferable for a group to be allowed to establish its own standards. A consensually-reached agreement is bound to be more effective than a therapist's arbitrary edict, and they find it hard to imagine a group that would establish a standard permitting the violation of confidentiality. Similarly, they believe that outside contact among patients does not usually become a serious problem. Such contact could conceivably emerge as a temporary restrictive solution in an early stage of the group (in that it permits the patients having contact to avoid discussing certain matters in the group), but inevitable shifts in the group's focal conflicts will lead to an eventual modification of these solutions. Like Wolf and Schwartz (see Chapter 3), Whitaker and Lieberman discourage the therapist from having individual sessions with group members, believing that such contacts constitute an evasion of issues that are best explored in the group.

In the present chapter, we have reviewed the models created by Foulkes, by Ezriel, and by Whitaker and Lieberman in their efforts to incorporate Lewin's group-dynamic orientation within a fundamentally Freudian approach to group therapy. In the following chapter, where we survey the existential-experiential model, we shall encounter another attempt to broaden and to partially revise the psychoanalytic approach to therapy groups without altogether discarding it, although this time along different lines.

References

Adler, A. 1927. *The practice and theory of individual psychology.* New York: Harcourt, Brace & World.

Bateson, G., Jackson, D. D., Haley, J., & Weakland, J. H. 1956. Toward a theory of schizophrenia. *Behavioral Science, 1.* 251-264.

Durkin, H. E. 1964. *The group in depth.* New York: International Universities Press.

———. 1972. Analytic group therapy and general systems theory. In C. J. Sager & H. S. Kaplan, eds., *Progress in group and family therapy.* New York: Brunner/Mazel.

Ezriel, H. 1973. Psychoanalytic group therapy. In L. R. Wolberg & E. K. Schwartz, *Group therapy: 1973.* New York: Intercontinental Medical Book Corporation.

Foulkes, S. F. 1965. *Therapeutic group analysis.* New York: International Universities Press.

———. 1973. The group as matrix of the individual's mental life. In L. R. Wolberg & E. K. Schwartz, eds. *Group therapy:* 1973. New York: Intercontinental Medical Book Corporation.

——— and Anthony, E. J. 1965. *Group psychotherapy.* 2nd ed. Baltimore: Penguin Books.

Hall, C. S. & Lindzey, G. 1970. *Theories of personality.* 2nd ed. New York: John Wiley & Sons.

Marrow, A. J. 1958. *The practical theorist: the life and work of Kurt Lewin.* New York: Basic Books.

Whitaker, D. S. & Lieberman, M. A. 1965. *Psychotherapy through the group process.* New York: Atherton Press.

5

The Existential-Experiential
Therapy Group

Existentialism, while beginning as a formal school within philosophy, so altered the then-prevalent view of man that it was bound to have a critical influence on both psychiatry and social science. This it did in the United States, first through its effect on some psychoanalysts and psychotherapists during the late 1940s and the 1950s, and then a decade later through the emergence of an "existential-humanistic" branch of psychology that played an important role in the development of the human potential movement in general and the encounter group in particular (see Chapter 11).

Existentialism, which had been foreshadowed in the writings of such nineteenth-century philosphers as Kierkegaard and Nietzsche, reminded man that beneath the elaborate structure of his consensually validated, seemingly knowable, and apparently purposeful world there remained the palpable, yet indescribable, fact of sheer biological existence; this fact often leads to a felt awareness of "being" that can inspire both terror and awe and that defies succinct verbal articulation. It is this ephemeralness that accounts for our difficulty in giving words to this existential or ontological level of human experience; as others have pointed out, our language is much more able to detail the *characteristics* of the thing or organism that "is" than to elaborate or specify what we mean when we state that this thing or organism *"exists."* The kinds of phenomenological statements that might begin to approximate ontological awareness, though they are necessarily devoid of their associated emotional content, are: I am; one day I was not; one day I shall once again no longer be.

The philosophy of existentialism, then, cannot be divorced from the situation of the individual man who realizes that his relationship to the world is contingent and finite, and that the world, as experienced by him, will die with him. The more he faces this ultimate aloneness, symbolized by the inevitability of his death, the more he senses that the meaningfulness of life, which might *appear* to be substantiated by the seemingly purposeful activity ceaselessly taking place around him, can only be confirmed, or refuted, on the most personal and subjective level. This "decision" as to the meaning of one's own life cannot be evaded, since a stance reflecting an ignorance or neglect of the existential problem in itself constitutes a position of sorts, however unaware and "inauthentic." Hence man, born into a universe whose meaning is not manifestly given, and granted no guidelines as to what constitutes a legitimate purpose for his own existence, or even as to whether such a purpose is necessary or desirable, indeed finds himself in an "absurd" situation (Camus, 1955). Yet the fact that no one but himself can provide the measure of his life's purposefulness, and the possibility that he might be able to create his own meaning, may be seen as adding elements of dignity and courage to this absurdity.

Experientialism played an important role in what gradually became known as "ontology"—or the study of being—since the existentialist's emphasis on the awe that we feel at the simple realization that we *are,* and his emphasis on the pressure that we feel to discern some meaning in our existence, came straight from the data of his own conscious experience. In this sense existentialism was the direct offspring of the modern phenomenological movement in philosophy, which emphasized the importance of paying systematic attention to the precise phenomena of consciousness. Credit for the origination of the phenomenological school is usually given to Edmund Husserl (1928), and Husserl was a teacher of Martin Heidegger (1962), who is generally considered to be the single most influential figure in existentialist philosophy.

Freudian psychology had developed on a different philosophical basis. It tended to regard conscious experiences as secondary events that were derivative of more fundamental, usually unconscious, complexes and drives. Hence, for the Freudian, the fear of death, made so much of by the existentialists, often represented certain sexual wishes and the defense against them. Just as modern physics approached a physical phenomenon (like a table) in a way that violated the experience of the naive observer (that which appeared to the senses to be a hard plane was actually composed of trillions of subatomic particles in a constant state of motion), the scientific approach to man's experience, as it was embodied in psychoanalysis, similarly upset man's traditional trust in the primary reality of his own consciousness. Existential phenomenology, on the other hand, strove to give the person back to himself by conceiving him in terms that empathically adhered to his own view of himself and of his relationship to the world. For example, the subjective conviction that most of us have that we have some freedom of choice, despite what we may intellectually know and believe with regard to doctrines of determinism, led the phenomenologist to a belief that we do indeed have some measure of choice, for he refused to endorse a theory that is openly at variance with our fundamental psychological sense of ourselves. It is for this reason that existential-phenomenology eschews a strictly deterministic position.

Existential psychology essentially originated in Switzerland, during the 1930s, through the work of two psychoanalysts, Ludwig Binswanger (1963) and Medard Boss (1963), who had been intimately associated with Heidegger and strongly influenced by his theory of ontology. The phenomenological emphasis in Binswanger and Boss was such that they rejected the usual notions of causality implicit in the predominantly logical-positivistic cast of Western thought, and instead saw psychological experience as a "first cause" in its own right. For example, the greedy, incorporative approach to the world seen in a psychotherapy patient whom the Freudian would describe as "oral," was viewed by the existential analyst as a fundamental *dasein* (Binswanger, 1963), or mode of "being-in-the-world" in its own right that did not have to be explained in terms of earlier trauma or prior causes. The greediness constituted the way in which this particular person chose to relate himself to the world, and was both a cause and a result; until this mode of experience changed, the world would be perceived by him in terms of food and supplies, and his own self as a void that needed desperately to be filled. This subjective view of himself had elements of a self-fulfilling prophecy; so long as he viewed himself as weak and helpless, he probably felt compelled to establish dependent relations on others and probably sought out people who tended to be dominating. According to the existential school, it was important for the analyst to realize that the world-view of any patient had as much cogency and reality for the latter as did his own world-view for himself, since each of us in attempting to construe the world is constantly in the process of creating his own arbitrary meaning. Once the analyst is able to respect the patient's right to choose whatever world-view he wishes, he has more hope of effecting change than does the traditional analyst who, tending to view the patient as an object to be worked on and dealt with, often seemed to believe that the patient could not but change and accept the "correct" view of reality once the right analytic interpretations had been made.

The publication of *Existence* in 1958, which was edited by Rollo May, Ernest Angel, and Henri Ellenberger and which translated three of Binswanger's papers into English, went a long way toward making the ontological approach to psychotherapy available to American practitioners. May himself was to become one of the major proponents of this approach, and some psychotherapists—among them Carl Whitaker and Thomas Malone (1953), and Carl Rogers (1951)—had already fixed upon a strongly experiential approach to treatment independent of any specific indebtedness to European existentialism. However, the American clinicians who were to seriously and systematically revise their orientation along existential-phenomenological lines were relatively few in number and of those who did, only a small percentage developed a particular interest in experiential approaches to group, as opposed to individual, treatment. Three people who did specifically address themselves to an existential-experiential approach to group therapy were Thomas Hora (1959), Hugh Mullan (1955), and Milton Berger (1958). At a somewhat later point, Rogers began to experiment with an experiential approach to groups, but his work in this area involved Encounter groups rather than therapy groups.

Existential psychoanalysis, as we can see by its very name, saw no need to abandon some of the major concepts of psychoanalysis, particularly those involving unawareness, anxiety, and resistance (although each of these was to some extent redefined, in keeping with shifts in theoretical emphasis). Nor was there necessarily a marked revision of the therapist's techniques (see "Role of the Leader" below), since the analyst—whether in individual or group therapy—often listened to the spontaneous communication of the patient in order to better grasp its latent meanings. Yet the existential approach, in repudiating Freudian psychology's emphasis on the role of biological drives in human development and in emphasizing instead man's cognitive need to give meaning to his existence, did offer a different view of man's essential task and of the origins of his psychopathology. Shifts in attitude that constituted a step away from the orthodox psychoanalytic position toward a more existential orientation included the following: (1) a deepened respect for the patient's subjective experiences as constituting valid phenomena in their own right, rather than as representing pale, disguised manifestations of his "real" (unconscious) feelings and thoughts, (2) the belief that the patient's need to give meaning to his life was inextricably linked to his dread of death, and that both these concerns were inherent within the fabric of his being and not necessarily derivative of repressed biological drives, (3) the conviction that a person's unconscious contained within it forces for courage and for creativity as well as for violence and cruelty, (4) an "I-Thou" conception (Buber, 1958) of the analytic relationship wherein patient and analyst, whatever their respective degrees of expertise and suffering, were more equal than they were unequal since each had to reconcile himself with the close-to-insurmountable problems of existence, (5) a belief that the analyst's actuality as a real person would be a more potent factor for therapy than would be his availability as a transference screen onto whom the patient could project his neurotic fantasies, and a concomitant willingness to accept and to share those aspects of the therapist's feeling and fantasies about the patient that are normally construed as "countertransference," and (6) a willingness to "let the patient be" (Keen, 1970) in the sense of accepting all aspects of his being, both healthy and pathological, including his freedom to resist the therapist and the treatment.

ILLUSTRATION OF A TYPICAL SESSION

For our illustration of a typical session we shall take the same group therapy situation that provided the basis of our example in Chapter 3. We are able to do this because the overall setting and basic format of the existential and psychoanalytic models are fundamentally similar. In this way we hope to be able to indicate how, despite these similarities, interventions on the part of the experiential therapist typically have a more direct, sharing, and emotionally-involved flavor.

Our fictitious group has seven members—four men and three women— and is reasonably heterogeneous in terms of age, vocation, and personality; with respect to cultural factors, the patients are by and large urban and middle-class. They have met for two-and-a-half years, with five of them having been with the group for this entire period of time, and two other members having entered during the previous ten months. Now our therapist is Dr. Alan R.

> The group begins without any structuring from Dr. R. who is silent. Ruth, a "hippie"-type girl in her early twenties, is talking about the fact that Bob, the man with whom she is living, is probably having an affair with her best friend, Terry. She knows he is attracted to Terry, and each of them has recently, in talking to her about the other, made some ambiguous and erotically-tinged remarks. Ruth doesn't know what to do about this. She is annoyed with herself for being jealous, for she knows that whatever Bob has going with Terry is a purely "physical" thing. He made it clear to her when they decided to live together that he did not feel sexually bound by conventional notions of a monogamous relationship; yet she feels hurt and betrayed by Terry. Then at other times, she feels that she is being old-fashioned, that it is obviously just a sex thing for Terry, who is basically interested in another, unavailable man.
>
> Mort, a brunette man in his middle thirties, razzes her. He says: That's right, Ruthie; Bob just has too much love in him to share with just one woman; besides, you love both of them so much this is really just an act of generosity on your part—you're giving two people you love to one another!
>
> Ruth reacts with a slight giggle, and continues to discuss the problem. Mort continues to bait her. Felicia interrupts at this point, saying that it makes her uncomfortable to see the way Mort is baiting Ruth and the way she allows him to do it.
>
> Ruth interrupts, saying: But what difference does it make? I'm used to Mort's sarcasm. What I'm worried about is Bob. Felicia says: Yes, but you take the same crap from both of them. Mort joins in, saying: Yes, she's so goddamned dumb with those rose-colored glasses on; doesn't she know what the world is like? Boy, she really asks for it.
>
> Ralph then joins in for a moment: She may ask for it, Mort, but I notice you're always there firstest with the mostest to give it to her.

Felicia says in a quiet voice: Ruth isn't happy until she has something to make her really miserable.

Ruth then says: Would everyone stop talking about me as though I weren't here?

Felicia expresses pleasure at Ruth's ability to speak up. Dr. R then wonders when Felicia is going to start talking up for herself. Felicia at first reacts with defensiveness and confusion, saying: I *am* speaking up.

Dr. R replies: Yes, but on behalf of Ruth, which is your usual way of participating. Perhaps this is partly your way of testing out what you're learning as a social work student. Look, it's okay with me, I like having a co-therapist, but I find myself wishing that you'd find a way to take as well as give; sometimes I sense that underneath that competent, supportive exterior there's a needy, bewildered little girl looking for comfort.

Felicia responds: Yes, I know what you mean, and there are day-to-day problems that I could bring up and at times would like to bring up; but they always seem so insignificant alongside what the others introduce; I guess I'm not ready yet.

Dr. R replies: Okay—I just thought I'd give you a little nudge.

For a few moments everyone is silent. Dr. R asks the group members what they are experiencing. Alice speaks up and says she was thinking about Ruth's problem, and wondering why Ruth was suddenly quiet. Ruth speaks up, saying: I felt criticized by Al in a way—when he pointed out how rarely Felicia brought up her problems, I thought maybe he was also saying that I do the opposite—always take up the group's time.

Dr. R: No, Ruth, I don't feel that way; I feel you have the right to ask for as much from the group as you can.

Ruth: Well, anyway, I don't know what to do about Bob. I guess I should just wait and let this affair between him and Terry blow over— that is, if there *is* an affair; probably if I wasn't so insecure I'd just accept it for what it is.

Nelson: I don't know Ruth—I could see being plenty jealous. I know I would be if Harriet (i.e., his current girl friend) was making it with some guy.

Mort, with heavy-handed sarcasm, says: But Nelson, you're so square, so bourgeois; you have this monogamy hang-up; both she and Bob have complete sexual freedom—the only difference between them being that he can act on his while she can't act on hers; besides, she's supposed to understand that he loves her more than any other woman he screws because he's living with her—so what does she have to be worried about?

Ruth answers Mort: I'm not sure that the idea you ridicule is so crazy, Mort; Bob is a very unusual guy—he's able to love more than one woman at once, and he's made it clear that in many ways I'm very special to him—that's why I get annoyed with myself for being jealous.

Mort becomes angrier and raises his voice, shouting at Ruth: Bob has one helluva good deal with you because you're so fucking blind; he can ball anybody he wants and still be welcomed home by your bleeding heart!

Ralph says: Lay off her, Morty—do you want to help her or destroy her? Ruth then says to Ralph: I don't mind his tone—I just want to figure out if he's right.

Dr. R says: Mort and Ralph both seem to sense the same thing about you, Ruth—that without realizing it you let other people abuse you; Morty is concentrating on how you get it from Bob and Ralph is bothered by how Morty is talking to you.

Ruth asks: But if Mort is right, how is he abusing me?

Alice answers: By speaking to you with contempt!

Ruth says: I think he feels that's the only way he can get through to me; and if he's right—if I *am* being naive with Bob—I want to find out, and I don't care *how* I find out.

Dr. R says: Ruth, you keep so busy trying to figure out what is right and what is fair that you don't instinctively notice that Bob and Mort don't give two damns about whether or not they hurt you. But what impresses me is the irritation and impatience that I am beginning to feel. For just a second now I had the strong impulse to really start yelling at you, to tell you to stop letting everyone treat you like dirt—but then I would have in a sense been doing the same thing myself. So my hunch is that you have some kind of need to provoke anger.

Ruth, seemingly bewildered, asks: But why would I want to provoke you? Dr. R replies: I feel you continuing in the same vein; the innocent young girl, with a perplexed, almost eager expression on your face, still trying to figure it all out.

Ruth asks: But what's wrong with that? Aren't I supposed to discover the reasons for what I do?

Dr. R answers Ruth: Again I'm finding myself starting to become irritated; until you get in touch with what you're feeling right now I don't think we're going to get anywhere.

Ruth is quiet for a minute, while the rest of the group seem attentive. Then she says: I don't know—I guess I feel sad more than anything else, and somehow inadequate; I feel like you're all mad at me, and like you're probably right to be, but I can't figure out just why—mainly that I'm being stupid about something; if I could only figure it out, then I could stop doing it and you'd all stop being so impatient with me.

Dr. R intervenes: So you mainly are aware of our anger with you—not yours with us, right? Ruth answers in the affirmative. Dr. R says: And what you're mainly aware of is your intense need to reason it all out, so you can then find a way to get us to stop being irritated with you.

Ruth says: That's right; and this feels like the story of my life; since I was very young I somehow was doing things wrong enough for my mother to get very mad at me—but somehow I could never be sure why.

At this point Felicia speaks up and says: I can understand that feeling; it's like: I'll be any way you want, so long as you love me. Mort then speaks up, saying: That's very good, Felicia, very empathic. I think we should give you A+ in Casework Methods II for that particular remark.

Alice quickly says: You know, Mort, when you get nasty like that I really feel like killing you. Mort is silent, and no one talks for a minute. Alice suddenly says: So why don't you turn your hostility on me? I'm waiting—my heart is pounding. Mort asks her what she means. She answers: I mean that when I say something like what I just said I expect to get some of your venom, and I imagine some of it would reach its mark and really get to me; so when I don't get it—like Felicia and Ruth seem to—I wonder why am I so lucky? When will my turn come?—and then I resent being so damned afraid of you.

Mort comments: There you all go again; because I say what I think and remind people of the kind of crap that passes for brilliant insight around here and don't play your love-in game, I become some kind of hostile monster who everybody is terrified of.

Dr. R breaks in, saying: Maybe if you allowed yourself to believe that people could be scared of you you'd have to start getting in touch with your own terror. Mort responds: Gee, Doc, you're getting more profound than Felicia—are the two of you in some sort of competition?

Dr. R says: Mort, level with me—do you believe the group when they say they're afraid of you? Mort answers: No. Dr. R. rejoins: Well, I don't know how to convince you that they are; I know that *I'm* feeling it right now—as I often do when I start to tangle with you.

Mort says to him: You're just saying that to make your theoretical point. Dr. R answers: Bullshit! I don't tell you I'm feeling something if I'm not! Mort asks him: But what are you scared of? Dr. R: Probably of what you'll do if your rage gets great enough; I don't feel it right now, but I remember asking myself that same question last session—what *am* I afraid of in you?—and my immediate fantasy was of your going really berserk and wrecking the office—but *completely* wrecking it, and of us standing by helplessly letting you do it.

Mort says to him: I still have the feeling you're putting me on. Dr. R replies: But isn't that your mistrust of everyone? Who does level with you completely as far as you're concerned? Mort answers: I don't know for sure—I'm never sure. Dr. R says: My guess is that if you had to admit that others are terrified, you might have to begin wondering why you never get frightened; you're very comfortable with your anger, but you don't ever express fear.

Dr. R then adds: By the way, Mort, I think my fear of your physical destructiveness is irrational, and probably has something to do with some uncomfortableness I still have with my own anger. But I also know that Alice's feeling of being intimidated by you is real.

At this point Mort doesn't say anything; he seems a bit red in the face, as though caught off guard. After a few seconds, Felicia says to Dr. R: I don't think you should have told him your fantasy—it probably will make Mort that much more afraid of his rage. And it sounds a bit pat to me—the same thing as what Mort likes to make fun of you for when you overplay the part of the "for-real," experiential therapist, letting us know just where you "are at" with everything.

Dr. R says: Well, Felicia, I invite you to become your own kind of therapist in your own style real soon—I sure as hell don't have a monopoly on technique; I do know that I felt quite genuine in saying what I did to Mort, and that it also felt great to hear you criticize me like that just now.

Felicia says: I can't imagine ever feeling that way about somebody's criticism of me. Dr. R rejoins: Well, I didn't get there overnight; I can remember in my earlier days not liking it one bit when my patients had something negative to say about me—or when anybody else did for that matter, but I was a rather different person then.

And so the session continues. As was the case in our illustrative psycho-analytic session which concerned essentially the same group (but with a different therapist—see Chapter 3), interaction in the present situation remains reasonably lively, and by the end of the meeting all participants have spoken up spontaneously, although a few have been considerably more active than others. While the analyst, Dr. M, remained silent for periods as long as seven or eight minutes in the psychoanalytic group, Dr. R, our existential-experiential therapist, is more active; for example, from the beginning of the session from which we drew an illustrative segment to its end, the longest period of time during which he said nothing lasted about five minutes.

KEY CONCEPTS

Since many writers and thinkers formally fall within the existential school of philosophy, a great number of conceptual terms have been intro-duced into various discussions of ontology. Therefore we shall limit ourselves to a few central and widely encountered concepts which we believe will give some flavor of this approach. These concepts are quite abstract and gener-alized, and involve a philosophical analysis of the human condition, rather than a more specific concern with the process of psychotherapy, whether individual or group. The general implications that the conceptual scheme has for the behavior of the group therapist will be presented in the final section, "The Role of the Leader."

In general, the ramifications that an existential approach has for psycho-analysis have centered on individual treatment, and within the latter frame-work have largely emphasized the nature of the therapist-patient relationship. In a somewhat similar fashion, the single variable emphasized most in dis-cussions of existential group therapy (e.g. see Mullan 1955) continues to be the therapist's attitude toward the patient. Consequently, as was the case with the initial psychoanalytic group model, the existential-experiential model tends to neglect the special properties of the group qua group, and instead simply transfers a theory of individual psychology and of individual therapy to the group setting. However, the existential therapist did see a specific value of the group in terms of the demands it placed on the individual patient for authentic relating, not only to the therapist (as in individual therapy), but now to other patients as well (Hora, 1959). Hence our discussion of the special uses of the group will be presented below under the concept of "Authentic vs. Inauthentic Existence."

Being vs. Non-Being. The concept of "being" can only be grasped on a phenomenological basis. It refers to our felt awareness that we "are," that we "exist"; therefore it is extremely personal and is difficult to articulate in abstract and symbolic terms. It has many elements in common with what is often called "self-consciousness," since it involves an awareness of physical existence and of individuation (and an envisaging, however vague, of death) that we assume to be unique to the human animal because of his better-developed conceptual capacities.

In short, man *is;* and, with the exception of the alternative of suicide, he has little choice as to when he will no longer be. He has similarly little control over the biological, social, and historical circumstances into which he is born. These accidental conditions surrounding his physical existence—his sex, his race, his bodily features, his century—constitute aspects of what Heidegger (1962) called man's "throwness," and set limits on his existence. Yet they cannot fully determine the shape of his life, for man, despite his throwness and despite social pressures to live "the good life," is able, by virtue of his awareness of some of the influences impinging on him, to say "No" to these influences, or to even attempt to say "No," thereby "transcending" his immediate situation. The person who is open to his sense of "being" feels his future open up before him full of emergent possibilities, some of which will be actualized by him, and some of which will not.

Hence the concept of being has connotations of choice, of identity, and of autonomy. It is an existential, as opposed to essentialistic, concept for it implies that "human nature" is ever evolving and never fixed; a person continues to redefine himself in a continual process of "becoming." The more he experiences himself as a "subject" in the sense of an active agent who has a determining effect on the world, the more he is open to that aspect of his experience subsumed by the concept of being. The more he experiences himself as an "object" who is acted upon, and whose life-pattern is somehow "given," the more his sense of being is attentuated, and the more he experiences himself as approximating the model of man offered by behaviorism (see Chapter 8) and psychoanalysis, both of which—according to the existentialists—tend to regard him as an "object" and thereby rob him of a considerable degree of autonomy.

The price of a well-developed sense of being is the dread of non-being, for the two are in a fundamental and dialectical relationship to each other, much as are the "figure" and the "ground" of Gestalt psychology (see Chapters 4 and 7). Each moment of life becomes more precious and more fully "owned" the more one realizes that existence is finite. Just as the figure of a black circle must be contrasted with a lighter background in order to be perceived, so being can only be fully savored in a context that involves the always threatening possibility of non-being or death. Awareness of this threat confronts the individual with existential anxiety (see below); neurosis, and psychopathology in general, are viewed as resulting from efforts to evade existential anxiety.

Being-in-the-World. This concept was originally introduced by Heidegger (1962) and was integral to the theoretical formulation of Binswanger. Again it expresses a dialectical relationship, this time between self and world; hyphens are used to indicate that without self there is no world (at least for the perceiver), and without the world there is no self, for the very notion of a "self" implies some sort of background or "world" against which oneself is figured or contrasted. Hence the expression "being-in-the-world" connotes much more than a purely spatial relationship.

This concept represents an attempt to overcome the subject-object dichotomy, which had bedeviled Western epistemology since Descartes first attempted to distinguish a mind or "soul" that was separate and detached from the sensory input impinging on the organism. According to existentialists, the Cartesian conception fragmented what man had initially experienced as a holistic relationship to the universe into a division between "inner" and "outer" reality, isolating the knower from the known, and alienating modern—or existential—man from the world he inhabits. In this model of reality, two people, each with his essential "self" buried deeply and obscurely within him, can only become indirectly known to each other. Such a view contrasts sharply with the existential notion of an I-Thou, dialogic relationship wherein each person can fully and directly encounter the other; this kind of mutuality ideally characterizes the patient-therapist relationship (see "Role of the Leader" below). In this conception there is no essential self that is secreted away in one's "soul"; instead the self develops and actualizes itself directly through intercourse with the world, and one's access to the world is immediate.

By insisting that each of us constructs his world in the act of perceiving it, existential phenomenology emphasized the creativity and activity involved in man's formation of his own reality. Traditional Western philosophy, in particular logical positivism, had on the other hand devalued subjectivity, implicating it as a source of potential error in man's effort to acquaint himself with "objective" reality. As the existentialists viewed it, at the point where the world pole of the self-world polarity is experienced as more important or more "real" than the self or the perceiver, the "being" aspect of one's existence is starting to become devitalized.

What the existentialist regarded as a person's mode of being-in-the-world, the Freudian saw as his characterology or life-style—for example, an oral, anal, or phallic orientation. And whereas the Freudian was not at all reluctant to distinguish between healthy and pathological life-styles, the existential analyst, in keeping with his phenomenological approach, preferred to grasp the patient's world empathically, without judgment. While the Freudian conceived of the patient's psycho-sexual orientation as having been "caused" by an earlier collision between his drives and the socialization forces impinging on them, the existentialist bypassed a cause-and-effect analysis altogether, and instead perceived the patient as an active agent in constructing his particular mode of being-in-the-world; the patient had created it and therefore only he could change it. According to the existentialist, if the analyst saw himself as someone who, through judiciously timed and worded interpretations, could *cause* the patient's world-view to change, he reinforced the patient's perception of himself as object and as victim, this time with the analyst, rather than the parents, being experienced as the active subject. In a more existential orientation, the analyst might point out to the patient the liabilities involved in the latter's mode of being (for example, if his world is experienced as one in which all good things come at the initiation of others, it follows that he will suffer prolonged periods of deprivation and will often feel powerless), and he might also remind him that alternative modes of being-in-the-world are available to him should he wish to change. Of course the patient may often blame others for his difficulties—for instance, for his dependency and his timidity—but for the existentialist the projection of responsibility onto others constitutes a mode of being-in-the-world in its own right. Such a mode increases whatever feelings of dependency and weakness the patient already has; the analyst's job is to help him see how defining himself as weak eventually makes weakness into a "truth."

If we look to the illustrative session described above, we can describe Ruth's mode of being-in-the-world as one in which she looks to the outside world in an attempt to figure out "correct" or "incorrect" ways of defining sexual relationships; hence she attempts to utilize the group as a means of determining whether she "should" give in to her jealousy, and she turns away from what is happening to her at the hands of Mort in the group. She makes a similar use of Bob, and is tempted to substitute his truth (namely a conviction that sexual fidelity is an outmoded ethic) for her own. In this process, she looks to cognition and reason as a way of orienting herself to a locus of values that she experiences as outside of herself.

Existential vs. Neurotic Anxiety. While the threat of non-being provides the most dramatic context for existential anxiety, other contingencies in human existence also account for its emergence. One is the necessity to act and to make choices in the face of uncertainty, with the result that there is no one to blame but ourselves for actions that are bound to have unpredictable consequences; even behavior that is designed to benefit another person can inadvertently bring harm to him or to others. Another source of existential anxiety is individuation, which guarantees that despite the possibilities of communication and empathy, we can never fully discover exactly what it feels like to be someone else.

Existential anxiety is not pathological. It is an inevitable response to a human condition wherein one is required to make decisions in the absence of the clearcut guidelines provided by religion and other cosmologies in an earlier era. Neurotic anxiety results when a person evades existential anxiety by failing to confront it directly and to make active choices in spite of it. While neurotic anxiety and neurotic symptomatology can take many forms, existentialists usually see it as involving some diminishment of the sense of self-as-subject and a corresponding increase in the self-as-object (Keen, 1970). Hence the individual ceases to relate to the world as an active agent who can structure some degree of meaningfulness for himself; with the breakdown of his usual relatedness to the world, experiences of disorganization, depersonalization, and meaninglessness occur. The more he experiences himself as an object, the more he fears potential abuse or harm at the hands of others.

Hence one fairly frequent symptom of neurosis is overt anxiety attacks. A form of neurosis that is more characterological in nature reflects an experience-mode in which the self is treated more as object than as subject. Here one lives for the expectations and love of others, and behaves as he ought to behave in terms of externalized criteria, and does not choose his activities on the basis of those that spontaneously appeal to him. In these situations, the self is taken as an object in that it is viewed in essentialistic terms; the self, treated much like a thing, must have particular static characteristics: e.g., punctuality, productivity, courtesy, etc. Once the self is experienced in more "being" and process-like ways, then what it is to be at any particular moment is determined more by context and by its current state of being-in-the-world.

Again Ruth—from the illustrative session above—provides an example. Experiencing herself as a satellite to Bob, who then becomes the "subject" in her existence, she objectifies her self in that she strives to develop "modern" sexual values that are in conformity to his. Were she more able to experience her self in the sense of "self-as-subject" (Keen, 1970, 17-19) she would probably come into contact with her genuine wish for a nonadulterous relationship. Of course, we don't know what Ruth would choose, since only she herself can make that decision and she has not yet begun to do so in an autonomous way, unclouded by Bob's definition of what she should want. Here again the Freudian and the existentialist clash to some extent, since the latter seems more willing to regard any of Ruth's decisions as "right" for her so long as they are autonomous ones. The Freudian, on the other hand, is more prone to see some sexual orientations—e.g., those involving promiscuity or homosexuality—as inherently pathological.

Existential vs. Neurotic Guilt. According to the existentialist, orthodox psychoanalysts too often ignore the question of actual guilt, and regard a patient's guilt feelings as inappropriate and irrational. For the phenomenologist, however, there is such a thing as ontological or genuine guilt; such guilt is experienced by all of us whenever we neglect certain potentialities within us; since we can never fulfill all our potentials, some degree of existential guilt is inevitable.

As was the case with existential anxiety, ontological guilt, when it is evaded, becomes neurotic guilt. And as with anxiety, the neurotic form of this emotion usually involves a curtailment of the person's sense of himself as an active subject; instead he objectifies himself, blaming himself for having failed to meet arbitrary standards involving fair and loving treatment of others. Of course many of our actions do bring hurt to others, however inadvertently. To the extent to which we take responsibility for these actions and feel pain because we genuinely care about these other people and their unhappiness, we experience either existential anxiety (in anticipating the possibility of hurting them) or existential guilt (after the hurt has occurred). All too often, however, guilt involves a breakdown in the experience of self-as-subject, in which our caring for the other person is paramount, and becomes instead a concern with meeting societal standards of correct behavior and of the way one should be; here the self is taken more as object than as subject.

Authentic vs. Inauthentic Existence. The concepts described above pave the way for understanding the existentialist's definition of authentic and inauthentic existence. In authentic existence the person confronts the ever-emergent possibility of non-being, makes decisions in the face of existential doubt, and takes responsibility for them. In inauthentic existence he seeks to confirm himself in ways that he hopes will evade the dread of non-being; often these are based on grandiose and competitive notions of existence in which the self is perceived, not as an experiencing process that is open to the world and therefore always in flux, but as an essence that must achieve certain fixed characteristics. The person imagines that once he actualizes this arbitrary self-image he will find security; since the security he longs for involves protection from the threat of non-being, his quest is doomed to failure. In trying to confirm himself inauthentically, one plays status-seeking games and keeps "busy" in conforming to the demands of mass man and mass society, but in doing so he fails to become what he truly is (thereby giving himself a heavy load of ontological guilt). To the extent to which his fellow man is treated as a means of gaining applause for his life "performance," the latter is being exploited and "thinged" by him. In a more mutual relationship he experiences himself as a subject who chooses both the relationship and how he wants to be with the other, but is also able to appreciate the other as a "subject" with wants, needs, and a world-view of his own.

It is around the concept of authentic vs. inauthentic relating that existential analysts tend to emphasize the unique value of group therapy. In individual psychotherapy, the existential therapist cannot possibly offer so great a range of "dialogic" relationships (Hora, 1959) as is provided in the group setting, because: (1) he is but one person, and (2) he cannot despite his greater openness, relate in so full a way as he could if he did not have to attend to his therapeutic task. Since every group participant constitutes a different person—and a different mode of "being-in-the-world" for a patient to relate to—what better laboratory exists for actualizing Buber's conception of the "I-Thou" relationship? Group therapy can be expected to push inauthentic ways of relating into bolder relief than does the one-to-one relationship, since the presence of other people typically engenders an unusual amount of anxiety. Silences in the early stages of the group create particularly intense anxiety as members struggle to fill them. The participant is doubtless aware that it is inappropriate to engage in social chatter—an awareness that constitutes still another source of tension—yet will find it hard not to fall back on his habitual and "inauthentic" ways of relating, particularly since he is the recipient of more intense interpersonal pressures than are presented by the relatively benign therapist in individual treatment. The group also offers a strong sense of support to a patient as he strives to find more authentic bases for relating, since each of his fellow patients is embarking upon a similar quest.

The transferential nature of member-to-member relationships within the group are not so emphasized within the present model as they are within the psychoanalytic model of the group. Instead, just as is the case with the leader-patient relationship, the actual and the emotionally committed nature of inter-patient relationships receives more stress than do their fantastic or unreal aspects. Where the existential group therapist might focus on distorted or inauthentic ways in which patients relate to one another, he attends to the here-and-now aspects of these distortions rather than to their specific genesis in earlier family relationships. Also less pronounced in the existential group model than in the psychoanalytic group model is the distinction between authority and peer vectors, since the special status of the leader becomes less important in the experiential group, where he tends to present himself as another—albeit "most experienced" (see below)—patient.

ROLE OF THE LEADER

As we indicated earlier, the existential-experiential model tends to take issue with the psychoanalytic one when it comes to theoretical and philosophic concerns regarding the nature of personality development and the origins of psychopathology. Yet the existential group leader's overt behavior—at least to the naive observer—does not necessarily provide a dramatic contrast to that of the psychoanalytic group therapist, for in both models the group is itself primarily responsible for initiating and maintaining interaction. Material relevant to events both inside and outside the group is considered pertinent, and patients talk about their problems and narrate their life histories in a straightforward fashion (unlike the Psychodrama and Gestalt-therapy models; see Chapters 6 and 7). The therapist's primary goal continues to be the enlargement of the patient's awareness and he attempts to do so within a framework that recognizes such concepts as resistance, transference, and interpretation. Therefore Dr. R , the existential therapist in the illustrative session above, focused on aspects of his patient's behavior that were similar to those attended to by Dr. M, the psychoanalytically-oriented therapist who led the same patient group in Chapter 3's illustrative session: Felicia's reluctance to present personal problems in the group, Ruth's masochistic inability to defend herself against sadistic exploitation by others, and Mort's counterphobic rage.

However, in his role as "the most experienced patient" (Whitaker and Warkentin) within the group and in his search for a more spontaneous and mutual involvement with each patient, the existential therapist is more willing than the psychoanalyst to reveal both his immediate experience in the session and various aspects of his own past. This is partly because he emphasizes real, as well as transferential, features of the therapist-patient relationship and because he has a tolerant and accepting attitude toward his own countertransference. While he is aware that some of his countertransference may reflect regressive and unworked-through parts of his personality, he also appreciates that the positive dimensions of countertransference include genuine concern and caring for the patient. Indeed, some existential analysts go so far as to say that without this care, which represents a kind of love, the patient cannot experience a symbolic rebirth or a true transformation of character, although he may experience symptomatic improvement and some change in his relationships. Of course, as some writers have been at pains to point out, the original spirit of psychoanalysis respected countertransference feelings as constituting important data that could shed significant light on pathological aspects of both the patient's intrapsychic functioning and the therapist-patient relationship; however, two subsequent generations of training analysts and training analyses would seem to have left the average analyst fundamentally wary lest any emotional involvement with the patient somehow be "wrong" or dangerous (e.g., see Durkin, 1964, 270-272).

In his wish to promote an atmosphere within the group of an authentic "happening" in which each person, including himself, feels free to express all aspects of his "being," however realistic or fantastic, however healthy or sick, the experiential therapist strives to ferret out, and even exaggerate, whatever countertransference feelings and fantasies he may have. For if he is not open to the conflictual elements of his own character, how can he help the patient to tolerate his? Hence Dr. R., albeit acknowledging that there is probably a neurotic aspect to his fear of Mort's physical aggression, shares his fantasy of Mort's destroying the office. Other personal actions and experiences revealed by him include his personalized image of Felicia as a needy little girl, his spontaneous pleasure at her ability to criticize him openly, his past difficulties in comfortably tolerating criticism, his momentary anger when Mort accuses him of feigning fearfulness, his immediate correction of Ruth's original perception of him as wanting her to take up less of the group's time, and his subsequent impulse to attack her verbally. While he is not uninterested in the past, he is most involved in the nuances of the patient's immediate experience—just how the latter is "being-in-the-world" at this very moment. There-fore, unlike Dr. M in Chapter 3's illustrative session, Dr. R does not directly ask Ruth whether she can connect her reactions to Bob and Mort with childhood events. Instead Ruth spontaneously remembers her past, perhaps as a response to her having had a meaningful emotional experience during this session.

The therapist, in his eagerness to be candid about his own experience, must rapidly select those of his subjective reactions that seem intuitively to be most related to significant aspects of the patient's being. In this process he would seem to be guided by something akin to Cohn's concept of "selective authenticity" (Cohn, 1972; see Chapter 12) wherein a leader either conscious-ly or preconsciously decides to share those personal feelings and thoughts that seem most helpful in promoting fruitful group interaction. However, any prolonged attention that he might give to the possible "censoring" of material that could prove irrelevant or that could go beyond what a patient "can take" violates the spirit of existential experientialism, which emphasizes the impor-tance of freedom and spontaneity in the therapist and a respect for the patient's ability to take responsibility for whatever reactions he in turn has to the therapist's revelations. Indeed, although it is tempting to discern a specific strategy in the therapist's authenticity—e.g., a kind of modeling function wherein a patient is "shown" how to be open—this kind of goal-oriented conception, emphasizing as it does the use of specific means to reach particu-lar ends, tends to reduce the patient to the status of an object, or of one who is "done to" and "done for." Thus experientialism is more accurately viewed as a way of "being with" the patient. This is more an inevitable concomitant of what the existentialist refers to as the therapist's "presence" (May, 1958, pp. 80-85) than it is a therapeutic technique.

This nonmanipulative attitude toward the patient is frequently described as "letting him be" (Keen, 1970, pp. 169-173), and this freedom to be-in-his-world on the patient's part includes all manner of pathology and resistance. Of course, the therapist is equally free to express his own reactions to the patient's mode of being; indeed, his role as an experiential leader makes it incumbent on him to do so. However, the patient is under no obligation to change for the therapist's sake. As was the case with the concept of counter-transference, there is little in psychoanalytic theory proper that is antithetical to this way of regarding resistance (Durkin, 1964, p. 272). However, according to the existentialists, orthodox analysts began to gradually move away from this respectful orientation to resistance, and started instead to become con-vinced that their interpretations, if valid and properly timed, could not but lead the patient one step closer to insight and therefore to eventual cure. Hence the existential therapist's suspicion that the average psychoanalyst all too easily loses sight of the patient's inherent freedom to resist his thera-peutic efforts, however benign in intention and brilliant in execution. It is the recognition of the patient's right to choose his own mode of "being-in-the-world", in the face of any and every therapeutic intervention, that constitutes in this model a major stimulus to continuous growth and individuation.

References

Berger, M. M. 1958. Nonverbal communication in group psychotherapy. *International Journal of Group Psychotherapy, 8.* 161-178.

Binswanger, L. 1963. *Being-in-the-world: selected papers of Ludwig Binswanger.* New York: Basic Books.

Boss, M. 1963. *Psychoanalysis and daseinsanalysis.* New York: Basic Books.

Buber, M. 1958. *I and thou.* New York: Charles Scribners, Sons.

Camus, A. 1955. *The myth of Sisyphus.* New York: Alfred A. Knopf.

Cohn, R. C. 1972. Style and spirit of the theme-centered interactional method. In C. J. Sager & H. Kaplan, eds. *Progress in group and family therapy.* New York: Brunner/Mazel, 1972.

Durkin, H. E. 1964. *The group in depth.* New York: International Universities Press.

Heidegger, M. 1962. *Being and time.* New York: Harper & Row.

Hora, T. 1959. Existential group psychotherapy. *American Journal of Psychotherapy, 13.* 83-92.

Husserl, E. 1928. *Vorlesungen sur phaenomenologic des innern zeitbewusstseins.* (Halle a.d. Saale, 1928).

Keen, E. 1970. *Three faces of being: toward an existential clinical psychology.* New York: Appleton-Century-Crofts.

May, R. 1958. Contributions of existential psychotherapy. In R. May, E. Angel, & H. F. Ellenberger, eds. *Existence: a new dimension in psychiatry and psychology.* New York: Basic Books.

Mullan, H. 1955. The group analyst's creative function. *American Journal of Psychotherapy, 9.* 320-334.

Rogers, C. R. 1951. *Client-centered therapy.* Boston: Houghton-Mifflin.

Whitaker, C. A., & Malone, T. P. 1953. *The roots of psychotherapy.* New York: Blakiston.

Whitaker, C. A., & Warkentin, J. Spontaneous interaction in group psychotherapy. Atlanta: Atlanta Psychiatric Clinic.

6

Psychodrama

Psychodrama is a group therapeutic approach designed to evoke the expression of feelings involved in personal problems in a spontaneous, dramatic role-play. In its purest form, Psychodrama consists of a therapy group or workshop, centered around acting out of emotionally significant scenes for the purpose of both catharsis and the acquisition of new behaviors. Group members role-play past, present, or anticipated conflict situations to release pent-up feelings and to practice more adaptive behavior. The major thrust of the method is to help participants relive and reformulate their problems in dramatic form in order to face their concerns directly and immediately in the living present. Experience in action, rather than the recapitulation in words and thoughts that is characteristic of most psychotherapeutic approaches, is the touchstone of this method.

HISTORICAL BACKGROUND

The term, Psychodrama, and the name, Jacob L. Moreno, are so closely tied together that it is scarcely possible to think of the one without the other. The method of Psychodrama is clearly his creation and has its roots deeply embedded in his personal history. Moreno was born in 1892, somewhere in eastern Europe. *Who's Who in America* (1966) gives his place of birth as Rumania. Moreno, himself, (Moreno, 1964) claims that his birth took place on a boat cruising the Black Sea.

Moreno historically locates the beginnings of Psychodrama as occurring when he was four and one-half years old. He was playing with some friends in the basement of his house in Vienna, the city in which he spent most of his formative years, and he suggested that they all play God and angels. There

108

was a large table in the center of the room on which were stacked a number of chairs. Moreno climbed to the very top and he played God and had the other children go around the table flapping their arms as if they were wings, taking the roles of angels. As the children assumed the roles of angels and thought of themselves as flying, one suggested that Moreno, perched high atop the chairs, fly too, and he attempted to do so. He quickly fell and broked his arm, but was left with a sense of the exhilaration and spontaneity of the experience. Both elements—spontaneity and exhilaration—were to become central concepts in the later development of Moreno's theory.

When Moreno was sixteen and a premedical student, he spent time walking in the gardens of Vienna and engaging in fantasy play with the children he met there, acting out fairy tales and stories. He was again struck by the freedom, openness, and creativity of the young people and also began to notice the positive emotional effect that the primitive fantasy play in which they engaged had on the children. After earning his medical degree in 1917, Moreno continued to pursue his interest in spontaneous play, an interest which culminated in the opening of a Theater of Spontaneity in Vienna in 1921. Moreno was much interested in drama, but over time he began to view theater presentations with prepared scripts and well rehearsed actors as stultifying and anticreative. In his Theater of Spontaneity there were no scripts; he introduced the concept of "The Living Newspaper" where actors and audiences played out events from the daily newspaper in an unplanned fashion. At this point in Moreno's work, he emphasized unrehearsed drama more as an art form than as a therapeutic endeavor, but when the personal problems of one of the actresses was brought to Moreno's attention by her fiance, he hit upon the idea of using unscripted role-playing in an effort to resolve personal problems. This incident gave birth to the therapeutic theater of Psychodrama.

Moreno moved to the United States in 1925 and continued the development of his psychodramatic method. Some years later he opened a sanitorium in Beacon, New York, where he built the first stage for Psychodrama in the United States. His years in the United States have been extremely productive ones, in the sense that he has been extremely prolific in his writings on both Psychodrama, Sociodrama, sociometric studies and related areas. He has produced a number of books, has edited journals, and has continued to be extremely active in teaching Psychodrama and in demonstrating it throughout the United States and abroad.

Moreno is frequently credited with introducing the term "group psychotherapy," and he has clearly played an important role in the growth of interest in the field of group therapy in general. According to Moreno, the concept of Psychodrama, as he developed it, has now been in existence for more than sixty-five years, a fact which clearly places it as the longest existing specialized group therapeutic technique in current usage. Yet it is difficult to assess the impact that Moreno's techniques and thinking have had on the development of group therapy. There are between fifty and one hundred Psychodrama theaters in various institutions around the country, and this fact is often cited as an example of its widespread usage. In addition, Psychodrama is, of course, used in situations where no specialized theater has been constructed. Nonetheless, it is fair to say that Psychodrama, as such, is not among the most common group therapeutic techniques in use today. In addition to Psychodrama as a technique used by itself, it is frequently considered to be a useful adjunctive technique to other group methods (Siroka, et. al., 1971; Blatner, 1970). Corsini (1957) has developed a modification of the technique which he calls psychodramatic group therapy, and an innovative approach to research on attitude change based on Psychodrama has been described by Greenberg (1968). Moreover, a variety of role-playing techniques, all of which have their roots in Moreno's work, have become increasingly popular in a number of group approaches, spanning the broad range from Gestalt to Behavior therapy groups.

Perhaps it is unfair to assess the impact of Moreno by examining only the frequency of usage of the psychodramatic technique. It is important also to note the influence of his ideas and techniques on the development of other group therapeutic and personal growth methods. His introduction of and emphasis on action, as opposed to analysis, his focus on the "here and now," his development of a variety of special techniques for use in groups, are all echoed in other group methods that we will be describing. Particularly illuminating in this regard are some comments by Schutz (1971), who is best known for his contributions to the Encounter group model. When he was scheduled to meet Moreno for the first time, he heard that the latter claimed credit for many of the Encounter techniques that he himself had developed. To prepare for their meeting, Schutz perused some of Moreno's works; as he did so it became increasingly clear to him that years earlier Moreno had indeed anticipated most, if not all, of the techniques that he was now using in his Encounter activities. During their discussions, Schutz acknowledged that many of his methods were derived from Moreno, even though he was unaware of it at the time he developed them. However, Schutz went on to say that he was at least sure that the fantasy methods that he was employing were derived from the work of others; yet Moreno was quick to point out that even those techniques had been anticipated in articles published many years earlier in his journal, *Sociometry*.

While it is clear that Moreno has had a major impact, it is also clear that that impact has been both less than direct and never fully acknowledged. Perhaps some explanation for this fact lies in three characteristics of Moreno and his approach. First is a self-acknowledged immodesty; undoubtedly his manner, his rather overbearing style, and his concern about being properly credited for his productions, have tended to put people off. Second, although he has written voluminously, he has not written with the greatest of clarity and directness of expression. His writings tend to be rather complex, not very succinct and they introduce a variety of dramaturgic and philosophical notions in ways that obscure the main outlines of the group therapeutic and group process conceptualizations underlying his theory. Third, Moreno's emphasis on the nonanalytic nature of the technique, stressing as he did the person's relatively public and conscious attitudes, ran counter to the main *zeitgeist* reigning then, which stressed essentially private, intrapsychic data. All of these factors have contributed to Moreno's writings being less widely read than might otherwise be expected.

In recent years, however, as we have indicated, Moreno's contributions to the understanding of group interaction and group therapeutic methods has been more frequently acknowledged. It has also become increasingly clear to many that his influence on the development of group techniques has indeed been an extremely important and insufficiently credited one.

DESCRIPTION OF A SESSION OF PSYCHODRAMA

We shall try to describe a session in Psychodrama as it might take place in Moreno's Theater of Psychodrama in Beacon, New York. The setting is a stage for Psychodrama designed by Moreno. It is in a small auditorium equipped with seats like a theater but with no proscenium. The stage itself comes close to the first row of seats and is made up of three circles of increasingly smaller size placed one on top of the other giving three different height levels. It has sometimes been described as looking like a three tiered wedding cake. In addition, there is a semienclosed area at the back of the stage and a balcony. At the back of the auditorium there is a raised area with some simple lighting equipment.

The persons who will be participating in the Psychodrama include the chief therapist or *director*, the patient-protagonist (or several people who may play that role at various points in the proceedings), people to serve as auxiliary egos to represent important figures in the protagonist's life, or at times different aspects of the protagonist's self. Additionally there may be other members of the audience including staff members, visitors, or other patients who are not yet ready to participate.

Since spontaneity is of particular import in the Psychodrama experience, Moreno emphasizes the role of the "warm-up period" in getting participants ready for the experience. An important function of the warm-up procedure is loosening up the members of the group, and getting them ready to act in as spontaneous a fashion as possible. This desired effect may be accomplished in a variety of ways. Moreno himself has a tremendous personal appeal, a quality of charisma, and the ability to generate a considerable excitement about, and interest in psychodramatic procedures. Such an emotional tone is viewed as desirable in all Psychodrama leaders. Anything that creates laughter or humor that the group can share serves the warming up process in an effective way. Some more specific techniques are sometimes used, many of which are quite similar to those techniques later developed in Encounter procedures. For example, a participant might be asked to pick another person out of the group who attracts him and to approach that person and to describe what his reactions are. Techniques involving communication without words, such as picking a person and looking into his eyes, are also utilized. In sum, anything that facilitates the ability of participants to express themselves openly and directly as well as helps to create a feeling of comfortableness and of shared mutual interest in the group is a useful element in the warm-up.

The role of the director is of particular importance in the warm-up period and in the initial stages of the Psychodrama procedure itself. He must function as a person who makes things happen, who helps people to be comfortable enough to use their spontaneity and creativity in examining their personal concerns. The director may have already chosen a person to be the first protagonist prior to the beginning of the meeting or he may choose somebody after the warm-up. If the person had not been previously selected, the director might approach a group member and ask him to bring up a problem he is concerned about and wants to explore further. Using another approach, the director might choose a topic, such as work-related problems or difficulties with family members, and ask everyone present to say something about his concerns in this area. After some discussion is generated, the group would focus on the problem of one of the persons and this person would then be encouraged to become the first protagonist. If he were shy or was showing signs of stage fright, the director would try to ease him into the role by asking him to come to the front of the room while continuing to talk with him. The director might continue facing the group and have the member with his back to the group in order to make him feel more comfortable. The director might also try to comfort him physically by putting his hand on his shoulder while at the same time easing him up onto the stage.

Once the protagonist is on the stage, the director begins to set the scene. Let us take an example of a problem whose central focus is a work difficulty, a conflict between the protagonist and his immediate supervisor. The director should rely as much as possible on the protagonist to give directions on how to play the scene, making certain that the latter provides a description of the situation in which the conflict manifests itself with as much specificity as possible about the setting, how the furniture is arranged, and what other people, if any, are present. Once the scene has been set the dramatic situation is already under way and the protagonist hopefully beings to "feel" himself in the performance, and to experience those emotions associated with the real life situation.

Now other participants or auxiliary egos (see below) are needed in order to bring the drama to life. Someone to play the supervisor and another person to play a fellow employee would be required as additional participants. The auxiliary egos should be chosen by the protagonist whenever possible, but may be chosen by the director, if he knows the members of the group well enough to decide who might fit the roles as they have been described; or they may be selected in consultation between the two. Once all the participants have been chosen, the plot needs to be outlined in somewhat fuller detail. The roles of the auxiliary egos have to be explained by the protagonist or the director. The protagonist should give a personal description of the supervisor, including some idea of his behavioral style. In this instance he describes the supervisor as being gruff and overly critical, loud and overbearing. The protagonist, Donald, outlines a situation in which his boss criticized him in the presence of a fellow worker, named Joe, a worker with whom Donald felt a great rivalry. In the Psychodrama Donald develops a plot in which he has it out with his supervisor. He begins to tell him as directly as he can that his criticisms would be much more constructive if they were given under different circumstances. The auxiliary ego playing the supervisor, reacting in terms of his perception of the protagonist's needs rather than in the role as described, responds warmly, encouragingly and apologetically, indicating that Donald is quite correct in pointing out the inappropriateness of his behavior. At this point the protagonist stops the action and explains that his boss would never act that way and he then repeats his description of the boss to the auxiliary ego and gives further instructions as to how the role might be played. Then the role play starts anew with Donald speaking to his boss.

Donald again begins now by telling his boss that he wished he would not embarass him by "calling him down in front of Joe." The boss this time responds tauntingly, telling Donald that he will never amount to anything because he cannot take a little honest criticism and he always wants to be coddled and to get special treatment. Donald, shaken by the comment and even more shaken by the memory it evokes of his father's repeated criticisms of him, angrily blurts out that the boss is unfair and mean to him in the same way that his father was, never giving him a chance to show what he can do and never being satisfied with anything he does do. Then Donald becomes silent, surprised by the feelings that have come to the surface. The supervisor begins to apologize but the protagonist doesn't respond. After a minute of silence the director asks why the action has stopped. Donald thinks for a while and then realizes that neither his boss nor his father have ever apologized to him, but he is also aware that he never expressed his anger and resentment directly to them.

The director takes the opportunity to question the protagonist, who is a shy, unaggressive man: "Would you really speak up like that to your boss?" The protagonist replies that he hasn't before and it would probably be very difficult for him to do so and goes on to say that he had not previously been aware of the similarity of his feelings and attitude toward his boss and his father. Donald is immediately impressed by both the emotional release he feels and the insight he has gained into his reactions; and he begins to wonder if he encourages his boss to "put him down" by always reenacting the role of the incompetent son that he had played with his father.

When the scene has been completed, the protagonist and the others return to the audience. At this point a variety of alternative activities might be introduced: included among these would be a continuation of the evaluation by the protagonist of his emotional response to the scene with other members of the audience offering their observations or describing their personal reactions; the director as well might raise questions or offer interpretations. He might wonder about the kinds of gratification Donald might be getting from being criticized and taunted or he might focus on what makes Donald so fearful of speaking up for himself. A technique called "sharing" is sometimes used in which members of the audience try to respond to what occurred in terms of relevant experiences of their own. Yet another alternative might be an interpretation of the scene by the director and/or other members of the audience including some suggestions to the protagonist about ways of changing his behavior arising from their reactions to his role in the scene.

Following completion of the work on the scene the same protagonist may move into another scene or a variant of the same scene, or a new protagonist may take center stage. Sometimes, for additional benefit of the original protagonist, the same scene is replayed with a member of the audience taking his role so that he has the opportunity to observe in a fresh way the experience he has just had.

In our example, catharsis and sudden awareness occurred swiftly and dramatically. At other times a slower, more painstaking effort is required to bring feelings to the fore. The emotional reaction that Donald experienced would of course be only a beginning of the psychodramatic work. Further scenes might well be developed to explore the protagonist's reactions to those in authority and his typical behavioral style in his contacts with them. A still later step is the development of new possible ways of behaving and role-playing in a behavioral practice fashion. Trying out these more desirable behaviors would become a central focus of the psychodramatic work.

KEY CONCEPTS: PHILOSOPHICAL AND THEORETICAL

Action and Acting. In many respects the concepts of action and activity seem to be Moreno's most basic theoretical notions. Like psychoanalysis, Psychodrama was developed in Vienna, some years after Freud first began his work. Moreno takes a most disparaging view of the passivity of psychoanalytic technique and at times almost seems to have chosen action because it represented the polar opposite of the psychoanalysts' insistence that the patient remain relatively immobile during the analytic hour and confine himself to thought and fantasy rather than action. He viewed the psychoanalytic method as being extremely stultifying and constricting, as encouraging a kind of rumination that bordered on the trivial, and as supporting the mediocre and uninspired. Moreno believed that emphasis on action, on the other hand, opened up and expanded awareness and made it possible for people to get in touch with aspects of themselves of which they had previously been unaware.

Moreno (1946) has suggested that some of the early opposition to Psychodrama was due to the widely held belief among mental health workers that action was dangerous while verbal interchange was the tried and true method. He felt that Psychodrama received a more favorable reaction in the United States than in Europe because Americans were much more a people of action than were Europeans, and therefore, could accept an action orientation to education and behavior change.

For Moreno, acting in an open way, acting out one's dreams and wishes, and desires and aspirations, represented a step in the direction of making man more God-like. Being God-like involved becoming so open and in touch with one's feelings, so spirited and creative, as to be able to extend oneself to the limits of emotion and achievement. Indeed, one of Moreno's basic aims in the development of Psychodrama was to help man reach a higher state of being than he had thus far reached. In part, his stance developed in opposition to the then current attitude in Vienna's psychiatric circles, one which was becoming increasingly receptive to psychoanalysis; Moreno's orientation had much more in common with the existential-humanistic emphasis on motives such as self-actualization. That Moreno was very firm in his conviction that people should be helped to stretch themselves to their creative limits is evident in a description of his one meeting with Freud, a meeting which took place just after he heard Freud lecture. Moreno states that he responded to Freud's questioning him about the kind of work he did by saying that the emphasis of his work was opposite to Freud's. "You analyze their dreams, I try to give them the courage to dream again. I teach people how to play *God*." (Moreno, 1946, p. 6).

The concept, action, then, for Moreno clearly represents his conviction that openness and nonconstriction are important elements underlying successful human functioning.

Spontaneity and Creativity. Closely related to the concept of action and, indeed, in many respects overlapping with it, are Moreno's ideas about spontaneity and creativity. It will be recalled that Moreno's first approach to Psychodrama began in his Theater of Spontaneity, which was originally more closely tied to a dramatic format than to a therapeutic one. He was fond of pointing out that dramatic works of a traditional nature that are written, directed, and performed in a preplanned fashion are at best, uninteresting, and at worst deadening. His approach to theater, stressing experiencing in the moment and acting out those experiences, was to create an alive and vibrant experience, both for the actors and the observers.

In a sense, Moreno's view of traditional theater had much in common with his view of psychoanalysis in that he considered both essentially closed and countercreative.

Moreno was impressed by his early experiences of developing impromptu plays in the parks of Vienna with children. He was struck by the fact that children, in contrast with adults, are much more ready to act and seem to be much more in touch with their fantasy lives and their feelings, as well as more able to enter into a role-playing situation. Along with this he felt that children have not yet stifled their imagination and their ability to be creative. It was these characteristics of children that Moreno sought to reactivate in adults through the method of Psychodrama.

It is difficult to define spontaneity adequately, but it seems to have at least two important components for Moreno. One is the ability of a person to experience his own state of being or feeling, with minimal interference from external impediments or internal inhibitions. The other element in the concept focuses on an aspect of spontaneity that is truly responsive to reality demands—the wherewithal to respond to new situations immediately, appropriately, and yet creatively. One of the important functions of learning to be more spontaneous, as one does in the Psychodrama situation or in specific exercises for spontaneity training which Moreno also introduced, is that of freeing a person from stereotyped behaviors rooted in his past, and helping him develop new and more creative approaches to current experience.

Here and Now. Moreno, as so many of the other developers of group methods described in this volume, puts great stress on the importance of experiencing in the present, in the moment, in the "here and now." Psychodrama emphasizes not "talking" about problems or about the past or about current relationships, but rather experiencing them in action, in the present. Therefore, even if one is replaying a situation that in reality is quite similar to an actual situation that occurred in the past, or rehearsing a situation that one anticipates might occur in the future, the here and now emphasis should predominate, since what is important is the spontaneous experience in the moment, and dealing with current feelings and emotional reactions. Psychodrama, then, emphasizes living in the moment and in the present, and reacting to the situation as it is created in the immediate moment of the Psychodrama situation, rather than to a real event, as it actually occurred in the past or is likely to occur in the future. The emphasis is always on the learning that comes from the reality of present experience and one's reaction to it, as opposed to verbal rehashing of past events or buried feelings.

Catharsis. Moreno (1946) developed his concept of catharsis as an extension of the idea originated by Aristotle, an idea that was but one aspect of the latter's more general writing on poetry and drama. Aristotle believed that good drama, particularly tragedy, had the power to arouse strong emotions in an audience; experiencing these emotions even in a vicarious way, had a purgative effect on the members of the audience. Moreno's view of catharsis goes beyond the Aristotelian conception. It is the actors, rather than the audience in Psychodrama, who are in the best position to experience total catharsis. The actors in an already written and formulated play are unable to truly experience emotional release since they are not portraying events and emotions from their own experience, and the audience of a formal drama can only feel such release in a secondary or vicarious fashion. The audience in Psychodrama, on the other hand, can develop almost total involvement and empathy and the attendant cathartic experience, because of the immediacy and reality of the enactment.

Moreno saw himself as taking up where Aristotle left off by creating the Psychodrama, wherein the participants—the actors—were able to experience total catharsis. According to Moreno's view, Freud and Breuer had begun to make headway in the therapeutic use of catharsis when their patients experienced emotional release under hypnosis, but they too quickly rejected it as a useful method. They did not go far enough in the exploration catharsis and cast it aside before they understood its true potential; they did not use the process of emotional release in a situation comparable to the psychodramatic one, and therefore, were not able to observe the potential benefits of catharsis to their full extent.

Moreno's conception of catharsis is intimately related to his constructs of action and spontaneity, discussed above. Total catharsis is most likely to occur in a situation where the person is allowed to deal with real life experiences and concerns by using an action oriented technique that facilitates spontaneous expression. In other words, the Psychodrama, with proper warm-up and readiness to respond, is an ideal situation for the experience of total emotional release, because the patient or protagonist serves as both the author, who formulates the experience and brings up his own emotional concerns for consideration, and also the actor, who lives out the experience with the help of other actors, who, in turn, experience emotional release from their own involvement in the role-play. The co-mingling of these two aspects, along with the facilitative role of a director and the receptivity of the audience serve to set the stage for the most complete cathartic experience.

KEY CONCEPTS: METHODOLOGICAL OR OPERATIONAL

Role of the Director-Therapist. Moreno (1946, 1953, 1964) described the role of the director as having three important components: producer, therapeutic agent, and analytical observer. He is the producer in the sense that he is the organizer of the dramatic situation; he plays the role of warming up the group members and he continues to oversee the proceedings throughout the dramatic presentation. The director is a therapeutic agent in the sense that he helps the patient develop and set his scene, he encourages spontaneity, creativity, and catharsis, and he subsequently helps in the gaining of insight and meaning from the experience. As analytic observer the director may have to stop action for clarification, making certain that roles are being properly enacted; he must also be attendant to audience members in an attempt to insure the achievement of any therapeutic or educative effects that they might gain from the experience.

The role of the director must vary with the nature of the group with which he is dealing. For example, in working with a group of regressed patients in a hospital, his role has to be an extremely active one. In the warm-up process he must get people involved and willing to participate; it often requires great expenditures of energy and an ability to help people relax and to feel comfortable. Under such circumstances the director may have to begin working with a patient around hallucinatory experiences that are occurring in the moment; his task may be especially difficult because the patient is so extremely withdrawn as to give only very minor clues as to how to set the psychodramatic scene. Under these circumstances the director's ability to empathize and to tune in to the patient's experience, as well as his having the charisma and spontaneity to get the action moving are particularly crucial. On the other hand, with a group of outpatients or a group of people using the Psychodrama experience for personal growth and development, the director's role in the warm-up period might be a much less active one since the participants already have considerable readiness to participate in the psycho-dramatic experience. In a continuing psychodramatic group in a state mental hospital, the patient-protagonist may have been chosen in advance and the general nature of the scene to be enacted may already have been anticipated. In a growth and development group, the major task of the director in the warm-up period would be to find topics of common interest to the group members. The director might begin by posing questions to the audience at large, or question an individual member of the audience about something of concern to him; he might pick a topic such as problems in marital relations, or functioning effectively with supervisors in a work situation and settle on a problem area with a high level of interest among group members. Such topics as work problems or family conflicts are likely to have some meaning for most members of a group.

Once the warm-up is completed and the group members are relaxed and ready for the psychodramatic experience, a protagonist is chosen to begin the first psychodramatic scene if he has not been selected beforehand. At this point the director's role, particularly in groups not involving seriously disturbed patients, becomes much less active and the protagonist assumes the role of setting the scene and, in a very real sense, becoming the organizer of his own drama. It is the protagonist who chooses the persons to serve as auxiliary egos and gives them directions as to how to behave. A director, of course, should keep particularly alert during this period since he must oversee the proceedings and might be called upon to help in directions to the auxiliary egos or to assist the protagonist in clarifying the scene that he is developing. Again, with more disturbed patients the director will have to be more active during this period. In any event, the protagonist needs to feel trust in the director and be able to look to him for guidance throughout the Psychodrama. It is important that the director remain constantly attentive to what the protagonist is feeling and be ready to intervene should the proceedings take an unproductive turn, or should the auxiliary egos be playing their roles in ways that do not seem to accurately capture the characteristics of the persons to be portrayed in the Psychodrama. At some points the director might intervene to suggest a variety of specialized techniques, to be described later, that would add to the cathartic effect and potential insight the scene might afford.

Once the scene has been completed the director might engage in a variety of techniques to extract additional gains from the psychodramatic situation. He might interview the protagonist directly in an effort to clarify and make more understandable the scene that was just enacted. Moreno feels that the protagonist is still in a state of intense involvement immediately following the scene and has a readiness for further exploration. Since Psychodrama is a technique that should always have benefit for all members of the group, it is important to make efforts to involve those who have not already directly participated and thus enable them to gain something from the experience. One technique to serve this end is called "sharing." In the sharing period members of the audience try to relate their own life experiences to what has occurred in the Psychodrama by describing similar kinds of experiences or similar emotional reactions of their own and discussing them with the group. Another post-Psychodrama technique would be an interpretive session in which all members of the group, coordinated by the director, respond to the scene by describing their reactions to the role behavior of the protagonist and the auxiliary egos. All of these techniques encourage maximal involvement of the total group and, beyond the emotion release of active participation, they encourage the development of insight into the motivation that underlay the behavior portrayed in the psychodramatic scene.

Protagonist-Patient. Once a protagonist has been chosen, he becomes the principal architect of the Psychodrama to be played out. In a continuing group, where the members know each others' histories, backgrounds and concerns, it is possible to quickly begin the enactment of a scene without a great deal of information to set the scene. In a new group, or one that is meeting only for a relatively brief period of time, the protagonist must set the scene by giving some information about himself, about the nature of his concern, and about the other characters that will be portrayed. The protagonist must also literally set the stage; the setting of the stage assists him in getting into the scene, as well as increasing the involvement of the other group members.

The protagonist must also select, often with the help of the director, persons from the group to serve as auxiliary egos. Then the protagonist must instruct the auxiliary egos about the specifics of the roles they are to play. These instructions should include identifying characteristics and some background information about the person, guidelines about the role the person plays in the protagonist's life and his particular role in the scene to be portrayed, and a feeling for his behavioral style. Sometimes the protagonist himself might have to take the role briefly to give the auxiliary ego an idea of how that person acts or at least how that person appears to the protagonist to act.

The development of the scene itself is, of course, a spontaneously evolving role-playing situation. The experience must grow out of the unrehearsed dramatic playing of both the protagonist and the auxiliary egos, out of the developing emotional feeling among members of the group, particularly among the players of the actual scene. As we saw in the case of Donald (described above), the protagonist, after an incorrect role interpretation by an auxiliary ego, had to stop the action and give additional instructions before the Psychodrama could meaningfully develop.

At the end of a scene the protagonist might suggest replaying it in the same form or with certain modifications. He or the director might also suggest modifying his own role in the scene in order to see if he is able to change his own behavior and observe what effect any changes might have on others. The possibility of playing and replaying a scene with modifications and of elaborating on it with the assistance of specialized techniques (described below) is almost infinite.

Clearly the benefits to the protagonist are the most direct of any group member—the experience of spontaneity, catharsis, reliving of emotionally charged or conflict ridden experiences, insight into his own behavior in these situations, and the potentiality for learning alternative modes of behavior.

Auxiliary Egos. In the presentation of any Psychodrama, unless the protagonist is engaging in a soliloquy, other actors are required in the performance. Moreno termed these persons "auxiliary egos." In the portrayal of a scene, involving the protagonist and other important persons in his life, other members of the group are called upon to play roles in the drama. For example, auxiliary egos may play any of a variety of persons in the protagonist's experience—parent, spouse, child, friend, nurse, doctor, to name a few.

They are given directions by the protagonist and/or the director as to the characteristics of the persons whose roles they are playing. Those who play the roles of auxiliary egos vary under different circumstances. In a training group or an outpatient group, the auxiliary egos are likely to be other group participants. In working with more disturbed patients, in addition to other group members, specially trained people may function as auxiliary egos. Moreno found that persons who were formerly psychotic and have recovered can be particularly effective in this role.

The role of the auxiliary ego is two-fold. First, the auxiliary ego must be able to empathize with the protagonist and with the nature of the conflict involved in the scene to be portrayed; he must be able to follow the protagonist's leads to develop an impression of the person to be portrayed. Second, the auxiliary ego functions as an observer so that he may later comment about his own feelings in the role he played as well as about the reactions he had to the protagonist, both of which might assist the protagonist in better understanding the conflict portrayed in the scene. In addition to playing the roles of important others in the Psychodrama, there are some special roles for auxiliary egos required by certain of the specialized techniques which will be described below.

Many of the statements made about the role of the protagonist also apply to the auxiliary ego; that is, he must also get ready to play his role through a warming up process, be involved in the scene setting, and have a readiness to engage in a spontaneous and creative effort required by the psychodramatic activity.

The Audience. The audience of the Psychodrama in some respects is like the audience in any dramatic presentation. It should be recalled that Moreno viewed Psychodrama as an extension of drama into the realm of psychotherapy and catharsis, such that it had a far greater potential for catharsis than Aristotle ascribed to drama or classical tragedy. The audience of the Psychodrama may benefit, as may the audience of any effective dramatic presentation, from experiencing empathy with the characters and cathartic emotional release through identification with them.

However, in Psychodrama, the role of the audience has other features as well. Because the focus in Psychodrama is clearly on human problems and conflicts, there is great opportunity for the audience to empathize and to relate the events to its own life experiences. In addition, the audience has a role of assisting the protagonist. It will be recalled that after the psychodramatic scene is completed, a variety of alternative follow-up techniques are available, many of which involve participation of the whole audience. In the sharing following the Psychodrama audience members respond to the scene just played in terms of their own experiences. When interpretation is focused on the audience, the members enter in by offering their reactions to what occurred or by making interpretive comments or suggestions to the protagonist.

SPECIAL TECHNIQUES

Although the basic and central activity of the Psychodrama is the spontaneous portrayal of scenes created by the protagonist, a number of special techniques have been developed. The introduction of these techniques is typically at the discretion of the director, who must be alert for occasions when the therapeutic or training effect of the Psychodrama would be enhanced by the introduction of one or another technique. Moreno (1953) cautions that these techniques should not be used to change the spontaneous Psychodrama into a static dramatic performance but rather should be used in the same way as the Psychodrama itself, to enhance the possibilities of spontaneity, catharsis and insight. The range of special techniques that might be created is infinite; the director may always spontaneously develop techniques that seem to be facilitative during the course of a particular psychodramatic session. Some of these have been used, modified, and used again and again until they have reached the status of regular parts of the psychodramatic director's armamentarium. Many of the most commonly known techniques have been summarized and described by Zerka Moreno (1959) and J. L. Moreno (1959). We will present a brief description of some of the more widely used techniques.

Soliloquy. As its name suggests, soliloquy is a technique in which the protagonist speaks directly to the audience in a spontaneous expression of feeling. Like the soliloquy in the drama, it is a monologue, but unlike it, the soliloquy technique involves a spontaneous emotional expression. The director may elect to suggest that the protagonist try a soliloquy when he thinks that the patient is unable to express his feelings adequately in the psychodramatic scene, or that the intensity of his emotional involvement in the scene is causing him to become unproductive. The soliloquy then provides an opportunity for the protagonist to gain some distance from his emotions and to explore in his own mind the reactions that he has been having.

Double. This technique might be employed when the director feels that the protagonist is being overwhelmed by the other characters in the drama or when he is having difficulty in expressing his true feelings. It consists of assigning an auxiliary ego to stand behind the protagonist and act with him and in some instances for him. It requires great empathy on the part of the auxiliary ego to feel what he thinks the patient is experiencing and to help him express it. Sometimes simply standing behind and following the emotions and bodily movements and attitudes of the protagonist is all that is required to give him additional strength to express himself adequately; at other times the double, or as he sometimes is called, "the alter ego," may react in ways that he thinks reflect what the protagonist is feeling.

Role Reversal. The role reversal technique requires the protagonist and an auxiliary ego to switch roles. The director might suggest the use of this technique when he feels that the protagonist would profit from an understanding of how the person with whom he is in conflict is feeling, or when he wants to give the protagonist an opportunity to act the role of a significant person in his life as he would *like* that person to behave. Since an auxiliary ego is playing the protagonist's role, it also affords the latter an opportunity to gain some knowledge about how others see him.

Mirror Technique. This technique emphasizes the last mentioned function of role reversal, that is, affording the protagonist an opportunity to see himself as others do. The director might suggest the mirror technique if he feels that the protagonist could profit from standing back from himself for a while and having the opportunity to see how another person would enact his role. The technique is particularly useful when a protagonist has great difficulty in appreciating the impact that his behavior has on others. The protagonist becomes a member of the audience and an auxiliary ego is assigned the role of the protagonist with instructions to play the role as much like the protagonist himself played it as possible. When the protagonist is unable to "get into" his role, the director might suggest a variation of the mirror technique. In this instance, he would instruct the auxiliary ego to deliberately distort the protagonist's behavior through exaggeration of some characteristic with the aim of arousing the latter into becoming more actively involved. The auxiliary ego might exaggerate a whining, demanding quality, and thereby arouse the original player to take over his own part again to show how he *really* behaves.

Behind the Back. This is a technique in which the protagonist ceases being an actor but sits with his back to the other group members who then, led by the director, discuss their impressions of him. This, like the mirror technique, is viewed as a method through which the protagonist might learn something about how others see him and react to him.

Magic Shop. This technique is considered useful when the protagonist is uncertain or confused or ambivalent about what his real wishes and goals in life are. Either the director or one of the auxiliary egos plays storekeeper in a magic shop that sells not objects but values or personal characteristics or general desires in life, such as success or courage or brilliance or wealth. In the magic shop, however, the method of exchange is not payment for what one wants but bartering. In order to have one's wishes granted, he must exchange some valued characteristic or aspect of himself for what he desires. This technique is seen as giving the person an opportunity to evaluate what is really important to him, as well as what aspects of himself really stand in the way of getting what he wants.

These are just a few of the many techniques that have been developed, all of which endeavor to further the process of exploration and emotional understanding in the psychodramatic setting.

SOCIODRAMA

Another form of spontaneous dramatic experience created by Moreno is called Sociodrama. As we have seen, Moreno always had a strong interest in and a great desire to contribute to the improvement of the human condition. The creation of Sociodrama was inspired by that desire and by the wish to put the dramatic expression of spontaneity and creativity to a useful purpose on the large scale group or social level. It was one of Moreno's hopes that human conflict could be diminished and understanding among people increased through an open exploration of socio-cultural differences using his dramatic methods.

It is difficult to draw a clear distinction between Psychodrama and Sociodrama, but in the latter the main emphasis is on group-related needs and issues of general social significance, whereas in the former, as was evident in our earlier description, stress is placed on the unique personal concerns of the individual. Yet the two forms are always intermingled to some extent. A useful way to distinguish between the two is to think in terms of the concepts of figure and ground. Psychodrama, as indeed all personal problems, always has a socio-cultural aspect, and Sociodrama is always colored by some individual concerns. In Psychodrama, the concerns of the individual are the figure and the social or group concerns are the ground, while in Sociodrama the reverse is true.

Despite the fact that Psychodrama typically occurs in a group setting, the focus of interest is basically on the individual and his particular problems. While it is true that other members of the group are able to profit from the experience either through playing roles of auxiliary egos or from the various aspects of audience participation that are involved, they are not the center of attention. Sociodrama (Moreno, 1946, 1953, 1964), on the other hand, is viewed as a collective type of group therapy that deals with sociocultural parameters. The problems dealt with are those of intercultural conflicts. Therefore, those playing roles in the Sociodrama are not enacting their own personal problems, but are rather serving as exemplars of problems that affect the group at large or the interface between several groups that are involved in cultural conflict. Sociodrama is the technique of choice when large numbers of people, or all members of a group, or indeed, society as a whole, are faced with a common problem. For example, problems in relating between blacks and whites in contemporary America, or conflicts between two groups—one pushing for industrial development and the other for environmental protection, would be appropriate topics for a sociodramatic session.

In many respects, Sociodrama follows the outline already described for Psychodrama in terms of its formal characteristics—the use of the stage, the role of the director, a protagonist, the use of auxiliary egos, and the like. As already suggested, in Sociodrama the emphasis is not on dealing with purely personal concerns, but rather on dealing with collective experience and group concerns. While it is of course true that the way in which any protagonist plays his role will be affected by his own idiosyncratic approaches and feelings, to as great an extent as possible the actor should be playing the role, not for himself, but as an exemplar of the group. Of course, all roles in Psychodrama and Sociodrama have both their personal and collective elements. One is not only a mother of a particular child but is also a member of a particular culture and living in a certain time and certain place, and these factors clearly affect the development of a role in Psychodrama and in Sociodrama as well as do one's personal idiosyncratic experiences. What is important in differentiating the two is the focus of concern in the group activity: when the focus is on an individual's personal concerns and his personal desire for change, then one is dealing with Psychodrama; when the focus is on collective concerns, on intergroup relations and collective ideology and group catharsis, then one is dealing with Sociodrama.

The participation of the whole audience is much greater in Sociodrama than in Psychodrama. In the latter, members of the audience may share personal concerns with the protagonist and achieve a secondary catharsis through their involvement in the protagonist's role experience. In Sociodrama, the focus is on collective rather than personal roles and members of the audience are likely to share in the problems that are of a collective cultural and not personal nature. Obviously the cathartic effect in Sociodrama will be the greatest when it deals with issues about which most members of the audience have strong and conflicting feelings, or when there are strong polarities between two subgroups of participants. Many of Moreno's examples of Sociodrama deal with intergroup conflicts such as racial and religious conflicts. Black-white relations have long been of concern to Moreno and he has advocated the use of sociodramatic techniques in helping to achieve group catharsis. Sociodrama as a technique is considered to be particularly useful under circumstances of very active intergroup conflict, such as the time following a large-scale interracial conflict, or, in a preventive way, when intergroup conflict threatens to develop into disruptive outbursts.

Since the group is the focus of attention in Sociodrama, there is no one exactly comparable to the personally conflicted protagonist of a Psychodrama. Rather, there is a cast of audience members and auxiliary egos who must submerge their personal concerns and play their roles for all members of the culture—a protagonist must be all blacks, all Jews, all Christians, all white Anglo-Saxon protestants. Some individuals who are more heated about the issues at hand—e.g. those who have been involved very directly in a racial disturbance—may be unable to separate strong personal feelings from shared cultural concerns and therefore would not be effective protagonists. Nonetheless, Moreno suggests that their role in the Sociodrama is an important one; they may be used as informants to assist the protagonist or auxiliary egos or as persons who help give the feel for what has happened in a group conflict. For example, a black woman, extremely angered at being turned down for a job at a white employment agency may not have enough distance from her anger to be an effective Sociodrama protagonist. Another person with instructions from her would be better able to play the role in terms of its larger social implications, and thus more successfully serve the sociodramatic goal of group catharsis and learning. The relative importance of shared group concerns versus individual problems is highlighted when one considers that the woman who was rejected for employment might seek personal catharsis as a protagonist in a Psychodrama workshop.

Again, in Sociodrama, Moreno developed a technique which for a long time went relatively unnoticed and unappreciated. In recent years—particularly around issues of black-white relations—the technique and derivatives of it have been more widely used, although Moreno has rarely been given credit for its initiation. For example, many of the confrontation groups that have been developed to facilitate communication between intercultural groups clearly draw upon sociodramatic technique and theory.

Moreno, himself, has also responded to the outbreaks of violent racial tensions in the recent past, and has become an active advocate for the use of Sociodrama as a means of understanding the black revolution in the United States as well as for working out intergroup tensions related to it. The *Boston Sunday Globe* in May, 1968, reported a meeting held at the 124th Annual Meeting of the American Psychiatric Association at which Moreno presented a Sociodrama demonstration entitled, "Origins and Causes of the Black Revolution and the Revolution of the Hippies in the United States Based on Sociometry, Small Group Research, Sociodrama and Group Pathology." A large audience gathered for the demonstration and many of the members participated. Among the issues suggested by members of the audience were problems such as how to achieve black unity, the problem of the white liberal, and the role of the black middle class "square." The interaction became extremely heated at times. For example, when the person playing the role of a black power advocate refused to accept the assistance of a white liberal, the white liberal couldn't understand why; the black power advocate insisted that at that time it was extremely important that black unity be permitted to develop without the involvement of whites. Many people in the audience spontaneously reacted with angry outbursts around their own ambivalence or their lack of understanding of the attitudes expressed. At the end of the demonstration, Moreno stressed the fact that no final answers had been found, but at least there was some opportunity to observe the nature of the cultural conflict, the range of attitudes that existed, and the strengths of the disagreements. All this represented an important first step in dealing with the continual human problem of intercultural conflict.

References

Blatner, H. A. 1970. *Psychodrama, role-playing, and action methods.* Thetford, England: Howard A. Blatner.

Corsini, R. J. 1957. *Methods of group psychotherapy.* New York: McGraw-Hill.

Dietz, J. 1968. Psychodrama: possible answer to the nation's race problems. *Boston Sunday Globe,* May 19, 1968, 50.

Greenberg, I. A. 1968. *Psychodrama and audience attitude change.* Beverly Hills, Calif.: Behavioral Studies Press.

Moreno, J. L. 1946. *Psychodrama.* Vol. 1. Beacon, N.Y.: Beacon House, Inc.

———. 1953. *Who shall survive?* Beacon, N.Y.: Beacon House, Inc.

———. 1959. Psychodrama. In Silvano Arieti, ed. *American handbook of psychiatry.* Vol. 2. New York: Basic Books, Inc.

———. 1964. *Psychodrama.* Vol. 1. (Rev. ed.) Beacon, N.Y.: Beacon House, Inc.

Moreno, Z. T. 1959. A survey of psychodramatic techniques. *Group Psychotherapy, 12.* 5-14.

Schutz, W. 1971. *Here comes everybody.* New York: Harper & Row.

Siroka, R. W., Siroka, E. K., & Schloss, G. A. 1971. *Sensitivity training and group encounter.* New York: Grosset & Dunlap.

Who's who in America. 1966. Vol. 34, 1966-67. Chicago: A. N. Marquis Co.

7

The Gestalt Therapy
Workshop

Gestalt therapy is famous for its founder, Fritz Perls, and for its innovative approach to individual and group psychotherapy, an approach that usually involves the patient in a highly theatrical dialogue with himself and in which he gives dramatic expression to the feelings, conflicts, and preoccupations of the immediate moment. Looked at from this purely technical aspect, Gestalt therapy would seem to represent a repudiation of psychoanalysis and of the latter's emphasis on a more cerebral, discursive, and historically-focused dialogue between analyst and analysand, and to constitute instead an extreme form of experientialism. Perls himself made much of his repudiation of psychoanalytic procedures. However, as we view it, Gestalt therapy represents a complex conceptual and methodological heritage composed of several influences, some psychoanalytic, some existential-experiential, and some even psychodramatic. These parts combine together to form the unique and coherent "gestalt" that is Gestalt therapy.

Fritz Perls and Gestalt therapy are nearly synonomous. Credit for its origination belongs to him, despite the considerable assistance that he received from his wife Laura and from the colleagues that were drawn to his unorthodox techniques. Perls' life, which ended in 1970 when he was seventy-six years old and is described in a book of autobiographical reminiscences (Perls, 1969a), was one of considerable searching, excitement, frustration, and growth. He was in many ways a restless rebel, antagonistic toward entrenched, establishment-oriented ways of thinking, and frequently fighting off boredom and discontent. For him, the psychoanalytic movement had come to be characterized by authoritarian close-mindedness, and he took out in a pioneering direction not dissimilar to that taken by Freud many years earlier in relation to the conceptions of psychiatry and neurology prevalent during his own time. Change was a central theme in Perls' personal life, which suffered frequent interpersonal disruptions and geographic shifts, and in his theoretical orientation, which emphasized the constant ebb and flow of healthy, present-centered awareness.

Perl's first dislocation occurred when he left his home city, Berlin, for Frankfurt. His second occurred when he emigrated to South Africa in response to the growing Nazi menace. Still another dislocation was his move to New York City, which was succeeded by one to Miami Beach, which was in turn followed by his establishing himself in Los Angeles. In 1966 Perls joined the staff of Esalen Institute in Big Sur, California, and in 1969 he went to Vancouver Island, Canada, where he founded a Gestalt community. Although he had published *Ego, Hunger, and Aggression* (1969c) in 1947 and *Principles of Gestalt Therapy* (1951) in 1951, it was not until the late sixties, which coincided with his residence at Esalen and with the explosion of interest in the human potential movement, that the man Fritz Perls and his therapy began to achieve national recognition. In the last years of his life Perls led an increasing number of workshop demonstrations and was an active participant and speaker at the 1968 meetings of the American Psychological Association. In 1969 two additional books appeared—*In and Out of the Garbage Pail* (1969a) and *Gestalt Therapy Verbatim* (1969b). Also produced during these years was a large amount of audio-visual material, films and video tapes demonstrating Perls at work.

Whether in individual or group settings, Gestalt therapy can be practiced in a variety of ways. In an individual context, it can be applied in a puristic fashion in which the patient's direct interaction with the therapist is minimal. The patient tries to translate his moment-to-moment experience into an ongoing, self-enacted psychodrama in which he personifies all the body sensations, feelings, thoughts, and persons that he is aware of; even his concern with the therapist and with what the latter might be thinking are directed into conversation with the-therapist-in-the-empty-chair wherein the patient's dialogue is not with the actual therapist but with his fantasy-projection of the therapist. On the other hand, individual therapy might proceed in the context of a more conversational, ongoing dialogue between patient and therapist; here the latter would reveal his Gestalt orientation in his consistent attention to the patient's nonverbal behavior, his occasionally suggesting various exercises or "experiments" (e.g., "Try exaggerating the motions you are making with your foot and see what you experience"), and in his reminding the patient that he is more interested in the patient's actual moment-to-moment experience than in any arbitrary "program" as to the kind of person he "should" or "should not" become. Consequently the therapist might frequently reassure the patient that, in calling the latter's attention to his constant tapping of his foot, he is not saying that the tapping is "wrong" and should be stopped, but is trying to make the patient *aware* of the tapping and of the feelings that it expresses.

In the group setting, the therapist might again practice Gestalt method in a pure way and discourage the participants from having spontaneous contact with one another; instead, they would watch while the therapist worked with a single patient. Or he might proceed less puristically, and allow the group to interact spontaneously, restricting his use of Gestalt techniques to particular interventions at selected moments when they seemed most appropriate; usually such interventions would be directed toward a particular patient in an attempt, via specific techniques, to heighten and exaggerate various awarenesses and various resistances. For example, if a participant began to focus on his perception of other groupmembers as quite critical of him, the therapist might suggest a specific reversal exercise wherein the patient would go to each member and deliberately find something negative in him that he would then criticize.

Like most psychoanalytic, experiential, and eclectic therapy groups, the Gestalt therapy group often meets on a weekly basis over a sustained period of time. However, it can also meet on an intensive basis over a short period of time. Such a format is appropriate in a training context, since it enables professionals to be introduced to Gestalt techniques in a direct and experiential way, and it can also be used in Encounter and sensitivity-training settings (see Chapter 11), where an attempt is made on a short-term basis to deepen the personal awareness of relatively healthy people. Esalen Institute sponsors Gestalt therapy workshops on just such bases as these; some are primarily for professional therapists and are oriented toward the more technical side of Gestalt approaches while others are geared for laymen.

The Gestalt therapy workshop format with which Fritz Perls became most identified toward the end of his life—at Esalen and Vancouver Island and in the several taped and filmed demonstrations of his work—was noncontinuous; its participants, whether professionals or nonprofessionals, met together anywhere from a half-day to several weeks, and their formal contact ceased at the workshop's end. Perls worked with the group in a pure way; his contact was focused on a single patient rather than on the group-at-large, and in this work the patient's attention was diverted away from the reality of the group and the therapist and directed toward his own internal self. This particular variant of the Gestalt therapy approach to groups represents the model in its purest form, and it is the one that we shall present.

The workshop begins with the therapist's asking who in the group wants "to work". Whoever volunteers then takes the "hot-seat", which is a chair facing the therapist. The participant at this point becomes the "patient". He may begin by stating a particular life problem that disturbs him; if silent, he may be asked by the therapist to express his immediate awareness. However he begins, the focus is on his moment-to-moment "here-and-now" experience as much as is possible; intensification and exaggeration of this experience is encouraged by a variety of exercises to be described below. The patient's "therapy" develops much as it might in the context of individual Gestalt therapy. Here, in the group setting, the other participants function much as a kind of "Greek chorus" (Denes-Radomisli, 1971) that hopefully resonates and empathizes to a point where it too, through processes involving identification, gains from his experience. At certain points the group might be called in by the therapist, but usually in a structured way for the purpose of furthering the therapist's work with the patient. For example, a go-around exercise might be suggested wherein the patient goes to every participant with the same sentence-beginning—"I want you to like me for my . . . ."—and then is to finish it differently for each person. The patient might remain in the hot-seat anywhere from ten to thirty minutes; he works until he and the therapist have some sense of closure. Typically from three to six participants take the hot-seat in any single session.

The Gestalt therapy group format, as it gradually evolved in the hands of Perls, became a means whereby anyone, whether professional or nonprofessional, whether "therapist" or "patient" in his extraworkshop life situation, could gain greater contact with his immediate experience. Unlike psychoanalytic and experiential groups, Gestalt group therapy did not involve a prolonged relationship to a group with which one slowly reconstructed his original relationship with his family of origin and through which he gained insight into his life as it had been lived historically. Perls' approach simply required one to focus intensively on his "stream of awareness" via the guidance of a therapist who, much like a Zen master, facilitated this meditative process. Such an approach was bound to have particular appeal for already analyzed therapists who, reluctant to re-enter formal treatment, yet searching for a vitalizing and re-integrative experience, could avail themselves of an extremely short-term form of therapy, often in the company of fellow-professionals. Despite the model's reliance on such terms as "therapist" and "patient," it departed markedly from the medical model of psychotherapy, in which a "sick" patient suffers from a specific psychological "disease" that is then "diagnosed" and "treated" by a "doctor." Now the patient could be a reasonably healthy therapist who, like all other men, has "problems in living" (Szasz, 1961) or, in Gestalt language, "blocks" and areas of "avoidance," and these problems could be approached in a workshop setting that, however charged emotionally, bore some resemblance to educational classrooms and seminars. Hence the Gestalt workshop, like its Psychodrama predecessor, constituted one more step away from time-extended group psychotherapy toward a short-term educational-therapeutic experience that would gradually evolve into the "Encounter" model (see Chapter 11).

We have already mentioned more than one parallel that Gestalt therapy has with Psychodrama. Both models can be employed in noncontinuous, workshop formats in which their respective methods are demonstrated to, and utilized by, relatively healthy people. Even more fundamentally, both encourage the patient to dramatize and personify various aspects of himself or his own behavior, although in the Gestalt setting the patient himself plays all these parts, whereas in Psychodrama the roles of significant others are assigned to various group members. It is curious that Moreno and Perls, coming from different theoretical backgrounds, hit upon techniques that were similar in terms of formal characteristics, yet different in underlying philosophy and in specific group procedures. Both models are rooted in the theatre, and Perls' youthful experience as a student-actor with Max Rhinehart in Germany might well have been influential in this respect. To what extent Perls was directly influenced by Moreno's technique remains a matter of speculation, since his writing makes almost no mention of Moreno or of Psychodrama.

KEY CONCEPTS

The Gestalt; Figure-Ground Dynamics. In reviewing Kurt Lewin's field-theory and its application to group-dynamic psychotherapy (see Chapter 4), we have already presented the perceptual theory of the three original Gestalt psychologists, Kohler, Koffka, and Wertheimer. These theorists had emphasized perception as a process involving organization and the apperception of patterned relationships in which some elements were perceived as "figure" and others as "ground." Moreover, certain perceptual elements or stimuli were perceived in the context of the overall whole in which they were embedded. For example, a black circle could be clearly perceived as such by the perceiver if it were shown against a white background; however, if it were embedded within a sufficiently complex gestalt involving many lines and patterns, it might well be "hidden" to the observer.

Gestalt perceptual psychology had been strongly phenomenological in that it regarded one's conscious perception of the world as constituting significant and instructive psychological data. It also was holistic in that it emphasized the person's capacity to impose pattern and meaning on discrete events and to organize phenomena into ever-more-complex wholes. Perls extended these phenomenological and holistic emphases to personality functioning, for along with his stress on immediate experience was his holistic conviction that one of the therapist's tasks was not so much to help the patient *resolve* conflicts as to *integrate* them more coherently (e.g., conflicts between thinking and feeling, activity and passivity, etc.). He was not, however, the first personality psychologist to be influenced by Gestalt theory. Along with Kurt Lewin, Kurt Goldstein—who was a teacher of Perls—had applied Gestalt concepts to the field of motivation, insisting that the human personality is not made up of an aggregate of discrete habits but instead strives for some sort of unity. What made Perls' relationship to Gestalt psychology unusually direct was that, in making the transition from simple perception to the whole gamut of personality functioning, he both retained the "figure-ground" concepts of the original theory and concentrated with unusual specificity on the moment to moment flow of awareness.

Let us now extend the attention that the original Gestalt psychologists gave to visual stimuli to a more everyday life situation, as Perls attempted to do. As a mother listens to her baby's cry, hoping that it will cease, all other noise becomes background of which she is largely unaware. Once his crying has stopped, she may then become aware of a sound that had previously been "ground"—e.g. the whirring of a fan. After this latter sound has been "figure" for a while it too will return to the background of her perception, to be replaced by another figure. Usually no one stimulus can be figure for any great amount of time; human attention doesn't work that way. Once a figure reaches a certain point of saturation, it begins to recede into ground. This principle provides the explanation for some well-known figure-ground reversals, e.g., two white silhouetted profiles face-to-face against a black backgound that—once reversed—become the silhouette of a black vase against a white backgound.

What was "perception" for the original Gestaltists became "awareness" for Perls. In bringing in the dimension of awareness he extended Gestalt phenomenology beyond mere sensation, to feelings and to thoughts. While awareness involves all three elements, Perls claimed that it was within the realm of awareness of *feelings* that the human organism experiences the greatest difficulty. Neuroses, he said, develop at that point in the flow of awareness where feelings that would normally become figure are blocked off by the patient and kept in the background, because of the latter's "phobic" attitude toward them; he "avoids" them because of their unpleasantness. The Gestalt therapist's task is to pay careful attention to the patient's "continuum of awareness" and to locate those precise points where he becomes "stuck"; usually these points involve avoidances that disturb the rhythmic ebb and flow of healthy, present-centered awareness. In balanced awareness various emotions, perceptions, and needs intensify to a point where they become clearcut gestalten. Once fully figured they will obey the law of all perception, and eventually become background. If these gestalten involve actual physical needs—like hunger and thirst—the person is functioning most organismically if he turns his attention to those aspects of reality that can best satisfy them; once satisfied, they too, like other perceptions, should gradually fade from awareness.

Perls did not ignore the sensory aspects of the patient's phenomenology. When working with a "stuck" or blocked patient, especially when the latter was caught up in ruminative attempts to discover what he was *really* feeling, Perls often directed him toward the simplest perceptual level: "What do you see? hear? smell?" This was the point of his oft-quoted motto: "Lose your mind and come to your senses!" As the latter statement implies, he was not impressed with the value of thinking per se. Unless it was directed toward genuine problem-solving or scientific pursuits (which Perls claimed it all too rarely was), thinking was largely a form of computing, such computing usually taking the form of fantasies in which we "rehearse" the various roles we intend to play with others in order to impress them. Therefore, for most patients, thinking was in the service of phobic avoidance. For Perls, then, normal awareness, despite its inclusion of feelings and thoughts, would have to take careful account of the physical environment, an account that returned it to the perceptual context in which Gestalt psychology had originally developed.

Now and How. These are two central emphases in Gestalt therapy theory. The "now" refers to our awareness which—in a fundamental, almost metaphysical sense—must always exist in the immediate "here and now," however much its content may involve the past or the future. Our specific memories and our anticipations of the future, both constitute fantasy-images, however "realistic," occurring in the present; however vivid, they can only remove us from the immediacy of the present in general, and from our sensory and affective experience in particular.

Perls believed that Freud's method of free-association was somewhat parallel to his own method in the sense that it too attempted to help patients report on their immediate experience. The problem, according to Perls, was that in asking a patient to report everything that came to his *mind* and in reducing the amount of environmental stimuli available to him (through his placement on the couch), Freud was minimizing the patient's opportunity for genuine contact with the environment. Perl's aim was to help the patient contact his experience with vivid immediacy, rather than to simply talk "about" it. Thus if the patient stated that he was aware of some sadness, the Gestalt therapist might ask him: "What does your sadness say? *Be* your sadness." Or, if the patient reported: "I think I try to bully people a lot of the time," the therapist might reply: "O.K. Be as big a bully here as you can. Bully me, and go and bully every person in the room." The emphasis is on intentionally demonstrating in the therapy session itself attitudes and behaviors that in psychoanalytic sessions are discussed discursively. Perls argued that in the absence of these intensifying techniques, the patient would all too likely lapse into a useless speculation about *why* he felt sad, *why* he liked to bully, and so on. According to Perls, "why" questions lead to an endless, arid, and cerebral rumination about the past that only serves to encourage the patient's obsessive resistance to present experience. As a phenomenologist, the Gestalt therapist has enough to do merely to attend to the *what* of the patient's immediate experience. If past figures are significant, they will probably emerge in the here-and-now work with the patient, either spontaneously ("Now I'm beginning to think about my mother") or through the therapist's alert attendance to cues ("The way you're ordering yourself to 'Start getting down to business!'—does that sound like anybody else's voice? Whom does that remind you of?"). Hence, for the Gestalt therapist "What?" "Now," and "How?" replace the psychoanalytic concern with "Why?".

The question of "How" becomes relevant at those points where the patient manifests a phobic attitude toward his experience, and attempts to avoid painful affect. Here the therapist must be extremely sensitive to all physical cues; for example, it may be that the patient manages, at the first sensation of tearfulness, to prevent weeping through specific muscular tensions and he may be unaware of this behavior until the therapist draws his attention to it ("Are you aware of your jaw? Try to speak for it.") Or when the therapist notices that a patient breaks eye contact with him, and asks what he experiences at that point, the patient may answer that he becomes preoccupied with an outside concern—e.g., a future event. The therapist now has an important clue as to how the patient uses withdrawal to avoid contacting emotions that are beginning to build in him. It may emerge that the patient breaks contact with the therapist at those moments when his anxiety is beginning to reach intolerable proportions. He has now progressed from knowing only that he was preoccupied with something that he had to do later in the day, to being able to connect the emergence of this preoccupation with his moving his eyes upward, and with a dim awareness of rapidly mounting tension.

If the patient is aware of the painful affect that he is attempting to avoid, the therapist can urge him to remain with the feeling ("Stay with your emptiness—Try to feel as empty as you can!") Through the therapist's reassuring presence, the patient may be enabled to face feelings that he has fought for a long period of time, and may find that he has a greater tolerance for them than he had suspected. Also, by allowing the affect to become fully felt and fully "figured," he may learn that no figure (or feeling) lasts forever and may therefore become less afraid of his feelings. The paradox here is that by having repeatedly prevented the affect from becoming fully figured (i.e., by having kept it at a point just below the threshold of awareness), he has held on to, and subtly nursed, his fear.

On the other hand, the therapist can encourage the patient to intensify his avoidance rather than the feelings against which it is directed. Essentially he has no other choice so long as the patient has no idea what the experience is that he wants to avoid. This strategy, although entirely consistent with Gestalt philosophy, also has something in common with what some psychoanalysts view as a "siding with the resistance" (Sherman, 1968). For example, if the patient says "I feel myself withdrawing; I want to get away from here!" the therapist might encourage him to do just this: "Go in your fantasy to the place you would most like to be in; describe it to me in detail." By "going with" the avoidance and making it as fully figured as possible, the therapist is gradually paving the way for the moment when the need for it will reach a point of saturation and then gradually recede into the background. At this point the patient may be ready for renewed contact with the feelings that he finds hard to tolerate. However, there is another possibility, and this is that the fantasy itself will reveal some of the immediate problems that the patient is trying to avoid. For example, if he imagines himself to be beside the ocean, the therapist can ask him to become, or "speak for," the ocean. If he were to respond: "Shore, I'm going to pound against you and pound against you until you gradually wear away!" he might well be starting to express some of the central conflicts that he initially used the fantasy to evade.

Let us go back to our earlier example in which a patient holds back tears through specific muscle tensions, like the contractions of certain mouth and throat muscles. A typical Gestalt procedure at this point would be to ask the patient to intensify his resistance by squeezing these muscles *harder.* Instructing the patient to allow himself to cry would probably be fruitless, since it is unlikely that crying is within his control. However, the patient's muscle contractions, once he is aware of them, are within his control. In addition, the therapist's request that he stop his avoidance would tend to repeat the toxic experiences of the past in which the patient's parents refused to accept him as he was. Gestalt therapy embraces the paradox that change is most likely to occur when the patient's right *not* to change is accepted. This tenet reflects the existentialist's emphasis on "Letting the patient be" (see Chapter 5). According to Perls, the patient's attempt to "program" and force change is largely what led him into his neurotic bind in the first place. For the therapist to ask the patient to stop avoiding would encourage the patient to believe that he can control that which he cannot automatically control. However, by asking the patient to intensify his avoidance, the therapist is still paradoxically giving him some control over this behavior, and by making him aware of the behavior, the therapist is also asking him to assume responsibility for it.

It is because it is hard not to read "conscious" for "figure," "unconscious" for "ground," and "defense" for "avoidance" that we stated at the outset of this chapter that we viewed psychoanalysis as one of the significant influences on Gestalt therapy. The present model clearly retains the kind of psychodynamic thinking that characterizes psychoanalytic theory, and some terminology—like "phobic," "projection," and "introjection"—has been incorporated directly into Gestalt language. Yet it is equally clear that Perls sought to give a strongly phenomenological emphasis to his theory and to pay more attention to the raw data of actual behavioral events than to theoretical speculation about the contents of the unconscious or about hypothetical connections between a particular constellation of childhood events and later psychopathology. Instead he preferred to concentrate on the minutiae of a patient's overt behavior (e.g., the twitching of a mouth, the averting of an eye), claiming that they embodied all the significant aspects of his experience, even those of which he was unaware. Hence he found a comfortable niche between the intrapsychic emphasis of psychoanalysis and the habit-oriented focus of behaviorism (see Chapter 8); for this reason we find his description of Gestalt therapy as a "behavioristic phenomenology" (Perls, 1969b), exceedingly apt.

Body Language. The patient's nonverbal cues furnish the therapist with extremely important information, since they often betray feelings of which the patient is largely unaware. "What do your hands say?" is a frequent Gestalt question. Or, if the patient is grasping one hand tightly with the other: "What does your right hand say to your left hand? Have them talk to each other." Similarly, the therapist may wish to direct the patient's attention to aspects of his vocal style, e.g., the whine implicit in his voice. As a means of getting the patient away from verbal content and more in touch with his style, the therapist might ask him to intensify aspects of his nonverbal behavior; e.g., "Hear that whining sound in your voice? Could you exaggerate it—just make the sounds, and make noises—Don't say words," or: "Notice that chopping motion you are making with your arm? Intensify it." At the point where the therapist gives these directions he has no preconceived idea of where he will go with it; "programming" is antithetical to Gestalt theory, since it implies a fantasy of the future. His intent is to stay with wherever the patient is "at" and to follow it as closely as possible. If the patient's arm-chopping becomes a kind of hitting or smashing, he may ask him to accompany it with sounds so as to intensify the experience for the patient and to enable himself to get a clearer sense of the emotion that the movement expresses. If the patient starts to make angry sounds, the therapist might ask him to give words to the sounds. If the words are: "I hate you!" he may ask the patient who the "you" is; if the patient says "Grandmother" the therapist might eventually encourage the patient to have a dialogue with Grandmother and so on. In this manner, "unfinished business" (see below), ill-buried resentments, and preconscious fantasies are woven into the here-and-now.

The therapist should be especially alert for nonverbal cues that are incongruous with the patient's verbalizations, e.g., the patient's smiling as he tells the therapist that he is angry with him. The therapist tries *not* to interpret ("You're afraid you'll displease me, so you tell me via your smile that I shouldn't take you seriously.") but, in keeping with his phenomenological orientation, simply tells the patient what he sees: "I see that you smile even though you claim to be angry with me." Or he may go a step further and ask that patient to "speak" for his smile, i.e., to give it words.

Projection. Perls' use of this term is broader than the meaning initially encompassed in Freud's use of that term (Freud, 1911, p. 449). Freud primarily employed projection to refer to the attribution of a repudiated internal feeling or impulse (e.g., I hate him) to another person (he hates me). Since Freud's initial coining of the word, projection has been used in looser ways, as in the term "projective tests", in which *any* aspect of the test-taker's personality (including conscious ones) may be "projected" onto an outside stimulus—like a Rorschach ink blot. Certain totemistic conceptions, in which aspects of nature may be seen as representing forces for good or evil, can similarly be seen as projective in nature. These looser definitions of projection resemble Perls' use of it, since for him "projection" refers to an almost universal human tendency to locate outside the self-boundaries properties of the self that properly belong inside. Indeed, he traces to projection our frequent tendency to view particular people as inherently good or bad, since what we are essentially doing is to describe as "bad" that which makes us *feel* bad.

This aspect of Perls' theory receives its most radical expression in his theory of dream formation; for him, every person and even every object in the dream represents a projected, or disowned, aspect of the dreamer. For example, a tyrannical figure in the dream may represent the patient's need to control, i.e., the "controller" part of himself. Perls refused to interpret or "explain" a dream, as is the traditional function of the psychoanalyst, and instead helped the dreamer to discover its meaning for himself by having him "play" or enact each of the significant figures in the dream, including both its people and its nonhuman content (e.g., a house). This approach to dream-work is consistent with two aspects of Perls' philosophy: (1) it discourages the patient from talking *about* the dream and encourages him to instead become the dream, and (2) it enables the patient—as opposed to the therapist—to take major responsibility for understanding the dream.

In Perls' thinking, the person who experiences frequent self-consciousness is disowning and projecting his own powers of observation and criticism; in giving up his "eyes" he becomes focused on what the eyes of others see in himself. Some Gestalt techniques are aimed at helping the patient to "own" (i.e., to reidentify with, and reintegrate into himself) his projections. For example, if he perceives the therapist or other group members as critical of him, the therapist might encourage a "reversal" whereby the patient criticizes the therapist, or goes around the group, making a negatively critical remark to each person in turn. The therapist might say: "Take anything in the other person that is the least bit negative and exaggerate it—blow it up." If the patient claims that he cannot find anything negative in the other person he might be encouraged to "make something up"—i.e. play-act it. Through this technique the therapist encourages the patient to begin to exercise once again his now dormant critical faculties.

Another Gestalt technique that is often used when a patient claims that others in the group are bored or annoyed with him is to have him "check out" his hypothesis to see if it holds true for the other members. The checking-out procedure is a way of helping the patient to distinguish between what is really out there versus what he imagines to be true via his projections.

The Empty Chair. Because of the relative ease most of us have in projecting outwards, it should be a relatively easy task to take certain aspects of ourselves and intentionally externalize them. This is what Perls required the patient to do in his "empty chair" technique; taking an empty chair (or stool or hassock), he would put it next to the patient and direct the latter to "put into" the chair an aspect of himself that is presently within his awareness. Let's say that the patient is beginning to get in touch with, and to complain about, his greedy feelings; the therapist might then direct him to first "put" his greed into the empty chair and talk to it, to then leave the hot-seat and go to the empty chair and in the role of his "greed" say something back to the hot-seat, which represents himself, or an aspect of himself. Usually a dialogue ensues in which the patient moves back and forth, alternately being his "greed" and then himself. He may say to Greed: "Greed, you are the bane of my existence! Go away and leave me alone!" And Greed might reply: "I have no intention of leaving. Don't you know my main joy in life is torturing you?!", etc.

This technique can be viewed in several ways. First, it helps the patient to get in touch with his greed on a different level—to become it, rather than to talk about it. Another is to discourage him from dissociating it—to help him recognize that it is as real a part of himself as the "ego" or "I" part of him that rejects it, as when he says: "I don't like my greediness!" The patient might also begin to sense that his "greed" represents a spiteful, torturing, clinging part of himself, perhaps even a particular parental introject. If the therapist sensed that this might be true, and observed too that the patient seemed to adopt a somewhat different posture and voice when assuming the "Greed" role, he might ask him: "Does Greed remind you of someone you've known? Think back—who talks in that voice?" If the patient replies, "That's Father's voice," the therapist might then have him talk as his father, and then move on from there to wherever the patient goes. As with Perls' splitting technique (see below), these dialogues have as their aim the promotion of a higher level of integration between the polarities and conflicts that exist in the healthiest of us. While "self" and "greed" approach each other as if in a life-and-death struggle, Perls' aim was to help them live more comfortably with each other. Too much human effort is directed toward an attempt to force change; according to Perls, the "self" cannot force "greed" to disappear, just as "greed" cannot force the "self" to accept it.

Introjection. This mechanism is the opposite of projection; it involves taking into oneself aspects of other people, especially the parents. Without the ability to take in from others there probably would be no significant forms of interpersonal influence, or learning, in life. Hence Perls implies that some sort of taking in process is inevitable and even desirable; his frequent use of eating as a biological analog to introjection confirms this impression. For Perls the crucial variable was the extent to which we are discriminatory in our taking in of others; are we careful to take in only what we value and to discard that which makes us feel anxious and/or hateful? Do we take in because we really want to or because we are overly-awed by the power of the significant other? The more selective process, in which unwanted parts can be discarded, is called "assimilation" in Gestalt theory.

Uncritical introjection results in inadequately assimilated introjects that can give the organism the psychic equivalent of "indigestion." Especially toxic was that form of the introject termed "top-dog" by Perls; his notion of the top-dog is roughly parallel to Freud's concept of the superego. Tyrannical top-dogs often instigate internal, tense dialogues where the person is told by his top-dog what he "should" be like and how far he falls short of certain ideals. Top-dog is then answered spitefully and defiantly by another part of the personality—i.e., by "underdog," who refuses to change, thereby re-enacting the role of the disobedient child. This top-dog/underdog struggle helps to explain why our frequent promises to ourselves (e.g., to finish an incompleted task) remain unfulfilled while our procrastination persists: our underdog continues to evade the moralistic imperatives of our tyrannical and toxic introjects. These kinds of internalized recriminations can result in what Perls described as repetitive and destructive "self-torture" games. This is why he tended to be wary when a patient sat down in the hot-seat with a request that he be helped to rid himself of a troublesome habit or symptom—e.g., smoking, nail-biting, masturbation, etc. To Perls this sounded like the persecutory demands of the top-dog; the patient was essentially inflicting upon himself a "program" that, in attempting to control that which cannot be controlled (i.e., his own experience and behavior) could only further estrange him from his spontaneous feelings and impulses.

The empty-chair technique offers a ready means for getting a patient to "externalize" an introject. If we take the situation cited above, Perls might quickly have the patient sit in the empty chair, turn back to the hot-seat, and tell "himself" how he must stop procrastinating, smoking, nail-biting, etc. Again, one consistent aim of such a technique is to promote integration between conflictual elements within the personality. In this specific situation, though, there may be two additional gains: (1) by "telling off" the introject (let's say it turns out to be Mother), the patient might get into firmer contact with the spiteful, underdog part of himself that has a stake in sabotaging her demands, which are in reality self-imposed demands—e.g., his actual mother may have been long since dead, and (2) he may, particularly if he is prodded by the therapist, begin to get in touch with benign, as well as toxic aspects of the mother-introject. One means that the therapist has for facilitating the latter process is to ask ·the patient to tell the mother-in-the-empty-chair what his "appreciations" of her are, as well as his "resentments."

Self-torture games that are linked to introjection can be handled by the therapist in another way, one for which the entire group is essential. The therapist asks the patient to go to each person in the group, to begin the sentence "I want to torture you by . . . ," and to then finish the sentence in a way that seems fitting for each person. This technique has several functions:

(1) it directs the patient's inwardly-directed aggression outward, where it was doubtless initially directed at some point in his past, (2) it may bring him in touch with the fact that he *still* tries to torture other people (like those who have to live with his endless self-criticism and doubt), but through indirect means: enervating and unproductive self-castigation, (3) it enables him to release energies that have been bound up in self concern, and (4) should the patient have been working on the hot-seat for a long period of time, this activity forces him to come into contact with the group once again; the request that he finish the sentence differently as he goes around hopefully results in his responding to the unique attributes of each participant. This kind of exercise also leaves the therapist free to "withdraw" for a few minutes should he wish to.

Retroflection. "Retroflection means that some function which originally is directed from the individual towards the world, changes its direction and is bent back towards the originator" (Perls, 1969c, pp. 119-120). Self-directed love, in the form of narcissism, and self-directed hatred and revenge, in the form of masochism and depression, are examples of this phenomenon. The original impulse is oriented toward contact with the outside world, but contact with the self is substituted because of primitive repressive forces involving fear of punishment, ridicule, and embarrassment.

The patient's frequent self-castigation may express critical, angry attitudes toward others, and his attempts to program and control himself (which can, as suggested above, reflect introjected forces) may retroflect an original wish to dominate and control others. If the therapist suspects that the patient is retroflecting energies that are meant for the environment, he will encourage the patient to turn them outwards, particularly toward the group. He may be instructed to criticize each participant in turn, or to dominate them by ordering them to do something. Self-directed aggression, in the form of hitting, scratching, or picking at oneself can in turn be channeled outward; here the therapist might introduce inanimate objects, like pillows, with the request that the patient perform against the pillow the same actions that a few seconds before were displaced onto the self.

Retroflection has much in common with Wilhelm Reich's notion of "character armor" (Reich, 1949, p. 44). Sensorimotor impulses that are directed toward living, sexual, or angry contact with the environment are opposed by negating and inhibiting impulses. As a result there develops points of chronic muscle tension, consisting of one set of muscles that are set for contact outward and an opposing set that counteract the first; these points of tension are often manifested in characteristic facial grimaces and postural rigidities. The example referred to earlier (see "Now and How" above), in which a patient holds back his tears by contracting the musculature around his jaw, reflects the cancelling-out and balancing effect of a retroflection. Just as in the previous example, the therapist can help to make the patient more aware of his jaw-clenching by instructing him to squeeze these muscles harder.

The Organismic Self. Central to Perls' theory is the organismic, autonomous self which, if left to its own natural biological rhythms and not contaminated by the toxic "shoulds" of a moralistic and pressuring society, can find its way to an aware, authentic existence. The problem lies in actualizing the real self, as opposed to the *self-concept;* the neurotic, in attempting to actualize his self-image, has a need to please others, to live up to external expectations of perfection, and is hereby led to "phony" and role-playing behavior. Perls' emphasis on the person's search for an authentic existence—toward a way of becoming what he fundamentally *is*—owes much to existentialist philosophy and to phenomenology. As we indicated in Chapter 5, this latter viewpoint sees man as being born into the world without self-evident purposes; his existential task is to cast aside the externalized life-structure imposed by the dominant moral and religious philosophies of his era and by the interaction "games" current in his particular social milieu.

A technique that directly grows out of this concept is the following: the Gestalt therapist might ask the patient with whom he is working to identify his primary life-game to each person in the group and to then add in each instance: "And this is my existence!"—e.g. "My main aim is to prove to you how strong and independent I am—and this is my existence!" The therapist's aim here is to encourage the patient to take full responsibility for this particular "game" and to impress upon him that this is how he chooses to spend the finite amount of time that he has allotted to him in life.

The constant aim of the Gestalt group is to enable the patient to function with "self-support" as opposed to "environmental support." The more infantile the person, the more he "plays" helpless and dumb as a means of manipulating others into giving him the comfort and support that he really doesn't need. One way of helping the patient to contact his pseudo-helplessness involves the kind of exaggeration-technique mentioned above: "O.K., be as helpless as you can." Or: "Go to each person in the group and ask him for something that you think you need from him." Should the patient complain that the therapist is not giving him what he needs, a technique occasionally employed by Perls was to direct the patient to go to the empty chair and to "play Fritz." In many instances the patient, as Fritz, was able to give himself quite constructive advice—e.g., "You know, you can take much better care of yourself than you realize," or "You look and act as though you're suffering, but I have the strong feeling that you're not really that bad off!", etc. The patient, on subsequently returning to his own chair, often reports that he felt less frustrated than he had just before the intervention—despite the fact that it was he who had essentially ministered to his own need.

In the example just cited, one can conceptualize the patient's relief in terms of his having discovered that he was less dependent on the environment than he had thought. Another explanation, one that is consistent with Gestalt-introject theory is that the patient is now better able to contact and to use the mothering part of himself, (The Gestalt personality-model postulates a constellation of "selves"—e.g., male-female; good-mother, bad-mother; etc.—rather than a single "self" or "ego." The more these selves are integrated, the stronger the personality.). One reason that the patient is unable to utilize the mothering, nurturant aspect of himself as a means of self-support might be that he totally identifies the mother introject with the toxic bad-mother. In other words, he is not allowing the positive aspects of his mother-introject to become actualized. One means that the therapist has at his disposal for facilitating the latter process is to help the patient acknowledge whatever appreciation he has for his real mother (see "Splitting" below).

Another very popular device for encouraging a patient to assume more responsibility for himself is to have him change "it" statements into "I" statements. For example if he says "It is trembling" (referring to his hand) or "It is sobbing" (referring to his voice), the therapist encourages him to say: "I am trembling," "I am crying." Whether or not he has volitional control over these responses, they are *his;* this semantic exercise can at least help him to *begin* to perceive himself as an active agent in his life, and to identify with his own feelings.

Unfinished Business. This is a key concept within Gestalt theory. It usually involves unexpressed feeling, although highly distinct memories, fantasies, and images may be connected with this affect. Because such feeling has never been allowed to become fully "figured," it stays in the background, is carried over into the present, and interferes with effective "contact functioning," that requires a present-centered, reality-bound awareness of oneself and other people. Since figure-ground relationships are essentially fluid, feelings excluded from awareness would, if they were allowed to become fully figured, eventually reach a saturation point; the ebb and flow of awareness would return and another feeling or "gestalt" would inevitably take its place. This conceptualization also explains Perls' conviction that it is only when we fully accept something about ourselves that it can change; once a disowned characteristic becomes figure and is acknowledged, it too cannot remain a central organizing motif for very long. Hence the Gestalt command to the patient on the hot-seat: "Go ahead, be as compulsive, or bitchy, or confused as you can!" Negative qualities, once made figure or "owned," can be more comfortably integrated.

Unacknowledged feelings create unnecessary emotional debris that clutter up present-centered attention and awareness, usually in the form of excessive preoccupation and rumination. The most frequent unfinished business concerns resentment and incomplete separation; a spiteful, clinging, "biting on" attitude toward another person which, according to Gestalt theory, often involves unworked through anger toward that person. The irresolution of the anger prevents the possibility of a genuine separation. Unacknowledged grief is another common kind of "unfinished business" and it, too, can prevent a more complete separation from a lost love-object. Therefore "saying good-bye," which often involves placing the living or dead person in the empty chair and speaking to him, is an often-employed Gestalt exercise. It may include a listing of both appreciations and resentments of that person, since one or the other may predominate in the patient's consciousness and thereby keep its opposite side from reaching awareness—(e.g., the dead father may be mercilessly blamed) and the patient's difficulty therefore lies in acknowledging his good feelings about his father.

Splitting. "Splitting" describes hot-seat work that is oriented toward having a patient express both sides of a conflict, polarity, or ambivalence. This is partly the rationale for the therapist's directing him toward stating first his resentments and then his appreciations, or speaking for the greedy part of himself and then the part of himself that rejects this greed. Another frequent kind of splitting involves confusion around a specific decision. The therapist might first have the patient go with one part of the conflict: I want to get a divorce, and then with the other half: I don't want to get a divorce. Going with each side of the conflict may acquaint him in a fuller way with them; in actual life he may be so conflicted that he doesn't let himself experience either side of the ambivalence for more than a few seconds. Psychic integration and *not* specific conflict resolution is the Gestalist's aim in this exercise. The person may emerge from it with the feeling that the question of his marital status no longer constitutes the "whole story" of his life—that either way, married or divorced, his life will go on and some of his abiding concerns, e.g., his children, his career, will continue. Such an attitude would seem to indicate a different level of integration; some of the psychological pressure has eased, although the person will eventually have to resolve his indecision one way or the other.

Some polarities, unlike a marital impasse, need never be "resolved." Perls rejected the idea, more characteristic of Western and of Eastern thought, that good and bad, male and female, active and passive, are antitheses. According to him, one did not have to choose one or the other alternative. A splitting exercise aims at a more harmonious combining of these elements within the personality.

Contact and Withdrawal. This last is perhaps the most fundamental polarity within Gestalt thinking. Healthy functioning, in Gestalt thought, involves effective contact boundaries; this is letting one's own feelings and sensations become fully-figured, just as it is letting the reality of other people, unencumbered by distorting projections, become fully figured. Yet there can be no real contact without withdrawal, which provides opportunities for renewal and reintegration. Too often we meet the overly-externalized person who permits himself little solitude; here there is a semblance of contact, but the over-satiation often makes genuine contact impossible. The issue for Perls was one of *organismic* regulation, which permits a more aware appreciation of when one wants to be alone—in contemplation, revery, or fantasy—and when one wants to be in contact with stimuli, either human or non-human. Too often the question of contact and withdrawal can become a matter of "should's": I *should* spend more time with people, or I *should* spend more time alone.

While withdrawal can be seen as an avoidance of contact, especially in hot-seat work, Perls had great respect for this avoidance, as he did for others. Frequently he allowed the withdrawal to become "figured," so that if the patient said he felt an impulse to leave the situation psychologically, Perls would encourage him to do so and would attempt to accompany him into whatever revery began to absorb him. Again the concept of saturation applies; once the individual's need for withdrawal is *accepted* rather than fought, it too recedes into the background. These paradoxes are reminiscent of Zen thinking; they encourage man to "relax" and "let be," since nothing need last forever. Indeed, it is the Western penchant for forcing, insisting, *making* things happen that can guarantee the kind of fixity we most fear. When the patient is fully ready to return to the here-and-now of the group, and can therefore *choose* to return, the therapist may encourage contact.

As we suggested in an earlier section (see "Now and How" above), a key task of the Gestalt therapist is to investigate precisely how and precisely when the patient avoids contact. His aim is to enable the patient to take responsibility for these mechanisms through becoming more aware of them, and to help him sense some of the experiences against which they are directed. Let us take a specific example. Suppose a patient tends to often break contact with the therapist by averting his eyes. Inquiry may reveal that he does this at those points where he becomes anxious about what he will say next. If the therapist asks him to speak for this anxiety, the patient might soon reveal fantasy-projections wherein he assumes that if he is silent others in the group become impatient with him. He might then be directed to speak for various group members by imagining what each of them is thinking. In this way the patient is brought into contact with himself, the therapist, and the group. The Gestalt therapist is careful to remind the patient that he is fully free to continue to avoid contact and that he is not being told that he *should not* break contact. What he wants to do is to enable the patient to make a more informed and deliberate, and therefore less automatic, choice as to contact versus withdrawal. Despite the codification of Perls' ideas into a formal theory, there can be no law stating that contact is good and withdrawal, bad. The existential spirit of Gestalt therapy encourages us to choose to let ourselves experience both contact and withdrawal, and to thereby make a more autonomous decision as to which of the two we want at any particular moment in time.

ROLE OF THE LEADER

In the remarks that follow we shall confine our attention to the Gestalt workshop as it was conceptualized and conducted by Perls.

The expertise of the leader lies in his skill in suggesting techniques that will help the patient to intensify his experience, in his alertness to nonverbal cues, and in his ability to identify contact-avoiding behaviors. While steeped in experientialism, he focuses on the experience of the patient and keeps both his own person and his own continuum of awareness in the background. Any preoccupation with him on the part of the patient is seen in terms of the light that it sheds on as yet unrevealed aspects of the latter's inner life, in particular his projections and introjects. Hence Perls, rather than directly encountering the patient (as is encouraged in the Existential-experiential model; see Chapter 5), usually had the latter speak to him in the empty chair, then go to the empty chair and, as Perls, answer back, etc.—thereby hoping to promote a dialogue between various parts of the personality.

When we look at the overall workshop situation, we see that both the leader and the group take subsidiary roles, while the patient-protagonist and his moment-to-moment experience come strongly to the fore. It is important to recall that in Perls' conception the presence of the group was inextricably, almost mystically, related to the work of the hot-seat occupant; each enabled the other to have a significant emotional experience. It is difficult to be specific about the precise ways in which each gains from the other because the Gestalt literature has not commented in detail on this matter. The implication is that the patient gains through the implicit support of the group and through the potential contact that it provides as he encounters it via exercises prescribed by the therapist. The other participants gain because each of them has been an empathic witness to a highly authentic experience that closely touches aspects of his own experience and his own attempts to tone down emotional responsiveness to life.

The leader's role in this process is catalytic and it demands a curious combination of activity and passivity. He is active in the sense of constantly instructing the patient as to what to do, much as a stage or film director might do; yet it is the patient who leads and writes the script, while it is he who follows. Although neither has a program as to just where to go, it is the patient who, guided by his awareness, sets the direction. He is the authority on what he senses and feels, and the therapist observes in an effort to detect specific behaviors of which he may be unaware. Once a particular behavior is pointed out to the patient it is again he who must ultimately lead in discovering its meaning and the therapist who follows. Suppose, for example, that the patient "leads" in the sense of touching his face; the therapist then "follows" by suggesting that he speak for his fingers as they caress his skin. The patient leads when he says "I feel a surface that is strangely like clay," and the therapist follows by saying "Speak for the clay." At no point does the therapist interpret the meaning of the patient's experience; instead he tries to create an atmosphere and to facilitate a process whereby the meaning, rather than being stated by him in the form of verbal conceptualizations, emerges in the spontaneous action of the Gestalt dialogue. For instance, in the illustration above it may soon become clear that the clay-like face is essentially a mask; however, it is the patient who finds this out in speaking for the clay, not the therapist. The Gestalt process thus bears a resemblance to dream-work, for it hopefully recapitulates, via concrete symbols and dramatic action, just where the patient "is at," much as the dream, through its own spontaneous artistry, portrays the immediate tensions of the dreamer.

The patient, especially if he has arrived in the hot-seat with a predetermined idea of the problems he wants to attack, may well be surprised by the hot-seat work that gradually evolves. The therapist, much like a Zen master, disarms him by asking him to do that which he feels he must not do, and by showing a benign acceptance of those features of the patient that the latter strives to change. He tries to show the absurdity of all programs, standing for acceptance rather than control, for what "is" rather than what "should be." Since all natural processes are characterized by flux, no gestalt—whether an attitude, feeling, need, or specific motor behavior— necessarily remains fixed, particularly if it is allowed to become figured as opposed to being fought and suppressed. Nothing need be forever, since there is essentially only the Now. And because no Now can ever be fully determined by previous Nows, it will always contain emergent and creative forces for change; however, it is beyond the patient's power to regulate this change. The Gestalt therapist's most fundamental and inclusive task is to enable the patient to embrace with more openness and trust the mystery of the eternal Now.

References

Denes-Radomisli, M. 1971. Gestalt group therapy: sense in sensitivity, 1971, Unpublished Paper delivered at a conference on Group Process Today, Adelphi University Postdoctoral Program in Psychotherapy.

Freud, S. 1911. Notes upon an autobiographical account of a case of paranoia. In S. Freud (E. Jones, Ed.), *Collected Papers, Vol. III.* New York: Basic Books, 1959.

Perls, F. S., Hefferline, R. F., and Goodman, P. 1951. *Gestalt therapy.* New York: Julian Press.

——. 1969a. *In and out of the garbage pail.* Layfayette, Calif: Real People Press.

——. 1969b. *Gestalt therapy verbatim.* Lafayette, Calif: Real People Press.

——. 1969c. *Ego, hunger, and aggression.* New York: Random House.

Reich, W. 1949. *Character analysis.* New York: Orgone Institute Press.

Szasz, T. S. 1961. *The myth of mental illness.* New York: Hoeber-Harper.

8

Behavior Therapy in Groups

Although behavior therapy, like most psychotherapeutic techniques, initially had its main area of application in work with individuals, it was inevitable that the approach would gradually be extended to the group context. The behavioral approach has had an enormous influence on the development of psychological science, and the social sciences in general, particularly as they have developed in the United States. Founded by John B. Watson in the 1920s and building on Pavlov's historic discovery of the conditioned response, behaviorism viewed personality as a complex constellation of stimulus-response connections learned during the long period of the individual's development. Because of its foundation in animal learning, which can be studied under precise and controlled laboratory conditions, behaviorism developed as a part of experimental psychology and its major thrust was in the area of basic research on learning processes. Yet its emphasis on man as responding both differentially and stably to stimuli in his environment was bound to have important applications not only to education, but to psychotherapy. If a troubled person could learn new and more adaptive responses to stimuli to which he was exposed, a potentially powerful therapeutic tool was made available. Behavior therapy or behavior modification, as the method came to be known, has been—as an alternative approach to psychotherapy— one of the major recent developments in clinical psychology.

It is rather difficult to describe a single model of behavior therapy in groups since there is no specific or unified technology of group methods within the behavior therapy framework. Thus this chapter represents, in a sense, a departure from the format that we have followed in most of our other chapters—that is, a presentation of a detailed, well articulated, single group method in its pure form. Nonetheless, because of the considerable

148

interest in behavior therapy and its increasing usage in a variety of different settings, we felt it pertinent to present a general outline of the behavioral approach and to give an account of some of the specific group procedures that have developed in the context of that approach. The group procedures that may be put under the rubric of behavior therapy represent, in some cases, modifications and extensions of specific individual techniques, and, in other more limited cases, simply the introduction into a group setting of techniques typically used with individuals.

HISTORICAL BACKGROUND

Behavior therapy, a designation which originated in Great Britain, or, as it is frequently referred to in the United States, behavior modification, has its roots in the experimental methods of psychology, particularly in learning theories and approaches. Behavior therapy as a widely-employed method of working with individuals has a relatively short history, dating back to the early 1950s, although there were clearcut precursors several decades earlier. As far back as 1924, Mary Cover Jones described her successful effort to eliminate fear of animals in a child using conditioning procedures. She presented a caged rabbit to the child, placing it at some distance from him while he was in a chair eating his favorite food, and through subsequent simultaneous presentations of the positive reinforcement (the favorite food) and the previously feared object at closer and closer ranges, she succeeded in getting the child to pat the rabbit and was thus able to eliminate his fear of the animals.

The more immediate theoretical precursors of behavior therapy and behavior modification as practiced today came from diverse roots and developed in a variety of places. Pavlov (1941), who introduced the paradigm of classical conditioning, made some initial efforts to apply the conditioning method to the understanding of neurotic behavior. The work of H. J. Eysenck (1960) in London and Joseph Wolpe (1958), originally in South Africa and later in the United States, grew out of the Pavlovian model and the learning theory of Clark L. Hull as well as the work of Jacobson (1938) on relaxation techniques. Simply stated, they attempted to apply reward or reinforcement and extinction principles derived from learning theory to change or modify overt problem behavior in individuals. They very clearly eschewed any consideration of underlying dynamics or causes of behavior, and believed that all behavior change could occur through the acquisition of useful new habits and the elimination of problematic ones.

The Pavlovian, or classical conditioning, model posits that learning takes place only under conditions of reward and involves the pairing of two previously unrelated stimuli, one of which reflexively produces the response (e.g., salivation to the stimulus of food). The condition of extinction, on the other hand, deals with eliminating already learned behavior by insuring that it occurs when no reward is offered. In dealing with human learning, rewards may be material, but may also consist of social reinforcement (the desired presence or praise of another individual) or reinforcement in the form of tension or anxiety reduction. Behavior therapy techniques that attempt to eliminate problem behaviors by replacing them with successful new responses that are incompatible with existing problem responses (e.g., relaxation in place of anxiety) are typically based on the classical conditioning model.

A full account of the range and kinds of behavior therapy techniques based on this model is presented by Bandura (1969), and Yates (1970). One of the most frequently employed and the most intensively studied of these is systematic desensitization. The basic idea is to present conditioned stimuli for anxiety responses while incompatible responses are being made. Relaxation responses are the responses incompatible with anxiety that are typically used. The usual procedure involves training in muscle relaxation, the developing of anxiety hierarchies—that is, lists of related objects or experiences in descending order of the degree to which they create anxiety in an individual—and lastly, the experiencing of the anxiety-producing images, from lowest to highest, while in a state of deep relaxation. In this way the anxiety is reduced by being paired with the incompatible response of relaxation.

The development of behavior modification in the United States followed more directly on the theoretical heels of B. F. Skinner (1938). Skinner's approach was that of operant or instrumental learning. The instrumental learning model requires that the learner himself take action to get a reward, and is most simply seen in the situation in which a hungry rat learns to press a bar for food. The typical experimental situation involves the animal learning to make a response in the presence of a particular stimulus, such as a sound or a light appearing. When the response is made in the presence of that stimulus then a reward is forthcoming, and the animal quickly learns only to respond at the appropriate time, i.e., when the reward stimulus is present. Most behavior therapy or behavior modification procedures involving the acquisition of new responses have very clear roots in the Skinnerian model, and involve the use of reinforcement for increasing appropriate behavior and of the removal of reinforcement to reduce or extinguish inappropriate behavior.

The development of group approaches based on the behavior therapy model is a relatively new extension of the procedure. As yet, no very well specified or articulated group model has emerged. Most typically, behavior therapy groups have centered on the introduction of individually-oriented behavioral techniques into a group setting. Thus groups have been developed using techniques of systematic desensitization, acquisition of new behavior, and behavior control that had previously been applied to individuals. There has been very little specific discussion of group phenomena from the theoretical point of view of behavior therapy. Although a number of positive effects that arose from the group experience itself were observed, work with groups by behavior therapists was attempted mainly because of an interest in providing services to more people in a more economical way. The usual style of group leaders working within the behavior therapy framework is a model that stresses communication from the group leader to the individual members, and tends to deemphasize member-to-member interaction. It is interesting to note in this connection that much of the impetus for the development of behavior therapy and behavior modification techniques came from reactions against psychoanalytic and psychodynamic approaches, because they were considered to be ineffective and were based on theories of hypothesized internal processes far removed from the concrete reality of observable experience. Yet with respect to the interaction style of the leader, the behavior therapy group leader seems most similar to the Psychoanalytic group leader (see Chapter 3) in the degree of his attention to individual members and his relative inattention to the experience of the group qua group.

Behavior therapy approaches to groups grow out of the theoretical and philosophical concerns of the approach as a whole. There are several characteristics that behavior therapists believe make their approach unique and distinguishable from other psychotherapeutic approaches. One is the degree of *specificity* with which the behavior therapist tends to approach each case; he makes a very careful and clearcut delineation of the specific behaviors, situations, objects and the like that are problematic for an individual and then attempts to help the person overcome the reactions and behaviors that make these circumstances problematic for him, using any of a broad range of learning-based techniques.

A second unique characteristic is the research orientation that has historically been associated with the behavioral approach. There has been a much greater emphasis in this method than in any other therapeutic approach on outcome studies and follow-up of cases in a systematic fashion to determine the efficacy of the techniques used. In focusing on the single case attempts have been made to study the learning course required to change specific problem behaviors. This would include efforts to determine the particular conditions that serve to reduce the frequency of or to eliminate the behavior and those that serve to increase or exacerbate it. A number of outcome studies and clinical reports surveying the treatment efforts in groups of cases have shown that behavior therapy has a very high rate of success, particularly in eliminating specific fears and phobias. Recently, however, Arnold Lazarus, who has been among the strongest advocates of the behavioral approach and one of its most prolific writers, did an extensive follow-up study of individuals treated by behavior therapy techniques. His results created considerable doubt in him about the persistence of changes brought about by behavior therapy. He found a much higher rate of relapse than had previously been reported (Lazarus, 1971). Whether or not the behavioral approach is as effective as some of its most ardent supporters insist, it is of note that most people working within the behavior therapy framework tend to give a higher priority to evaluation of their techniques than have the proponents of virtually all other techniques of psychotherapy.

In the remainder of this chapter we shall describe three rather distinct categories of group approaches developed within the behavior therapy framework: systematic desensitization groups, behavioral practice groups, and specific behavior control therapies. We shall endeavor to give the reader a sense of the kinds of usage in groups to which behavior therapy has been put.

SYSTEMATIC DESENSITIZATION GROUPS

Most desensitization groups have represented a rather direct application of the individual techniques in a group setting. The basic structure of the desensitization procedure, whether applied individually or in a group, is most fully described by Wolpe and Lazarus (1966), and involves three steps. First the patient is given instruction in the process of deep muscle relaxation. In this procedure the therapist suggests that the patient get as comfortable as he possibly can and try to let go of all of the tension that he experiences. Next he is told to tense up and experience all of his tension, and then to stop tensing and experience the feeling of relaxation *and* the contrast between the two states. Through a series of successive approximations to total relaxation with a heavy dosage of hypnotic-like suggestion, most people are easily able to become quickly relaxed in their therapeutic sessions. The second task is to construct an anxiety hierarchy. This is most easily illustrated in the case of a person with a specific phobia, for example, a phobia about snakes. A person with such a phobia is likely made most anxious by the actual physical presence of a snake, having to look at and perhaps touch a snake. Further on down the hierarchy would be anxiety created by knowing that a snake might be present or seeing pictures of snakes. Less anxiety-provoking still are situations where the person thinks he might see a snake, such as entering a zoo or museum, knowing there might be live or stuffed snakes in the area, hearing someone talk about snakes, or picturing a snake in one's own mind. Lowest on the hierarchy, creating only minimal anxiety, might be reading the word "snake." An important element in the procedure is making certain the patient is able to imagine "scenes" of the items on the anxiety hierarchy. As the third step, the systematic desensitization procedure requires that the patient relax as fully as possible and begin imagining the scenes on the hierarchy, step by step through the progression of anxiety-provoking stimuli, beginning with the weakest. At any point at which he begins to feel anxious and lose his state of relaxation, the procedure stops and the patient is helped to induce the relaxed state once again. Then he again relaxes and begins to imagine the ascending series of scenes on the hierarchy another time. The underlying principle said to be involved is that anxiety responses will be weakened if antagonistic responses (in this case, relaxation) can be evoked when stimuli usually creating anxiety are present.

Lazarus (1961) was one of the first to describe the use of this procedure in groups. He advocated the use of the group procedure for patients who are made anxious or fearful by specific objects or situations. As he initially described the group, it consisted basically of an individual procedure carried out in a group setting; the group was typically composed of members with very similar fears or anxieties. Most other reports describe group activities that have been essentially experimental in nature, i.e., they are more concerned with varying elements of the procedure so as to study aspects of systematic desensitization technique than with endeavoring to further develop the procedure itself. In general, the advocacy of the use of such groups has been made in terms of greater efficiency and economy when compared with individual treatment. More recently, however, emphasis has been placed on the use of the group atmosphere as a supportive and reinforcing agent. The group members serve to support one another in their efforts at behavioral change outside the group and to reinforce each other for successes. Furthermore, the success of a group member gives evidence to others in the group that change is, in fact, possible, and thereby gives additional encouragement to work for change.

At present it is possible to distinguish two general types of desensitization groups. One, such as that described by Fishman and Nawas (1971), focuses almost exclusively on the desensitization procedure and attempts to create a situation whereby all participants may proceed through their total anxiety hierarchy within a specified period of time. To facilitate this the authors developed a standardized anxiety hierarchy and followed a standardized time schedule. All of the participants were people with snake phobias so that it was possible in that instance to create a hierarchy, such as the one we described earlier, that would have some relevance to all members. Desensitization groups of this variety last five to six sessions, with the first session being devoted to teaching deep relaxation, following the Jacobson method. In subsequent sessions the hierarchy is presented and the desensitization procedure followed in the standardized manner described. Each member is given one minute for the imagining of a scene, and each scene is presented about six times. In this approach there is little or no group interaction or patient participation in developing hierarchies, nor any other mutual group activities.

Lazarus (1968) has applied a similar kind of procedure to people with sexual anxiety, including groups of men with impotence and women suffering from frigidity. He added a period of didactic instruction which involved descriptions, explanations, and verbal instruction about manual and oral sexual techniques for satisfying one's mate without actual sexual intercourse. In addition some information about the physiology of the sexual organs and some explanation of how their dysfunction might be related to anxiety and tension were presented. In the group of impotent men, which had three members, the second session was chiefly devoted to relaxation training and instruction in directing attention away from thinking about their problem in gaining an erection while engaged in sexual activity and instead focusing on the pleasure they could give their partner using the other techniques they had been taught. The third session introduced this anxiety hierarchy: kissing, mild petting, undressing, nude love play, getting ready for insertion, and finally, changing position after insertion. The scenes were imagined under deep relaxation during the remainder of the third as well as in the fourth session. In the fifth session, discussion was devoted to potent sexual encounters which group members had actually experienced. One patient attributed his increased potency to desensitization, but the other two felt that their wives' willingness to engage in a wider range of sexual activities was the more important factor in their improvement.

The second type of desensitization group emphasizes greater interaction among group members than the first, but still group discussion is limited to certain periods, usually at the end of the session, and very much directed by the leader. McManus (1971) and Paul and Shannon (1966) provide descriptions of this more broadly conceived approach. This type of group is also distinguished by the fact that participants more commonly exhibit diffuse anxiety rather than specific phobias. McManus worked with college students experiencing test anxiety, while Paul and Shannon worked with people with social anxiety, which manifested itself in stage fright or fear of speaking in public. Although their approaches differ in some particulars, we will endeavor to present an overview of how such a desensitization group might function.

The group typically lasts for between six and ten sessions and begins with the group members discussing the similarities in their experience with anxiety. The therapist focuses his remarks on emphasizing these similarities, referring questions to the group as a whole, and attempting to apply the comments of one member to the others in the group. Also in the first session, relaxation training, such as previously described, begins. After the first relaxation training session is completed, the group members share their reactions to the experience with each other. In the second session the group begins to mutually construct a desensitization hierarchy that will be usable by all the members. Of course it is only possible to make a composite hierarchy when the presenting problem is essentially the same for all the membership. In constructing a group hierarchy care has to be taken to find mutually meaningful and acceptable wording so that each group member can successfully apply the items to himself. Later in the session additional training in relaxation occurs and the therapist begins to instruct the participants in the visual imagining of scenes on the anxiety hierarchy. At the end of the session, each member evaluates with the group his ability in employing imagery.

In the third session the anxiety hierarchy is completed, there is further training in relaxation, and the desensitization begins. The therapist then leads a brief discussion of the desensitization procedure. The remaining sessions consist of inducing the relaxation experience, simultaneous presenting of the various items on the hierarchy, and group discussion of the experience. Users of the group desensitization method are careful to point out the necessity of gearing movement through the hierarchy to the slowest member of the group; that is, one should not move on to the next higher item on the hierarchy until all group members feel completely relaxed in the presence of the anxiety-producing scene that they are presently imagining.

Both the group desensitization procedures of McManus, and Paul and Shannon were conducted in the context of experiments designed to determine whether such procedures achieved their desired effects. In the case of the test anxiety group of McManus, a follow-up indicated a significant increase in grade point average of the persons who received the group desensitization experience compared with no significant change in a control group. Paul and Shannon's subjects, who were anxious about public speaking, were also evaluated by a battery of personality and general anxiety measures. This group, when compared with a control group and with groups employing other treatment alternatives, showed a significantly greater decrease in anxiety and in other indices of personality dysfunction. Moreover, a two-year follow-up study (Paul, 1968) revealed greater continued positive effects of the group desensitization procedure in comparison with the other group methods.

In summary, then, the group desensitization procedure involves the application of a common technique to all of the group members. In contrast to most of the other group approaches described in this volume, it is more highly structured and has more clearly specified goals that emphasize specific desired changes in behavior. Typically, such groups are advocated for persons having similar problems or anxieties, although it is possible to compose such structured groups of patients with different problems. In the latter instance, each person would be working on a separate hierarchy that was individually developed.

BEHAVIORAL PRACTICE GROUPS

Behavior rehearsal, or behavior practice, groups are designed to help individuals develop more effective ways of behaving in interpersonal interactions, or more specifically, to learn appropriate responses to situations that have been problematical for them. In essence, the focus is that of role-playing or practicing new interpersonal skills in order to overcome behavioral deficits, or inadequacies, such as the inability to assert oneself effectively or to express feelings openly.

Despite the rather striking differences in orientation and approach between Psychodrama and behavior therapy, the role-playing in behavior rehearsal groups has clearcut roots in Moreno's method, described in Chapter 6. Role-playing in behaviorally oriented groups is devoted almost exclusively to practicing behaviors that participants have been unable to perform successfully, whereas, in Psychodrama, of equal or greater importance is role play with the aim of reliving, for the purpose of catharsis, emotionally charged past or present life situations. In the behavior rehearsal group, leaders assist group members in specifying and clarifying the nature of the ineffective behaviors, the kinds of situations in which they are evoked, and in determining what new responses would be more effective. Group members, then, role play attempts to try out new responses to these problem behaviors, discuss the strengths and weaknesses in the role play, and evaluate the performance of the member whose problem is under consideration. Then the role player has the opportunity to rehearse the situation a number of times, continuing to get feedback about where his performance needs improvement. Sometimes the leaders will play the role of coaches by directly modeling the desired behavior while engaging in the role play activity themselves. As the group progresses group members are instructed to try to apply the new behaviors learned to actual life situations outside the group and their successes and their problems in performance are discussed in subsequent group meetings. Relaxation training is often included as a part of the group's activity to serve as an additional aid in counteracting unrealistic anxiety experienced in social situations.

Members typically interact at two levels in groups of this type: (1) as actors in role-playing situations that most often occur in dyads but occasionally involve more than two people if the situation demands it; and (2) as a group, helping to develop problem situations for role-playing and discussing an individual member's performance in the role play. Therapists serve at both these levels also: (1) in the role-playing, they coach, reinforce, and serve as role models; and (2) in the group discussions they participate as expert members lending special guidance to the development of role play situations and offering feedback to members about their performances.

Perhaps the most highly developed version of behavior practice groups is that devoted to what has been termed "assertive training" or "expressive training" groups. Lazarus (1968) and Fensterheim (1972) have provided extensive descriptions of this approach, which originally dealt with difficulties in direct communication of annoyance and displeasure, and more recently has been broadened to include work with inhibition in expressing warm, tender, and other positive feelings as well.

The assertive training group is typically composed of eight to ten members of homogeneous backgrounds; group meetings last for two hours. Lazarus suggests that the procedure works most effectively when members are all of one sex, while Fensterheim has worked with groups made up of both sexes. Like most other behaviorally oriented groups, it is characterized by a fairly high degree of leader-provided structure. Since members are selected on the basis of a history of difficulty in asserting themselves, the first session begins with a didactic presentation on the nature of unrealistic social anxiety. This formulation sets the stage for the forthcoming behavior change activities by underscoring the point that the members have learned to be unrealistically anxious in situations that do not present any actual dangers to them; the learning task then is one of unlearning these unfortunate internal responses on the one hand, and learning new assertive behaviors on the other. Following the presentation members introduce themselves and the introductions are tape recorded; subsequently the introductions are played back so that each member may get the group's comments on the ways in which his performance was unsuccessful. Such discussions tend to focus on the manner in which the individual's anxiety and defensiveness were presented in the actual behavior of introducing himself. When relaxation procedures are included, the beginning of relaxation training usually occurs at the end of the first session.

In the second session effort is devoted to further training in relaxation and to each member's description of behaviors that he feels are particularly problematical for him. One member might, for example, complain that he is unable to tell a waiter in a restaurant that he finds his dinner unsatisfactory and another might find it difficult to say that he has other plans when his boss asks him to work late in the evening. After each member has stated a concern, he then commits himself to attempt to carry out the previously avoided behavior during the coming week.

In the third session the members describe the assertive behaviors that they tried and evaluate the degree to which they were able to carry out their attempts. Since these first attempts are typically not entirely successful, the group turns its attention to the core activity of the assertive training group— role-playing. For example, if the member who had problems in asserting himself with waiters angrily blurted out a volley of dissatisfactions to the waiter so that he got only an angry response back, the group would try to help him role play, modulating his assertive behavior in a way that would get him a more satisfactory reaction. After further portrayal of the scene there would follow a discussion of its successful and unsuccessful aspects with suggestions from the other group members or the leader about how to improve the behavior. Role-playing the scene again, this time incorporating the suggestions, would conclude the session. The fourth meeting is very similar to the third in that there is additional relaxation training and further discussion of attempts to engage in assertive behavior outside of the situation of the group meeting, followed by analysis of the behavior and role-playing.

From the fifth session on the process is much more dependent upon the specific needs of the members and the particular assertive activities that concern them. In some instances groups tend to focus regularly on role-playing procedures; other groups devote more effort to the discussion of the attitudes and values that underlay the difficulty in engaging in the assertive behaviors; still others are characterized by an equal combination of both role play and discussion.

Lazarus contends that assertive training groups are successful and useful for between fifteen and twenty sessions; after that they tend to become rather repetitious. Efforts to shorten the length of assertive training groups have been attempted by employing less input of specific member problems and using canned or "pre-scripted" scenes in which assertive behavior would be appropriate, but difficult for the members to successfully express. Incidents such as being kept waiting by a friend for an hour or being brought by a cab driver to the wrong address by a rather circuitous route are employed. Members work in dyads on practicing certain scenes, with the leader offering suggestions and making observations about their success. Other groups have used even more specific scripting with actual dialogue provided for the group members; this creates the opportunity for behavioral practice without requiring the generation of responses by the participants. Such approaches have been more frequently used with relatively less well-educated and less verbally facile people. In these latter groups the leader plays a particularly important role in directing the activities of the group; the degree of interaction among members is quite minimal except for the role-playing interaction within the dyad.

SPECIFIC BEHAVIOR CONTROL THERAPY

This type of behaviorally oriented group therapy is concerned with alleviating specific behavioral excesses such as extreme overeating or excessive smoking. Groups are composed of members with similar unwanted behavior patterns and typically involve a direct application of individual behavior therapy techniques, such as stimulus saturation (see below) in a group setting. The majority of interaction in such groups occurs between the therapist and the individual member or between the therapist and the group as a whole. However, in some groups discussion of the difficulties and discomfort encountered in the efforts to eliminate the behavior seems to be valuable in providing group support for continued participation in the group experience. Moreover, group approval or disapproval can also be highly potent as positive or negative reinforcement.

Pinick and his colleagues (1971) describe a group behaviorally oriented technique for working with obese patients; the main focus of the approach is on helping group members to become better observers of their eating behavior and then to learn new ways of controlling the behavior more effectively. The group met weekly for three months for a five-hour program that included a two-hour behavior therapy session, and exercise session, and a low calorie lunch. The group procedure began with the therapist asking members to describe the behavior that is to be controlled and the circumstances surrounding the occurrence of the behavior, that is, eating behavior in this instance. After the first meeting members were required to keep records of the time and place of eating, the speed with which they ate, and the kinds of food they consumed, as well as any discernible emotional and attitudinal reactions related to eating. This procedure had two important effects: (1) it required group members to become cognizant of a number of characteristics of their eating behavior that previously had gone unnoticed, and (2) it directed their attention to the attitudes and emotions that seemed to accompany excessive eating behavior, for example, noticing that when one feels angry he eats even more than he customarily does.

The next set of procedures, after having gathered information about the circumstances and external stimuli related to eating behavior, dealt with efforts to control the stimuli governing eating activities. The therapists instructed the patients to see to it that their eating did not occur in the random way that they had observed it happening. For example, they suggested that patients confine eating to one place in their homes, that they eat at certain specified mealtimes and not whenever they felt like it, and that they separate their eating experiences from other activities such as watching television, talking on the telephone, or engaging in other distracting activities. In addition, there was instruction in techniques for controlling the act of eating itself. Group members learned to decrease eating by counting each mouthful, by putting their forks on their plates after a specified number of bites, and by chewing more slowly.

The authors did not describe any efforts to encourage group interaction, but did indicate that the group sessions included members' describing difficulties in maintaining eating schedules, sharing with each other "tricks" that they played on themselves to help them stick to their schedules, mentioning successes that they achieved in lowering food intake, and recounting problems encountered in performing the self-observation homework assignments. When compared with traditional discussion therapy groups focused on weight problems, patients in these groups showed significantly greater weight loss, with 53 percent of the members losing 20 pounds or more.

Another specific behavior that has been dealt with in behavior control groups is excessive smoking (Marrone, *et al.*, 1970). One technique used, labelled stimulus saturation, requires group members to engage in smoking behavior continuously over an extended period of time and with so great a frequency that the pleasurable aspects of smoking become overshadowed by the discomfort created by excessive usage. Sessions were arranged in two formats in two different groups; group one had twenty hours of treatment in a forty hour period, and group two had ten hours of treatment in a thirteen hour period. Patients were permitted to engage in any kind of group activities they wished with one proviso—they had to smoke continuously throughout the period. A one dollar fine was charged if a patient was seen not holding a cigarette or not inhaling at least once every two to three minutes. An important leader task was constantly monitoring the smoking behavior. Typically, patients became nauseous and about 50 percent of them vomited during the treatment period. This form of aversive conditioning led to the majority of members of both groups giving up smoking initially; a follow-up after four months showed that group one had significantly more nonsmokers than group two, with 60 percent of the former's members continuing to abstain.

KEY CONCEPTS

As indicated earlier, writings concerning the application of behavior modification approaches to groups is relatively sparse. Therefore, it is not so possible to specify key concepts in the application of the technique with the degree of specificity to groups that has characterized our discussion of most other models. Nonetheless, since there are certain key concepts underlying the development of behavior therapy and behavior modification in general that are as relevant to work done with groups as with individuals, we consider it useful and appropriate to review and summarize these points.

Focus on Overt Behavior. In contrast with many group methods that have developed theoretical constructs dealing with hypothesized internal motivational states, the behavioral approach eschews such constructs and instead concerns itself as much as possible with overt and observable behavior. The basic therapeutic questions become: What are the behaviors that the individual wishes to change, and what are the new behaviors that he wishes to learn? For example, in the assertive training group, the focus is on practicing behaviors that the individual has found himself unable to perform. Oftentimes what is required as a first step is the very careful observation of the patient's actual behavior, paying close attention to subtle characteristics of the behavior and related situational factors that have previously gone unnoticed. Such close observation was required in the obesity group described; the reader will recall the importance in that instance of group members' keeping close track of all of the circumstances in which eating took place. The major therapeutic concern is first with isolating the problem behavior and second with creating the means of changing it.

Specificity. Closely related to the focus on overt behavior is an emphasis on detailing conditions that control behavior and specifying as clearly as possible the nature of the problematical behavior under consideration. The behavior therapist must never be satisfied with a general statement of the problem but he requires a very careful delineation of its nature, the circumstances under which it occurs, and unsatisfactory concomitants of it. Vague descriptions of problems are unacceptable. Thus the behavior therapist would not allow someone to describe himself as anxious and let it go at that, but rather would inquire into the specific behavior that the patient is referring to when he offers that adjectival description. Knowing when, and how and where the feeling is experienced is quite relevant. Thus, becoming aware of the sepcific conditions that control the existence of problem behavior so that new conditions may be created to facilitate behavior change is a central principle.

Determining Treatment Goals. Many of the treatment methods that we have discussed throughout the book, whether applied to individuals or to groups, have goals or aims which most behavior therapists would view as extremely vague and undelineated. Many would further comment that with extremely amorphous goals one is never certain whether he has achieved them or not. In rather sharp contrast, the behavior therapy approach attempts to state in very concrete ways the kinds of behaviors that an individual finds problematic and wishes to change; it also attempts to detail the nature of the change that needs to take place. The behavioral approach is typically directed toward one or another of the following goals, or some combination of several of them: acquiring behavior, maintaining behavior, strengthening behavior, and eliminating behavior. There is, of course, a range of specificity of goals within the behavior therapy model. For example, at one extreme would be very delimited changes such as stopping smoking, or losing a predetermined number of pounds in a certain period of time; at the other extreme would be feeling more comfortable in social situations. But even the latter would not be left at such a vague level; it would be broken down into more particular observable kinds of behaviors that need attention, as we saw in the development of anxiety hierarchies in the desensitization group for students with fears of speaking in public and of being in social situations.

Behavior therapists have some data to support the fact that charges in delimited problematical behavior or elimination of specific symptoms have additional unanticipated positive effects that go beyond an alleviation of the specific symptom. For example, the level of general anxiety is frequently shown to be diminished when only one specific phobia is focused on in the treatment situation. A number of variables centering around general level of personal comfort, greater ease in social situations, and feelings of increased adequacy have been found to occur concomitantly with the more circumscribed treatment goals.

Treatment Plan. As we have seen, there is a diversity of group and individual methods that generally come under the rubric of behavioral approaches. After developing specific goals, it is necessary to choose the most appropriate method for successfully accomplishing those goals. The careful analysis of the individual's overt behavior and the development of specific goals should lead to a reasoned choice of method by which to help the individual change the behaviors. The body of knowledge that has developed in the area of behavior therapy has led to the association of certain techniques with certain problems, such as desensitization techniques with phobias and other circumscribed anxieties and behavior practice techniques with behavioral deficits, as in the use of assertive training to increase the ability to express dissatisfaction or annoyance. While a particular technique is commonly used with a given problem, a predominant emphasis remains on attempting to customize the technique and treatment plan to the specific manifestations in each individual.

Objective Evaluation of Outcome. Traditionally there has been a great emphasis in the behavioral approach on evaluating the effectiveness of techniques used and on continuing to carefully reexamine them with an eye toward their evolution and improvement. Many of the behavioral techniques have been developed in the context of controlled studies comparing these techniques either with other existent treatment approaches or with no treatment conditions. This emphasis on evaluation clearly articulates the roots of the behavioral approach in the experimental-scientific method.

ROLE OF THE LEADER

Throughout our discussion we have pointed to a variety of leader characteristics; let us now briefly summarize those that have some relevance to the behavioral techniques we have discussed. The leader in behavior therapy groups frequently fills the role of teacher or expert. His approach is typically a very authoritative but not necessarily authoritarian one. He presents himself as knowledgeable about the problems under consideration, frequently has didactic information to impart, and in general is the organizer of the proceedings. The group interaction is characterized by instructions and comments from the leader to a particular individual in the group or to the group as a whole, although there are some exceptions, notably in those instances where group discussion plays a relatively prominent part.

In contrast with group process or group dynamics approaches, character-ized by a considerable amount of member to member interaction, low frequency of input by the leader, and tolerance for periods of long silence, the leader in the behavioral approach is typically quite intent on keeping the proceedings going and leading the group through a predetermined set of specified activities. He is active, directive, and is looked to by the members for instructing, pacing and sequencing, and assuming overall responsibility for the proceedings.

References

Bandura, A. 1969. *Principles of behavior modification.* New York: Holt, Rinehart and Winston.

Eysenck, H. J. 1960. *Behavior therapy and the neuroses.* London: Pergamon.

Fensterheim, H. 1972. Behavior therapy: assertive training in groups. In C. J. Sager & H. S. Kaplan, eds. *Progress in group and family therapy.* New York: Brunner/Mazel.

Fishman, S. T., & Nawas, M. M. 1971. Standardized desensitization method in group treatments. *Journal of Counseling Psychology, 18.* 520-523.

Jacobson, E. 1938. *Progressive relaxation.* Chicago: University of Chicago Press.

Jones, M. C. 1924. A laboratory study of fear: the case of Peter. *Journal of Genetic Psychology, 31.* 308-315.

Lazarus, A. A. 1961. Group therapy of phobic disorders by systematic desen-sitization. *Journal of Abnormal and Social Psychology, 63.* 504-510.

——. 1968. Behavior therapy in groups. In G. H. Gazda, ed. *Basic approaches*

to group psychotherapy and group counseling. Springfield, Ill: Charles C
Thomas.

————. 1971. *Behavior therapy and beyond.* New York: McGraw-Hill.

Marrone, R. L., Merksamer, M. A., & Salzberg, P. M. 1970. A short duration
group treatment of smoking behavior by stimulus saturation. *Behavior
Research & Therapy, 8.* 347-352.

McManus, M. 1971. Group desensitization of test anxiety. *Behavior Research
& Therapy, 9.* 55-56.

Paul, G. L. 1968. Two year follow-up of systematic desensitization in therapy
groups. *Journal of Abnormal Psychology, 73.* 119-130.

———— & Shannon, D. T. 1966. Treatment of anxiety through systematic
desensitization in therapy groups. *Journal of Abnormal Psychology, 71.*
124-135.

Pavlov, I. P. 1941. *Conditioned reflexes and psychiatry* (trans. by W. H.
Gantt). New York: International Universities Press.

Penick, S. B., Filion, R., Fox, S., & Stundard, A. J. 1971. Behavior modification in the treatment of obesity. *Psychosomatic Medicine, 33.* 49-55.

Skinner, B. F. 1938. *The behavior of organisms.* New York: Appleton-Century-Crofts.

Wolpe, J., & Lazarus, A. A. 1966. *Behavior therapy techniques.* New York:
Pergamon.

Yates, A. J. 1970. *Behavior therapy.* New York: John Wiley and Sons.

9

The Tavistock Approach
to Groups

The Tavistock approach to training in group dynamics, like that of the T-group and Laboratory Method to be discussed in the next chapter, usually takes the form of an institute or conference in which several distinctive types of groups are organized. However, just as Chapter 10 will focus on the T-group as the core learning experience within the laboratory method, the present chapter will emphasize one particular kind of grouping—the "small study group"—as that which is most central to the overall Tavistock approach. The small study group is the group about which Tavistock trainees usually feel most intense and with which they feel most closely identified. It is the group that most dramatically manifests the latent forces that Bion believed to be characteristic of small groups, and it is the one that most frequently convenes over the course of a conference's life. Therefore when we mention the "Tavistock model," we are referring primarily to the small-study group, rather than to other group events occurring during the conference, like the application group or the intergroup event.

The Tavistock model bears important similarities to the three group-dynamic therapy models persented in Chapter 4. Like them, it reflects a unique blending of concepts derived from both psychoanalysis and Lewinian field-theory. However, unlike them it is not a psychotherapy model and is instead geared toward relatively healthy people wishing to learn more about group dynamics, especially as they involve problems of leadership within bureaucratic organizations.

From a conceptual point of view, credit for the development of the Tavistock group is to be given to Wilfred Bion, whose theory of small group processes provided the model's basic foundation and led to the development of the small study group. Later, A. K. Rice and Margaret Rioch were to become prominently involved in the design and administration of Tavistock conferences, which were constructed around the core experience of the small study group initially created by Bion. Bion's intensive work with groups had begun during World War II when, as a British army officer, he was given responsibility for selecting candidates for officer training and for heading a hospital unit of psychiatric patients. In connection with this latter function, he became heavily involved in group treatment and soon was impressed with its therapeutic potential. For him, its value lay not so much in its efficiency as in the way in which the group situation repeated in microcosmic form the patient's fundamental difficulty in becoming integrated into his larger society. In this sense, Bion's ideas are reminiscent of those of Foulkes (see Chapter 4), who similarly viewed the individual as a sociobiological unit whose psychopathology represented an inability to adapt to the interdependence necessary for effective role-functioning in the modern community. Just as the patient's difficulties developed within a sociocultural matrix, so he must then be treated and cured within such a matrix.

Bion's fascination lay with the ways in which groups continually form resistances to the reality-demands of the task-at-hand (Bion, 1959); these resistances take the form of "basic assumption" matrices wherein a group regressively looks for magical solutions to the hard work before it. While such resistances were observable in therapy groups, Bion's thinking was essentially that of a generalist who saw the specific phenomena before him as instances of considerably broader and more universal principles. Hence the ways in which the therapy group resisted its essential task (i.e., the resolution of its members' psychological difficulties) was but a concrete example of the general tendency for all groups to engage in similar avoidances. Not many more steps were needed before Bion was to arrive at the idea of the small study group, whose primary task was to study its own behavior. The role of the leader, or "consultant", would be to interpret at selected moments the latent meaning of the group's behavior, much as a psychoanalyst might do with an individual patient. The small-study group began as a means of training group therapists and other mental health professionals; several such groups were run by Bion at the Tavistock Clinic in London and were his first civilian training groups subsequent to the War. Because of the association of study groups with the Tavistock Clinic, and later with the Tavistock Institute of Human Relations, they became known as "Tavistock groups." Then, starting in 1948, there was a seven-year hiatus during which small study groups were discontinued at the Tavistock Clinic, which had begun instead to focus on group therapy and on other kinds of professional education.

A major revival of the small study group took place in 1957 at a conference organized under the joint auspices of the University of Leicester and the Tavistock Institute of Human Relations, and Tavistock conferences and

Tavistock groups have been occurring ever since that date. Between 1957 and 1965, seven additional such conferences were run under the same organizational collaboration, while others were sponsored by the Tavistock Institute in cooperation with other organizations, and still others by the Institute alone. Prominently involved in the organization and directorship of these conferences was A. K. Rice, an Englishman who had been associated with Bion's first civilian training group at Tavistock, and whose background included many years as a government administrator in both Africa and India. It was this latter work that had initially led to Rice's interest in organizational psychology and to his wish to learn more about the psychodynamics of leader-follower relationships.

Primary credit for the introduction of Tavistock thinking into America belongs to Margaret Rioch, a psychoanalyst on the faculty of the Washington School of Psychiatry. Rioch attended a Tavistock conference held at the University of Leicester in the early sixties, returned home, and stimulated enough interest in some of her colleagues for them to attend a subsequent Tavistock conference in Great Britain. The first such conference held in the United States occurred in 1965, on the campus of Mt. Holyoke College, and was sponsored by three organizations: the Washington School of Psychiatry, Yale University's Department of Psychiatry, and the Tavistock Institute. Such conferences have been held annually at Mt. Holyoke since 1965, and other national conferences based on the Tavistock model have taken place at Amherst College. Figuring importantly in the organization of these Group Relations conferences has been a semiautonomous institute within the Washington School of Psychiatry; this unit was formally dubbed the A. K. Rice Institute in 1970, one year subsequent to Rice's death.

In addition to sponsoring conferences, the Rice Institute offers management consultation to interested organizations. In 1971 a somewhat similar group was incorporated in New York City; calling itself the Institute for Applied Study of Social Systems and existing on a nonprofit basis, this institute provides consultation services and holds roughly four training conferences per year. Parallel organizations in England are the Grubb Institute and what is now known as the Tavistock Center for Applied Social Research. While businesses and schools have shown an interest in this model, psychiatric and psychoanalytic institutes have also been particularly receptive to its theory. For this reason, such groups as Mt. Zion Hospital (in San Francisco) and the Menninger Institute (in Topeka, Kansas), along with Yale's Psychiatry Department, have become informal centers for Tavistock learning.

Bion's unique contribution to the Tavistock conference was the original small study group. The gradual elaboration of other conference events around the basic unit of the small study group to a large extent represents the contribution of Rice (1965). We shall first describe the course of a typical Tavistock conference below, after which we shall present the key concepts involved in Bion's conceptual framework.

DESCRIPTION OF A TYPICAL CONFERENCE

The nature of Tavistock conferences is most succinctly and comprehensively described in Rice's *Learning for Leadership* (1965). In order to be able to give concrete examples of a specific conference, we shall sometimes refer to a weekend institute sponsored by the Institute for Applied Study of Social Systems in May, 1972, which constitutes the Tavistock conference with which we have had direct familiarity. This specific institute, while having a specific theme—the Exploration of Male-Female Work Relations in Group Settings—was clearly designed to be consistent with the Tavistock model.

The conference begins with a relatively brief Opening Plenary which is acknowledged to have some ritualistic aspects (Rice, 1965, p. 36). Yet it also serves to bring the entire membership together for the first of what may be several plenary review sessions. Moreover, in those conferences where members live in residence certain important "housekeeping" details—like meals—might be mentioned, and the conference's Administrative Secretary introduced. The conference's purpose is summarized in a brief statement that also appears in whatever written brochures or program-booklets participants are given. This statement serves to establish the set for all the group events that follow, and is very rarely repeated by the consultants: members are told that the main task of the institute is to explore covert group processes, particularly as these relate to issues of authority, and they are reminded that there is no specific prescription as to what anyone will learn; in other words, they are encouraged to assume active responsibility for what they get from the experience and to relinquish any expectations that their primary learning will occur via specific cognitive inputs—or "lessons"—from the staff.

The Small Study Group. The small study group ideally is composed of from eight to twelve people. The number should be small enough for every member to be able to feel some degree of personal relatedness to each of the other members, and large enough so that no one member need feel continually pressured to speak or to be "on stage." Conference planners attempt to maximize the heterogeneity of study group participants, so that the group life can start "from scratch," with a minimum of conventional customs carried over from members' prior associations with one another in either formal or informal settings.

The small study group almost always convenes shortly after the Opening Plenary. It is thought that it should constitute the first primary group event because (1) it is the most frequent and most intensive event of the conference (2) it is the event about which members usually have the most anxiety, and (3) as a face-to-face group it can offer the participant a primary group identification with which to approach subsequent conference events. The schedule is arranged so that the study group ends during a period that precedes the official conference ending; hence the study group, which will meet both regularly and often during the first three-quarters of the conference's life, might drop out altogether during its final quarter. It is believed that this procedure enables the participant to have an initial separation-termination experience that helps him to more realistically anticipate—and therefore better prepare for—the eventual conference ending; through this procedure he does not lose both his small study group, which gradually comes to be a strong source of support and belongingness, and the entire conference membership simultaneously. Furthermore, Rice and others think that ending the conference with group events that have a closer direct relationship to outside life—like the Application group and the Intergroup event (see below)—helps to furnish the participant a smoother, less abrupt transition as he moves from the relatively cloistered and intense conference experience to his "back-home" existence.

Typically the study group's leader-consultant is a member of the Conference staff. Usually he makes no formal introduction to the group, and simply waits for members to begin to speak and to interact. One reason for this silence is his wish to establish a culture within the group that is divorced from the more formal culture of most task groups, where the leader tends to take on a more authoritative role; another reason is the fact that the conference's primary objective—the study of covert processes—has already been outlined in the opening session and in the literature sent out before the conference.

As Rice defines it, the goal of the study group is to "provide an opportunity to learn about the interpersonal life of a group as it happens" (1965, p. 57); therefore its focus is on the here-and-now. Individual behavior is invariably seen as an expression of group forces; hence, all the consultant's interventions are directed toward what the group as a whole, rather than toward what a specific individual, is doing. Consequently, no attempt is made by this method to make a person more aware of how his functioning within the group renders him unique, or different from the other members.

The consultant's interventions are almost always referred to as "interpretations" in the Tavistock literature. However, this term is a broad one, and covers a variety of different kinds of statements. Although many of the consultant's interventions would seem to be interpretations in the more traditional sense of exploring what particular behaviors might mean, others are more behaviorally-oriented in that they point out overt aspects of the interaction without any speculation as to its covert meaning. For example, after about twenty minutes of random, seemingly innocuous discussion at a group's inception, the leader might point out that the topic of conversation has been entirely about outside affairs and that no one has said anything about the situation immediately confronting him. However, while the overt level of the leader's intervention refers to behavior that is evident to everyone, its covert effect is to sensitize the group to the possibility—and indeed probability—that these behaviors constitute avoidances that are attempts to defend against anxiety. Again, then, there is a fairly direct parallel to individual psychoanalysis, where the analyst's interpretations are geared toward pointing out the patient's resistances and avoidances, particularly during the early stages of treatment.

According to Tavistock theory, the primary experience against which most study-group resistances are directed is the participants' here-and-now awareness of their feelings and fantasies about the leader. Consequently, when a group led by Rice (1965, p. 59) began with the participants discussing a murder that had recently been featured in the press, he eventually broke in and stated that so far as the here-and-now was concerned, he was the murder victim, for the group was studiously ignoring both his presence and preventing him from helping it to more effectively pursue its task. And, in a later instance (p. 60), when a participant had slapped his hands on a table and loudly said: "Well, that's cleared the decks!" after a particularly desultory sequence in which members had continued to avoid looking into their feelings and instead struggled in vain for some kind of arbitrary activity with which to occupy themselves, Rice wondered if these decks were to be cleared for a fight that the group wished to have with him for having refused to give them the kind of leadership they had expected.

Much of the group's initial activity is directed toward trying to get the consultant to tell it what to do. He doesn't satisfy this demand, but instead indicates through his interpretations that this behavior constitutes a somewhat infantile attempt to avoid responsibility for working at its own task. Yet the leader, via his interpretations, implicitly demonstrates and encourages a particular kind of activity that is potentially available to everyone within the group—namely a concerted attempt to make rational sense of the raw data of its own behavior. The consultant is in effect saying: "I have no special magic to wield; what I do have is the power of observation and the ability to use it in an attempt to understand what's going on; I invite you to use your capacities for observation and for rational analysis in a similar way." In outside task groups there is a similar tendency to expect magic from the leader, to blame him for failure as a defense against feelings of helplessness, but also to see him as the source of all the good feelings that one experiences during the group. However, the authoritative and managerial role that the leader plays in most task groups, and the need to direct most of one's attention toward the "real" work to be done—e.g., the preparation of a program, a budget, a plan, etc.—mitigate against the likelihood of the group's becoming aware of these tendencies within itself. The small study group is unique; as in the psychoanalytic situation, the person's attention is turned away from outside stimuli and diversions and is instead turned toward examining the normally unexplored data of group life, particularly feelings. And the leader, by not fulfilling a participant's expectations, makes him more aware of the infantile fantasies that are often masked in ordinary groups.

Following an initial period of discouragement and confusion, members often take strength from the consultant's dispassionate, almost clinical attitude; there is no aspect of their collective mental life that cannot be explored—no fear or wish, however primitive, that in the cool light of day does not appear to be but another aspect of "the human condition." In addition, the fact that whatever participants reveal about themselves is interpreted as something that they all share in common as a group, rather than something that distinguishes each of them from one another, also helps to reduce their defensiveness. After a while members may begin to value the group for its candor and its permissiveness. Gradually there is an expression of very positive feelings toward the leader for having made these developments possible. Yet the leader is unequivocal in his pursuit of analytic understanding, for he interprets this need for self-evaluation and self-congratulation as a denial of the fact that theirs has been an essentially mixed experience, that all learning and progress is uncertain and incomplete, and that the members must soon prepare for the pain of the group's ending. In his refusal to collude with the group in its attempt to evaluate what it has learned (and, by implication, to "pat itself on the back"), the consultant is once again frustrating its expectations, since this kind of assessment often occurs in organizational meetings.

The theory of how learning takes place in the small study group receives an implicit, not explicit, statement in the Tavistock literature. Such learning seems to be conceived of along lines running closely parallel to the theory of change in psychoanalysis. A Tavistock assumption is that learning is maximized in an ascetic atmosphere in which needs for approval and for structure are denied, and in which powerful fantasies and affects are mobilized. Distortions are thrown into relief by the consultant's nonauthoritarian behavior, feelings become less fearsome as they are openly expressed and accepted, and members are presented a leadership model that shuns omnipotence in favor of a more limited, but nonetheless useful, ability to observe, to weigh possibilities, and to come to tentative conclusions.

The insights to be gained in the study group are often intuitive and personally felt, and therefore more unique to the situation immediately-at-hand than they are "scientific" and generalizable to a wide variety of situations. As we see it, the trainee is not so much learning universal laws of group behavior directly applicable to his back home work group as he is getting a feel for *some* of the enormously subtle and complex processes that *can* occur in groups. Each group has its own idiosyncratic problems, however, and once back within his organization he will have to be his own master and will have to decide for himself how best to account for whatever specific tensions seem to be interfering with maximal performance in his on-the-job groups.

Lectures. A Tavistock conference sometimes includes a series of lectures, perhaps one per day, in which an attempt is made to provide purely cognitive content. Often the series is divided into two parts, the first relating to theories of group behavior and the second to an application of these theories to actual work settings. Although the overt purpose of these presentations is didactic, the lectures, by bridging the gap between traditional approaches to education and the strongly nondirective and experiential approach employed by the conference itself, can help to render the conference atmosphere slightly less foreign and anxiety-producing for the membership.

American conferences, especially the briefer ones, tend to omit straight lecture presentations. This omission becomes feasible since participants have become increasingly sophisticated about the experiential approach inherent in the Tavistock orientation and therefore less likely to expect that they will be "taught" in a format even remotely akin to that of the academic classroom.

The Large Group Event. The Tavistock model, more than any other, has devoted systematic attention to the specific dynamics of large groups. The task of the large study group is very similar to that of the small study group, but now the group contains anywhere from twenty to fifty people, and this number often constitutes the entire conference membership. Because of its size, its dynamics are more complex than those of the small group, and it therefore has two consultants assigned to it.

Usually the small study groups have met a few times before the large group event is introduced, since a small group is more quickly conducive to a sense of identification than is a large one (Rice, 1965, pp. 33-34); such an identification should help to ease a participant's anxiety about the conference and to simultaneously illustrate for him one of the basic dynamisms of group life. The large group may convene several times during the conference; yet its ending precedes that of the small study group, so that the participant can use the more familiar and more congenial atmosphere of the small group to work through the tensions and the conflict in loyalties that tend to arise in the somewhat overwhelming large group.

The consultant's role in leading the large group in no way differs from that of leading the small group. He makes no formal introduction, since members have already been informed as to the group's purpose, and he waits for someone to start the discussion. As in the small group, his interventions mainly take the form of observations and interpretations. Therefore our discussion will concentrate on the ways in which the dynamics of the large study group tend to differ from those of its small group counterpart.

Rice (1965) offers a phenomenological analysis of how a participant's situation changes as he moves from the small study group to the large group event. Although the anticipation of exposing oneself to a group of any size doubtless involves some anxiety, the lesser intimacy of a large group might well intensify this feeling, at least for some. Furthermore, if a member should gather up the courage to speak, he might feel guiltier about taking up the time of a large group, because of the larger number of people competing "for the floor." However, just as the large group can be viewed as a source of increased tensions, it can also maximize the opportunity for defense, through anonymity and "hiding," for any participant's silence is less likely to be noticed or commented upon.

The fundamental problem confronting the large group is in some way to define itself and its essential boundaries, because the usual things that large groups normally share in common and that help to give them a sense of collective identity are not available to this particular large group—e.g., a well-defined task or purpose, a motto or flag, a parliament or governing counsel, a common heritage or enemy. Moreover, the one source of identification that is readily at hand for most participants—the small study group—is as much a source of fragmentation as it is of unification. Finally, the large group, simply by virtue of its greater size, is less likely than the small group to unite behind a coherent regressive-defensive strategy for resisting the group task. The paradoxical result of all these factors is that the large group is often forced to unite around the theme of the contending parties and fragmentations within it; as Bion points out, a cogent interpretation of this phenomenon on the part of the consultant might well be stated as follows: "It seems we can be united only if we are split; we can become one only if we are more than one" (1959, p. 80). Often this preoccupation is overtly acted on by some participants in the form of a suggestion that the group divide into two smaller groups, which might then prove more manageable. Usually a sub-group then arises that is opposed to this idea, with the result that without the groups having to split physically there is now an issue on the floor that unambiguously divides it.

As we have indicated above, the concern with the group's fragmentation partly reflects a reality of the group—namely that it lacks a clearcut inner coherence or structure. However, Rice points to a psychodynamic factor that also accounts for the emphasis on splits within the group, and this is the participants' fear of the large group as a potentially violent and destructive force; so long as the group is kept fractionated this danger is reduced. In accounting for this fear, Rice relies primarily on the mechanism of projection; in other words, because the large group is less definable and more diffuse than the small group, it offers a readier target for a member's projected and disowned impulses, particularly hostile ones. Yet it would also seem that the greater potential for a "mob psychology" in a large, unstructured group than in a small face-to-face one provides some realistic basis, however minimal, for this fear; the potential for primitiveness and anarchy in a mass of people is a phenomenon that was originally underscored by Freud in his attempt to create a psychology of groups (1922) and that has also received support in the social-psychological literature (Milgram and Toch, 1969).

The Intergroup Exercise. As we indicated above, the study group constitutes the first main event of a Tavistock conference, and the large group event the second. After the large group has met once or twice, the intergroup exercise begins. At this point a member has faced both his study group and a large-group situation in which all the study groups have been brought together. Now, with the intergroup exercise, he is thrown into an even more complex situation in which he must, as a member of a small face-to-face group which we shall call a "membership group" and which has a different composition from that of his small study group, begin some sort of formal negotiations with other, similar face-to-face "membership groups." The kinds of learning that are promoted in this event relate to the phenomena that occur when groups begin to negotiate with one another. For the first time in the conference, members are faced with a task that, albeit vague, goes beyond the study of group process per se; now they must try to communicate with other groups, and at this point the conference life begins to more closely resemble the problems of organization and of political power in the institutions with which most members are involved in their "back-home" situations.

In early Tavistock conferences, the study of intergroup relations had proceeded by assigning face-to-face groups the task of filling up some days of the conference schedule. Members were told to divide into groups in any way that they wanted and for the groups to in some way reach a consensus as to the content of four of the program's sessions. Hence the primary task would be the planning of these sessions, and members would, as a by-product of doing this task, learn something about what goes on among groups as they interact around a specific assignment. However, Rice and others decided that if the main purpose of this exercise was to learn about intergroup relations, this should become a primary, rather than secondary, focus. Therefore, the conference membership, after being given some general directions at the beginning of the exercise, are nowadays given a less explicit assignment. They are told that their primary task "will be to study the relations between the member and staff groups—in other words, the entire conference institution." Just what the face-to-face membership groups will do in order to fulfill this agenda, what messages they will send to other membership groups that are meeting simultaneously and facing the same dilemma, and how they will set up the political machinery for sending these communications and for making intergroup decisions, constitutes the rather formidable problem that the participants face.

In order to illustrate how this exercise is typically introduced, we will take as our example the three-day residential conference on male-female work relationships that we referred to earlier. For the initial, and rather brief, orientation to the intergroup event, men and women met separately. Members were told that directly after the orientation, staff-consultants would be available in specifically assigned rooms (a single consultant to each room) in order to aid members in their performance of the intergroup task. The task in this initial session was for the members "to form groups among themselves and to study the relations among these groups as they interact with each other" (The Institute for Applied Study of Social Systems, 1972). Hence participants were free to form face-to-face membership groups by going to a room in which there was a particular consultant or by forming face-to-face groups on some other basis without the presence of a consultant, the one limitation being that they meet in a room specifically set aside for this exercise. Starting with the second session and for the remainder of all subsequent intergroup events, the staff would constitute itself a separate membership group and meet in its own, specifically designated room. Staff members would be available as consultants to separate membership groups or to meetings between groups; in other words, unlike both the small and large study groups, where a consultant-leader is always present, the use of consultants is optional in the intergroup exercise and therefore at the discretion of the various membership groups and inter-groups.

The members were also informed that a membership group, if and when it prepared to send one of its members as an emissary or representative to another group, could give this person three different levels of representative-ness: (1) observer status; here the representative could try to observe and to gain information from other groups but was not empowered to articulate viewpoints or to act on behalf of his group; (2) delegate status; here the representative could deliver a message in the name of his group or state his group's opinion on a particular issue; however, he could not modify these messages, no matter what he learned once he left his group, nor could he take any further action without returning to his group for consultation, (3) plenipotentiary status; here the representative had flexible negotiating powers in that he was allowed to take action and to make decisions on behalf of his fellow group members without referring back to them for consent.

One can well imagine the kinds of basic political problems that member-ship groups face as they go about attempting to set up a structure for dealing with other groups. As soon as representatives from other groups begin to knock at a group's door (or, in Tavistock lingo, "to cross boundaries"), the group is forced to make a fundamental decision as to whether to receive such messages and whether to admit observers and possible new members to its meetings. It might decide to station a "gatekeeper" at the door and to leave these decisions to him, but even to do this the group must develop some basis for arriving at a consensus. Once a group has sent out a plenipotentiary it must come to terms with the amount of power it has given him; a Tavistock plenipotentiary has had the experience of returning to a group only to find that it had in his absence decided it no longer is to be bound by whatever commitments he may have made to other groups on its behalf. And a group, on the other hand, sometimes has learned that its delegate overstepped the bounds of his authority by firmly committing it to an intergroup decision without returning for consultation.

As groups go about constructing this elaborate machinery for negotiating with one another, they are still left with the basic question of how to fulfill the function of the exercise. Should they set before the conference a petition demanding that one of its female consultants have her status enhanced by being designated as a co-director of the conference? Should they form larger groups for the discussion of male-female relationships? Since the theme was men-women relations, our actual Tavistock conference considered both these possibilities. Despite their intellectual realization that they are free to adopt any agenda they wish and are responsible for their own learning, members tend to become convinced that the staff has some definite notion as to what will constitute successful task performance; once they are so convinced, some members will attempt to formulate a program that will "please" the staff whereas others will "rebel" against the exercise by evading its instructions altogether. Yet the membership, however struggling, uncertain, and awkward it may appear to be in its efforts to meet the task, *cannot but perform* it, for from the moment a group selects a representative from among its ranks it is beginning to engage in some form of intergroup relations. Whenever a member observes what is happening in a concerted attempt to draw conclusions from it, he is studying the intergroup process at the same time that he is engaged in it.

The membership is also free to utilize this exercise for learning about relationships between membership and management, since the latter, from the second session on, constitutes itself as a separate group. Staff is the one membership that meets throughout the intergroup event, whereas other members are free to "cut" the exercise altogether, to leave their groups, or to reorganize into new groups. Members are allowed to observe the staff meetings at any point. The staff can serve as a model in two distinct ways: (1) it will hopefully illustrate some adaptive ways of making decisions, of delegating authority, and of expressing feelings, and (2) it can, through its errors, its blind spots, its dissensions and disruptions, demonstrate that conference leaders, as they assume membership in their own group, are as vulnerable to the irrational forces of group process as are conference members.

As we indicated above, membership groups have the option of calling in a consultant at any point that they decide that his services might be useful. Consultants leave the staff meetings one-by-one during the intergroup exercise, usually in alphabetical order. They are committed to consulting with a particular group only insofar as they perceive the group as having a legitimate need for consultation. It is important to remember that the authority-membership mistrust is such that members may well have as their unconscious purpose in requesting consultation a wish to in some way weaken the staff and to "win over" the consultant to its cause. If paranoid enough, a group may begin to feel that the consultant, while seemingly interested in helping, is actually attempting to sabotage its attempt to fulfill the task. Furthermore, since the staff is prey to its own irrational hostilities and projections, these "paranoid" fears on the part of a group may occasionally be justified.

Increasing the tensions and confusions that already exist on the basis of task ambiguity, membership frustration, and staff-member hostilities, are severe time and space "boundaries" (see "Key Concepts" below). Staff is extremely punctual in beginning and ending the intergroup events, and some rooms are available only for *intergroup* meetings (as opposed to a meeting of a single membership group). In the Tavistock conference in which we participated, these tensions were heightened by the staff's further limiting space resources by suddenly removing a room from the list of available rooms. Membership anger eventually reached such proportions that one group acted out its defiance by "occupying" the staff's room during a coffee-break and refusing to yield it upon the staff's return. As Rice points out, the entire intergroup event is a kind of game or charade that is supposed to mirror its real-life organizational equivalent. Yet, as the just-cited behavior demonstrates, it is a game that mobilizes tremendous emotion and that most members play in deadly earnest.

The Plenary Reviews. The precise structure and content of plenary sessions have been surrounded by more uncertainty than any other single conference event. They typically occur at the end of a conference and have as their overt purpose a recapitulation of what members have experienced there. It is here that the entire membership will have an opportunity to explore collectively its brief history as a group, to review the meaning of its various crises, and to integrate some of these emotionally-charged events with conceptual material. Originally there had been a tendency for the staff to regard the plenary session as a study group and to interpret the members' behavior during this session in terms of its latent meaning. This problem was partly alleviated by the subsequent introduction of the large group event; since the purpose of the latter was to exclusively focus on understanding the covert processes involved in large-group interaction, the plenary reviews could now, at least in theory, concentrate more directly on their summing-up and integrative function.

However, it is our impression that ambivalence remains and that plenary sessions are viewed in a somewhat perfunctory and ritualized way. This ambivalence is hardly surprising when one remembers that Tavistock theory views learning in a way that fundamentally challenges all traditional modes of teacher-student discourse. Therefore it seems difficult for the Tavistock staff to comfortably and directly satisfy the kind of learning needs that tend to be expressed by the membership at such a session (the one exception to this is the final Application Group, which is discussed immediately below). For example, at the conference on men-women work relations, staff consultants were reluctant to share their interpretation of other conference events and instead primarily confined themselves to interpreting the here-and-now events of the plenary session, particularly the membership's need to know how the staff had conceptualized earlier conflicts and crises. This focusing on latent meanings on the part of the staff was probably exacerbated by the fact that this particular conference, because it had omitted large group events, had not provided any other vehicle for the processing of large-group behavior.

The Application Group. If not actually the final conference event, application groups come very close to the end of a conference. They have as their explicit focus an exploration of what has been learned and the application of this learning to a member's vocational setting. For this reason, an attempt is made to keep the group homogeneous, i.e., to assign to it people from similar occupations. The placement of this event at the conference's conclusion is designed to help ease the member's emotional transition to his outside life.

Because the consultant makes a concerted attempt to be more cognitive and didactic than in other conference events, this group often is experienced by members—even by those who welcome it—as "flatter" than the other groups (Rice, 1965, p. 117). Members are encouraged to remember back to their signficant learning experiences and to relate them to analogous events and situations in their work environments. Rice believes that the group leader need not be exceptionally familiar with the members' employment specializations; what is important is that he be able to grasp some sense of a member's unique organizational situation from the latter's description, and that he then be able to help him relate the insights he has developed during the conference to that situation.

The three-day conference on male-female work relations had a single application session as its very final event. While members did not concentrate on the relevance of the conference learning to their jobs, they did bring up conference incidents that had meaning for them in a highly informal and relaxed way. The consultant was unusually direct in discussing his own feelings, in introducing theoretical concepts, and in discussing some of the general application possibilities of conference events—especially the intergroup exercise—to larger organizations. Hence the group's atmosphere was considerably less charged than is typical in a study-group, and began to resemble that of a rather comfortable academic seminar.

KEY CONCEPTS

Bion's theory of group behavior has been mainly set forth in a collection of his papers called *Experiences in Groups* (1959). Rioch has conceded that his writing tends to be obscure, and it was in an effort to clarify some of his concepts that she wrote her paper *The Work of Wilfred Bion on Groups* (1970). Despite the clarity of Rioch's writing, it seems to us that it is still sometimes difficult to understand these concepts very precisely, partly because Bion's highly abstract and conceptual theory is always several steps removed from the concrete data of everyday group life.

The Work Group. Bion thought of any group as simultaneously consisting of two groups, or as having two coexisting aspects: a work group, and a basic assumptions group. At any point in time a group's behavior is expressing some sort of balance between the two kinds of groups; neither one is ever operating in a pure culture. The more a group is functioning toward the work-group end of this polarity, the more it is rationally and maturely focusing on the performance of its overt task in as efficient a manner as possible; the more it is functioning toward the basic-assumptions end of the polarity, the more it is behaving in a regressive manner wherein the group takes on primitive, familial connotations for its members and begins to be used for emotional gratification and tension release. Hence, like Freud's concepts of the ego and the id, and of the reality principle and the pleasure principle (to which they bear an obvious correspondence), the work-group and the basic-assumptions group are metaphors—or, more technically, "theoretical constructs."

If a task-group were to function solely as a work group the number and content of its meetings would be determined solely by the nature of its task; its leader would be determined not by virtue of charisma but only in terms of his ability to do the job and his leadership would last only so long as that job remained to be completed. Members would have a strong enough sense of personal autonomy and individuation to cooperate without fear of loss of self and without undue competitive feelings. And because their interest in, and identification with, the task would outweigh their libidinal investment in either the leader or one another, they would not permit either emotional gratification or emotional deprivation to interfere with effective task performance.

If the Tavistock small study group were to perform within a pure work-group culture (and this state of affairs can only exist in theory), its consultant would not need to intervene, since the group would immediately begin to process its own data without any avoidances and regressions. For example, he would not have to wonder why the group so studiously ignores him, since the group would either not be ignoring him or, if it were, would comment on this behavior of itself and by so commenting would already begin the process of paying attention to him.

Basic Assumption Groups. When a group is in a state of emotional regression (and it always is in such a state to a greater or lesser degree) it acts *as if* it believed certain things to be true that really are not true. For example, if the group is behaving in accordance with the basic assumption dependency, it seems to assume that the leader is omniscient. Basic assumptions are oriented more toward the way we would like reality to be than toward the way it actually is; therefore they constitute resistances to the rational task of the work group.

In the typical task-group situations of everyday life, several factors tend to obscure these basic assumptions to a point where they function in an implicit and partially disguised fashion. These factors are: (1) as Freud discovered many years before the emergence of the Tavistock model, most people tend to be unaware of the more infantile aspects of their emotional life, (2) since basic assumptions are essentially *shared* fantasies, they belong more to a group's unconscious than to any single individual's unconscious; as such they constitute a kind of "collective unconscious" (Jung, 1917) and therefore are *even more easily* denied by an individual than are his more personalized and idiosyncratic unconscious fantasies, (3) task group leaders do not as a rule encourage their groups to pay attention to the more subtle aspects of their fantasy life, and instead direct their attention outward onto concrete projects that focus the members' attention outward rather than inward, and (4) the fantasy needs of the typical task-group leader have enough in common with the fantasies of his followers for him to collude with the group's fantastic expectations of him; since he tends to go along with these expectations, the discrepancy between fantasy and reality is less marked and the group-member consequently has less chance to gain insight into the infantile nature of his attitude toward authority.

The small study group is a special kind of task group, however. Although the study group's consultant can do little in the way of a direct modification of the first and second factors listed above, he attempts to directly offset the third and fourth factors. He gives the group no task other than the understanding of its own emotional processes (factor number three), and by flatly refusing to meet the group's emotional needs, he directly attempts to foil—and thereby highlight more dramatically—their fantasies (factor number four). For example, while the fantasy lying at the heart of basic assumption fight-flight (see below) is that the leader will rally the group against a common enemy, the consultant refuses to do this. Hence it would seem that the role of basic assumptions in the small study group is almost the precise theoretical counterpart of the role played by transference resistance in psychoanalysis, both individual and group. However, a basic assumption is characteristic of a group as a whole, while a transference resistance is from a conceptual point of view the property of an individual.

Bion distinguished three main kinds of basic assumption groups. Like the more general concepts of the work group and the basic assumptions group, these specific basic assumption states do not emerge in an absolutely total way. At any particular point in the group interaction, some members may be operating more in accordance with one kind of basic assumption, and other members, with another. However, careful attention to the group process will usually reveal one of the three basic assumptions to be predominant.

A. The Basic Assumption Dependency Group. To the extent to which a basic assumption of dependency prevails, a group lives for and through its leader. He and his infallibility are the source of all wisdom, comfort, and security; neither one's own resources nor those of one's peers count for very much. The leader's observations are regarded more in religious terms involving unswerving faith than in scientific terms involving balanced and empirically-oriented judgments. The primary axis of relatedness for each member is between himself and the leader, and it is only in this context that other members have significance for him. Hence the person who presents himself to the group as weak or sick may be eagerly confirmed in this position by his peers, who vicariously use him to force some display of nurturance from the leader. Since members relate in a greedy and demanding manner and since their infantile expectations cannot be completely met, considerable jealousy, disappointment, and resentment are activated, however much suppressed.

B. The Basic Assumption Fight-Flight Group. While the main focus in basic assumption dependency is a fantasy relationship with the leader, the primary focus in the present basic-assumption is the preservation of the group through some kind of action, either fight or flight. Both fight and flight stem from the same motivational dynamic—i.e., a defensive escape into activity for its own sake. Bion implies that whichever of the two is chosen in any particular instance may relate more to incidental factors than to the basic dynamics of the group; it is as if the group is ready for some kind of action and will seize on whatever comes its way. Therefore if a member who has been absent from the group returns, he may be attacked (fight), whereas if a particularly charismatic member begins to talk about a well-publicized event outside the group at a time when it is ready for such a diversion, it will most likely mobilize around and pursue this digression (flight).

Bion does not make clear what events or stages are needed to prepare for the emergence of the fight-flight culture. One senses that it requires some degree of group identity and cohesiveness. Once aroused, this group spirit acts as a strong force, with the result that members struggle to preserve the group at all costs. Since a group is more than the sum of its parts, each member is able to imagine its surviving intact despite the fact that some of its other members have been hurt or destroyed in the process. Unlike the dependency culture, then, which treats the ailing individual with compassion in the hope that he will arouse the leader's sympathy, the fight-flight group can be ruthless in its disregard for his welfare, much as a retreating army may leave its wounded behind to die. Indeed, there may be times when the group's "fight" is directed toward one of its own, now scapegoated, members. Since this group culture is oriented toward action, it is responsive to the kind of leader who rallies it against a common enemy (e.g., a team-captain, an Army sergeant, etc.), but unresponsive to a leader who embodies the values of intellectuality, introspection, and understanding (e.g., the study group consultant).

How realistic is the group's concern with its own survival? To qualify as a basic assumption it must be primarily irrational. If this need to preserve itself physically were actually the main basis of the group's existence together, as in the case of an army platoon under attack, the fight-flight orientation would begin to constitute a more appropriate basis for a work-group culture and in this sense would no longer offer a pure example of a basic assumptions culture. Indeed, in situations where a group is under physical attack, the basic assumptions group and the work group tend to converge, and the basic assumption of fight-flight can—in the hands of an effective leader who knows how to harness and exploit it—prove quite supportive of the group's real task.

However, most groups need not survive beyond the rather limited purpose that called them together—e.g., the development of a marketing plan, the writing of some legislation, etc.—and should they find they are not "making a go" of that which has united them, their most adaptive response would be to disband. Yet the fantasy element in any fight-flight group culture, whatever the group's real purpose and situation may be, is the individual's assumption that his survival and that of the group are completely synonomous and codetermined, that he will die if the group should die. It is probably when we are very young that we most consistently and most consciously perceive our survival as inextricably linked to the survival of our "small group"—i.e., our family—and in this parallel we see the strongly archaic pull of the fight-flight culture.

C. *The Basic Assumption Pairing Group.* Here the individual member-to-individual member axis becomes paramount. One possible indication that a pairing culture is in the making is the group's gradual focusing on a colloquy between two particular people; in the group's unconscious mental life there begins to arise the hope that this "pairing" will in some way affect the life of the group for the better. Pairing is more obvious if the dyad consists of people of the opposite sex, and if their conversation is relatively personal and intimate. Yet the pairing basic assumption may exist when the two people are of the same sex and seem to be focusing on something relatively innocuous— e.g., what the group should discuss at that particular moment. The basic assumption then, is that "there could be no possible reason for two people's coming together except sex" (Bion, 1959, p.62). The second basic assumption is that out of this sexual relationship something or someone is to be born— perhaps a new idea, or a new leader—that will "save" the group. An atmosphere of attentiveness and optimism gradually permeates the group—the sense of a Utopia-about-to-be-born that will extricate it from its present frustration, irritation, and uncertainty. Even without direct evidence of a distinct member-to-member pairing, feelings of hopefulness are almost always a clue as to either the existence of a basic assumptions pairing group or its imminent emergence. A second, slightly less reliable sign is the way in which the group allows one particular dyad to become prominent; it would seem that somewhere in the group's attentiveness there is some expectation, however submerged, that this interaction will bring something different, and hopefully something better, to all. This is why the group nurtures the dyadic focus—i.e., it promises something for everyone.

In order for the pairing culture to persist, it is essential that the *promise* (and not the actuality) of a new idea or a new leader be present; should such a Messiah or idea emerge he or it will inevitably be rejected and hope be killed, for the "complete solution" that the group longs for exists only in fantasy. Real "solutions" are all too temporary and incomplete; whatever understanding that could be reached would gradually be replaced by confusion as the group began to focus its attention on new tensions and new problems; whatever good feelings come into the group would gradually dissipate. Such is the life of groups on earth; what the pairing culture strives for is group-life as it is commonly imagined to exist in Heaven.

As we have described the three basic assumption groups, we have moved from themes of being nurtured and supported (dependency), to mobilization and aggression (fight-flight), to reproduction (pairing). Hence, while the Tavistock literature does not contain a reference that directly links the three basic assumption cultures to Freud's three psychosexual stages of oral, anal, and phallic, this correspondence seems to us to be fairly clear. Moreover, the three basic assumptions are almost always described in the order in which we listed them, even though Bion does not imply that in any given group they will necessarily emerge in this order, or that one kind of basic assumption is more mature than any other. We mention the parallel in order to indicate the extent to which fundamentally psychoanalytic notions prevail within this model and also to show how the laws of group behavior are considered to directly embody and continue, albeit at another level, the same archaically-determined dynamisms that account for the laws of individual behavior.

"Sophistication." Thus far we have primarily viewed basic assumption groups as having negative effects in that they interfere with the goal of the work group. However, some basic assumptions, if put to a "sophisticated" use, can be supportive of the work-group. For example, as we indicated above, the army batallion's assumption that it must fight to the death to preserve itself might well make it more effective in combat, just as the parishioner's dependency on his pastor might help to strengthen the effectiveness of their church. And the one group in social life that ideally has pairing, reproduction, and the maintenance of hope as its essential functions is the family. In these situations, where the goal of the work-group requires some of the primitive affect released by the basic assumptions groups, it is the leader's skill in mobilizing and channeling these emotional forces that most often makes the difference between success and failure in the task. To be effective, he must actually embody some of the qualities that the basic assumption culture wants in its leader, though he can never possess them to the degree that the archaic mentality underlying basic assumptions demands (Rice, 1965, p. 72). In other words, the basic assumption dependency group yearning for an infallible leader might settle instead for one who is nurturant; the fight-flight culture longing for an unconquerable leader might accept one who is merely courageous, and the pairing culture, wishing for a leader who is "marvelous but still unborn," might manage to live in reality with one who is only "creative" (Rioch, 1970, pp. 64-65). Since the work-group aspect of any task group is always in force to some degree, along with whatever basic assumptions groups exist, these sophistications and compromises are often possible.

What is the role of the basic assumption cultures in the study group, and can they too be exploited in a sophisticated way? On the surface they would seem entirely unadaptive and unsophisticated. Surely they are treated as such by the consultant. According to him, the group's inappropriate expectation that he will save it from its confusion only postpones the point at which it might begin to take responsibility for itself and make some sense of what is occurring. He is equally quick in challenging the group's magical conviction that fighting, or pairing, or escaping into trivia will somehow extricate it from the morass of frustration and despair into which it is sinking. Hence it would seem that the leader, rather than harnessing these basic assumptions, is instead exposing them as infantile attempts at delay and avoidance.

Yet there is a paradox here, for if no basic assumptions existed within the study group there would be no reason for the group's existence. The study group convenes in order to better understand the irrational forces of group life and the way in which it can most effectively do this is to observe these forces as they emerge within the life of its own here-and-now group. If the emergence of basic assumptions did not threaten the life of work-groups, task groups in business and government would go about their projects with maximum efficiency, group-dynamics would not be particularly complex, and there would be no need for the Tavistock model. In essence, then, the work group that the consultant repeatedly tries to summon into existence is an inherently unrealizable ideal; if it were ever to actually exist in a prolonged and stable form the study group would no longer have meaningful data to process. In this respect the basic assumption concept again parallels the concept of resistance in psychoanalysis, for resistance is claimed to "impede" the work of free association, just as the study group's basic assumptions are said to interfere with the work-group's task. Yet both methods exploit and indeed depend on these "impediments," for at the point where the patient can free-associate with complete success (again an unrealizable ideal) he has adequate access to his unconscious and is therefore "cured." Similarly, once the study group is able to do what the consultant asks it to do from the outset—to effectively work at the task of understanding its own data—it is at the end of the process rather than at its beginning. Thus it turns out that the study group, like the family, the Army, and the Church, is quite adept at making a sophisticated use of basic assumptions, albeit in a paradoxical and surprising fashion. Indeed, we would argue that it makes an unusually sophisticated use of the sophistication principle in that it not only manages to make constructive use of *all three* basic assumptions, but also denounces them at the same time that it exploits them.

Valency. Individuals differ in their propensity for subscribing to any one of the three basic assumptions: dependent people will be more responsive to a dependency culture, antagonistic ones to a fight-flight culture, and sexual ones to a pairing culture. Bion (1959) used the term "valency" to refer to a person's predisposition to respond in terms of a particular basic assumption. Knowledge of a person's valency can be useful in deciding which groups he should join as a member. Leaders would probably have reciprocal valencies in the sense that some are readier to respond to certain basic assumptions than they are to others. This returns us to our earlier discussion of a leader's "sophisticated" possession of qualities looked for by a particular basic assumption culture. For example, a leader with a high valency-nurturance would best be placed with a group whose individual members tend to have a high-valency succorance or dependence.

Boundaries. According to Bion and to the Tavistock leaders who subsequently implemented his model, effective functioning of the work-group depends on a clearcut appreciation of boundaries and limits. For example, a work-group is most likely to be actualized if its task is clearly delimited and if each member has a well-defined role to perform; members will then resist activities that are not required for efficient task-performance. Again Bion's constructs for group life are analogous to similar constructs designed by Freud to account for an individual's psychological functioning: the work-group parallels Freud's "secondary processes" (Munroe, 1955, p. 35) which, in their acknowledgement of fixed categories of time and space and in their ability to differentiate fantasy and reality, enabled the person to survive. Basic assumption groups, on the other hand, resemble "primary processes"; in their search for effortless fluidity they tend to deny the distinction between task-performance and emotional gratification, and between the individual and the group.

In addition to boundaries involving task and roles, other boundaries are important to the work-group, including those between one task group and another, and those involving time and space. The press of basic assumptions is such that the work-group may all too quickly: (1) lose sight of why the group is convening in the first place (task boundaries), (2) forget that it has at its disposal only a finite amount of time and space resources (time and space boundaries), (3) want the leader to step "out of role" to a point where he gives emotional nurturance (role boundaries), (4) attempt to deny its members' individual identities through a cozy, warm, oceanic coming together wherein each becomes the group and the group becomes one (personal boundaries), and (5) cast aside the selectivity required to determine how other groups can best be used and communicated with in pursuit of the work-task (group boundaries).

ROLE OF THE LEADER

Because the function of a consultant to a study group is different from that of a consultant to a task group (such as the groups forming the intergroup event), we will consider these two roles separately.

1. The Study Group Consultant. The role of the study group consultant is best understood in the context of a few theoretical assumptions or premises that are basic to the Tavistock model: (1) any comments made by an individual reflect concerns that are shared by almost all other members to some degree, (2) the single most difficult and emotionally charged issue facing any group involves coming to terms with its leader and the authority that he symbolizes, and with the discrepancy between its fantasies about authority and the reality of authority, and (3) transference feelings and needs expressed in the group should be interpreted rather than gratified. Based on a Freudian model that views peer and sibling relationships as a reaction to, and a way of handling, a far more powerful and emotionally crucial parent-child axis, the Tavistock orientation views the leader as a recipient of extremely ambivalent and primitive feelings; he is alternately loved as wise and grand, feared as powerful and potentially destructive, competed with as a rival, and hated as the source of all the bad feelings in the group. Member-to-member issues primarily reflect the vicissitudes of the member-leader relationship, and the group interaction is conceptualized as a dynamic oscillation between an expression of feelings about authority and a concomitant attempt to defend against them. The members' irrational fantasies about authority emerge as especially inappropriate and paradoxical in view of the fact that the consultant has been voluntarily hired by the group, his degree of power over group-members is minimal since they are relatively free to do as they like within the group (including leaving it), and he gives no direction as to what should be talked about. Instead, his rather limited authority is based on his expertise in understanding group dynamics.

Although the consultant is in a formal sense a member of the group, he holds himself separate from and outside of the group. For example, he rarely expresses his feelings directly, especially as they involve particular individuals. However, he tries hard to be silently aware of these feelings so that he may use them to infer what the group is unconsciously experiencing at any particular moment. He restricts his interventions to interpretations and these are invariably pitched to the group level, e.g., "It is as though the group is saying . . . ," "Is it possible that what the group most fears . . . ?", etc. These interpretations are frequently couched in highly metaphorical and symbolic terms (e.g., the group might be likened to an animal wallowing in its own excrement), with the result that they are often, at least initially, experienced by participants as cryptic and deliberately obscure.

The leader is relatively formal in manner, careful not to step "out of role," and scrupulous in his attention to time boundaries. It is clearly not in role for him to reinforce particular behaviors, either through praise or overt disapproval. As Rice puts it, "learning is its own reward; lack of learning its own punishment" (1965, p. 67). His only function is to interpret; how the group chooses to use these interpretations is its own decision. This is by design a somewhat aloof role and Tavistock consultants, even outside the confines of the study-group setting, are usually careful to limit their overt fraternization with members, at least until close to the conference ending. Essentially the leader is a firm and remote figure; he respects the autonomy of each member to the extent that he frequently reminds the membership that it bears the major responsibility for what it does and doesn't learn, he refuses to evaluate the amount of learning that has occurred, and he embodies as his primary value an interest in understanding the "truth" of the group's unconscious, however unflattering this truth may be.

2. The Task Group Consultant. Study groups have as their sole function the understanding of their own internal processes. On the other hand, the groups involved in the intergroup event resemble task groups in that they have a somewhat more tangible agenda that directs their attention outward toward other groups in an effort to coordinate some sort of specific program or project. If they are to even attempt to accomplish this goal, they must make some concrete decisions. For example, plenipotentiaries may assemble in an effort to design a large-group session that will bring together in a dynamic way, and with a meaningful agenda, all the face-to-face groups involved in the intergroup excercise. However, they may find themselves hopelessly bogged down with the question of how the diverse ideas of the plenipotentiaries are to be resolved into a coherent consensus. Now that it is no longer so necessary for the consultant to sharpen and foil the group's basic assumptions via a strictly nonauthoritative stance, he is more willing to directly share his knowledge about organizational life and organizational procedures. If he notices that a group has difficulty in maintaining its group boundary—e.g., in laissez-faire fashion it is allowing members to walk out and visitors to walk in—he might state this observation. Other things that he might note and share with a group can include any of the following: the group's failure to provide maximum role differentiation of its members, with the result that there is no formal designation of a leader; its ambivalence about delegating authority, with the result that plenipotentiary powers are granted but subsequently revoked; the lack of preciseness with which it defines the mandates and responsibilities granted to its representatives; its inefficient use of time and space resources; the absence of any unanimity as to the definition of the task facing it; etc.

One point that the consultant to a Tavistock task group consistently emphasizes is that the group's task is no longer that of studying its own internal processes. The resistance of the group to its new task and its eagerness to remain with the old one of group-processing stems from two factors, one cognitive, the other emotional. On the cognitive side there is the fact that all trainees up until that point have been involved in study groups, either large or small, and self-processing has therefore become the activity with which they are most familiar; furthermore, the task of the intergroup event tends to be rather ambiguous. On the emotional side, the intimacy and the opportunity for self-revelation inherent in the study group exerts a strong pull on the membership. While perhaps initially resistant to this focus, participants might now be starting to experience some of the emotional pay-offs that can come from the lowering of defenses and the sharing of feelings.

A concrete example of this kind of resistance occurred in the conference on male-female relations mentioned above. The small study groups in this conference had segregated men and women. Now that a face-to-face group composed of both sexes had formed for this first time—in response to the intergroup task (which had asked participants to spontaneously form small membership groups of their own choosing)—these groups wanted to "process" what felt different, and what happened that was different, when both males and females were in the group. However, leaders who were requested to consult at these meetings consistently refused to do so, claiming that the group was not dealing with the intergroup task, which required the "to study the relations between member and staff groups" (and not to focus on their own dynamics, despite the fact that a new dimension had been added to these dynamics).

A leader also declines to consult with a task-group when he suspects that the group might be more interested in using him in the service of basic assumptions than of legitimate work needs. Such a possibility is rather likely in the intergroup event, where angry feelings toward the staff, and the opportunity for acting them out, are maximized. For example, it is conceivable that a membership group that has become thoroughly enmeshed in a fight-flight culture has defined the staff as its common enemy; they think that by asking for a consultant and removing him from its ranks the staff will thereby be weakened. Once a consultant determines that a task group is genuinely trying to cope, however inadequately, with a legitimate task he remains with it until he reaches a point where he has given it all the rational help he can.

Complicated emotional dynamics and basic assumption cultures will of course continue to arise in task groups, as in study groups, and the perceptive consultant is aware of them. However, he takes pains to remember that an awareness of these dynamics is no longer the primary task of the group, and he discourages it from examining them for their own sake. As a result, he might highlight latent processes only when they have begun to become serious impediments to the task group's effective pursuit of its goal and have not yet been commented upon or tackled by any of its members.

Whether functioning as a consultant to either the small study group or to the task group, the Tavistock consultant is, as we have seen, somewhat aloof; the great majority of his remarks are addressed to the group-at-large, and often take the form of an interpretation. Rarely is the consultant's participation very extensive. In the next chapter we explore an alternate approach to group-dynamics training, the T-group, where the influence of orthodox psychoanalysis has been considerably less and where the leader's style of relating has consequently become more personalized, more emotional, and more informal.

References

Bion, W. R. 1959. *Experiences in groups.* New York: Basic Books.

Freud, S. 1922. *Group psychology and the analysis of the ego.* London: Hogarth Press.

The Institute for Applied Study of Social Systems. *Bulletin:* for a Three-day Residential Conference to Explore Male-female Relations in Group Settings, May 1972.

Jung, C. 1917. *Collected papers on analytical psychology.* New York: Moffat, Yard, and Company.

Milgram S. and Toch, H. 1969. Collective behavior: crowds and social movements. In G. Lindzey and E. Aronson, eds. *The handbook of social psychology, Vol. IV.* 2nd ed. Reading, Mass: Addison-Wesley.

Munroe, R. L. 1955. *Schools of psychoanalytic thought.* New York: Dryden Press.

Rice, A. K. 1965. *Learning for leadership.* London: Tavistock Publications.

Rioch, M. J. 1970. The work of Wilfred Bion on groups. *Psychiatry, 33.* 56-66.

10

T-Groups and
the Laboratory Method

T-groups (T standing for "training")—or as they have been alternately called, Sensitivity Training groups and Human Relations Laboratories—have, since their inception in 1946, been among the most widely attended "educationally focused" group experiences. A T-group may be briefly defined as an intensive effort at interpersonal self-study, and an attempt to learn from the raw experience of member participation in a group how to improve interpersonal skills and to understand the phenomena of group dynamics.

HISTORICAL BACKGROUND

In a very real way Kurt Lewin may be thought of as the spiritual father of the method. He created the field of group dynamics, and of action research, which emphasized basing decisions on information from relevant and well analyzed data. He continually stressed both the use of valid data as the basis for action and the study of impact of that action, thereby generating more useful data for future decisions. All of these conceptual developments provide the background and undergirding of T-group theory.

The idea of the T-group came into existence almost by accident, during a workshop that focused on helping community leaders to implement the Fair Employment Practices Act. The workshop, held in Connecticut in 1946, was under the direction of the Research Center for Group Dynamics at MIT. Kenneth D. Benne, Leland P. Bradford, whose backgrounds were in adult education, and Ronald Lippitt, a social psychologist, were in charge of the training. At the same time, research on the conference experience was being directed by Lewin and Lippitt. The format of the conference was quite different from what subsequently emerged as T-group training. It began with a

series of discussions about how to comply with the Act, and various participants brought in experiences that had caused them problems in dealing with
its provisions. The task of the other group members was to try to develop
solutions to these problems.

Interestingly enough the concept of the T-group developed not in the
context of the conference but rather grew out of evening meetings that were
originally planned for staff members to discuss the observations that the
researchers had made during the course of the conference. Several participants
who had free time in the evenings asked if they might attend and were
permitted to do so. It was an unusual circumstance for the Group Dynamics
staff to discuss observations of conference members in their presence. As
might now be obvious but then came as a surprise, a number of arguments
developed among group members and staff about the accuracy of the research
staff's observations. While these discussions became quite heated, they were
also extremely fascinating to both staff and participants; before long all of the
participants began attending the evening meetings, some of which lasted for
several hours. Thus, in an unexpected way the training staff of the Research
Center for Group Dynamics hit upon the idea for an extremely powerful
educative tool, the now widely known method of learning about group-process
and one's impact on others through observing one's own behavior in a group
session and receiving feedback about that behavior from other group members.
That is to say that until this time, Lewin's research on group process had not
directly involved group participants in examining the data of their own
experience. Previously these two processes had been kept separate; the group
members had engaged in their group task activities, and the researchers had
gathered data on how group process variables affected the work of the group.
The T-group brought these activities together in a strikingly unique way; the
very same participants produced data and then processed and examined those
data in an effort to learn about group dynamics from their own experience.
An entirely new way of studying group dynamics had been discovered.

Although much of the impetus for the development of T-groups came
from the work of Kurt Lewin, and although he was present when the method
was conceived, he died in early 1947 before the T-group format was fully
developed. As a follow-up effort to the initial experience, the participants of
the conference met in 1947 at Bethel, Maine, a town whose name subsequently became almost synonymous with laboratory training. Here the idea of the
"basic skills training group" (a forerunner of the T-group) was developed, a
group which had two broad purposes: (1) it served as a medium for learning
how to encourage planned change in social systems and (2) it provided an
opportunity to understand and to facilitate individual and group growth and
development.

As the laboratory method evolved, a division of the functions of the
basic skills training group was made; its purposes were subdivided and assigned

to two separate groups: T-groups, which focused on learning about small group dynamics and interpersonal styles through studying the group's own behavior, and A-groups (or action groups), which had more of a sociological orientation and focused on strategies of social action and social change in large social systems, and which employed a more traditional teaching method of didactic presentations and group discussion of reading and lecture material. The attention to interpersonal dynamics that had become characteristic of T-groups seemed to have such a powerful lure for most participants that this style of analysis tended to spill over into the A-groups, with the result that the two frequently became very similar in format. A variety of efforts to resolve problems around the different aspects of learning in the laboratory method characterized the course of the experience over a period of years. Eventually the A-group was abandoned, and a laboratory format that combined T-groups and other didactic experiences evolved.

The backgrounds of the participants played an important role in the developments that took place at Bethel. The original group that developed the laboratory method was comprised almost entirely of social psychologists, who, following Lewin's action research model, were basically concerned with the use of group dynamics to influence the process of social change, and with discovering more effective ways to function as agents of social change. Later on, when a number of new staff members from clinical psychology and psychiatry were invited to participate, the T-groups began to focus on processes of individual behavioral change in addition to the original orientation around group dynamics, group development, and decision-making processes. When the more clinically oriented participants gained a major voice in the development of T-groups, learning about oneself, that is, learning how one behaves in groups and the kind of impact one's behavior has on others became the major group purpose.

The interpersonal learning emphasis in T-groups grew out of the desire to make large-scale bureaucratic organizations more human and thereby more productive. While it is true that over a period of time many T-groups continued to focus on effective and creative functioning within large-scale organizations, they tended more and more to emphasize interpersonal interaction in its own right, divorced from its role in the improvement of organizational functioning. This, of course, was a major departure from the original action research and social change orientation of Lewin and his group. Perhaps it was not only the influence of the clinicians who entered the movement but rather also a characteristic of the time in which T-groups were developing—the later 1940s and 1950s—a time in which psychoanalysis and other dynamic theories of personality were having a major influence on developments within academic psychology as well as having a tremendous impact on the public at large. These factors may have contributed importantly to the manner in which T-group styles evolved.

It is also interesting and perhaps ironic that when in the mid-1960s a great emphasis on changing large-scale institutions again came to the fore, the methods and purposes of T-groups were not in the main refocused on learning about influencing social change, which had represented an important thrust in the T-group's origination. The tremendous complexities involved in large-scale societal change, coupled with a T-group style that was increasingly emphasizing smaller-scale interpersonal dynamics, undoubtedly made a shift in emphasis unlikely to occur. However, one outgrowth of the model that moved in the direction of planned organizational change has come to be called Organization Development or OD. Organization Development is seen as a group of intervention strategies used to help organizations function more effectively, and is differentiated from the T-group, whose focus is on individuals becoming more effective organization members. Although OD practitioners emphasize its supraindividual focus, Bennis (1969) points out that the T-group is the most frequently employed focal activity of OD interventions. Furthermore OD has not been directed toward attempts at major social change nor been much used as a strategy to mediate between opposing community factions. Bennis expresses concern that OD has failed to create techniques to deal effectively with confrontative situations, as well as at the fact that its main successes have been in working with affluent business institutions, rather than with disadvantaged groups.

The establishment of the National Training Laboratory in Group Development in the Washington, D.C., area, later called the National Training Laboratory or NTL, provided a formal organizational structure for the development of the laboratory method. Initially NTL sponsored summer training laboratories at Bethel and eventually was involved in year-round activities. In its early years NTL served as the main organizer for T-group training. Later, a number of other organizations became involved in similar kinds of training activities, but NTL still plays a major role in the training of leaders for such groups, and providing internship experiences and accreditation for those who have completed the requisite training.

T-groups have been used in an almost infinite variety of ways and in many settings. They have run from one meeting to weekend, almost marathon-like, meetings to weekly meetings spread over months or even a year. It will not be possible for us to go into detail about all of the many variations that have occurred. Indeed, recent modifications have involved the merging of T-group technology with other group methods, such as the Encounter and Gestalt models. Our effort here will be to describe the structure of the T-group, as it evolved from the original laboratory method begun by the Lewinian group, a format that consisted of an intensive one-to two-week experience in a setting removed from the usual home and workplace of the participants. Let us turn now to an examination of how this experience is organized.

DESIGN OF A RESIDENTIAL LABORATORY

The essential form of the laboratory experience may be seen most clearly in the two-week residential laboratory. Detailed descriptions of such laboratory experiences are provided by Benne, Bradford, Lippitt (1964) and Schein and Benne (1965).

One important feature of the residential laboratory is the creation of a *cultural island*. The residential laboratory typically takes place in a bucolic setting in which participants are able to feel removed from their everyday work and familial circumstances. Functioning in such a cultural island may have a variety of different effects on participants, but two characteristics are considered to be of especial importance. (1) Removal of the participants from a setting with built-in expectations and props for behavior puts them in a position to be much more open to new inputs and experiences. (2) The unusualness of the setting serves to heighten anxiety and uncertainty about the laboratory experience. Although didactic sessions dealing with small group theories, large general meetings and social activities are part of the residential laboratory, the T-group sessions are considered to be its major learning vehicle.

One of the main characteristics of the T-group in the laboratory experience that is stressed again and again, and one that is facilitated by the removal of the delegate from his everyday life circumstances is the emphasis on learning a different style of approach to problems. Perhaps this can be most vividly seen if one thinks of the typical participant in the T-group experience as a person from middle-management in a large organization whose usual manner of functioning emphasizes activity and productivity. The experience in the T-group would essentially represent the antithesis of his ordinary everyday experience. The T-group presents an unstructured situation with no clearcut set of expectations, with no agenda, with no guidelines as to appropriate behavior or expectations of others; the participants are faced with a vacuum. The T-group has a nominal leader, but he is one who functions not as a chairman or authoritative person, but only as a facilitator or helper in learning. In fact, one of the roles of the "leader" is to create a vacuum which the participants must fill with their own behavior. Part of their agenda is learning to analyze their own group data. The behavior that emerges and the understanding of that behavior in its multi-faceted forms becomes the basic content of the learning, but the fact that the members' own behavior is the grist for the learning mill is not evident to the participants as they enter into this experience. Although the typical laboratory experience starts out with an overview and explanation of what the T-group experience will be like, it is presented at a fairly high level of abstraction; furthermore it is believed that the members are unable to incorporate the knowledge in a way that will be meaningful to them until they have had the experience of the T-group itself.

A typical T-group might begin with the "trainer" saying that he imagines that the group members have come to learn about how people behave in groups by learning from their own experience of becoming group members. He offers neither agenda nor any suggestions as to how to proceed. In the vacuum that is created, group members begin to act in characteristic ways; some may try to provide structure by suggesting the formulation of an agenda or the election of a chairman, others may complain about the leader's failure to lead, while still others may comment about the anxiety that the lack of structure creates in them. These comments are likely to be interspersed with periods of silence. Group members experience considerable tension as they attempt to cope with the ambiguity of the situation. Although a number of suggestions may be offered by group members as to how to proceed, none is followed up. The group looks to the trainer for guidelines, and the trainer in turn reflects back the group's desire for guidelines. Finally a member suggests some easily agreed to action, such as all of the members introducing themselves, and the group, seizing on it, agrees to proceed in this manner. The first session typically ends with members feeling confused and bewildered about what happened during the session and about how they ought to proceed next.

The succeeding few sessions provide further evidence of group members' efforts to cope with the frustration of ambiguity and lack of structure. Abortive attempts at leadership develop; the group may become divided into two camps—those who very much want leadership and structure and those who are opposed to organizing until the group decides what it wants to do. The trainer's suggestion that the members explore their feelings of frustration at their inability to get the group going is typically ignored. There may be a variety of other abortive attempts to organize, set up committees, elect chairmen; and the sense of frustration grows. Eventually the group responds to the trainer's comment suggesting that it examine the members' contributions to the lack of group progress.

At this point focus shifts to an examination of member behavior and interpersonal style. Attention might be first directed to a member who has been particularly active in an earlier effort to elect a chairman. Let us say that Alex, a hard-driving, production manager, has played this role in the group. He begins to get feedback about the bossy and authoritarian way in which he insists his procedure is correct, his inability to consider alternatives once he has formed an opinion, and his open attack on those who stand in the way of his drive for leadership. He initially reacts defensively, unwilling to consider the comments, but several warmly concerned members convince him that their comments are meant to help in exploration, and are not the cruel attack Alex believes them to be. Slowly he begins to look at his over-concern with performance, with getting the job done properly, his distrust of others' capabilities, and his consequent inability to share responsibility. In a similar fashion the characteristics of other members are explored, sometimes at the person's own initiation, at other times with assistance, prodding, or feedback from other members or the trainer. Don, another member, who had vacillated among supporting a number of alternative ways to proceed earlier, spontaneously begins talking about his inability to take responsibility and his constant hedging and avoiding, touched off by the stark contrast with Alex's account. Others chime in with concerns about being too aggressive or too passive, too involved or too cool, too emotional or too stolid. Finally Ned, a member who has been quite inactive, is turned on by the group for not wanting to reveal his feelings, not letting other people know him.

The mutual support members have given each other during the period of feedback may lead to a great deal of expression of positive feeling between members; for example, Don may be lavishly praised for his willingness to take a good hard look at himself. Group cohesiveness is now at its height. The concern of the group may then turn to comparing individual members in terms of their degree of involvement and efforts are made to "bring in" those who seem insufficiently involved. Ned is again focused on in an effort to make him feel more a part of the group. As the time draws to a close, attention is turned to evaluation and examination of what the members have gained from the group both in terms of greater awareness of the nature of their impact on others, and knowledge about how group process works.

The foregoing description illustrates the fact that learning in T-groups is different from what is typical for most participants in their usual experience in work and personal life. The learning involves observation and examination of one's own behavior and of the interaction among members of the group. It requires a radically different approach from the usual interpersonal style of the middle management participant. It is frequently pointed out that the kind of learning that occurs in T-groups can only emerge from the ferment of the immediacy of experience. In other words, didactic instruction alone about the same content would not result in acquisition of knowledge about individual and group phenomena in usable form. Laboratory training also includes theory sessions that are kept separate from experiences in the T-group; each is expected to have a mutually useful and productive effect on the total learning of the individual, but the experiential component provided by the T-group experience is seen as crucial.

In the residential laboratory the experience that takes place in informal contacts among participants is also important to the learning process. To facilitate such informal contacts members typically share rooms, take their meals together in groups, have arranged cocktail hours, and a considerable amount of free time available for "bull sessions" and interaction. Informality in dress is encouraged and usual status and role props, such as formal styles of address and organizational or educational titles, are discouraged. Members at a two-week residential laboratory will typically have the weekend between the two weeks free either to return home or to spend some time away from the residential setting in a nearby city.

Each of the two weeks of residential laboratory is seen as having a special role in the experience. The participants'—or, as they are sometimes called, delegates'—main task in the first week is to become immersed in the laboratory culture, which demands a whole new style of learning how to observe oneself and others. After this immersion has occurred, the focus of the learning then turns to applying the new style to real experience. To facilitate this, the didactic sessions in the second week stress application of the learning to actual life circumstances facing the participants, although the T-group experience continues to emphasize learning in the "here and now."

As has been noted, the laboratory method involves a number of different kinds of experiences—T-groups, lectures and intergroup activities—but the T-group carries the major burden of the learning that is to take place. The sessions of T-group meetings vary from one to three two-hour sessions per day, concentrated most heavily at the start of the laboratory. In a typical laboratory there is a total of about fifty participants, divided into four T-groups of from ten to fifteen members each. In addition to the T-groups, there are also theory sessions, which provide didactic information about the underlying learning principles of T-groups, and focused exercises which frequently involve intergroup competition. Theory sessions are designed to complement the experiential part of learning that occurs in the T-group with didactic material on group process, communication, and observation of behavior. Developing a conceptual framework to help in understanding the ongoing T-group experiences maximizes the learning opportunity. Tasks used in intergroup competition require cooperation among the members of each T-group, e.g., producing as many greeting card verses as possible or developing a system for democratizing an autocratic organizational structure. Observations on how the group deals with the task are then analyzed in a subsequent T-group session.

Most experiences of personal change are difficult to describe; T-group experiences are no exception, but a great deal has been written by and about participants and their reactions. It is not an easy task for a participant in a T-group, after he returns from a two-week laboratory or indeed even while he is in the process of experiencing it, to describe meaningfully exactly what he derived from the T-group. Participants frequently say that they feel different, that they learned a great deal, but find it difficult to specify precisely what they learned, or in what ways they have changed. A large number of participants in laboratory experiences seem to come away with very positive feelings, with feelings that changes have occurred, and that important learning has taken place. Some have suggested that the experience of intimacy and mutuality in the group is a very important part of the positive reaction. Feelings of freedom and openness to other people and to new experiences seem to characterize the response of many participants. Klaw (1961), writes graphically about the laboratory experience from the viewpoint of an observer not trained in group leadership. He recounts reactions of participants which range from the initial anxiety created by the ambiguity, to efforts at dealing with issues of openness and trust, and he describes how one learns about interpersonal impact. His conclusion indicates his skepticism about whether people are really changed by the experience.

KEY CONCEPTS: PHILOSOPHICAL AND THEORETICAL

Value Bases. When one considers the evolution of the T-group, it becomes clear that although the method had its roots in social science theory, its development has been based more on practice and experience factors than on systematic theory building. It will be recalled that the idea for the T-group came directly from the action research and group dynamics emphases of Kurt Lewin, and was based on the group's analysis of data that it produced itself. Theoretical concerns with the relationship of personal change to interpersonal or group influence, and to variables such as group cohesiveness and equilibrium also grew out of Lewinian theory. By the time the format of the T-group became set in the early 1950s, it had already become more a practice format than a vehicle for theory development and basic knowledge about interpersonal and group process. Therefore, no fully articulated theoretical structure has been produced to undergird T-group technology. There has, of course, been considerable interest in studying aspects of group process—ranging from ancedotal and observational to quite rigorous and controlled—but as yet no systematic and inclusive theory of group process has emerged.

There is, however, fairly general agreement (e.g., Schein and Bennis, 1965; Bradford, Gibb, and Benne, 1964) on the kinds of value bases that formed the ideological underpinnings of T-groups at their inception, and on the important values that T-groups hoped to inculcate. The focus on organizational change through the impact of individual efforts to modify hierarchical structure, it will be recalled, was a prominent concern of Lewin and his group.

Science and the Scientific Method. One important aim of early T-groups was to introduce ideas from behavioral science, particularly group dynamics, into the day-to-day thinking, planning, and frames of reference of responsible persons in organizations. The underlying hope was that through greater knowledge of behavioral science, a more rational approach to organizational development and a greater openness to inquiry might be introduced into the everyday life of the system. Being open to awareness, allowing oneself to utilize all relevant information in making decisions, being aware of how one's own values might influence the way in which one viewed a situation, were all seen as aspects of the scientific approach.

Democratic Orientation. Many of the participants in T-groups came from organizational structures which were viewed as, at least, hierarchically structured and, at worst, extremely authoritarian. To counteract this aspect of organizations which the developers of T-groups firmly believed to hamper productivity, an emphasis on democratic values was introduced. Earlier research of Lewin's group supporting the superiority of democratic decision-making in groups bolstered this belief (e.g., Lewin, Lippitt and White, 1939). While it was clear to everyone that bureaucratic structures were unlikely to change in such a way that all members of the organization could participate in all decisions affecting them, it was felt that a greater degree of cooperation, and a minimization of the kinds of covert dissatisfaction that hampered productivity could be achieved as the amount of participation of group members increased. One of the learnings, then, that might be fostered by T-group experience would be an awareness of how cooperation and collaboration facilitates group functioning and, in the larger sense, total organizational functioning. The expectation was that the learning that took place in the T-group would then have impact on larger organizational structures when the members returned to them.

Genuine Concern for Others. Important in the thinking of the originators of T-groups was the desire to introduce a greater sense of "humanness" into large impersonal organizations. Caring for others, being willing to help others, being concerned about the feelings of others, rather than hindering productivity in organizations, all facilitated effective functioning of an organization, while, at the same time, enriched the lives of its members. The T-group was seen as an arena for learning how all people profit from genuine, caring human interaction.

Goals. A second group of important theoretical concepts growing out of the values just described deals with goals of participation in T-groups. Attempts to articulate these range from those at a very general level of analysis to highly specific and articulated outlines with a number of subgoals suggested. For some representative discussions see Benne, Bradford, and Lippitt (1964), Schein and Bennis (1965), National Training Laboratories (1962), and Golembiewski and Blumberg (1970). Although there are minor variations among the various T-group theorists, there is a core of characteristics that are generally agreed upon. These will be described and discussed.

Learning How to Learn. Perhaps the most basic notion of a goal statement and the one almost universally mentioned is the central concept of "learning how to learn." The core idea is that in the course of their educational experience, most people have typically followed the model of looking to experts for accepted knowledge and have viewed teachers as authorities and pupils as absorbers of information. During the T-group experience a participant has the opportunity to learn that he has the wherewithal to generate new and useful knowledge and information himself. Thus one comes to "learn how to learn" by using his powers of observation, by stretching his imagination, by listening to what others are saying, by responding to others and observing their reactions to those responses, and by examining the impact of his own behavior on other people. The reader will recall that in our example of a typical group, Alex, during the early sessions, constantly looked for structure, demanded that the trainers provide structure, and finally offered his own suggestion for structure—i.e., that the group make an agenda and follow it. He quickly began to get feedback from others and had to deal with the single-mindedness of his preoccupation. By virtue of this sequence of events he became much more attuned to his own inner experience and to the behavior and reactions of others. Another important aspect of what is meant by "learning how to learn" is the task of developing greater acuity in observation and greater ability to scan and pay attention to observations of behavior, both one's own and that of those with whom one interacts.

Self-Knowledge. The goal of increased self-knowledge of self-awareness or insight can be considered as a special subcategory of learning how to learn, i.e., learning how to learn about oneself, one's behavior and reactions. The T-group is seen as providing an opportunity for a person to come to know himself better, by learning in an atmosphere of openness how others react to him, and by having the chance to observe himself more carefully than he typically does. Such observation of self would include tuning into his own feelings and responses to other people as well as attending more carefully to his own behavior. Don, in our example, was able to experience his own passivity because of its contrast with Alex's style. In this way he began to learn something about the effect on himself of his characteristic stance and its impact on others.

Effective Membership in Group Functioning. Another goal of the T-group method is to help people to become more effective in dealing with others in group settings. The opportunity for emotional give and take in a setting in which one gets constant feedback about how he is perceived serves to make one more observant both in the T-group itself as well as in subsequent group activities. As one becomes more aware of the range of needs that people in the group have and the variety of techniques they have for expressing them, and as well becomes more responsive to his own needs and desires in the group context, he will learn to monitor and to modulate his own behavior in group settings in more effective ways.

Leadership Techniques. T-groups provide the opportunity for people to learn how to be better leaders, not only in group settings, but in any organizational or managerial functions they perform. Perhaps leadership technique is an inexact term to express the idea of learning to be more responsive to the needs of others, to the needs of persons subordinate and superordinate to one in a hierarchical structure. The desired leadership style, then, based on the value of genuine concern for others, is one of a nonauthoritarian, responsive, caring person who pays attention to the wants and desires of others and tries to create a working atmosphere in which the needs and feelings of all are taken into account. This attitude is meant to have a softening effect on the dominant depersonalizing task orientation that exists in organizational structures, and in the long run would be expected to increase productivity as well as improve the quality of performance or output.

Impact on Organization. This goal is the one least directly related to the actual activities of the T-group. Nonetheless, one of the important motivations for the development of T-group and laboratory experiences was the wish to influence positively the functioning of organizations. Therefore, one of the goals of T-groups, particularly when there is involvement of a number of individuals from the same organization in the T-group, is to have an impact on the quality of human relations within the organization. When sufficient numbers of organization members become more self-aware, are more concerned with the human needs of others, are more effective group members, and more effective group leaders, they should eventually have positive influence on the total structure and function of any system. The kind of organizational impact advocated clearly emerges from the value bases of democratic orientation and concern for others.

KEY CONCEPTS: OPERATIONAL

In attempting to describe the important events, activities, or processes that occur in a typical T-group, one is again faced with the problem of an extremely broad array of dimensions that have been described by writers in the field. We have selected a limited number of operational concepts to describe. We have chosen those emphases that we judged to be most central and germane, and about which there was most consensus, although they are not universally referred to by the terms that we have chosen.

Here-and-Now Focus. The learning process in the T-group is extremely dependent upon observation of and response to what is, in fact, occurring in the group itself. Underlying the "here-and-now" focus is the assumption that learning about interpersonal style can best occur when observing immediate experience and feeling its emotional impact. Attending to feelings as they are felt and understanding what evokes those feelings is a constant concern. Thus, long digressions into problems members face on their jobs, into historical events in their personal lives, or attempts to explain dynamics of present behavior in terms of past relationships are very strongly discouraged. One learns from participating in the group process, from observing that group process, and from reflecting on it. It is the "here-and-now" focus of the learning experience that T-group theorists would most strongly agree is an essential ingredient of learning about group dynamics.

Unfreezing. "Unfreezing" denotes freeing people from their standard and typical ways of behaving and of viewing themselves and others in interpersonal situations. It is a complex process that typically occurs under conditions of abrupt and dramatic change. The "cultural island" of the residential laboratory both contributes to the unfreezing process and then, once it occurs, exploits it as a vehicle for learning. The T-group with its lack of structure, with the absence of any formal agenda, provides an opportunity, an impetus and a demand to take a fresh look at one's typical style of functioning. Ambiguity about group structure, the absence of role and status props, uncertainty about expected, desired or appropriate behavior in the group, are all seen as contributing to the unfreezing of the group member.

Group Support and Atmosphere of Trust. The process of unfreezing puts one in a position to view things in a new way, but the motivation, willingness, and feeling of security sufficient to do so is primarily a function of the developing group process. Concern of members for each other, toleration of failure or mistakes in others, the leader's attempt to create an atmosphere of psychological safety and his encouragement of risk-taking are all important elements in the development of a feeling of trust among the members. Underpinning all of these is the development of support of each member for the other because they are all in a common circumstance that is foreign to their previous experiences, making them particularly needful of each other's concern and interest.

Disclosure. A basic assumption in the T-group literature is that, to a greater or lesser degree, all members have motivation to learn in the T-group setting. Over against the motivation to learn is a counter-motivation created by anxiety resulting from ambiguity and uncertainty, fear of emotional involvement, or concern about exposing one's weaknesses. The T-group norm of self-disclosure, of revealing one's reactions, one's feelings, one's personal responses, is a very important aid in overcoming anxiety and making the motivation to learn prepotent. There is a danger that this expectation will create great pressure on members to disclose more than they can comfortably reveal. The trainer needs to be alert in guarding against such occurrences. In the T-group, members can only learn from each other by revealing their responses and reactions. Yet there must necessarily be some limit to *how much* is revealed, since this is a time-limited, nontherapeutic group. Therefore, realistic norms must develop about the degree of self-disclosure that is appropriate for the group. The development of such norms is central to effective learning in a T-group.

Feedback. It is fair to say that in the view of most T-group theorists, feedback—the response of members to each other about their reactions to the other's behavior—is the *sine qua non* of learning. An honest, straightforward, helpful sharing of reactions to one another provides basic, but rarely available (in most real life situations) information about how one is affecting others. In our example of a T-group described above, members' telling Alex about their reactions to his authoritarian manner *and* their convincing him of their genuine concern for him illustrates a highly desirable feedback style. When feedback is given in an atmosphere of interested concern, of trust, and of shared disclosure, optimal conditions for use of such information in personal growth and change have occurred. A cautionary note should be given about potentially harmful feedback. Feedback given in a hostile manner, in a way that the recipient cannot accept or learn from, or in a way that distorts the behavior of the individual in terms of the respondent's own perceptions represent circumstances that undermine the effective use of this very powerful tool. An important task of the trainer is to help the group create norms discouraging this kind of unhelpful feedback.

Developing Group Norms. Most of the typical norms that develop in T-groups grow out of the value bases discussed earlier and out of the other group process emphases, e.g., the "here-and-now" orientation just described. It is important to note here the possibility of a group's developing idiosyncratic norms that may be detrimental to effective group functioning. For example, the usual norm of openness and concern for others' feelings may at times become distorted to a norm of "Don't give negative feedback." The leader should be on the alert for norms of this type and raise questions of the group about its creating implicit and counter-productive norms, such as systematic turn-taking, excessive politeness or overprotection of a member. Such norms of course run counter to the group's basic aims and purposes.

TYPICAL COURSE OF A GROUP

Earlier in this chapter we briefly described a typical experience in a T-group to give the reader a "feel" for what occurs in such a group. At this point let us examine the phases of group development in greater detail. The T-group, perhaps more than any other model, has been subjected to careful observational study of group process, thereby making it possible to offer more specific detail about the course of a group than in most other instances. Of course, there are still many variations in group movement and emphasis that are dependent upon a wide range of variables. Leader personality and style, the make-up of the membership, including background, personality character-istics, occupational roles, variations in motivations of members, whether group members are affiliated or strangers—all play a part in the nature of group development.

Warren Bennis (see Bennis and Shepard, 1956; and Bennis, 1964) has formulated an interesting description of the vicissitudes in group processes at different phases of group development. He divides the time span of the T-group into two major phases each of which has three subphases, making a total of six subphases in all.

Phase I is termed *Dependence* and includes the following three subphases:

Subphase I: Dependence-Flight. The major issue at the outset of the group is to try to find a common goal and an agreed upon means to reach that goal. As mentioned earlier, an important characteristic of the T-group experience, that of ambiguity, creates within the members a dependency on the leader for structure, for direction, for advice on how to proceed, as well as a dependency on other members for action-guidelines. There is both a wish to have structure provided and a flight from structure, a desire for someone to take a leadership role and a blocking of any attempts that are made for leadership bids. There is a desire for the trainer to take some responsibility for providing structure and yet total indifference and inattention to the comments he makes.

Subphase II: Counterdependence-Flight. Now the members more actively seek to avoid the leader and begin to provide their own structure and own procedures. Typically two subgroups with opposing desires develop; one subgroup attempts to establish structure, develop an agenda, elect a chairman and the like and the other subgroup opposes all efforts to provide structure. Dissatisfaction with the trainer grows, but is not directly expressed. He is viewed as obstructionistic and oppositional and as not having the best interests of the group at heart. Members secretly consider him to be unable, unwilling, or at the very least unlikely, to meet their learning needs in the group.

Subphase III: Resolution-Catharsis. The most characteristic aspects of the first two subphases are their disruptiveness and their avoidance of any useful learning experiences. However, at the same time, but remaining very quiescent, another set of motivations exists—that is, the desires of members to make the best use of and to learn from the experience. One positive aspect of members' experiences in the subphases I and II is the development of a mutuality in working together, at least in the spontaneous subgroups, and the development of some trust among members. The more independent members of the group are seen as crucial in the development in this third subphase. Commonly one such member will suggest that the group is getting nowhere and perhaps would proceed better if the trainer would leave for a while. This is an expression of an attitude that seems quite counter to what members have felt earlier, i.e., that the trainer was absolutely central to the functioning of the group, even though he was as yet not successfully performing his duties. Such a direct attack on the trainer brings to the surface much that has been ignored up to this point, including resentment of group members toward the trainer as an authority figure. Beginning to recognize attitudes toward authority and how such attitudes have impeded effective functioning in the group helps to stir an incipient sense of autonomy in the group members, and some recognition of member responsibility for group development and learning within the group.

Phase II is termed the phase of *Interdependence*. During this phase power and relations with authority recede to the background and effective working together and caring about members for one another come to the fore. The subphases of Phase II are:

Subphase IV: Enchantment-Flight. This period is characterized by the focusing on positive feelings that members have for each other. They saw in subphase III that they could work together effectively as a group and now take the opportunity to relax and enjoy each other. Concern about the feelings of others and the enjoyment of group members predominates. However, group solidarity is not long-lived. The burden of everyone's being in harmony with each other is a heavy one to bear and soon resentments about submergence of the self for the sake of the group begin to come to the fore.

Subphase V: Disenchantment-Fight. During this period the group again divides itself into two subgroups. The issue, however, is different from that in subphase II at which time structure and independence were important dimensions; now degree of personal involvement seems to be the important issue. Thus the members divide themselves into those who want to be quite personally involved with each other and those who want to avoid a high degree of involvement. The underlying fears of all members during this subphase is viewed as the same: "How would others feel about me if they really knew me?" It is at this point that the sensitive issue of degree of disclosure, discussed earlier, becomes central. Some members react to their anxiety by drawing together in an intimate way and focusing on self-acceptance and acceptance of all members. Others attempt to ward off anxiety by rejecting all interest in personal involvement with the group.

Subphase VI: Consensual Validation. The impending end of the T-group experience and the need to complete the group's work of learning about group dynamics and interpersonal behavior—in particular an evaluation of what each member has contributed to the entire process—mobilizes all members. The two subgroups mentioned in subphase V both try to avoid the task of role evaluation, those avoiding involvement on the grounds of invasion of privacy and those seeking close contact because evaluation invites unfair comparison of group members. In the most positive circumstances progress in this subphase is again pushed by one of the more independent members of the group; for example, he might ask the group to focus on him and to provide him with feedback. Fear of being attacked becomes less pronounced when the task of evaluation is actually entered into. The important learning in this phase comes from each member's sharpening his awareness of how he responds to others. The task of this last subphase is to try to resolve the problem of interdependence of group members and to prepare for inevitable separation.

ROLE OF THE LEADER

The trainer in the T-group should bring a special set of role characteristics to the experience. He is not in the usual sense a teacher, or a group therapist, or a chairman of the proceedings, or a group leader. Rather, the trainer is viewed as a facilitator or helper in the learning experience. Because the leader provides little structure in the beginning of the T-group meetings, a kind of vacuum of structure and expectations is created. This vacuum is filled by members with their own behavior in deciding about how the group should function. That behavior and its analysis, of course, becomes the basic content of the group experience.

A central aspect of the trainer's role lies in his ability to create an atmosphere for effective learning. The creation of such an atmosphere involves a complex set of activities and characteristics. Setting the scene by making clear that he will not serve as an authority and helping the group to develop goals of its own is important. Just as central is the continual modeling of the behavior of a good group member—openness, responsiveness to others' needs, eagerness to understand and to explore ongoing group phenomena, and the requesting and offering of constructive feedback. Attention to and anticipation of changes in group process, and the ability to keep the group focused on group process in the present instead of becoming overly involved in personal concerns, are also important trainer skills.

Let us examine several special categories of leader characteristics which have been viewed as important in the T-group process.

1. Facilitation of Learning. Perhaps the most frequently stressed aspect of the trainer's role is his providing the opportunity for members to behave in a group setting and to observe their own behavior. The fact that the leader does not offer structure, does not respond to member demands to assume authoritative control, and does not offer specific action guidelines, all force members to respond in their characteristic styles, and all assist him in his role as facilitator. The fact that the trainer refuses to be an authoritative, directive leader, but attempts to help the group to seek its own path to development is central to this aspect of the role.

2. Protection. Helping to develop a climate of trust in the group situation is another important aspect of the leader's role. At times he may have to intervene when feedback from one member to another becomes so hostile, ill-timed, or inaccurate as to put the recipient of feedback in a position of great anxiety. For example, if in one of the early group sessions a very shy member begins to talk haltingly about how anxious the uncertainty of the situation makes him feel and is quickly attacked by a boisterous member for being perfectly absurd, the trainer might first turn to the rest of the group to elicit similar feelings of anxiety; if he fails to do so he might then tell the shy member that he can readily understand why he feels that way.

3. Balancing the Role of Helper, Member, and Expert. The trainer's role includes elements of a number of subroles; as indicated earlier, the helper or facilitator role is an important one. In addition, the trainer functions as a member; particularly when a group develops a more truly egalitarian atmosphere, a greater degree of sharing with other group members on an equal basis becomes possible. The trainer should serve as a model of openness, concern for others' feelings, and attention to behavior in the here-and-now—all of those attributes that constitute good T-group member behavior. Also, the trainer must, at times, function as an expert; he is more knowledgable about group process and group dynamics than is a typical member, and that fact is better acknowledged than denied. Furthermore, certain aspects of the role of the trainer involve specific expertise; for example, he may have to introduce training exercises such as competition among T-groups in producing greeting card verses or the presentation of role-playing techniques. The important point is that flexibility, balance and ability to shift from one role to another—from helper, to member, to expert—is central to an effective training repertoire.

4. Group Process Orientation. Another aspect of the role of the trainer is that he must carefully observe interaction among group members. He must be in a position to make interventions that are useful to the "here-and-now" learning of the group and to constantly develop hypotheses to anticipate the nature of group movement. In the case of our example, once Alex had accepted the fact that his overbearing attitude created discomfort in others, the trainer might have taken that opportunity to help group members explore their reactions to such demands from one individual, while at the same time anticipating that for some members the structuring aspect of that stance remained a very positive lure. Group process orientation is also seen as important in helping the trainer to avoid several pitfalls of the training experience: becoming too directive or too clinically oriented or too much invested in the "there-and-then" rather than the "here-and-now." The group process orientation, then, is particularly facilitative of the kind of learning that the T-group is structured to provide, that is, learning about group interaction, and one's impact on others in groups. Here again, trainer behavior in pointing to group process issues serves as a model for the development of a similar orientation among members.

5. Controlled Interventions. A matter which requires constant attention and constant decision-making is the issue of how the helper role is most effectively carried out in any given circumstance. Is it better carried out by letting the group search and try to find its own way? The issue here, of course, is one of balance, of the trainer's not taking on too much of the responsibility for intervention facilitative of group functioning. For example, if a group member suggests electing a chairman and making an agenda, the experienced trainer knows that this suggestion will come to naught, but he knows, too, not to cut off discussion of the issue, lest the group feel that he is impeding their progress in an autocratic way. He must let the group consider the issue until enough members are sufficiently disenchanted with the idea to begin to examine the role that the efforts at structuring played in fleeing from ambiguity.

VARIED USES OF T-GROUPS

As previously indicated, at their inception, T-groups were called basic skill training groups and focused on the development of knowledge about group dynamics, leadership skills, and awareness of interpersonal relationships. With the increased participation of clinical psychologists and psychiatrists the social psychological emphases waned a bit, while the personal growth focus increased. Over a period of years there has been a noticeable shift in orientation from a group focus to an individual or self-fulfillment focus. This is clearly reflected in the changing terminology, such that by the mid-1950s the term "sensitivity training" became increasingly common. The term sensitivity training clearly emphasizes the self, one's own feelings, and a concomitant de-emphasis on understanding of group processes. While it is fair to say that this general trend has occurred, it is important to quickly point out that there is tremendous variation from group to group, leader to leader, and situation to situation. Some trainers adhere to the earlier emphasis on group dynamics and leadership skills much more fully than others. This is particularly true in the laboratory method that has been the main focus of our discussion. Indeed some view T-group trainers as having broken into two camps—one organization focused, one interested in the growth and change of individuals.

Another way to examine the range of uses of the laboratory method is to look at the kinds of situations in which T-groups have been utilized. Here again the range of situations is very broad. The two groups that apparently have most frequently made use of the laboratory method are business organizations on which much of the initial work focused (Blake and Mouton, 1964), and groups in the helping professions trying to learn more about ways to function more effectively in their work—e.g., psychologists, social workers, psychiatrists, school counselors, and nurses. More recently use of T-groups in community action groups, cross-cultural groups, and interclass, interracial groups has become more common.

We may also consider the ways in which T-groups have been used by comparing the kinds of backgrounds and statuses of the various participants in T-groups. T-groups have been organized around people functioning in comparable roles, but in different organizations—e.g., middle management personnel from different companies. This was the original and initially the most common model. Subsequently other patterns have been introduced. One such pattern is to have several members of an organization at different levels in the hierarchy attend the same T-group at a site away from their usual place of employment. A more recent innovation involves bringing a T-group into an organization and having a group of people who all know each other or at least have worked together—usually at different hierarchical levels—in the same T-group. For example, a T-group might be held for the staff at a mental hospital, with psychiatrists, psychologists, social workers, nurses, attendants, and secretaries participating. A number of arguments have been raised about the relative merits of T-groups composed of strangers versus those comprised of coworkers, whether at or away from the organizational site, with some feeling that the within organization T-group helped to create very difficult interpersonal relationships subsequent to the T-group meetings or made lower status members fearful of being open under circumstances where they might expect future sanctions; others have argued that it is precisely in this kind of situation that true learning about interpersonal functioning in an organization can take place. Only anecdotal evidence is available to support each point of view.

RECENT DEVELOPMENTS IN T-GROUPS

Although the original emphasis of T-groups still continues—the focus on group dynamics, on institutional and organizational change—and indeed many of the ongoing programs of NTL continue to be oriented in this fashion—the newer emphasis on groups with personal growth and development themes has become equally prominent. As noted earlier, a more "clinical" emphasis became prominent in the mid-1950s, but it was rooted in the context of the person functioning in an organizational structure. Subsequently groups with a more personal development emphasis began to draw participants from the population at large. In these groups there may be considerable overlap in method and technique with other models. For example, nonverbal techniques identified with encounter groups (see Chapter 11) have been introduced into the T-group methodology; NTL has sponsored groups or workshops with specific themes which tends to create overlap with theme-centered groups (see Chapter 12).

Let us mention some of the kinds of laboratories and workshops offered by NTL in order to give the reader a sense of the movement and change of format in recent years. In its recent program brochures, NTL described the following workshops: (1) *Developing Individual Potential*—a personal growth oriented experience to promote authentic, honest and trusting relationships in the context of the small group experience. (2) *Couple's Interaction*—an effort to learn new creative ways of sharing life together. (3) *Being A Woman*—an opportunity to develop a personal sense of identity outside of the expectations of husband, children, and parents. (4) *Family Relationships*—participation of the whole family in learning better ways to express their needs, their anger, their affection. (5) *Between The Generations*—an opportunity for younger and older people to get together and examine the generation gap. It should be noted that many of these groups feature nonverbal exercises and techniques and leadership styles of such kinds that it becomes quite inaccurate to refer to them as T-groups; however, both their style and format make them relatively indistinguishable from encounter groups as described in the next chapter.

There appear to be two distinct aspects to the trend illustrated by the content of the laboratories described above. The first is the very clear emphasis on individual growth and development, on identity, authenticity and freedom in human interaction. The second emphasis is on the specificity of content in these workshops. Whereas in early days the themes of laboratories were much less specific in focus and content, and generally were concerned with functioning in occupational roles, one emphasis that now seems to have emerged is that of learning to broaden and enrich certain very pervasive but nonwork-related roles—e.g., husband and wife, youngster, woman, member of the family, oldster. It is interesting to follow the history of a movement that was initially concerned with helping people to personalize roles—e.g., their work roles in presumably authoritarian organizational structures, roles that were not usually thought of as personal in nature. Although the original residential laboratory still continues, some more recent workshops deal with roles that historically have been presumed to be the most highly personal. One may assume, considering the demand for attendance at these workshops, that many people are not finding the degree of satisfaction and openness to intimacy in living that they wish. This trend, while pertinent to the history and development of the laboratory method, is clearly of broader interest since it relates very importantly to the development of a variety of group endeavors that have been generally categorized as the human potential movement. This trend will need to be examined in greater detail in the final chapter.

References

Benne, K. D. 1964. History of the T-group in the laboratory setting. In L. P. Bradford, J. R. Gibb, and K. D. Benne, eds. *T-group theory and laboratory method.* New York: John Wiley & Sons.
——, Bradford, L. P., and Lippitt, R. 1964. Designing the laboratory. In L. P. Bradford, J. R. Gibb, and K. D. Benne eds. *T-group theory and laboratory method.* New York: John Wiley & Sons.
Bennis, W. G., and Shepard, H. A. 1956. A theory of group development. *Human Relations, 9.* 415-438.
——. 1964. Patterns and vicissitudes in T-group development. In L. P.

Bradford, J. R. Gibb, and K. D. Benne, eds. *T-group theory and laboratory method.* New York: John Wiley & Sons.

——. 1969. *Organization development: its nature, origins, and prospects.* (Addison-Wesley series on organization development). Reading, Mass.: Addison-Wesley.

Blake, R. R., and Mouton, J. S. 1964. *The managerial grid.* Houston: Gulf Publishing Co.

Bradford, J. P., Gibb, J. R., and Benne, K. D. 1964. *T-group theory and laboratory method.* New York: John Wiley & Sons.

Golembiewski, R. L. and Blumberg, A. 1970. *Sensitivity training: the laboratory approach.* Itasca, Ill.: Peacock.

Klaw, S. 1961. Two weeks in a T-group. *Fortune Magazine.* August, 1961.

Lewin, K., Lippitt, R., and White, R. K. 1939. Patterns of aggressive behavior in experimentally created "social climates". *Journal of Social Psychology, 10.* 271-299.

National Training Laboratories, *Issues in human relations training.* Selected Readings Series, No. 5. Washington, D.C.: NTL, 1962.

Schein, E. H., and Bennis, W. G. 1965. *Personal and organizational change through group methods.* New York: John Wiley & Sons.

11

The Encounter Group

The Encounter format offers an intensive group experience that is designed to put the normally alienated individual into closer contact—or "encounter"—with himself, with others, and with the world of nature and pure sensation. As a result, Encounter groups are somewhat global in their purpose: they include both the psychotherapeutic aspect of therapy groups and the educational function of growth and development groups. They are similarly global in their methodology in that they incorporate several aspects of the various models thus far presented. For example, although Encounter participants are free to talk with one another in the conventional and discursive style that predominates in analytic, experiential, and T-groups, the typical Encounter leader will also employ, where they seem appropriate, the expressive and action-oriented techniques emphasized by the Psychodrama and Gestalt therapy models.

Consequently the present model represents a more diverse approach to group-leading than do most of the models that we have presented thus far. Unlike such group models as Psychodrama, Gestalt therapy, or Theme-centered (see Chapter 12), which developed out of the theoretical conception of a single person, the Encounter model represents the accumulated thinking, practice, and writing of several people. Moreover, unlike the Tavistock and T-groups, which evolved out of the close collaboration of colleagues working within a common theoretical framework, the practitioners responsible for the development of the Encounter group tended to work in isolation from one another and to represent somewhat disparate conceptual traditions. For example, William Schutz, who developed one form of the Encounter model, came from a psychoanalytic orientation, whereas Carl Rogers, another influential figure within the movement, drew from his own school of "client-centered" psychotherapy (Rogers, 1951) which, when viewed within the frame-of-reference employed in this book, comes closest to an existential-experiential approach.

Therefore our task in this chapter is to present a cluster of models, just as was the case in Chapter 4, where we described three distinct variants, or submodels, of the group-dynamic psychotherapy group. While ongoing therapy groups can employ Encounter methods, we shall primarily concern ourselves in this chapter with time-limited groups that meet intensively for a period of several days in a residential setting, and that are open to the public at large as opposed to being open to troubled people seeking psychological treatment or to professionals having an interest in further human relations training. One particular model, Schutz's Open Encounter, will receive major emphasis, since it has been the most influential and representative of the several approaches to Encounter, and it is to this model that our "Illustration of a Typical Session," "Key Concepts," and "Role of the Leader" sections will apply. At the end of the chapter we shall describe Mintz's Marathon Encounter group in order to illustrate how a clinician can integrate Encounter techniques with an ongoing psychotherapy practice and with a theoretical framework that is essentially psychoanalytic.

An aspect of the Encounter model that contributes to its complexity and ambiguity is the fact that it has within it elements of a social movement (Back, 1972). Encounter proponents, while claiming a therapeutic function for their groups, do not make a distinction between neurosis and health and instead insist that alienation from ourselves and from our bodies is sufficiently endemic in contemporary culture for each of us to suffer from it to some degree. As a result, the Encounter model, more than any other thus far presented, is at least in part based on a reaction against the conditions of rational-bureaucratic society and it attempts to offer new values for guiding day-to-day existence outside the group as well as in it. Elements within this ideology include a greater emphasis on feeling and sensation than on thinking, an involvement in the immediate present, and a favoring of spontaneity over reflection and continued delay of gratification. As an aspect of their negative attitude toward bureaucratically imposed regulations, Encounter theorists often support the use of nonprofessional or "lay" leaders who have received little formal training in psychotherapy, in group-leading, or in social science in general (Schutz, 1971). All of these factors indicate the extent to which the Encounter model has become identified with elements within our society that are often described as comprising a "Counterculture" (Reich, 1970, and Roszak, 1969). It has been suggested that the philosophy-of-life common to both Encounter and Counterculture comprises elements involving the stress on spontaneous impulse and the rejection of authority cited above, a repudiation of a concern with future goals (along with the emphasis on structure and on appropriate role-behavior that accompany such a concern), and a championing of experience, in particular strong emotional experience, for its own sake. These elements obviously interrelate with, and complement, one another.

Some of the factors already mentioned help to explain why the Encounter movement has had a widespread appeal. People *are* burdened by the powerful demands of an increasingly externalized and materialistic society and doubtless miss the emotional outlets afforded by more traditional opportunities for ritual and celebration, such as those encompassed by conventional religion and by more dramatic forms of patriotism. Moreover, the Encounter experience promises something akin to a feeling of mutual concern and of a close-knit community that is similarly lacking in an increasingly fragmented urban culture in which most people find themselves participating in a wide variety of disparate and isolated reference groups—familial, occupational, social, civic, and religious. Encounter gives the person a chance to immerse himself in an intensive group experience in which he comes as himself rather than as a representative of a particular social or vocational role, and does not have to define himself as either a "patient" or as a teacher, businessman, or mental health professional seeking further clinical or human relations training. In addition, the typically time-limited format of the Encounter group permits him to attend one that may take place at a considerable geographic distance from his home, thereby enabling him to be in a group that is led by a particularly well-known or expert leader or situated in an unusually beautiful setting.

The Encounter culture's emphasis on group leadership that bypasses traditional notions of professional competence and accreditation helps to give the movement a strong grass-roots and Populistic flavor. What is stressed is the need for people to be more in touch with their feelings, and less with arbitrary standards of "appropriate" role-behavior. A natural vehicle for achieving this is a group experience where members stop striving to impress one another and instead just let themselves "be," where the leader makes no claim to a rational and scientific body of knowledge that separates him from the rest of the group, and where the real person behind the facade and the actual body underneath the clothing is revealed. Hence the nude Encounter (Bindrim, 1968), another variation of the model, seems a logical and concrete extension of this thrust. Implicit here is the influence of what was becoming, in the early 1960s, an increasingly humanistic psychology that emphasized the importance of man over "the machine," of self-determination, and of authenticity.

Despite the diversity of format, procedures, and leadership styles found within Encounter, we shall focus on one particular model as reasonably prototypical, and this is what Schutz describes as his "Open Encounter" group (Schutz, 1971). Because Schutz's work evolved within the setting of Esalen Institute, which has played a role in relation to Encounter that is roughly analogous to that played by NTL in relation to T-groups, because it is defined as directed toward relatively healthy people, because it has a specific focus on the release of bodily feeling and bodily energy, and because it minimizes the group-dynamics emphasis inherent in a T-group orientation and instead concentrates on the liberation of the individual, we consider it to be the single most representative Encounter model yet developed.

Before tracing the history of Schutz's model, we would like to give a feeling for what an Open Encounter session might be like. The setting for the illustration to be presented below is a five-day Encounter workshop as it might have been led by Schutz, or by one of the members of what he termed his "Flying Circus", at Esalen during the late 1960s. These groups usually had their first session on a Sunday evening, and continued through the morning of the following Friday.

ILLUSTRATION OF A TYPICAL SESSION

A total of fifty-two people are in residence at Esalen for our five-day Encounter. On Sunday night after dinner they assemble for their initial Microlab session which involves the entire membership. Its purpose is to introduce them to the kind of communication games and exercises that they will participate in throughout the week, to prepare them for some intense emotional experiences, and to help them feel more comfortable in physical encounter with one another. The leaders begin by directing the audience in exercises that involve concentrated breathing, careful and quiet attention to their inner bodily and emotional experience, "blind milling" (which requires people to move around the room with their eyes closed and to engage in whatever nonverbal contact they wish with whomever they happen to touch), and "face touching" (here each person selects a partner and attempts, via direct visual and tactile contact with other's face, to form a distinct impression of him) (Schutz, 1971, pp. 132-148). Now the audience is asked to divide itself into ten or so smaller "Microgroups" having approximately five people each. The leader guides the smaller groups through a series of exercises designed to help their members get to know each other more deeply. For example, the groups are instructed in a fantasy game in which each person imagines what part of his body he would instinctively try to cover were he to have no clothes on. Later he places this body-part in an imagined "empty chair" and, in the manner of Gestalt-therapy (see Chapter 7), engages in a dialogue with it while the rest of the group observes. (For example, a woman might ask her breasts why they are so small. As her breasts, she might reply: "Because you don't deserve any better!"; and so on). Microlabs can also be used to demonstrate Encounter techniques and to provide a brief Encounter experience in large groups that are meeting for a short period of time, like a single afternoon.

Following the Microlab, our fifty-two participants are split into five Encounter groups, each having ten or so members. One of these groups is to be led by the leader of the Microlab session, and the remaining ones by four other leaders, some of whom are graduates of the Esalen training program for Encounter leaders and have been supervised by Schutz himself. The small group now constitutes the primary medium of the participant's Encounter experiences, and it will meet throughout the remainder of the week, usually with the leader but sometimes without him. General sessions involving all fifty-two participants, scheduled for the middle of the next four afternoons, will demonstrate particular techniques or methods—e.g., body movement, graphics, Yoga. In one of the afternoon sessions the theme of encountering the world of nature will be introduced via Esalen's famous "Blind Walk" exercise, which requires a blindfolded person to be walked around the grounds by his partner, who will present many natural objects to him through non-verbal means, including touch, taste, and smell. The two will then reverse roles. In this exercise the issue of trust is admixed with a sensory dimension.

As our illustrative excerpt from the opening of one of the small groups will show (see below), many of the Open Encounter sessions have a specifically therapeutic focus. However, the overall Encounter experience aims for nonprogrammed personal growth in the most general sense of this term. The emphasis is on an individual's expanding his awareness along any one of an infinite number of dimensions, and also on his own responsibility in choosing which of these dimensions is most appealing and important to him. Since most Encounter proponents believe that contemporary Western man has over-developed his intellectual faculties at the expense of his bodily and sensory experience, the major stress is on the latter. Once concentration and contact with the inner self is sufficiently strengthened, the possibility of achieving experiences that are variously described as "peak", "mystical", or "transcendental" is increased. Again, peak experiences can occur in a variety of ways. However, they are most likely to occur in moments where the participant allows himself to live fully in the immediate present and to feel at one, be it with others in the group or with nature. Situations wherein he experiences himself as truly cared for and nurtured by fellow members can be especially intense (see Mary and the "Roll and Rock" excercise below).

Let us follow one of the smaller groups as it meets in its first session with its designated leader, Ted. It is now about ten-thirty in the evening, and the group is composed of eleven people—six men and five women—ranging in age from nineteen to fifty-five. They are seated in an informal circle on the floor of a relatively bare, but carpeted, lodge. The leader begins by reminding the participants that each of them bears the primary responsibility for what happens to him in the session; if he wishes to either go with or resist group pressure, to let himself get injured physically, or to become extremely upset, the decision is basically his. This is stated, in part, to bring home to participants the fact that they have both more responsibility for, and more personal control over, their own behavior than they usually exercise.

The leader now suggests a warm-up exercise in which people give their first impressions of one another. He stops, giving no further directions, while the group is silent for a few moments. Then Alex, a man in his mid-forties who has had some previous Encounter experience, leaps up and positions himself in the center of the group. Other participants begin to make spontaneous comments, not necessarily going in order. "He tries to look kind, but I have a sense that he could stab you in the back," says one man. "He's sexy," says a woman. From another woman: "I sense a scared little boy underneath." When almost everyone has been heard from, Alex returns to the circle and is replaced by Meredith, a pretty girl in her early twenties, who stoically seats herself before the group as though grimly steeling herself for the worst. Again the participants offer comments in no particular order. Several participants, most of them male, make some appreciative comments about her attractiveness. Participants replace Meredith in the center of the room in random order; Doris, who follows Meredith, laughingly says that it makes no sense to drag out the anxiety, so she "may as well get it over with." The exercise is over once each participant has taken his turn in the center of the circle. (The Encounter leader can start off the session with any one of a number of warm-up exercises, and some leaders prefer to begin in a totally unstructured way, much as in the T-group format. Once the group atmosphere is sufficiently loose, Encounter exercises are introduced in a more discriminating and specifically therapeutic way in that the leader will usually introduce them only when he thinks that they will facilitate his work with a particular participant.)

At this point Ted, the leader, asks the participants for their reactions. Alex leads off by saying that he was hurt that more than one person had reacted to him as a frightened little boy. He knows that this is an aspect of himself, but it is one that he has been trying to change, both through psychotherapy and previous Encounter groups, and he expresses disappointment that this part of him still shows through so strongly. Mike, a husky, vital-looking man in his early thirties, begins to show impatience with Alex, and says that the latter, by his whining and self-pitying behavior, is still acting the role of the little boy and subtly asking for the group's sympathy and reassurance. "If you were really a man," says Mike, "you wouldn't need us to tell you you are!"

Alex initial reaction to Mike's irritation is one of hurt and defensiveness, but as Mike continues to needle him, he becomes increasingly attacking. Finally he lights into what he calls Mike's "cocksureness," and says that Mike has the same self-doubt as does he, Alex, but chooses to cover it over with a facade of super-virility. Ted interrupts at this point, and suggests the "High Noon" exercise (Schutz, 1971, pp. 140-141), which requires the two men to go to two opposite corners of the room and then face each other. Their instructions are to refrain from speaking and to walk slowly toward each other slowly. Once they have approached each other, they are to spontaneously let their bodies lead and to go wherever their impulse leads them. As the two men begin to follow his directions, he reminds them to not plan their actions beforehand, and encourages the group to remain silent as the exercise proceeds.

Once the two men are opposite each other at the room's center, they pause. Alex stands rigidly still, as if determined that it be Mike who makes the first move. The latter seems awkward and uncertain; he reaches out as though to playfully hit Alex on the shoulder, but then impulsively embraces him. Alex seems surprised, then responds by putting his arm around Mike. The latter hugs harder and harder, and then, with his head on Alex's shoulder, begins to weep.

Ted moves swiftly over to the two men, as Mike begins to sob more loudly, asks him what he is experiencing. Mike, still crying, says that he is thinking of the gulf and the antagonism that has always existed between him and his father. He feels suddenly in touch with the positive aspects of the relationship that existed between them when he was very young, and he is remembering the longing for affection and comradeship that he felt in relation to his father long ago. Ted, attempting to improvise a spontaneous Psychodrama, asks Mike to talk to Alex as though the latter were his father, and to try to express some of these feelings. Mike does so, and finds himself trying to explain to his father why it seemed that they could never get together. Suddenly he lashes out: "It was Mom who didn't want us to be friends—somehow she kept spoiling it." Ted intervenes, and asks "How?" Mike responds: "By speaking about him derogatorily to me, and by tearing him down in front of me—and, you—you shmuck" (here he turns back to Alex) "you let her!"

Ted asks Mike to select from the group the woman who most reminds him of his mother. He picks Mary, a youthful-looking woman in her mid-fifties. Ted tells Mike to begin to express his feelings toward his mother. He instructs Mary to listen, and to begin to respond as she senses Mike's mother might have. Mike begins to upbraid his mother for her behavior toward him and his father; taking his cue, Mary responds in a slightly scared and defensive way. Mike corrects her, and says "No, my mother would counter-attack much more forcefully," and for a moment he takes the mother role, in order to show Mary how he perceived his mother to behave. Mary resumes her role-playing in a more forceful way as Mike struggles to get his anger out; perceiving him as too timid, several members of the group spontaneously, without any direction from Ted, assume alter-ego roles and try to shout down his mother. Mike begins to shout too, but in a few minutes turns to Ted in frustration, saying: "I still can't get it out—I'd like to kill her, the bitch!"

Ted suggests that he go to the couch that is against the wall, that he stand next to it with his feet about a foot apart, and that he begin to beat it as hard as possible, all the while shouting at his mother whatever angry words come to mind. Ted cautions Mike that the activity might seem quite artificial at the beginning, but that he proceed in an attempt to see what feelings emerge. Mike begins; as he proceeds to throw his body more and more into the beating, he starts to pound more savagely, his cries become louder, and his curses against his mother more vehement. After several minutes of this, his pounding gets weaker; he turns to Ted, saying that he feels exhausted and "finished," and Ted suggests that he stop.

The group is silent for a few minutes while Mike continues to lie by the couch, breathing heavily. Doris comments that Mary seems to be in great pain. With some encouragement from Doris, Mary begins to talk about some of the feelings that she experienced during her role-playing with Mike, and about how she was reminded of the guilt that she feels in relation to her daughter, Nancy, who died several months ago at the age of thirty. Mary feels that most of the criticisms that her daughter had begun to direct at her during these past few years had been valid ones; she expresses regret that she had not been a better mother, and that Nancy had probably died without realizing how much Mary had loved her.

Ted now encourages Mary to proceed in a Gestalt therapy exercise (see Chapter 7), in which she places Nancy in the empty chair and speaks to her. She begins by describing for Nancy the loneliness she has felt since her death; as Nancy, she directs angry complaints against her mother. Once again in the role of herself, Mary expresses and is surprised by the anger that Nancy's accusations arouse in her; she defends herself and states her love for Nancy. Returning to the role of Nancy, she expresses great wonderment at the extent of her mother's love, which she (i.e. Nancy) had never permitted herself to fully feel before. At this point, as she plays Nancy in the empty chair, Mary is overwhelmed by her feelings and begins to sob uncontrollably. With some encouragement from Ted, a few of the other participants draw slowly to her side, comforting her and tentatively embracing her. Once Mary has regained some composure, Ted insists that she continue the Gestalt therapy dialogue and say Good-bye to Nancy.

At the end of this exercise Mary is softly weeping. Ted quietly gestures toward the other participants, who slowly gather around her. Performing the "Roll and Rock" exercise (Schutz, 1961, pp. 145-146), the group lifts Mary to her feet and form a circle around her. Ted instructs her to close her eyes and to let herself go completely limp; as she does so, the other participants gather closely around her and pass her around the circle. After a while, they move her to a horizontal position, and lift her above their heads; holding her in this position, they rock her back and forth for several minutes, while softly singing a lullaby. Then they continue their rocking motion, while they slowly lower Mary to the floor.

By now it is two o'clock in the morning. Nothing is said while Mary continues to lie on the floor with her eyes still shut. Her face appears to be in a peaceful repose, while some participants continue to gently touch her or stay close by her side. Other members are off to the side, either singly or in groups of two or three. Most appear to be exhausted; all are silent. Ted says that he is ready to quit for the night, unless anyone has some reaction or feeling that is immediately pressing. Since no one responds, Ted reminds members that they are to reassemble in the same place at ten o'clock that morning, and he bids them good-night.

The format of the small-group sessions does not change during the remaining four-and-a-half-days. Now no warm-up exercises are necessary, and the leader waits for members to spontaneously bring up problems and concerns. Many of them do so in response to the previous work of other participants, much as Mary, in her role as Mike's mother, had been moved to speak of her own personal anguish. While participants are given free rein to talk about the past, they are encouraged, through the use of Gestalt-therapy,

Psychodrama, and other communication games, to connect these concerns to the immediate present, their fellow participants and their shared group experience. By Friday morning, every participant has revealed something of his own life circumstances through having had a chance—like Mike and Mary—to take "center stage."

HISTORICAL BACKGROUND

As we have stated more than once, the Encounter model can be viewed as a logical extension of all the group models that preceded it. The group-work and psychoanalytic models had taken the initial steps in encouraging the participant to shed his more social and stereotypic masks and to reveal the less conscious and more authentic person underneath. The experiential model took another significant step when it encouraged the leader-therapist to do the same. Then came Psychodrama and Gestalt therapy, which claimed that therapeutic results could be gained in a time-limited workshop format and which encouraged the participant to stop talking *about* his difficulties and to act them out directly in more expressive and vivid ways. And at a subsequent point there emerged the T-group, which offered an experience in interpersonal sensitivity that went even further than Psychodrama and Gestalt in being expressly for normal people and that, like the latter two models, attempted to give something to the participant who attended the group for a short period of time.

As the growth and development group that inaugurated the sensitivity-training movement, the T-group is the most conspicuous and immediate predecessor of the Encounter group. Initially the T-model was relatively strict in emphasizing two distinct foci (see Chapter 10). The trainer was to (1) encourage the group to become consciously aware of its own processes, and (2) insure that the group maintain a continuous concentration on the here-and-now; by restricting the introduction of there-and-then material (especially past events of a particular participant's life) the trainer avoided the kind of individual focusing that might easily begin to constitute psychotherapy. For reasons which we reviewed in our first chapter, the T-group leader gradually began to relax his adherence to these two paramenters, and at this point the first distinct introduction of an Encounter thrust into sensitivity groups was taken. Other steps toward a strong Encounter focus, including an emphasis on hugging and physical contact, soon followed. In retrospect it can be argued that once the explicitly personal focus of group psychotherapy models was introduced into groups that were designed for nonpatients, once the spirit of experientialism was interpreted as granting the leader complete freedom to be himself (to the point of having extensive physical contact with the participant), and once the more expressive and less verbal procedures involved in Psychodrama and Gestalt therapy were introduced into a sensitivity-training format, the relatively unstructured Encounter group was probably an inevitable outcome.

However, the path taken by sensitivity-training as it proceeded from the more structured and social-science oriented T-group to the more loosely organized and experiential Encounter group involved several disparate developments. One step in this sequence involved the work of Carl Rogers, who in developing what he called the "Intensive group Experience" or "Basic encounter" introduced into the training-group model a strongly humanistic and personalized emphasis. A second step involved the Marathon model developed by Bach and Stoller, two psychoanalytically-oriented group therapists who, although proceeding from a different theoretical orientation, hit upon a time-limited group format having significant similarities to Rogers' approach. A third and final step in this sequence involved the evolution of what is sometimes referred to as the "Synanon" or "attack" approach to group interaction. Here the group meets on a continuous basis, in relation to a specific, drug-related symptom. Yet, despite this resemblance to a therapy group, the Synanon group's focus on an essentially leaderless format in which members relate to one another in highly confrontational ways played an instrumental role in the movement toward Open Encounter, and Synanon groups were eventually organized for "straights," as well as for addicts. We shall summarize each of these three approaches below.

Rogers Basic Encounter Model. Rogers' orientation to working with groups is a clear-cut outgrowth of his "client-centered" approach to an individual therapy (1951). His group model emphasizes a strongly phenomenological dimension wherein an individual counselor or group leader responds in terms of the client's internal frame of reference and refrains from imposing his own interpretations of the latter's experience. Rogers' pervasively humanistic orientation predates by many years the emergence of all encounter methods and has much in common with the Existential-experiential model (see Chapter 5); indeed, his initial experience with groups goes back to 1946 when he began to work with counselors-in-training on a group basis. In this sense, unlike most other Encounter leaders, Rogers bypassed both the psycho-analytic and T-models, and while revising some of his concepts, has remained remarkably consistent in his basic approach to the people with whom he is working.

Starting in 1964, when he became a Resident Fellow at the Western Behavioral Science Institute (W.B.S.I.) in La Jolla, California, Rogers had a considerably increased opportunity to nourish and follow up his interest in what he refers to as the "Basic Encounter" or "Intensive group experience" (Rogers, 1967). These opportunities were even further enhanced four years later when he shifted to the newly formed Center for the Whole Person (also in La Jolla), which he had helped to found and which embraced even more openly than did W.B.S.I. the pursuit of humanistic and unorthodox approaches to the expansion of consciousness.

Three distinct aspects of Rogers' Basic Encounter helped to place it within the mainstream of what, at that time, was a rapidly developing Encounter movement (Rogers, 1970):

1. Rogers did not worry about making a careful distinction between growth and development goals and therapy goals. While he strove, as the group's leader, to bring out into the open the participants' here-and-now affective reactions to one another, he did not deem the recounting of past or personal events as irrelevant or inappropriate, and he viewed the group experience as able to effect permanent changes within the individual.

2. He emphasized the value of honest confrontation, even if the feedback presented seemed negative and potentially hurtful. Rogers believed that an honest expression of negative feelings cannot but be helpful in the long run to the person receiving the feedback. While he did not deal explicitly with the problem of confrontational feedback that is offered more in the spirit of outright sadism than of genuine interest in the recipient, it seems likely that in such a situation either Rogers or another participant would state such an impression to the person offering the feedback. The important point here is that an emphasis on the relevance and palatability of feedback, which was a feature of the T-group model, was no longer prominent.

3. Rogers had little interest in directing the group's conscious attention to its own processes. As has always been the case with him, the primary emphasis is on the awareness, expression, and acceptance of feeling, rather than on an appreciation of the patterns of interaction that are developing within the group. This is not to say that Rogers has little awareness of, or respect for, group-dynamic processes. To the contrary, he emphasized that a trusting and cohesive group climate—which he, as a leader, continually attempted to facilitate—is one of the most therapeutic properties of the Basic Encounter. Rogers' extremely accepting personality in the Encounter situation appears to embrace the group as a coherent entity; his preference is to facilitate its self-regulative and curative powers to a point where his interventions can be minimal and each participant can become, at particular moments, a facilitator or therapist for other participants in the group;

Although meeting on an intensive and noncontinuous basis, Rogers' Basic Encounter resembles analytic and experiential therapy groups in that members communicate verbally with one another in relatively discursive and conventional ways. Hence, other Encounter models were to go much further in the direction of the leader's interposition of catharsis-oriented games and exercises. Rogers claims that he uses devices involving role-playing and body contact from time to time, but his utilization of such techniques seems relatively sparing; where they are employed, his concern is that they be in touch with the feeling of the moment and devoid of artifice or theatricality. He is anxious lest leaders feel that as facilitators of groups labeled "Encounter" they ought somehow to introduce fadlike and increasing popular Encounter techniques, which are usually nonverbal, psychodramatic, or Gestalt in nature. His preference is for the participant's stating himself clearly without being directed by a leader into techniques that for Rogers smack of gimmickry.

Stoller and Bach's Marathon Encounter. Fred Stoller (who died in 1970) and George Bach, two psychoanalytically-oriented group therapists, were interested in extending the format of conventional group therapy to the point of having participants remain in one another's presence for periods of time ranging from twenty-four to forty-eight hours. Because of the emphasis on the time factor, Stoller and Bach initially referred to these experiences as Marathons; within three years, perhaps influenced by the already-building Encounter movement, the term "Marathon Group encounter" was used (Bach, 1967 and Stoller, 1972).

In many respects, Stoller and Bach's model was not very different from that of Rogers; people admitted to the Marathon did not have to be seeking therapy, and a climate of openness and trust was encouraged in which group-members could shed their more habitual defensive and role-playing behaviors. The emphasis was on immediate feeling experience rather than on the narration of the past or on intellectual explanations of behavior. Participants were encouraged to "level" with, and confront, one another without concern as to what the other person could or couldn't "take". Formal communication games and exercises were kept to a minimum, and each participant was viewed as a potential therapist for every other participant with the designated therapists simply being the most experienced therapists present (and it was not considered inappropriate for them to become the focused-upon member in the group from time to time).

Rogers had come to Encounter from a client-centered tradition that from its inception de-emphasized the role of both diagnosis and interpretation in doing treatment. However, since Stoller and Bach had emerged from a strongly psychoanalytic and clinical tradition, their shift toward an Encounter approach represented a dramatic transition in their thinking. No longer did they deem it necessary for the group therapist to have a detailed knowledge of the patient's past or for the patient to have intellectual insight in order to change. In their thinking, the "working through" phase of psychotherapy, so integral a part of the psychoanalytic method, could be accomplished by the participant on his own in the weeks following the Marathon, with the expectation that significant personality change could occur on the basis of a single Marathon experience. In other words, traditional features of conventional treatment which underlined the importance of a treatment plan and careful support of the patient's defenses until he was ready to relinquish them were slipping away. Instead these two therapists stressed the positive forces for autonomous growth, reparation, and reintegration that existed within each group member. This emphasis on the need for the participant to assume responsibility for his own welfare—as opposed to his placing this responsibility in the hands of either the leaders or the group—was to become a fundamental feature of the Encounter model.

Similarly novel was Bach and Stoller's belief that if change were to occur it must occur *now*. This shift in emphasis wherein the emitting of new behavior was made primary, and the understanding of old behavior secondary, philosophically had much in common with the Behavior therapy model, and reversed the traditional priorities of psychoanalysis, which claimed that meaningful change could occur only in the context of a patient's emotional and intellectual appreciation of his own dynamics.

Rogers had been used to working with groups on the basis of an intensive and time-limited format, and therefore did not stress this aspect of his approach to Encounter. Stoller and Bach, on the other hand, made much of the time factor, because for them it was a distinct departure. As they saw it, the extended time format had several advantages: (1) the prolonged nature of the Marathon tends to produce fatigue, which in turn leads to a weakening of defenses, (2) paths of retreat that in traditional group therapy are normally open to patients who feel hurt by the negative reactions of others are less available in the time-extended group, where no participant is likely to escape the group's attention during the long session, (3) the fact that the group does not have to anticipate breaking within an hour or so (as in conventional group meetings) helps it to be less wary lest there be an insufficient amount of time to deal with the hurt and angry feelings attendant upon confrontation, thereby enabling its members to take greater risks in leveling with one another, (4) the participant has a considerably greater opportunity to see that his reaction-style—which he likes to think is primarily determined by either the situation or his mood of the moment—is recurrent and patterned in that it cyclically repeats itself throughout the extended Marathon sequence, and (5) the dramatic and keenly anticipatory nature of the Marathon helps to create an atmosphere of crisis and expectancy; this climate has within it elements of a self-fulfilling prophecy wherein the participant, expecting a breakthrough for himself, works hard to make it happen. Where he does not, his fellow participants, realizing that he has come for a distinct reason and has a strong investment in the outcome, are quick to remind him that there will be no next session to which pressing emotional issues can be deferred.

Initially, Stoller and Bach were so impressed by the time-intensity and fatigue factors that they advocated nonstop twenty-four hour sessions in which the group was given no opportunity for sleep. Later this position relaxed, and Marathons ran late into the night, and then broke until the next morning, thereby giving participants a chance to sleep. This is the procedure followed by both the Esalen Open Encounter and Mintz's Marathon Encounter (see below).

Synanon and Attack Therapy. Synanon, a residential setting for the rehabilitation of drug addicts, was initially established in Santa Monica, California, in

1958 by Charles Dederich, an ex-alcoholic and layman who conceived of a unique approach to the treatment of addicts. Those people wishing to be helped were required to submit themselves to a total program in which they agreed to live at Synanon, to keep strictly "clean" (and this entailed complete abstinence from alcohol as well as drugs), and to abide by a number of house rules, which included attendance at frequent group meetings and the performance of chores necessary to the maintenance of the house. The direct participation of professionals was kept to a minimum; those who were associated with the organization were there in a research capacity and had to become full-fledged members of the community (Casriel, 1963, and Yablonsky, 1955). Dederich's intent was to create a self-help community in which an autocratic family structure would help to provide a source of controls and stability for the initially anarchic and dependent addict and to pave the way for his gradual assumption of more self-directed values. Important steps in this process would be his chance to role-model those addicts who were higher within the organizational hierarchy and had had a longer record of "clean days," and to participate in the leaderless small-group sessions, or "synanons," which were the primary locus for the group approach known as "attack therapy."

Although synanons meet continually throughout the life of the house, their membership is not fixed, with the result that the membership of the groups is constantly shifting. It is believed that one advantage of such an arrangement is that it prevents the kind of collusion that can develop among members of the fixed, ongoing therapy group, in which members might establish an unwritten pact to refrain from exposing particular vulnerabilities in one another. The average member participates in about three such groups a week. While most synanons are unstructured and spontaneous, some are held on special topics, like status-seeking or prejudice, and some are "rigged" ahead of time; for example, if it is known that two coworkers are having problems on their job they might intentionally be placed in the same group, and sometimes, in line with the attack approach to be described below, a few members prearrange to focus on a particular person or issue.

The attack phase of a synanon refers to an interaction sequence wherein a particular participant is cross-examined, ridiculed, and berated for certain aspects of his behavior or attitudes that are felt to be impeding his path toward greater self-reliance; the characteristics being focused on might include excessive self-pity, undue dependency on outside family figures, false humility, and laxness in performing his assigned job. An especial cause for contempt is the pseudo-insight, in which a member who is well-skilled in the rules of group therapy uses impressively worded psychological "discoveries" about himself and his past in order to give the appearance of confronting a problem that he prefers to avoid emotionally. Once under attack, the victim usually attempts to defend himself, but his defenses are shown up for the rationalizations and excuses they are. According to Synanon theory, the truly therapeutic confrontation requires a good deal of skill in that the attacker must know when to back off and at what point to offer support.

No one is immune from attack, and in a single session several people may have a turn at becoming a recipient. However, more often than not the attacker is a "Synanist"—i.e., an older member who, while attacking a new member, at the same time reminds the latter that he, the Synanist, once had similar problems and succeeded in overcoming them. In this context, the Synanist is functioning as a lay therapist. One advantage of his being a nonprofessional is said to lie in his greater willingness to expose his own problems, both current and past; another advantage is that his nonprofessional status reaffirms Synanon as a genuinely self-help community in which each member, whether "attacker" or "victim," suffers an equal degree of exposure and has an equal emotional stake in the basic viability of the organization.

To the outside observer, a prolonged attack may appear to be a sadistic "third degree" or inquisition. Synanon proponents, however, make several arguments in support of its effectiveness: (1) one of the addict's problems is that he has been treated too laxly and with too little recognition of his potential for toughness and strength, (2) the victim gradually learns that it is his problem that is being attacked, rather than his basic "self," (3) he might even realize that what seems like an overt attack is frequently an expression of caring and of genuine regard, (4) sometimes an addict's emotional blocks are of such an intensity that he can be reached in no other way, (5) attack therapy teaches the addict verbal ways of handling stress that are considerably more sophisticated and effective than his previous reliance on acting-out, and (6) new members slowly appreciate that while the content of his accusations is of genuine concern to the attacker, the attack format is in itself something of a game, with its own ritual and rules of play, including exaggeration.

Although Dederich has pointed out that attack approaches may work only within the very particular context of Synanon, the Synanon approach to group therapy had a strong influence on the Encounter movement. One manifestation of its impact has been the belief in the effectiveness of the relatively untrained leader. Another has been the increased use of confrontational styles, in which group members feel free to attack one another verbally and to fight physically. Also reminiscent of the synanon is the quite common interaction pattern wherein each Encounter member in turn, and for a fairly prolonged period of time, becomes a focus of the group's concern and attention.

Schutz's Open Encounter Model

The developments recapitulated above take us through the mid-sixties and helped to pave the way for Schutz's Open Encounter model. One additional event that was to prove instrumental in this model's final emergence occurred in 1967 when Bill Schutz joined the staff of Esalen Institute. Esalen had been established in 1962 when two Stanford University graduates, Michael Murphy and Richard Price, decided to use sixty-two acres belonging to Murphy in Big Sur, California, for the development of a center that would devote itself to the exploration of human potential. Murphy and Price, both nonprofessionals, were convinced that Esalen, if it were to remain consistent with its humanistic orientation, had to be nondoctrinaire. Therefore, while they wished to study further the sensitivity-training procedures initially developed by the National Training Laboratories, they were receptive to other techniques (including Gestalt therapy, Yoga, meditation) and to non-Western religions and cosmologies; hence there was an emphasis on Eastern philosophy, Zen-Buddhism, and mysticism in general. Starting with weekend retreats, Esalen's Big Sur program and facilities grew to a point where by 1968 it offered year-round events, had a permanent live-in staff, and ran two to three simultaneous workshops lasting anywhere from four days to several months; it was also in the process of developing a San Francisco branch that within a year would be sponsoring shorter workshops on a nonresidential basis. In this way, Esalen came to spearhead and to epitomize the human potential movement, and to develop into a prototype for scores of growth centers that subsequently sprang up through the United States.

At the point when Schutz arrived on the scene, some of Esalen's workshops were centered around a particular technique, like Yoga or meditation; others were thematic in nature and might concern marriage, divorce, loneliness, intimacy; still others had no specific focus apart from the kind of interpersonal exploration that is the general aim of all growth and development groups. These were workshops that were called "Encounter," and it was their development, along with the creation of a program for leaders-in-training, that became his primary responsibility.

Schutz was a social psychologist with a strong grounding in psychoanalysis. While on the faculty of Harvard, he wrote a book, *FIRO* (1958), that attempted to coordinate psychoanalytic approaches to group dynamics with the psychoanalytic theory of personality dynamics. He also received some training in group leading during this time from the National Training Laboratories at Bethel, Maine, and from Elvin Semrad, a Boston psychoanalyst whose theoretical orientation to work with groups was in the Bion-Tavistock tradition (see Chapter 9). In 1963 Schutz joined the faculty of the Albert Einstein College of Medicine in New York City. In New York he came under the tutelage of Alexander Lowen, the founder of Bioenergetic Analysis, a school of psychotherapy emphasizing the essential unity of mind and body; bioenergetics stresses the necessity of reawakening whole areas of a patient's body, often through extremely vigorous exercises involving thrusting and pounding movements of the entire skeletal musculature. According to Lowen

(1967), this kind of body work permits the patient to get into renewed contact with long-suppressed emotions; until these affects are felt and released, latent energies within the body are so blocked as to prevent a real feeling of aliveness. Lowen in turn had been a disciple of Wilhelm Reich, whose theory of character armor postulated that each emotional repression or blockage within us has a specific site of muscular tension associated with it (Reich, 1949); as a result, many aspects of our posture both embody and signal (to the sensitive observer) our defensive and/or characterological stance, and psychological treatment that ignores the body is bound to be superficial. During this period, Schutz, albeit impressed by the intellectual insights of Freud and his followers in the dynamics of human character formation, began to believe that formal analytic technique was usually unsuccessful in achieving any genuine transformations of character. His experience in personal analysis up until that time had done nothing to convince him otherwise. The Reichian and Lowenian emphasis on physical action and body-work seemed to hold some promise for a more potent means of reawakening long-dormant feelings.

Given this background, Schutz was in an ideal position to integrate theoretical strands emanating from Freud, Reich, and Kurt Lewin into the unique amalgam that he eventually labeled Open Encounter. He did not abandon a psychoanalytic understanding of character formation, but instead of exploring these processes in a purely verbal way with a participant-patient, he was eager to approach them through more immediate physical and bodily means. Similarly, he had both a theoretical and intuitive command of group-dynamics and respected them as important phenomena, but instead of desiring to help the group explicitly label and understand these processes, he preferred to employ them in such a way as to build a cohesive, trusting atmosphere wherein each participant could begin to liberate himself from the devitalizing effects of his chronic alienation.

KEY CONCEPTS

The Centrality of the Body. Following in the tradition of Wilhelm Reich and Alexander Lowen, Schutz makes the body the single overriding concept in his theory of Encounter. While the Gestalt therapy model, in its careful attention to body language, had already taken some steps in this direction, Schutz's model was to go even further, for Schutz, once he was aware of a particular emotional constellation within the participant-patient, consistently urged the latter to translate his feelings into a physical activity that would express it in a more primitive and tangible form. For example, if a participant expresses a sense of immobilization and constriction, the leader suggests the "Breaking Out" exercise (Schutz, 1971, p. 142), which requires the group-members to form a tight circle around him and to forcibly attempt to prevent his breaking through them. If he expresses mistrust, he is encouraged to engage in the

"Falling Back" exercise (Schutz, 1971, p. 138), which has him fall back in the trust that the person behind him will catch him. In the illustrative session above, both the "High Noon" and "Roll and Rock" exercises constituted attempts to put into the realm of physical action emotions that were at that moment the focus of the group's attention.

Implicit in Schutz's thesis is the following: Our very earliest experiences originated within the body before we had any symbols other than body language with which to code them. The earliest emotions, including feeling good (which probably relates closely to feeling loved and cared for), feeling bad, and feeling angry, were body emotions. Therefore, there is no more basic and fundamental way for experiencing ourselves and our being than through bodily sensations. As a result no amount of "head" talk to the man who wants to break through his self-containment as to why he feels so constrained or what he could do to feel less constrained will offer a learning experience that is equivalent to his expressing his problem motorically; in the "Breaking Out" exercise there is a higher probability of his experiencing the full extent of his rage, and of his becoming aware of how he sabotages himself through lack of sustained effort and through premature "giving up." Furthermore, any actual success that he has in escaping out of the group-circle will help him to feel more strongly the exhilarating possibility of breaking out in the larger emotional sense—again because the body furnishes the most powerful linguistic coding of this sense of self-expansion and transcendence. In a similar fashion, the risk taken in falling back into the arms of another, without any chance to visually check what lies below, furnishes a direct experience of trust that no amount of conceptual symbolization can parallel.

As Schutz points out, this technique reverses psychoanalytic method, which limits the patient's behavior in the analytic session to verbalization and reflection, and discourages overt action. Although impressed with the limitations of verbal interpretation when used alone, Schutz is not opposed to it, and claims that it can serve a role in consolidating an intense emotional experience.

The Facilitative Role of Fantasy and Inner Imagery. As we just indicated above, one way to give an emotional conflict more concrete form is to translate it directly into physical activity. Another way is to direct it into *imagined* physical activity. Here the activity is occurring at a more symbolic level than when it occurs in actuality; however, according to Schutz, a fantasy of physical activity still has a greater chance of making a problem emotionally alive than does an abstract discussion of the problem to which it relates.

Let us cite a specific example described by Schutz (1971, pp. 262-263). One of the problems that Jane was having with her boyfriend was that she, although quite bright, had had considerably less education than he. Schutz, as the group leader, decided to try the "Guided Daydream" technique (Schutz, 1971, p. 185), in which a leader encourages a participant to engage in spontaneous fantasy as a way of dealing with a particular problem; sometimes the leader suggests a specific image or symbol that the participant then uses to start his fantasy, and at subsequent points, where the fanticizer seems stuck or immobilized, the leader will supply some help.

In her fantasy, Jane visualized herself attempting to crawl through a long tunnel. She became frightened as the tunnel-opening became progressively smaller. Schutz viewed this as an analog to the impasse she felt she had reached in her love affair; therefore, while giving her sufficient encouragement to enable her to continue in the fantasy, he refrained from making any specific suggestions as to how to deal with the tunnel, his reasoning being that the more she used her own resources within the fantasy, the more the experience would carry over into her outside living. Despite some panic she broke through the tunnel's narrowest opening. Yet when asked to go through the opening again, she balked. Schutz hypothesized at this point that Jane's breakthrough, while real, had not yet been sufficiently consolidated for her to feel confidence in it. As her guide he urged her to try to go back through the opening, "using any instrument or people that would make the task easier." She fantasized a magic pick, and used it to enlarge the opening. Eventually it was big enough for her to walk through it, back and forth, again and again. She felt joy within the fantasy, and her body actually appeared quite relaxed. At this point the exercise was ended.

Had Schutz wished to introduce a cognitive dimension into the resolution of Jane's difficulty, he could have ventured an interpretation—e.g., "The obstacle in the tunnel represents the way you feel blocked in your life by your lack of education." Because he wasn't completely sure of the validity of this interpretation and also sensed it to be superfluous, he didn't offer it. His implicit assumption seems to be that in Jane's unconscious her mastery of the fantasy-block generalizes to, and eases, areas of her living in which she experiences herself as blocked. This is not an unusual conception; for example, some child therapists encourage a reworking of the child's neurotic solutions by addressing comments to the child's fantasy without indicating the parallel between the fantasy and the child's actual life situation (e.g. the therapist might say "I wonder if the sister-doll wouldn't need the brother-doll so much if she could find some friends of her own"). Like Schutz, they assume that the patient unconsciously applies the fantasy solution to his or her own emotional dynamics.

The guided daydream, which offers a quite representative example of how Schutz uses inner imagery in his work with individual participants, is an alternative to the overt physical activity involved in an Encounter game like "Breaking Out" (see above); here Jane's success in breaking through the tunnel-opening is the fantasy equivalent of a participant's actually succeeding in breaking through the group-circle. Although the activity is in this instance a fantasy, it is experienced by the fantasizer so vividly as to seem real; for Jane, it was as though she had broken through an actual, physical impediment.

According to Schutz, this immediacy makes for greater therapeutic effectiveness than would any verbal, and inevitably rational, discussion of the dynamics behind her troubled love affair.

The Dissolution of Blocks. All of the examples above can be seen as attempts to resolve one kind of block or another: mistrust, which blocks one's way to closer relationships; devaluation of the body, which blocks one's way to a fuller enjoyment of it; feelings of constriction, which block one's way toward a greater sense of expansiveness; and so on. Schutz seems close to Carl Rogers (and to an organismic theorist like Kurt Goldstein—see Chapter 7) in assuming that the fundamental human drive is toward growth, with the result that once blocks are removed the organism will resume the temporarily-interrupted movement toward greater self-realization. Growth does not necessarily continue uninterrupted, and the Encounter participant is always free to seek out future Encounter groups. Indeed, the Encounter model tends to see the Encounter experience as a psychotherapy for normals that is essentially available on a life-long, and periodic, basis. Such a view of therapy is different from that implicit in the psychoanalytic model, where an extended working through phase is devoted to the dissolution of resistances, the hope being that the patient's treatment will eventually be completed, at which time he will become a person who can care for himself and not require any therapy in the future.

Almost all the body-work that Schutz does can be conceptualized within the framework of block-dissolving. Body-tensions may be thought of as blocks against feeling; therefore reducing tension in specific body parts can help to effect emotional release. And certain feelings, like hostility, can serve as blocks against other feelings, like affection. Hence the leader has a hierarchical conception of personality, and is rapidly moving from one level to another; whatever the leader's formal training, intuition and clinical skill are necessary. Block-dissolution is therefore akin to resistance-analysis within the psychoanalytic model and it is more in their treatment approach that these two models are opposed than in their conceptualization of either personality dynamics or the role of the unconscious.

Perhaps the most fundamental way to try to help a person contact body feelings and feelings in general is through a relaxation and deepening of his breathing. Hence Schutz's very first exercise is the Microlab above involving breathing. Another technique involves "unlocking," in which people with shallow breathing and cramped closed-in postures (which can symbolize resistances against interpersonal contact) are encouraged to uncross their arms and/or legs and to breathe deeply. These are relatively "quick" techniques which are aimed at blocks closer to the surface of the personality. Similar techniques involve screaming, pounding, and pillow-beating.

The Energy Cycle. This is a concept that is partly derived from George Herbert Mead (1938) and is closely related to Schutz's emphasis on both the blocking, and the discharge, of tension. As a need is activated, energy is mobilized, and it begins to flow into muscle fibers. If a person's energy has been adequately discharged, he is left in a relaxed state; if not, it might express itself in various signs of chronic tension or nervous activity like headaches, clenched jaws, tapping fingers, etc.

Schutz uses this concept in describing how the group leader should make his decision as to which individuals and group issues are most in need of attention at any given moment. He encourages the Encounter leader to sense where in the group energy is strongest, and to avoid going after issues and feelings that are likely to turn out to be relatively superficial and lifeless. For example, the leader should hesitate before focusing on a participant who seems relaxed, since the latter at such a moment is unlikely to be experiencing very strong feelings. If the leader turns his attention toward someone who seems tense and constricted, he might try to activate more energy within the latter before beginning intensive work (usually through some of the block-dissolving techniques cited above, like breathing and unlocking exercises). And just as the leader must know when an energy cycle is ready to begin, he must be able to sense at what point it is about to reach closure, so that he does not linger over an emotional experience after it has begun to wane.

The Inclusion-Control-Affection Trichotomy. This concept is derived from Schutz's own interpersonal relations schema, which is based on his earlier research intergrating personality dynamics with group dynamics (Schutz, 1958). Called the Fundamental Interpersonal Relations Orientation (FIRO), this conception cites three fundamental issues that are predominant in human relatedness: inclusion, control, and affection. While these concepts are applicable to personality dynamics (for example, people might be characterized in terms of which of these three issues is most salient in their emotional living), they also can be applied to group-dynamics in that any particular interaction-segment might have one of these interpersonal orientations as its central emotional dynamic.

The first dimension, inclusion, is perhaps the most fundamental and primitive in that it involves feelings of acceptance from others, and from the world-at-large. In this sense it resembles Erik Erikson's conception of basic trust (Erikson, 1964) as the first crisis in human life, and Freud's concept of orality, which emphasized feelings of being loved and cared for. If we apply it to the Encounter group, inclusion touches on the question of the extent to which any particular participant feels that he is either "in" the group or "out" of it. Exercises requiring him to "break into" a circle formed by the group attempt to highlight this dimension.

The second interpersonal issue is control; it is related to Erikson's concept of autonomy and Freud's of anality. Issues predominating here involve power and authority. In the Encounter group this orientation focuses on competition for leadership and dominance within the group. Specific exercises that serve to highlight it involve competitive games, like pushing or wrestling, and "Dominance," in which participants are directed to form a line reflecting what they believe to be their order of dominance within the group. The key question here is: Am I on top or botton?

The final issue involves affection, and corresponds to Erikson's conception of intimacy and Freud's of genitality. As participants become enmeshed in this issue, the group as a whole recedes in importance, and concerns involving pairing and specific dyads become prominent. Who loves whom? is the central question, and heterosexual attraction within the group epitomizes this dimension. Exercises that are aimed at reflecting it involve pairings, dyadic communication, and the "High School Dance" (Schutz, 1971, pp. 134-135), in which a large group of people are asked to select partners for a dance. The key question for each participant is: To whom do I feel close, and from whom do I feel distant? Affection and inclusion are naturally related, since both emphasize love; however, affection is a somewhat more mature dimension since it involves giving, as well as receiving, and is more discriminating as to who is loved.

Schutz believes that as a group progresses in time, it moves from an initial concern with inclusion, to a focus on control, and finally to affection. Sensing which of the three issues is predominant at any particular point can help the leader determine what particular intervention would be most facilitative. For instance, if he senses that the men are competing for the three most attractive women in the group, he might wish to select an exercise that forces the latent competition among them to surface. By highlighting this problem, he would also enable himself to concomitantly gain access to whatever competitive feelings that exist among the women as to which of them are considered attractive by the men. Similarly, during the earlier stages of the interaction he would need to be on the alert for those participants who seem to feel not yet included within the slowly coalescing group.

ROLE OF THE LEADER

As with most other group models, the Open Encounter leader is most meaningfully viewed as a catalytic agent who helps to facilitate the group interaction. However, because of the somewhat looser format of Open Encounter, the leader has an unusual degree of freedom with regard to the kinds of methods he can use and the kinds of issues he may pursue. For example, while the group psychoanalyst almost always relies on verbal and discursive forms of communication, the Open Encounter leader feels free to introduce Psychodrama, Gestalt, and body movement exercises at those points where he believes they might help to facilitate either interpersonal communication or individual catharsis. While the Tavistock leader confines his interventions to those that highlight what the group is doing as a group, the Encounter leader may make comments that are addressed to either a single individual or the group as a whole. And while the T-group trainer strives, when dealing with a single individual, to avoid focusing on the latter's unconscious processes, the Encounter leader is not at all reluctant to do so.

In Schutz's conception of the leadership role, as in Rogers (see above), the leader does best not to make the group consciously aware of those forces that either promote or impede its cohesion, but instead tries to guide these forces in such a way as to make for a very close and trusting atmosphere. Rather than teaching the participant about group-dynamics in any kind of conceptual way, he tries—through an emphasis on trust, openness, and an exposure of his own painful experiences in the group—to produce on a feeling level a very strong sense of closeness and group cohesion. According to Schutz, once defenses are penetrated, the similarities among group-members become much more marked than their differences. The resultant sense of communality helps participants to realize that in a fundamental sense they are more alike than they are unalike, and can give an almost mystical feeling of unity to the group experience.

In this context the individual and the group reciprocally interact, with genuine catharses on the part of particular members serving to increase the group's cohesion, and increased feelings of group closeness in turn helping each participant to reach a higher emotional peak and to feel more emboldened to reveal himself. In this framework, then, group cohesion is to a great degree a by-product of the leader's skill in helping individual participants to become aware of, and to express, their tensions. However, a knowledge of group-dynamics theory can clearly be of help to the leader. For instance, an understanding of Schutz's inclusion-control-affection trichotomy can aid him in gaining a more secure grasp on the successive stages through which the group as a whole is passing, and also on those issues that are paramount for most participants as time moves on; for example, early in the group the average member is concerned with whether or not he is accepted in a global sense, and it is only later that particular liaisons and rivalries begin to become a specific focus of his interest.

In deciding whom in the group to approach, the leader should be alert to those individuals and those dyads where energy is most mobile (see "The Energy Cycle" above). Once he has determined with whom to work, his skill lies in sensing what emotional issues to concentrate on and in selecting those methods that will most facilitate his work; here the talents and intuitions of the experienced psychotherapist are probably most relevant. Wherever possible, the Open Encounter leader strives to have core emotional issues expressed via the body; hence affection becomes translated into touching and holding, hostility into shoving and pushing, possessiveness into clutching, and so on. Personal qualities in the leader that doubtless are of considerable help in enabling him to make these kinds of moment-to-moment interventions are self-trust, imaginativeness, and flexibility.

The Open Encounter leader encourages each participant to share with the group those current problems and concerns that have led him to seek out an intensive group experience. However, he endeavors to respect the member's right not to participate and also emphasizes each person's responsibility for himself when it comes to critical decisions regarding interpersonal confrontation and physical expressiveness. Although setting some (usually implicit) limits on the destruction of physical property, the leader tries to leave it to the participants themselves to determine how much they can take in terms of verbal and physical confrontation. Once group cohesion has started to develop, the leader typically can trust other members to intervene in those situations where two fighting protagonists go beyond the constraints he has placed on them—e.g., move from wrestling to no-holds-barred, face-smashing combat. In general, he prefers that the group, wherever possible, monitor its own behavior.

In summary, the Open Encounter leader attempts to provide an intensive emotional experience for as many participants as possible. In doing so, he is careful to remind the members that they have the main responsibility in trying to gain something for—and to protect—themselves. He does not make a precise distinction between personal growth and psychotherapy, and instead trusts the member's autonomous capacity to either disregard the experience or to use it for further growth—either through his own efforts or through the help of future Encounter and/or therapy experiences.

MINTZ'S MARATHON ENCOUNTER

Schutz's Open Encounter model synthesized the original T-laboratory model, Reichian therapy, and the increasingly humanistic spirit represented by Esalen into a unique amalgam that was distinctly his own. Yet despite this uniqueness the Open Encounter model typified Encounter as a philosophy of life in that it consciously went beyond an approach to group-leading and advocated a style of interpersonal relations and of human organization that could help to offset the negative effects of bureaucratic impersonality. Indeed, in setting forth his ideas, Schutz (1971, e.g., see pp. 266-273) went so far as to indicate what its specific applications to business, education, domestic politics, and international negotiations might be. On the other hand, Encounter methods can be approached from a more specifically technical (and perhaps more conservative) point of view in that they offer seemingly powerful tools for penetrating a patient's defenses. Hence there is no reason why Encounter, as a *technique* cannot be adapted to the ongoing practice of a psychoanalytically-oriented psychotherapist. Mintz's Marathon Encounter model is prototypical of such an approach.

Elizabeth Mintz is a clinical psychologist who was trained as a psycho-analyst at the National Psychological Association for Psychoanalysis in New York City. As a practitioner of both individual and group therapy, she soon found herself somewhat impatient with the classical concept of the therapist as a "blank screen"; albeit reluctant to adopt a wholesale experientialism wherein she was willing to share all of her feelings with a patient, she felt that the expression of warmth and spontaneous interest—and even boredom in selected instances—toward a patient could have a facilitative effect on the treatment process. Furthermore, this absence of impersonality, far from discouraging the development of transference, in many cases seemed to hasten its emergence. She also claimed, again contrary to the tenets of classical psychoanalytic method, that physical contact with the patient, if judiciously timed, could have extremely beneficial effects. Two further developments in the 1960s hastened what Mintz describes as her "path toward Marathons" (Mintz, 1971, pp. 24-46): her participation in some of Fritz Perls' Gestalt-therapy workshops and an experience in a marathon led by Stoller and Bach. Particularly moved by her participation in the Stoller and Bach West Coast Marathon, she returned to New York City from California determined to lead some similar intensive weekends herself. Now, a decade later, she is still enthusiastic about the therapeutic potential of the Marathon-Encounter.

Although sometimes conducting larger workshops in a country setting, Mintz usually holds marathons in New York City. Starting at noon on Saturday and ending around five o'clock on Sunday afternoon, the group, consisting of roughly twelve people, breaks up late on Saturday night for approximately eight hours; members arrange sleeping accommodations on their own and resume for the second session Sunday morning. Participants come from a variety of sources. Many are referred by other therapists with whom the participants are in treatment; others are referred by Mintz's own patients or by former marathon participants; still others are present or past patients of Mintz herself. If a participant applies who has no clearcut referral, Mintz suggests having a brief interview or a longer phone conversation with the person for screening purposes, her main concern being a weeding out of sensation-seeking and psychotically fragile individuals.

Despite the fact that prior therapy is not a prerequisite to admission, the majority of participants in any single marathon either have had, or are currently in, psychotherapy, some with Mintz herself, others with colleagues. Some of the participants have been in earlier marathons. Others may have had individual therapy, but are curious to find out what group therapy is like; still others may have had no treatment, but are considering the possibility of treatment. Hence the composition of the marathon is such that it is viewed by many of its participants as an adjunct or possible precursor to their personal psychotherapy, and should they want to see Mintz either for some follow-up sessions or for ongoing treatment, she would be available to them since she resides in the same general geographical area.

Like Schutz, Mintz is impressed with the extent to which particular Encounter techniques can facilitate the release of feelings, especially childhood feelings that the participant has long since dissociated. One of her favorite motoric techniques, for example, involves the hand-press, which she usually combines with a psychodrama improvisation. The person is asked to close his eyes and to exert his full strength on Mintz's clasped hands. After gathering information from him concerning how his mother addressed him and the style of her speech, she tries to reproduce his mother's way of talking to him as closely as possible and then says: "Now say to your mother whatever it was you always wanted to say and never did." The specific mechanical advantage of hand-press is that it permits the squeezer to exert an enormous amount of pressure on the symbolic mother's hands, provided that they are properly clasped. If he exerts his maximum strength there is often a release of strong emotion, usually involving helpless rage. The participant, having been encouraged to remember how he used to talk to and address his mother, often speaks in a more simple and childlike manner. A very common result of the exercise is a strong sense of relief, which is sometimes accompanied by a wish for physical contact—like an embrace—with the symbolic mother.

The exercise above is fairly typical of what Mintz aims for, since it involves three specific psychological elements: a catharsis, a reparative regression—however brief—in which the participant briefly and symbolically relives a childhood experience in a more wholesome way (in this instance his rage, rather than being disapproved, is accepted), and an opportunity for cognitive integration, since the person has some opportunity to discuss the meaning of this experience once it is over and he has regained his adult perspective. Although such a regression cannot be effected in every instance, the leader should, according to this model, be ever-alert to opportunities to initiate one. This kind of therapeutic regression constitutes, for Mintz, one of the major opportunities provided by the marathon environment; since it requires a considerable amount of time it cannot be accomplished during the hour-and-a-half provided by the conventional therapy group. Emphasis on affective and cognitive components are fairly balanced in the Mintz model. She believes that Encounter techniques can facilitate deeper levels of feeling than is normally possible in the relatively verbal atmosphere of psychoanalytically-oriented psychotherapy; yet she also recognizes the importance of cognitive interpretation as an aid to helping the participant to fully integrate the experience and to use it as a source of inspiration and insight in his subsequent living. While the regression can be facilitated in a variety of ways, psychodramatic procedures are probably most often employed in this connection. For example, Mintz again playing the symbolic mother, once encouraged femininity in a participant-daughter by taking the latter on a fantasy shopping spree, an opportunity that the participant was forever deprived of by her real mother. For mother-bound men she has sometimes played the "good" Oedipal mother who gives them permission to find another woman to whom they can totally commit themselves.

One very striking example of a therapeutically-induced regression involved Saul, (Mintz, 1971, pp. 87-93) a professional man who, although considerably helped by conventional psychotherapy, still felt traumatized and damaged—both physically and psychologically—by an extraordinarily painful mastoid operation that he had suffered as a child; because of other physical complications, it had not been possible to administer any anesthetic. Strapped to the operating table for a period of two-and-a-half hours and given absolutely no comfort, the six-year-old boy had screamed until he was hoarse to the point of voicelessness and at times lost consciousness. Two distinct sequelae to this experience, both of which became clear in the Encounter, were (1) a fantasy that the surgeon had wanted to destroy him, and (2) a sense that he had perhaps imagined or somehow exaggerated the extremity of the experience, since it had never been referred to again—either by the doctors and nurses, who said nothing about it afterwards, or by his parents, who had not been informed of the extraordinary pain involved in their son's surgery.

Saul's regression in the Encounter was geared toward enabling him to live this experience in a less helpless way. One clearcut residue of this experience had been a phobic attitude that he had toward the possibility of accidental physical pressure on the mastoid area. Therefore the therapist encouraged him to allow each person of the group to touch this area—but only when and if he wanted them to—thereby putting him in control of the situation. Other elements involved his playing of the role of the surgeon, threatening to mercilessly kill the fellow-participant who played himself as a young boy, again giving him a sense of mastery, since *he* was now the aggressor, someone else the helpless victim. The group was consistently called in to furnish the atmosphere of comfort and security that had originally been absent during this experience. At one point he was "rocked" by the group, (see "Roll and Rock" in the Schutz Microlab above), and at another he was joined in pounding the couch (as a means of venting fully his fury against his remembered tormentors) by another participant who also had reason to be angry with physicians. One very important function of the group, as Saul expressed it at a later time, was to "bear witness to" and to share—thereby making more real—an experience that until then had remained private in an emotional sense.

As can be gleaned from the above account, other participants often take roles in the center protagonist's Psychodrama. Sometimes this can happen in a uniquely fortuitous way, with the result that the auxiliary player is enacting a role that has a particular significance for his own life, thereby increasing his involvement in the protagonist's problem and simultaneously expressing aspects of his own (as was the case with Mary when she role-played Mike's mother in the illustrative session at the beginning of the chapter). The improvisation of psychodramatic scenarios gives the group members a unique role in Mintz's Marathon-Encounter model. Not only can they play various dramatic roles, but ideas for various symbolic reenactments can come from the group, which might then function as mourners at an improvised funeral, as an audience to a graduation speech, as guests at a wedding, and so on. At such times, the group atmosphere takes on strong elements of collaboration and ingenuity, and, despite a strong sense of shared pain, playfulness and humor also emerge. According to Mintz, this spirit of support and empathy characterizes the final stage of the Marathon-Encounter. The average participant, after an initial period of apprehension and "role-playing" that is followed in turn by hostility and defensiveness, gradually begins to reveal himself in a climate that he experiences as accepting. Mintz's description of this stage is highly reminiscent of the communality and feeling of unity emphasized by Schutz. In Mintz's conceptualization, the group "takes the heat" off the leader by providing a relatively benign and nonsymbiotic transference figure, thereby promoting a reintegrative process wherein the patient can "come out of" his regression fairly easily. The group is able to do this by virtue of consisting of many people, thereby diluting the intensity of what would be a one-to-one attachment in individual psychotherapy, and by having built-in limits on the amount of nurturance it is willing to give, since each participant has his own needs to pursue in the Encounter. Two factors, then—the opportunity for a prolonged amount of time in which to work and the presence of a supportive group—render the Marathon-Encounter a uniquely suitable format for the encouragement of reparative regression. While earlier Marathon leaders attested to the potentially therapeutic function of other participants, Mintz's model goes further than others in this direction, especially since members are encouraged to both introduce, and play a role in, the various Encounter techniques.

Mintz acknowledges that regression can render a patient vulnerable, and therefore emphasizes the importance of three safeguards in this procedure. The first is that the participant voluntarily enter the experience; the second is that there be some figure available to offer him support via a symbolic relationship; the third is that the situation permit a full working-through of the experience. As indicated above, the reintegration should include the opportunity for the patient to "return to reality" in the sense that he will, in the presence of the leader and the group, reflect on the experience and attempt to conceptualize it. It is the opportunity to relive the childhood experience *in a somewhat different way* that makes the regression reparative. The concept of the reparative regression is probably the single most innovative feature of this Encounter model; concomitant with it is a particular adaptation of Psychodrama wherein another person, usually the leader, portrays a "good" parent figure much as the child would have liked him or her to be in the past.

As has probably been evident, Mintz consistently employs a psychoanalytic framework when conceptualizing for herself what is transpiring in the group. For example, her work with Saul, mentioned above, involved a deductive use of psychoanalytic theory wherein she applied general principles—e.g., "identification with the aggressor" (A. Freud, 1946) as a positive step toward mastery—to her selection of those specific Encounter exercises that would be most helpful to him. No other Encounter proponent has so consistently adhered to a psychoanalytic formulation of how specific Encounter techniques effect change. For Mintz, the special valve of Encounter techniques is their frequent ability to penetrate defenses with greater potency than more traditional analytic methods.

ENCOUNTER GROUNDRULES

Unlike most of the other group-models, the Encounter model has some explicit and implicit ground rules which most of the leaders included in this chapter have specified in their writing. Not all of these "rules" are necessarily stated to the group; a few might be mentioned when they become relevant to the group interaction, and others might remain implicit. Schutz (1971) lists the most groundrules in his writing, Mintz mentions relatively few, and Rogers none (his reluctance to specify what is and is not allowed to happen seems consistent with his preference for an extremely open and nonstructured situation). Bach (1966) developed what he referred to as the Marathon "ten commandments"; therefore it can be assumed that these rules were generally subscribed to by his colleague, Fred Stoller. The main points covered by these rules appear below. The initials following each statement indicate which of the three leaders involved—Bach (B), Mintz (M), and Schutz (S)—mention that particular rule or principle in his written exposition of his procedures.

1. The group is to stay together and not leave until the prearranged time: don't form subgroups. (B., M., & S.)
2. Be as honest as possible; level with people—don't give advice and/or maudlin comfort. (B., M., & S.)
3. Stay in the here-and-now; don't "narrate" your life story. (B., M., & S.)
4. Emphasize feelings over ideas. (B. & S.)
5. You have the primary responsibility for getting from the session what you want. (B. & S.)
6. Try to do the thing you are most afraid of doing. (B. & S.)
7. Keep everything that transpires here completely confidential (B. & M.)
8. Talk directly to the person whom you are addressing. (B. & M.)
9. Aspirin is discouraged; it's better to try to explore the feelings and conflicts underlying your headaches. (M. & S.)
10. Smoking is discouraged; food and coffee are forbidden. (S.)
11. Give the statements underlying your questions and the feelings underlying your "I don't know's"; substitute "I won't" for "I can't." (S.)
12. Sit and stand in a position where you have easy physical access to others and they have access to you. (S.)
13. Whenever you can, express yourself physically as opposed to verbally. (S.)
14. If a fight occurs, protect the fighters from walls and hard objects. (S.)
15. Try to be tolerant of nudity when it is relevant to themes concerning one's image of and acceptance of his body. (S.)
16. Confine your attacks to words only. (B.)
17. Special techniques are to be used only sparingly. (B.)

RECAPITULATION

In the present chapter, we have reviewed how the models presented in the previous chapters, and the T-group in particular, paved the way for Schutz's Open Encounter, which we see as pulling together and epitomizing the various strands of both theory and method that comprise the overall spirit of Encounter. In tracing these developments, we described three earlier Encounter models: Rogers' Basic Encounter, Stoller and Back's Marathon Encounter, and the Synanon small group. We concluded with Mintz's version of the Marathon Encounter because it demonstrates the extent to which at least one Encounter approach systematically employs traditional Freudian concepts involving therapeutic regression, emotional reparation, and catharsis.

In view of Encounter's incorporation of both psychotherapeutic and sensitivity-training goals, the inherent looseness of its format, and the diversity of its techniques (which include methods originated by other models, like Psychodrama and Gestalt), it is inevitable that the term Encounter encompass a broad panoply of approaches and styles. As we see it, the majority of sensitivity-training groups existing at the present time fall within the Encounter framework. The more a particular group (1) bypasses the T-group model's emphasis on a group-dynamics orientation and instead focuses on personal growth, (2) is willing to include psychotherapy as one of its goals, and (3) emphasizes nonverbal and physical action techniques, the closer it approximates a pure Encounter model.

References

Bach, G. R. 1966. The marathon group: intensive practice of intimate interaction. *Psychological Reports, 18.* 995-1002.
———. 1967. Marathon group dynamics: I. some functions of the professional group facilitator. *Psychological Reports, 20.* 995-999.
Back, K. W. 1972. *Beyond words: the story of sensitivity training and encounter movement.* New York: Russell Sage Foundation.
Bindrim, P. 1968. A report on a nude marathon. *Psychotherapy: Theory, Research, and Practice, 5.* 180-188.
Casriel, D. 1963. *So fair a house: the story of Synanon.* Englewood Cliffs, N.J: Prentice-Hall.
Erikson, E. H. 1964. *Childhood and society.* 2nd ed. New York: W. W. Norton & Company.
Freud, A. 1946. *The ego and the mechanisms of defense.* New York: International Universities Press.
Henry, J. 1963. *Culture against man.* New York: Random House.
Lowen, A. 1967. *Betrayal of the body.* New York: Macmillan.

Mead, G. H. 1938. *The philosophy of the act.* Chicago: The University of Chicago Press.

Mintz, E. E. 1971. *Marathon groups: reality and symbol.* New York: Appleton-Century-Crofts.

Reich, C. A. 1970. *The greening of America.* New York: Random House.

Reich, W. 1949. *Character analysis.* New York: Orgone Institute Press.

Rogers, C. R. 1951. *Client-centered therapy.* Boston: Houghton-Mifflin.

——. 1967. The process of the basic encounter group. In J. F. T. Bugenthal, ed. *Challenges of humanistic psychology.* New York: McGraw-Hill.

——. 1970. *Carl Rogers on encounter groups.* New York: Harper and Row.

Roszak, T. 1969. *The making of a counter culture.* Garden City, N.Y: Doubleday.

Schutz, W. C. 1958. *FIRO: A three-dimensional theory of interpersonal behavior.* New York: Holt, Rinehart & Winston.

——. 1971. *Here comes everybody.* New York: Harper & Row.

Stoller, F. H. 1972. Marathon groups: toward a conceptual model. In L. N. Solomon and B. Berzon, eds. *New perspectives on encounter groups.* San Francisco: Jossey-Bass.

Yablonsky, L. 1965. *The tunnel back: Synanon.* New York: Macmillan.

12

The Theme-centered
Interactional Method

The Theme-centered model, as its name implies, has as one of its major innovations the setting of a clearcut theme that is kept in the forefront of a group's awareness with reasonable consistency and noncoerciveness on the part of its leader. This theme may be quite personal; in such instances the group might resemble sensitivity-training groups, though in a theme-centered format the theme would be explicitly stated—e.g., "Letting the 'Real Me' Show Through." In other instances the theme may be relatively impersonal, as in traditional community groups formed around a specific task or learning purpose, such as committees, staffs, seminars, and academic classes; here the theme might be: "Understanding *Huckleberry Finn*" or "Planning Next Year's Curriculum." However, a Theme-centered approach to these latter themes, unlike more conventional orientations, regards digressions from the overt theme as appropriate and even desirable. The leader aims for an optimum, rather than maximum, amount of theme-centeredness, and consequently may at times encourage a group to pursue issues that go beyond the theme, particularly if the discussion up until then has been so theme-focused as to have excluded an expression of the participants' more personal reactions—to their theme or task, to the leader, to one another, and to what has occurred during the session thus far. Especially relevant would be distractions to the theme, as when a participant finds himself too preoccupied with other concerns to listen, and resistances to the theme, as when a student has not done the assignment or feels no interest in the lesson at hand. What the Theme-centered format brings to sensitivity-training contexts, then, is a more structured approach wherein the leader more sharply defines and delimits the group's learning goals by means of a specific theme. What it introduces to task and education groups is a more psychologically-aware and humanistic orientation in which goals and purposes are pursued in a more open, communicative, and enlivened atmosphere.

The present model was primarily inspired by Ruth C. Cohn, a European-born psychoanalyst and group psychotherapist. Having fled Germany in the thirties, she had initially been trained at the Zurich Psychoanalytic Institute. Following her emigration to the United States in 1941, she began private practice in Englewood, New Jersey, and became a supervising analyst at the National Psychological Association for Psychoanalysis. It was in the context of a supervision group for psychotherapists that Cohn first began to practice the approach that was later to evolve into the Theme-centered method. Called a Countertransference workshop, this group was geared toward helping therapists become more aware of how the unresolved aspects of their own conflicts and feelings interfered with their usefulness to their patients; what quickly became apparent was the frequency with which a student's personal difficulties with a patient became in some manner reflected or reenacted in his behavior within the group. For example, in one instance a presenting therapist's inability to recognize the rebellion and anger implicit in his presented patient's nonpayment of fees was paralleled in the workshop by his difficulty in perceiving that he and a coparticipant, by getting into a discussion of the case before he had completed its initial presentation, were rebelling against the workshop structure and the leader's authority (Cohn, 1969, p. 260). Since the workshop's theme was countertransference, what we see in this example is a dovetailing of the theme (in this particular case the therapist's need to promote his rebellious patient's acting-out) with a specific interactional dynamic (the therapist's struggle against the authority of the workshop structure and the leader).

Cohn gradually began to see her task as that of keeping the workshop's focus evenly balanced between the countertransference theme and the emotional interaction of the participants. These two motifs, rather than being separate or independent aspects of the group process, were turning out to be interdependent, dynamically-related forces. She, as leader, was "hitting pay dirt," so to speak, when she could find a point of direct contact between a workshop's theme and an immediate event in the group that highlighted and illuminated it. While this kind of intermeshing was doubtless more likely when themes were of an emotional and interpersonal nature, as in the countertransference workshop, she began to wonder if the imaginative leader could not find similar points of contact in task and classroom groups if only he were willing to see the "theme" in its broader implications. For example, the history class has a common history as a group, the literature seminar reading a poem on loss might recently have lost one of its members, and the task group attempting to solve the organizational problems of its company might find itself facing not too dissimilar organizational problems within its own structure. If the theme-and-interactional dynamic initially developed in the supervisory workshop could be applied to these other kinds of groups, Cohn would be succeeding in an effort that she had begun to think about many years earlier, i.e., to bridge the gap between the psychoanalytic couch and the community (Cohn, 1969) by finding educational and organizational applications for the dynamic psychological methods that, while potent in their ability to treat individual neuroses, seemed terribly impotent with regard to effecting any change in collective ills.

The next application of this gradually-evolving model, and one that began to put to the test the question just raised, was to an industrial situation; Cohn was asked to tackle some of the organizational problems confronting a rather large company (1969, pp. 261-262). What had been hoped for emerged—the group process at times reflected in bold relief tensions and conflicts within the larger administrative structure, and so the theme and interaction dialectic of the countertransference workshop proved transferable to another setting. In this instance the theme, "Management Relations," slowly grew out of the workshop as it met over several sessions, rather than being formally stated at its inception. It became evident after a while, though, that it would be better to state a theme clearly at a workshop's outset, since it usually exercised a subtle, albeit strong, influence on the participants' initial set and on their subsequent orientation. Therefore a milestone of sorts was reached in a weekend workshop sponsored by the Los Angeles Society for Clinical Psychologists in 1963 when for the first time a noncountertransference theme was explicitly stated in advance—"Training in Emotional Skill" (Cohn, 1969, p. 264).

Cohn was slowly discovering that the thematic aspect of her approach provided an exceptional degree of versatility, since the number of possible themes that could be set for a wide variety of groups having specialized interests was virtually unlimited: psychotherapists might find themselves interested in "Freedom and Control in the Psychotherapy Relationship," parents in "The Teenage Drug Culture," writers in "Freeing Creativity," teachers in "Living Learning vs. Dead Learning," and so on. Principles and procedures that had evolved through an inductive, trial-and-error phase were now sufficiently experience-tested to be codified into a tentative "model," which could in turn be taught to leaders-in-training. For example, Cohn and her colleagues found that a workshop proceeded best if a leader first opened it with a formal statement of its theme and then encouraged a few minutes of silence, during which participants would have an opportunity, through guiding questions and directions from him, to come into deeper contact with the theme both intellectually and emotionally (1969, p. 265). "Ground rules" were developed that, while not coercive, provided a framework which helped members to relate to one another as autonomously and fully as possible. In addition, certain balancing principles were built into the model. Leaders were kept mindful of the need to keep both thematic and interactional motifs in proper balance so that neither was focused on to a degree that proved detrimental to the other; similar balances were to be established between a concentration on cognition and on feeling in the group, on intrapsychic awareness and on interpersonal awareness, on the here-and-now of the group and on the there-and-then of the outside world. And so the model was born.

In 1966 an organization devoted to the teaching and implementation of the Theme-centered interactional method was founded. Called the Workshop Institute for Living-Learning (W.I.L.L.), it was established in New York City; within the next several years branches were started in Atlanta, Georgia in Pittsburgh, Pennsylvania, and Basel, Switzerland. The Institute offers an ongoing training program for professional and community group leaders, organizes weekend workshops for both professionals and the general public, and consults with community groups and agencies to help them develop appropriate workshops within their indigenous settings.

Although Theme-centered workshops are almost always time-limited, the time involved may range anywhere from a single afternoon to an entire semester; the latter might be the case in a classroom or in a course given by the Workshop Institute for Living-Learning. Where something akin to a course or seminar is involved, an overall theme is given to the seminar and specific subthemes are set for each session. While the overall theme is normally determined ahead of time by the educational objective, subthemes can be flexible and need not be determined by the leader alone. He may invite the participants to join him in a consideration of possible themes; indeed, "Choosing Future Themes" might in itself constitute an appropriate subtheme for one or two sessions. Some workshop settings may be relatively open-ended, with members leaving and joining; the countertransference workshop would be an example of such a group. And some psychotherapists are experimenting with an application of Theme-centered methodology to group therapy, in which the therapist sets themes, either beforehand or spontaneously, in accordance with the predominant mood or concerns of the group.

ILLUSTRATION OF A TYPICAL SESSION

In order to give a feeling for what a segment of a typical theme-centered session might be like, we will take as an example a workshop for psychotherapists with the theme of "Freedom and Control in the Psychotherapy Relationship."

Let us say that a young psychologist Bob, in the context of what has been a relatively intellectual discussion about the concept of freedom, has begun to talk about his relationship to one of his female patients, Sylvia, because he wonders whether some of the limits that he has been trying to set for her—which could be viewed, said Bob, as attempts to constrain her freedom—have really been very effective. Sylvia, a highly labile woman with a severe character disorder, had made some dangerous suicidal gestures in the past month. Bob had strongly encouraged her to "talk out" rather than act out her feelings of depression and desperation, and emphasized his availability to her, at least by telephone, at all times. When Sylvia made a subsequent suicide attempt Bob told her that if this happened again hospitalization would probably be necessary. He had hoped that her shaky sense of self-control might be buttressed by his firmness. Yet Sylvia had become angry, and when she provocatively asked what would happen if she refused to agree to be hospitalized, Bob had surprised himself by replying, "Then I won't be able to treat you."

Bob had not yet gotten to the denouement of this situation when he was interrupted by Alice, who upon hearing about Sylvia's behavior had immediately begun to mention Sylvia's marked similarity to one of her own current patients. Bob, who had earlier expressed some discomfort with the theme-centered format, since he was looking for a more formal group-supervision structure, then turned to the leader, Helen, saying in effect: You see what's wrong with these workshops?! There's no rule as to who should speak and when—I like it better when there is a formal case presentation where the therapist first gives all the information and then everybody can discuss it.

At this point the leader asked the rest of the group what they thought about the issue Bob had raised. Joan said that although she didn't want quite that strict a format, she had felt annoyed when Alice inappropriately jumped in. Dorothy said that people should be able to speak whenever they felt like it—after all, wasn't that an advantage a workshop had over a seminar? Jim said: Yes, of course nobody can tell you when you can talk and when you cannot, but there are still rules of common propriety; if everyone felt free to utter his every random thought the result would be chaos. Roger then spoke, saying he was bored with the whole wrangle and wished the group would settle it so he could proceed to discuss a problem that had begun to concern him in relation to his own practice.

The leader said it was her impression that Roger wanted to talk about his problem right away, but was reluctant to speak lest he offend the group, which was struggling to define when it was appropriate to speak and when it wasn't. Roger said it was more simple than that—he didn't want to start talking when he felt that others weren't yet ready to listen. Joan remarked suddenly: You know it's true—the rules here don't give us any guidance as to what to do; they don't even tell us we have to stick with the theme; the funny thing is that Bob wants us to do with Alice what he is trying to do with Sylvia: he wants to make a rule as to when Alice can interrupt, just as he wants to give Sylvia a rule about not acting-out and about following his recommendations for hospitalization.

Bob then answered Joan somewhat heatedly: I can proceed in any way I want; I don't have to—and shouldn't—see a patient who's making me too angry and too uncomfortable to be of help! Dorothy laughed, saying to Roger: I guess that's the paradox of freedom—that you're *free* to control others, or at least to try to control them; but you're reacting to Joan as though she had given you orders as to what procedures to follow with Sylvia and what procedures not to follow; if she did that she'd be attempting the same control with you that you seem to try with Sylvia; I know that *my* feeling is that you make an error in not acknowledging her right to make her own free choice, even the choice to die, but that doesn't mean I'm insisting you follow my advice.

After a brief silence, the leader turned to Alice and told her that she, Helen, had been very aware of her silence. Roger then came in angrily, wondering why Helen had chosen this point to intervene when the group was obviously very much interested in the interchange among Bob, Joan, and Dorothy, which had been left hanging; furthermore, said Roger, Helen was oversolicitous of Alice; if Alice had hurt feelings she could doubtless take care of them herself. Alice then said: No, I have been smarting and feeling foolish and embarrassed; Helen made it easier for me to come in just now when she singled me out. Alice went on to report that she often spoke out at the wrong moment, probably as a means of getting attention, and she suddenly remembered some incidents in early adolescence when her mother had become very angry at her for the very same thing and shared these memories with the group. Alice added that even as a therapist she erred in the direction of overactivity and overintrusion into the patient's stream-of-consciousness.

Roger at this point asked the leader if she had been annoyed when he had criticized her intervention. She reminded him of a ground rule suggesting that participants try to state the thoughts and feelings behind their questions. He replied that she had looked slightly angry to him, and that this made him quite uncomfortable, since he always wanted to feel that people in authority liked him. Helen acknowledged that she had been somewhat irritated by his telling her how she "should" lead the group, and wondered if his comments hadn't reflected an overall group concern, perhaps inspired by the Freedom vs. Control theme, as to how other people should behave: Sylvia should stop her acting out, she as a leader should have both imposed a stricter format on the group and refrained from commenting on Alice's prolonged silence, Alice should not have interrupted, and Bob should not have attempted to set limits on his patient. Bob then smiled and said: That reminds me—I never did get to finish my story about Sylvia and the hospital! This remark produced considerable laughter and appeared to relieve tension in several of the members.

Our formal presentation of the model below will hopefully make clearer those ways in which this segment illustrates certain of its features. The primary methodological principle applied by the leader involved a linking up of the Freedom and Control theme, which nominally applied to the participants' work with patients, to the here-and-now of the group interaction. This could be conceived of as establishing a balance between "content" and "process" (see "The I-We-It Triangle" below). Other kinds of balances were also evident. Some of the material was cognitive, as when Dorothy wondered about what she thought to be an authoritarian attitude on the part of Bob toward his patient; other material was emotional, like the anger of Roger and of Bob, and Alice's hurt feelings. Most of the interaction was focused on the immediate present; yet Alice had mentioned some aspects of her past life.

And although the balance between an in-depth focusing on a specific individual and fluid group interaction favored the latter, Alice had said enough about herself to stand out rather clearly as to the kind of person she was, and Bob had had a chance to discuss specific clinical material in some detail.

KEY CONCEPTS: PHILOSOPHIC

Autonomy and Interdependence. These two concepts are not unique to the model presently under consideration. They have been attended to by psychological theorists, by philosophers, and by humanists for centuries. "Autonomy" refers to the "I-ness" of my experience, and all experiential phenomena relating to self-awareness and selfhood. As the receiver of all sensations emanating to me from the outside world and as a reactor to these sensations (I feel good about what I perceive, or I feel bad about what I perceive), I am at the center of my universe. I, in my awareness of you, am still at the center of my universe, although you are now part of my universe too. I am autonomous with regard to you in that I can choose the kind of relationship with you that I most want and can attempt to implement that desired relationship; you are autonomous in that you have a choice as to whether to accept, reject, or modify my definition of our relationship. Interdependence exists because my autonomy is not sufficient to the satisfaction of all my needs. Without another person or other persons with whom I can be intimate I will feel lonely; without a partner I will not be able to satisfy myself sexually or to procreate. This other person does not have to be you—to the extent to which I feel that *only you* can satisfy my needs, I have exchanged my interdependence for symbiosis. Man is separate, yet connected, and Donne's classic "No man is an island . . . ." remains a most poetic statement of this human connectedness.

Autonomy and interdependence are existential givens that can only be denied at the expense of one's fundamental sense of reality; the person who claims helpless and passive dependence blots out his sense of autonomy, just as the isolated, grandiose paranoid attempts to avoid a sense of interdependence. The Theme-centered interactional model elevates these two concepts to a place of central importance in its theory and practice by making it incumbent upon the leader to promote both the felt autonomy and interdependence of each participant; we say *felt* autonomy and interdependence because they belong to each member, whether he chooses to acknowledge these aspects of his being or not. The model's structure directs the attention of each participant to his own thoughts and feeling-awareness (his autonomy) and to his relatedness to others within the group (his interdependence). How the leader, through certain technical procedures, puts these aspects of the model into operation will be discussed below.

The "I-We-It" Triangle. This aspect of the model, along with the "globe," are conceptualized in visual-spatial terms. A flat, two-dimensional triangle bisecting a three-dimensional sphere is the physical analog of this metaphor. The meaning of the globe will be discussed in the next section.

The three points of the triangle represent the "I," the "We," and the "It" aspects of the group process or interaction. These are essentially constructs or abstractions that subsume particular group data. The "I" encompasses the psychological experience of each person at any one point in time, whether or not this experience is directly expressed. Without a finite number of the "I's" there would be no group. The "We" refers to the interrelationships within the group at any one point in time and to the awareness of the part of at least some participants that they are in a distinct, unique group with its own particular dynamics, interconnections, and concerns. "At any one point in time" is emphasized because the subtle psychological processes encompassed by these concepts are fluid and never fixed. The "We," then, embraces the cohesiveness of the group, and it is via the concept of the "We" that Theme-centered theory integrates group-dynamic concepts. It could also be stated that the "I" aspect of the triangle roughly parallels the concept of autonomy, the "We" aspect, of interdependence.

The "It" point of the triangle refers to the theme, or task, that the group meets to consider. It might be thought that the "It" relates only to Theme-centered groups, where a theme is formally presented for consideration. However, one of the major tenets of the Theme-centered philosophy is that all groups gather with some sort of focus, however implicit, and that the more this focus is explicitly stated and intentionally kept in the forefront of the consciousness of both leader and participant, the more successful will be the group-process and outcome. The implicit theme of a psychotherapy group is: I want to feel and function better, of an Encounter group: I want to get more in touch with the world inside me and the world outside me. The present model's proponents see as one of its major contributions the explicit attention given to both the emotional-experiential-interactional aspects of the group on the one hand (the "I" and the "We"), and to the group's cognitive-task-learning function on the other (the "It"). Traditional groups (e.g., the committee meeting or the classroom) pay too much heed to the overt task without sufficiently encompassing the affective and interpersonal components of the group—e.g., who is angry? bored? excited? In contrast, sensitivity groups give too much attention to the "I" and the "We" aspects of the group without giving enough structure and cognitive attention to the specific learning-agenda of the group. For instance, the T-group model's approach to teaching about group dynamics and interpersonal relations is almost entirely experiential; most trainers explicitly discourage an academic or intellectual formulation of group-dynamic principles in the T-group. On the other hand, a Theme-centered approach to such learning might well entail a leader's introducing some conceptualization into the discussion, but only at a point where the group process had been sufficiently intense and involving for these group-dynamic concepts to be meaningfully understood and integrated. Relevant here is the motto of the Workshop Institute for Living-Learning, "Sensitivity is Not Enough," which was designed to indicate that people, while sensing and feeling, also think, and that self-awareness, albeit important, cannot by itself constitute a solution to the problems confronting today's world. What is also required is the kind of rational planning, political action, and program development that is traditionally encompassed by the concept of "task," and in Theme-centered terms, by the concept of "It."

"Content" is another term that is traditionally applied to what Theme-centered leaders call "It," whereas "process," which is usually contrasted to "content," is embraced by the Theme-centered concepts of "I" and "We." For a certain segment of a group's session its members may find themselves attending to content. For instance, parents of autistic children participating in a workshop with the theme of "Constructively Parenting a Disturbed Child" might talk about the difficult parental situations that they share in common, especially in the early stages of the group; here the "It" or content aspect of the triangle would predominate, though with some attention to the "I" since participants are bound to include at least a few of their personal thoughts and feelings about the problems they face at home. During another segment of the time process, or "We," aspects of the group may become salient, with participants finding themselves in a discussion of what has been transpiring in the group. For example, a female participant might observe that it is the women in the group who have been the talkers; another member might wonder if this is because they, as mothers, feel more fundamentally related to the child, and still another member might suggest that another important factor is the leader's also being a woman. This "We" segment becomes more strongly tinged with an incipient "I" focus at those moments when a participant begins to elaborate on his personal reactions to the group-process. The reader may well wonder when a Theme-centered leader views the group process as focused on the "I" point of the triangle with minimal saturations of either the "We" or the "It." His answer would probably be: whenever an individual, with little overt reference to either the theme or the other people in the group, talks about aspects of his life outside the group—his past, his work, his problems, etc.

Usually content and process will coincide at several points within the group interaction; these connections involve the dovetailing of thematic and interactional motifs described at the beginning of the chapter. Let us say that in the parent-group mentioned above Lorraine describes herself as overly protective with her child. Ralph then points out to her that she tends to play the same mother-hen role in the group; several other participants agree, and one of them, Cynthia, states that this behavior tends to irritate her. At this

point Lorraine begins to talk about her chronic anxiety, which usually manifests itself in a compulsive concern with the welfare of others. In this segment
of the group scenario we have an intersecting of "I" (Lorraine and her
anxious feelings), of "We" (the other members are giving her feedback as to
her role-behavior in the group and the feelings that this behavior engenders in
them), and of "It" (Lorraine's overly anxious treatment of her child was also
briefly in focus).

The "I," "We," and "It" are not all-or-none phenomena; they must
always be a matter of more or less. For instance, at a point where a mother in
the example above talks about the problems faced by all parents of autistic
children she is being relatively abstract and is therefore centered on the "It";
nevertheless her statements are inevitably tinged with an "I" aspect since it is
her statement and *her* thought. At the point where she expresses her deeper
feelings about her particular situation and her child, the "I" focus becomes
larger and tends to balance the "It." At a point where she leaves the theme
altogether and discusses an experience she had on the way to the workshop
that upset her, the "I" focus becomes even larger, while the "It" begins to
diminish. If, after a few minutes, another person interrupts her in order to
express some of his feeling response to her, the "We" focus, which has thus
far remained dormant, starts to enlarge. In attempting to explain these triangle
points we have found ourselves envisaging them as three spotlights reflected
through a lens-diaphragm; they may expand and they may contract to a mere
pinpoint of light, but they never completely go out.

The "Globe." The globe is an extremely inclusive concept, for it encompasses
all aspects of the environment in which the workshop takes place, especially
those that are likely to impinge on a participant's awareness. This includes the
immediate physical environment, the workshop's location, its schedule, the
circumstances surrounding its development, its perceived purpose and rationale, and the extent to which members have had prior contact or acquaintance with one another. The globe may also include more remote national and
international issues, so long as these are in some way a matter of concern to
the group.

The leader needs to be especially alert to those aspects of the globe that
may be in some way discomfitting or confusing to the participants; these are
the factors that will have to be dealt with explicitly in the workshop. If a
serious international crisis has developed the day before the workshop, this
fact cannot be ignored. Sometimes there are extreme physical factors that
affect the globe, e.g., a breakdown in air-conditioning on a hot summer day.
Typically it is more immediate elements, such as the participants' goals and
expectations, that become salient aspects of the globe. For example, the
participants may be coworkers on the same job who feel that there has been
some subtle coercion to join the workshop on the part of their supervisor,

even though their entrance into the workshop was supposed to be a matter of free choice. These circumstances do not have to be changed for the workshop to be successful, but it is important that the leader know about them so that he can help the participants to reveal some of their apprehensions, suspicions, and resentments. In some instances the straightforward presentation of relevant information on the part of the leader can go a long way toward "clearing" the emotional atmosphere. In a workshop where participants are coworkers, the leader's explicit statement that he will not give any information as to its proceedings to their supervisor might prove helpful.

Globe factors involving possible feuds, hierarchical constellations, sub-factions, and contrary purposes within the group become especially crucial. Such situations are especially likely when the leader is an outsider coming into an ongoing agency and/or institutional setting. Whose decision was it that the workshop be held? If it was an administrator's, to what extent has the latter consulted participants as to their feelings about the workshop and been reasonably frank as to his own expectations? To become aware of such factors the leader must do a fairly intensive amount of investigation and information-gathering before the workshop proper. There are no guidelines as to what he does with regard to any or all of these global features. Again, his awareness is all; being aware, he can help participants to contact and express their respective awarenesses of these same factors.

KEY CONCEPTS: METHODOLOGICAL

Theme-Setting. Theme-setting concerns the selection of a theme and its precise wording. It may strike the reader as a relatively straightforward procedure and therefore of not major methodological consequence; yet Theme-centered practitioners claim that it is far less simple than it appears and hence have given it considerable emphasis in their conceptual structure.

Advertised workshops provide a situation where theme-setting is a relatively direct affair, since the leader knows the themes in which he is most interested—e.g., Marriage and I, Overcoming the Generation Gap, etc.; he, or his sponsoring organization, then attempts to attract a group of people, most of whom are strangers to each other, to a workshop centered on the theme. Situations in which a subcommunity, like a school, agency, or church, call in leaders for help with a concrete situation are more difficult. Here the work-shop-planners must attempt to diagnose the problem, since the agency directors, being close to the situation, may not be the most expert in labeling their interests and/or difficulties. Consequently, the workshop-planner, who will not always be its eventual leader, should be knowledgeable about organizational dynamics; an assessment of the problem precedes his selection of a theme. Is the difficulty one of indirect or faulty communication among the staff members? Or is the problem one of perceptions that are distorted but nonetheless clearly communicated?—i.e., two factions, let's say both adminis-tration and staff, may regard each other with antagonism and suspicion—un-realistically—and communicate quite accurately to each other this feeling of threat and hostility. Or is the perception a realistic one?—i.e., administration and staff have genuinely competing interests, and so long as they do they will not feel comfortable with each other and will look to replace the other with a new set of people. Themes involving empathy and communication would seem most appropriate to the first situation, themes involving prejudiced, stereo-typed, and distorted perception to the second, and themes involving a redefi-nition of goals and expectations to the third. The reader may wonder why Theme-centered theorists make so much of the theme, yet it must be pointed out that their rationale is consistent; if it is true that the theme has an important effect on the kinds of things that members bring up for discussion, then the extent to which the theme fits the circumstances and needs of the people attending it is extremely important.

Once the theme is selected there still remains the problem of its precise wording. Theme-centered leaders find that specific words, like overall themes, can have an important effect on participants' expectations. Therefore they have developed one or two specific guidelines. One is that themes should be worded positively rather than negatively; for instance, "Overcoming the Gen-eration Gap" would probably prove to be a better wording than "Faulty Communication Between Parent and Teen-ager." A second guideline is that the use of the pronoun "I" and the "-ing" form of verbs helps themes to become more personal and more energizing; for example, "Being Myself at Work" might well turn out to have a less deadening effect than would "The Impersonal World of Jobs."

Setting themes within a classroom can also require intensive considera-tion. The overall theme of a course is usually fairly clear, since it will in most instances correspond directly to the course's purposes as stated in a formal curriculum. More difficult is the session-to-session setting of subthemes. As we mentioned earlier, there is no reason why the teacher cannot invite the participation of his students in setting themes for at least some of the sessions. Ideally a subtheme will reflect the content of what is being taught and read, be broad enough to leave room for varying student reactions to the material at hand, and yet explicit enough for it to evoke meaningful associa-tions and feelings within each student. "Erik Erikson's Eight Stages of Man: Their Meaning in My Life and My Living" would be an example (Erikson, 1964).

Introductory Procedures. The Theme-centered leader, in beginning his group, proceeds in a more structured way than does the T-group leader, the group therapist, or the Gestalt-workshop leader. He resembles somewhat the En-counter leader who chooses to begin his group with some specific "microlab" or nonverbal exercises involving milling, touch, groping with eyes closed, etc.

In contrast to the Encounter leader, however, the Theme-centered leader's procedures are usually verbal. He has two primary aims: (1) to get the group to focus on the theme in a total, thinking-feeling way, and (2) to reduce anxiety as much as possible. His main means of minimizing anxiety, once the group interaction has started, is to respond in a somewhat positive and empathic way to the initial comments of participants. This kind of paraphrasing responsiveness is very similar to that mode of intervention encouraged by Carl Rogers (1951) in his model of client-centered psychotherapy. It helps members to feel less threatened, and it is especially useful in the early stages of a group, when a participant's initial statements are likely to receive no answering comment from another member; the participant's remarks (which however innocuous on the surface may have cost him dearly in a sense of premature exposure and personal vulnerability), unless quickly responded to by the leader, may instead be greeted by a deafening silence which only increases his discomfiture and probably acts as a deterrent to those who are silently debating whether or not to speak up.

One way that Theme-centered leaders like to begin their groups is through a period of silence in which the participants are asked to let their minds revolve around and associate to the theme, which is clearly stated by the leader at the inception of the group. The "triple" silence, wherein the participant is encouraged to internally relate the theme to both his past and the here-and-now, is a favorite of Ruth Cohn and her associates. It will be described and illustrated below. It is important to remember, however, that silence, because it can severely increase the anxiety of group members, works best with relatively sophisticated and motivated groups. Where groups are characterized by considerable apprehension and mistrust, the leader can begin in a somewhat informal way, asking people to introduce themselves and to state what meaning the theme has for them and what their expectations are in joining a group concerned with this particular theme. In a workshop entitled "Living Creatively", participants could be asked to discuss those areas of their lives in which they feel themselves to be least creative.

The three steps of the triple-silence ask the participant to perform three tasks: (1) to think about the theme, (2) to try to be in contact with, and to intensify, how it feels to be in the group, and (3) to connect a theme-oriented task with the present group. Let's take Ruth Cohn's example of a workshop for counselors and state as its explicit theme Improving My Counseling Skills (Cohn, 1972, p. 856). In step one, the participant is asked to shut out outside stimuli, and to get into himself, especially in relation to his feelings about himself as a professional counselor, both past and present; in order to intensify the experience of turning inwards, he is sometimes asked to close his eyes. This procedure invites a connecting of the "I" and the "It," but not the "We," since the group aspect of the experience is temporarily held in abeyance. In step two, the "I" is linked with the "We." If the participant has had his eyes closed he is asked to open them, to become aware of how it feels physically and emotionally to be in this room with these coparticipants. One way of implementing step three, which attempts to link the "I," the "We," and the "It," is to give the following directions: "Please remain silent and choose one of the participants to be your personal counselor. Tell him why you came to visit him and what you want to gain from this visit. Then reverse the situation. Choose another group member whom you would like to counsel. And imagine any reason why this counselee has come to you."

Following the silence, the leader invites the group to interact. One way of offering this invitation that embodies several of the Theme-centered ground-rules (see below) without listing them in a formal way proceeds as follows (Cohn, 1972, p. 856):

> Let us now communicate about whatever we want to—the theme, my suggestion to you, your experiences, thoughts, feelings, whatever you want to communicate about. Please be your own chairman and try to get whatever you want to get from the group and to give whatever you want to give. I will do the same being my own chairman, and the chairman of the group. Do interrupt when you are bored, distracted, angry or anything else which prevents you from full participation.

In most instances, these introductory procedures will be sufficient to produce some initial interaction around the theme. Subsequent leader-interventions are geared toward maintaining and deepening these processes.

Dynamic Balancing. Dynamic balancing refers to the leader's activity in making sure that the group-process does not remain overly-focused on any one part of the I-We-It triangle. His skill lies in detecting those decisive points at which the group is becoming stuck and is therefore most ready for a shift of some kind, e.g., from "I" to "We." His conceptual understanding of the triangle and an ability to sense which of its three aspects is being most seriously neglected will facilitate his ease in balancing.

Certain techniques are helpful in making these transitions. One such technique, the snap-shot device, is often useful in enabling a group to know where each of its members "is at." It works in the following way: the leader creates a "stop-action" situation by snapping his fingers and saying: "Please try to pinpoint just where you were at the moment I snapped my fingers and stopped the action. Now go around, each in turn, and give a *brief* statement of what your inner experience was at that point." It is important that this exercise be handled in a disciplined way; each member is to be as brief as possible, and each person should proceed in order without spontaneous interaction. In other words, even though Member X's experience may have involved negative thoughts about Y, Y is not given a chance to reply until a formal "go-around" has taken place. This is a relatively easy way to introduce a "We" focus and is designed to promote a greater sense of group cohesion.

Encounter techniques can be of aid in intensifying dyadic interactions; two participants experiencing conflict and tension vis-à-vis each other could be asked to come to the center of the room and to engage in verbal or nonverbal dialogue. Here too the "We" focus will be intensified, though now its scope will be reduced to two people instead of the entire group. If the formal theme relates to interpersonal relations, this technique will simultaneously strengthen the "It" point of the triangle. Should the group seem ready for shift to "I" at a slightly later point, the leader's focusing on a particular individual—should it meet a positive response—will effect such a movement. In the example of the Freedom vs. Control group cited above, this was precisely what was done when the leader commented on Alice's prolonged silence.

Expertise in the thematic area on the part of the leader is useful, but not absolutely necessary. It is rare for the skilled group-leader to have as great an understanding of "Management Relations" as do the executives he is leading. The teacher who uses the Theme-centered model in his classroom is conversant with his subject-area, but we can imagine a sensitive group-leader being brought into a high school class in order to lead a group discussion around poetry, so long as he—along with the participants—has read the relevant poems. Co-leading can be a tremendous aid in the dynamic balancing process, since it permits a division of labor wherein one leader takes primary responsibility for attending to the theme or task aspect of the group-process, and the other the interactional aspect.

Themes like "Training Empathy" or "Understanding Group Dynamics" are directly related to here-and-now interpersonal processes. They are what might be described as "Sensitivity" themes and in such contexts content and process tend to overlap (as contrasted with a situation where the theme might be "Understanding French Poetry.") The merging of the "I" and the "It," or the "We" and the "It," can make for greater excitement, but also more difficult group-leading, since it is harder to keep the three points of the triangle in distinct focus. The leader is able to introduce an "It" emphasis whenever he focuses on aspects of an emotional interaction that relate to the theme. For example, where the theme is "Training Empathy" he might ask two participants who are in conflict with each other to role-play each other as a means of helping each to contact what the other is feeling (thereby bringing the group back to the empathy theme); where the theme is "Understanding Group Dynamics" he might ask the group to conceptualize in dynamic terms the interaction that is occurring at that very moment (thereby bringing the group-dynamics theme explicitly into focus).

Ground-rules. In conducting a Theme-centered interactional workshop, the leader states several "rules" or procedures that participants should keep in mind in pursuing their dialogue. With the exception of the "Be Your Own Chairman" rule, which is often stated at the beginning in the manner already indicated (see "Introductory Procedures" above), these guidelines are usually introduced where they are appropriate. For example, the "Speak One At a Time" rule would probably not be mentioned at the beginning of a group, but would only be introduced at a point where several members were speaking at once, or where two members were making side-comments to each other secondary to the main group interaction. Participants sometimes view these rules as coercive restraints; however, it is thought that if the leader presents them with the right spirit, they will be seen as *facilitators* of the group interaction rather than as arbitrary impediments to it. Actually, there is no coercive power behind the rules; any participant is free to "break" them at any time. The leader can only try to make him aware that he is doing so and wonder what his need to flout them might mean. The five rules are as follows:

1. Be Your Own Chairman. The rule attempts to reinforce each participant's awareness that he himself is primarily responsible for what he does or doesn't obtain for himself during the session. It is an attempt to operationally implement the autonomy concept that the model emphasizes and to discourage the participant's dependency on an all-powerful leader who will somehow make certain that something meaningful will happen to him. Hence one of the prime responsibilities of the group-leader, as Chairman of the group, is to remind the various participants of their self-chairmanship. While this function constitutes something of a responsibility for the leader, it is a much less burdensome one than in a more authoritarian structure, where the fundamental autonomy of each group member is not made paramount and where the leader consequently becomes responsible for what happens to each member. For example, a leader might wonder aloud if Participant X, who has remained silent, is getting from and giving to the group as much as he would like. He might even encourage X to take a few moments, while the group waits, to silently develop his own "agenda" as to what he would ideally like to see happen within the remainder of the session—either in relation to himself or to others. The leader might then, once X has had the fantasy, encourage him to do his utmost to make whatever he fantasized happening actually happen. The ultimate choice of whether or not X participates belongs to X (autonomy); he may, of course, as a result of the leader's prodding, begin to participate more fully (interdependence). This autonomous "freedom" is an existential given and therefore is not within the power of any particular model of group interaction to either grant or revoke. The innovation here is that the Theme-centered leader frequently reminds the participant of this freedom, and encourages him to make maximum use of it. The careful leader is also at pains to remember that the choice to remain silent can be as authentic or "free" as the choice to speak.

2. Speak per I. This guideline is directed toward an attempt to encourage each participant to state his own experience as clearly as possible. Participants very often mask their statements in such a way as to appear to be making generalizations about human behavior; for example, "You find that as you get older ... ," "One never likes to ... ," etc. Even when a participant is instructed to speak from his own experience and to begin his statements with "I", he frequently—after some initial compliant behavior—finds himself lapsing into "You" statements. When the leader hears a second person statement ("You don't want to be cut off from your family, so you start giving in on small points") he may suggest that the participant try to speak for himself only. Perhaps some of the other people in the group have the same feelings, perhaps not; the participant concerned can always try to find out if others have had the same experience. Some people may argue that the tendency to begin statements with "You" is a habit of syntax, but the Theme-centered approach argues that on a deeper psychological level such linguistic customs represent somewhat defensive attempts to project out and to collectivize, rather than to fully *own* and assume responsibility for, one's experiences and convictions.

   3. Give the Statement Behind Your Question.   Like rules number one and number two, this rule encourages each participant to take as much responsibility for his own actions, beliefs, feelings, and concerns as possible. Most questions that one person asks of another hide an unstated concern or curiosity; for example, the very common question of "What do you do?" may mask a more authentic statement of: I feel competitive and am wary lest you have higher status than I—or it might even imply the less complex feeling: I am made more and more anxious by this silence between us. Often in groups, X's emotional reaction to Y becomes obscured by an attempt to "interview" him. For example, X may ask "Do you often get this nervous in a group?" The leader may then intervene with, "X, could you try to state what Y's nervousness does to you? How it makes you feel inside?" We do not wish to imply that all such questions on X's part betoken an egocentric concern; some questions addressed to another group member proceed from a genuinely felt, empathic response to this other person; yet rather than this feeling of closeness being stated more directly, it frequently becomes protectively "embedded" in an inquiry that tries to make the recipient, rather than the questioner, the focus of interest.

   4. Disturbances Take Precedence.   This rule recognizes the fact that no participant can be fully involved in the group-process so long as he is acutely bothered by something or experiencing emotional interference. This becomes an especially important issue in nonsensitivity groups like classrooms and committee meetings where it is often assumed that everyone is attending to the theme at hand. The leader, through the "disturbance" rule, encourages each participant to let the group know when he is too distracted or preoccupied to partake fully in the group discussion. However, this kind of autonomous self-chairmanship, which is a difficult affair at best, becomes especially burdensome at those moments when a member is upset; therefore it is important for the leader to be alert to the signs and signals of a disturbance in anyone and to encourage him to express his concern to the group. It is often sufficient for a member to simply talk about his feeling, especially if he then receives some sympathy and/or support from other members. At other times, this kind of direct catharsis might not be enough, and certain Encounter or Gestalt games might prove appropriate. For example, the participant who feels overwhelmed by a sense of group rejection might be encouraged to go around to each member and begin his statement with "I want you to like me for my . . ." which he then completes differently in each instance. The leader attempts to limit the expression of each disturbance to the here-and-now context as much as is possible, since the workshop's purpose—as a nontherapy group—is *not* to resolve disturbances originating in the past, but to temporarily relieve the participant of his distress to a point where he can return his attention to the group. This is not to say that participants do not find workshops therapeutic in their effect—but many experiences in life are "therapeutic" without constituting formal psycho-therapy.

During those moments that the leader works with a "disturbed" participant, the "I" aspect of the Theme-centered triangle becomes para-mount; yet to the extent to which the leader can get other members to join in (as in the Gestalt-therapy games cited above) or link the disturbance to the group's explicit theme (for example, the participant feels rejected by the group and the theme is: Collaboration vs. Alienation in Today's Society) a "We" or an "It" focus might also emerge.

5. Speak One at a Time. This ground-rule is, in a sense, the most practical of the five cited. It constitutes an attempt on the part of the leader to avoid mass confusion in situations where several participants speak simul-taneously. All those wishing to speak could be encouraged to "Fight for the floor," or the leader could instead ask each of them to say quickly what he wants to say, much like the snap-shot technique mentioned earlier.

This rule is also invoked when there is only one participant speaking as part of the formal group interaction and two or three members have a whispered conversation that constitutes an aside to the "main action." The leader often encourages such members to make their statements to the group at large, since they obviously reflect an unsuccessfully suppressed response to the group-process, and as such, are an invaluable part of the group process. Even if the overt content of this "side conversation" is totally "irrelevant" to the group interaction such content is usually an implicit statement of boredom and annoyance on the part of the conversers. To the extent to which the conversers are asked to share their side conversation in the spirit of an admonishment they will of course be reluctant to do so; to the extent to which they are asked to in the spirit of making the interaction as meaningful as possible, they might find their embarrassment at being asked to share their experience with the rest of the group less acute.

Selective Authenticity. This concept involves the extent to which the leader shares with the rest of the group his own inner here-and-now experiences, especially as they involve emotional reactions to specific participants. The leader, as Chairman of himself as well as of the group, finds that he, like other participants, has to monitor personal needs for giving and getting; for example, he may be tempted to express hostility toward someone who irritates him and to seek out positive feedback from others. Yet the expression of some of these needs conflict with his leadership-role since they may well impede the group-process. Hence the idea of *selective* authenticity: the leader selects from his stream of inner awareness those experiences that help to either facilitate the group interaction or to amplify the theme, and states them; he inhibits or delays the expression of those that do not.

An example of selective authenticity was provided in our initial session-segment, when Roger asked the leader if she had been angered by his criticism and she acknowledged that she had been irritated. Her directness doubtless facilitated the group interaction, since any evasion on her part would not only have frustrated Roger and made him that much more anxious lest she dislike him, but also have discouraged other participants from being candid in their expression of feeling. Three other factors could be seen as helping her in her decision: (1) she knew that her feelings were of direct interest to at least one participant (i.e., Roger), (2) the fact that her anger was not intense made it easier for her to be straightforward with Roger, and (3) her reaction was shared at a point where the group cohesion was sufficiently great for some negative feelings, even on the part of the leader, to be expressed.

It is difficult to formulate very general rules as to when authenticity on the part of the leader is growth-promoting for a participant or for the group and when it is not—partly because successful instances of a leader's authentic sharing depend on a subtle balance of many factors existing at an unique moment in a group's progression, and such moments are rarely repeated. A few guidelines, however, seem possible and we will state them within the framework of the I-We-It triangle.

It is with respect to the "It," or theme, that the leader has most leeway in sharing himself, particularly when he relates to aspects of the theme that are more intellectual or that relate to his experiences outside the group. For example, in a workshop having marriage as its theme he might wish to share some of his own experiences as a married person; in a theme on "Freedom and Control in the Psychotherapeutic Relationship," the therapist-leader might wish to discuss some of his own cases. Especially in the classroom, it is in the theme-area that the teacher-leader usually has most to give to his students. If, for instance, the topic under discussion were "Appreciating the French Novel," his own thoughts about the theme—along with those of his students—would be very relevant.

Greater sensitivity would be demanded in the areas of the "We" and of the "I". With regard to the "We," the leader would be expected to confine himself to observations that are conducive to the greater cohesion of the group; therefore, if he experiences feelings that he suspects are shared by at least some other members and that seem to be impeding cohesiveness, he might want to express them. In the case of his reactions to a specific participant, he tries to confine himself to feelings and observations that will promote the ego-integrity of that person. As in any encounter involving people, whether it be therapy, counseling, or group-leading, considerations of tact, timing, and sensitivity are paramount. As was indicated in the discussion of Introductory Procedures above, the leader has to take greater care in keeping all his responses positive toward the earlier stages of the group. We can envisage situations where a leader's statement of some irritated feelings toward a particular participant could be constructive, e.g., if it helps the latter to attain a deeper understanding of his effect on others without unduly wounding him. Also, the leader might want to share his fantasies about a participant—e.g., in a theme-discussion involving marriage, the leader might say: "When I imagine you with your spouse I picture you behaving in such-and-such a manner." Here the leader is functioning much as a therapist might—in the sense of using his inner life as a source of hypotheses—but his aim is to deepen the participant's experience in relation to the theme. It would not be appropriate for him, in the example just cited, to share his fantasy about how the participant behaves with his boss, or with his daughter.

It might also be appropriate for a leader to occasionally share his own "disturbances" with the group, particularly if these genuinely prevent him from attending closely to the discussion. Many factors would enter into such a decision, including the nature of what is bothering him, the cohesiveness of the group, the emotional maturity of its members, the group's theme, etc. Given a sufficiently trusting group atmosphere and a comfortableness on the leader's part with regard to sharing himself personally, this kind of authenticity can prove helpful: it might relieve the leader, at least temporarily, of his burdensome preoccupation and it might enable others to more readily identify with him, thereby promoting a feeling of closeness with the group.

ROLE OF THE LEADER

By means of its self-chairmanship guideline, each participant in a Theme-centered workshop is given primary responsibility for making sure that he tries to get something for himself from the discussion, and the leader's role, as "chairman of the group" is to constantly encourage members to exercise this autonomy. A second leadership role involves an enforcement of the ground-rules, wherein members are asked to state their feelings and ideas as directly as possible, and a third requires the leader to keep certain dynamics in a state of relative balance. These dynamics can be briefly summarized as involving: (1) the I-We-It triangle, (2) cognition and affect, (3) the here-and-now and the there-and-then, and (4) the intrapsychic and the interpersonal. Ruth Cohn has likened the leader's task in this respect to that of an organist who, through a skillful use of hand-stops and foot-pedals, which soften some sounds and resonances and amplify others, tries to make the richest music possible. Just as the organist's music must bear some relationship to the composition played and to the instrument he is playing, the group interaction, no matter how skilled the leader, cannot be independent of the theme, the globe, and the people participating.

If every person in the group were truly his own chairman, to the point of saying what was on his mind most of the time, minimal leadership would be necessary and the leader's sole function would be to enforce the ground-rules, particularly the one that asked people to speak one at a time. Because members would be actively involved, interaction would be fluid. And, given a diversity of members—some having intellectual interests and some looking for an emotional experience, some tending to be self-involved and some preferring to draw out others, some preferring to stay with the theme and some wanting to digress from it—the group would dynamically balance itself.

In actual experience such a group is rare. The over-talkative member is not necessarily interrupted—at least not soon enough; a digression is not offset by members wanting to find their way back to the theme; and the silent, suffering person who searches for contact does not have his need answered by another participant. Here the interventions of the leader are crucial, and his willingness to be quite active is often the key. If one or two people consistently monopolize the discussion, he might wonder aloud what is happening in the group that twelve people appear willing to listen, in apparent stupefaction, while two persons dominate. If he notices concerted efforts to avoid the theme, he would share this observation with the group; in fact, proceeding on the basis of selective authenticity, he might even express a growing conviction that the theme was either poorly selected or phrased, and attempt to rectify this.

The leader has no goals more specific than the balancing ones we have mentioned, especially when the theme under consideration does not involve a specific task or agenda. When it does, he usually hopes for task completion, but the latter will be as much a result of the members' efforts as of his own, and he can have no clear idea ahead of time as to what the final task-product will be. Where personal and learning themes are concerned, the leader strives to enable the group to have a maximally enriched experience around the theme wherein each member feels free to express his thoughts and feelings about it, and to relate to others as they similarly struggle to connect with, and associate to, the theme. Whatever learnings or significant experiences occur around such interchanges are necessarily somewhat amorphous and not easily measured, as is true for all the models of group interaction we have presented. This kind of unprogrammed and experiential learning, which gives considerable responsibility to the learner for what he gains, may appear to be closer to psychotherapy than to education; yet educators increasingly advocate that classroom learning involve a group-discussion process in which learning consists not so much of memorizing facts as of incorporating the ability to see relationships between events and things in ever more novel and diverse ways (Postman and Weingartner, 1969).

The leader relates to a participant's emotional needs only insofar as they either interpenetrate with the theme or distract the participant from the theme. To deal with personal needs other than in the context of the theme would take the workshop into the realm of psychotherapy, which is not its purpose. For example, in the sample session first presented, Roger, after having attacked the leader, worried lest he had incurred her disapproval. In a group therapy context, it would be entirely appropriate for the leader to point out the paradox involved in Roger's acting provocatively toward a transference-figure from whom he wants a positive response, but in the Theme-centered setting the leader intentionally bypassed this dynamic. Had Roger behaved similarly in a workshop having a theme more relevant to this behavior—e.g., "Learning to Express My Needs"—the leader would be more justified in commenting on the paradox. Even here, however, her efforts would be better directed toward helping Roger focus on how he frustrates himself in satisfying conscious needs, like his wish for approval, than on his unconscious need for aggression.

The leader strives to keep the theme in clear, but not perpetual, focus throughout the workshop. A major tenet of the Theme-centered method, and it is one that is closely allied to theoretical aspects of Gestalt therapy, holds that a continual theme-focus would produce oversaturation and fatigue. Just as the natural rhythm of the perceiver is such that he cannot keep a stimulus "figure" for too long without its become "ground," the theme-centered participant can better attend to a theme if it is occasionally allowed to recede into the background. Spontaneous interactions unrelated to the theme, statements of disturbance, humor and laughter, brief "snap-shots" in which each participant states whatever he was experiencing at a particular moment regardless of whether or not it is theme-relevant—all have a place in the workshop. The leader's task is to return the group to the theme—sometimes subtly, sometimes obviously—but only when this is not done by the spontaneous behavior of the participants themselves.

References

Cohn, R. C. 1969. From couch to circle to community: beginnings of the theme-centered interactional method. In H. M. Ruuitenbeek, ed. *Group therapy today*. New York: Atherton Press.

——. 1972. Style and spirit of the theme-centered interactional method. In C.

J. Sager and H. S. Kaplan, eds. *Progress in group and family therapy.* New York: Brunner/Mazel.

Erikson, E. H. 1964. *Childhood and society.* 2nd ed. New York: W. W. Norton & Company.

Postman, N. and Weingartner, C. 1969. *Teaching as a subversive activity.* New York: Delacorte Press.

Rogers, C. 1951. *Client-centered therapy.* Boston: Houghton-Mifflin.

13

Integration
and Perspectives

In this final chapter we return to the global focus of our historical introduction and attempt to view the models through a broader perspective wherein their areas of both overlap and divergence are systematically explored. We also devote particular attention to two issues which our comparison of the models (presented below) reveals to be pervasive and fundamental. The first issue involves the possible influence of group pressure and group norms; the effects of group pressure constitute a potential concern for any leader, and some of the models attempt to cope with this problem in relatively systematic and specific ways. The second issue concerns questions surrounding the Encounter group, for this model has been the subject of considerable controversy among both professional and lay people and has, on several dimensions about to be enumerated, taken a relatively more extreme position than have most other models.

To look at all eleven models simultaneously is of course impossible. What we have chosen to do instead, in the first section below, is to offer some systematic comparisons juxtaposing one specific model against another. Such comparisons are of necessity arbitrary and selective. In most of them, we have tried to differentiate models that, albeit somewhat parallel in purpose and in setting, are nonetheless different with regard to certain other features, usually involving their underlying philosophy or method (e.g. the Tavistock group and the T-group). In one comparison, that of Gestalt versus Theme-centered, we simply want to point out some interesting points of congruence that have not been noted before. (Another relevant comparison, that of the Existential-experiential approach with the Psychoanalytic, is omitted here because it was explicitly considered in Chapter 5, where we noted precise areas of congruence and divergence between the Existential therapy group and the Psychoanalytic therapy group.) While these comparisons naturally cannot encompass all the historical, conceptual, and methodological issues touched on in each of the chapters, our hope is that they will succeed in recapitulating those central points where theoretical cleavages occur. A review of these comparisons reveals that each of them can be related to one or more of four distinct and key parameters: (1) a focus on the group versus a focus on the individual, (2) psychotherapy goals versus growth goals, (3) gratification of needs versus frustration of needs, and (4) a relatively structured format versus a relatively loose format. We shall attempt whenever possible to consider these parameters in comparing models with one another.

One parameter, that of the individual versus the group, deals not only with the technical question of whether to view group interaction in terms of an intrapsychic focus as opposed to group-dynamic one but also with the broader question of whether group norms can undermine the autonomy and integrity of the individual participant. Some theorists fear that the participant in *any* type of group, often isolated from his usual moorings and anxious lest he incur the group's disapproval, might find himself impulsively embarking upon behavior about which he is actually quite ambivalent. Indeed, this potential tyranny of the group constitutes one of the reasons why Wolf and Schwartz (1962, pp. 207-237) take such a strong position on establishing an individual, rather than group-dynamic, emphasis in their analytic groups, why some Gestalt leaders place restrictions on the amount of spontaneous interaction in the group, why an Encounter leader like Schutz at the outset reminds the participant that the latter himself has the ultimate responsibility for what he does and doesn't experience in the group, and why the leader using Cohn's Theme-centered interactional method uses specific techniques (like periods of silence, and the "Be Your Own Chairman" groundrule) to help the participant get in deeper touch with what *he* is feeling and what *he* most wants at any particular moment (as opposed to what the group might seem to want). Because the group pressure issue has been responsible for some of these methodological variations and for some of the criticism that has been directed against particular models, we give it separate treatment.

Also meriting separate consideration is the entire question of Encounter groups. The Encounter model had taken what was, at least at the time of its emergence, a somewhat unorthodox position with regard to each of the four parameters noted above: it places the group in a position of especial importance in that it envisages as one possible peak experience that point at which the participant loses his sense of being different from the other members and appreciates instead "the unity of man" (Schutz, 1971, p. 221); it questions the meaningfulness of the distinction between therapy goals and growth goals; it encourages need-gratification in that it goes further than do other models in encouraging physical contact among participants and between the leader and the participant; and it minimizes the need for a somewhat fixed and predetermined procedure or format. In addition, some of its proponents question the necessity for the Encounter leader to have had professional training. Because of this unorthodoxy, and because of the enormous amount of interest and of actual participation that Encounter has engendered on the part of the public at large, we have included a discussion of some of the controversy surrounding this model.

PAIRED COMPARISONS

T-Group and Tavistock. Several similarities exist between the laboratory training institutes developed by the National Training Laboratory in the United States and the Group Relations Conferences originally sponsored by the Tavistock Institute in England. Both conferences, usually held in a residential setting and lasting a week or more, were sponsored for the purpose of helping their participants to learn more about group dynamics and organizational relations; both designed an institute schedule that placed the participant in a variety of groupings, including small groups, large groups, and intergroups (i.e., meetings between groups); both eschewed the kind of cognitive learning emphasized in the traditional classroom and championed instead a more experiential learning in which the student struggled to make his own sense of the raw data of the group experience; both had as their central learning vehicle a small group composed of ten to twelve people whose sole function was to study its own processes (designated the "T-group" by the laboratory training model, and the "small study group" by the Tavistock model). Indeed, Rice (1965, p.4), in describing Tavistock training, specifically sees as its American equivalent the training laboratory developed by NTL. In order to make our differentiation between these two models clearer, we will focus our discussion on specific differences existing between the T-group and the small study group; this presentation owes much to an unpublished paper by Klein and Astrachan (1969).

The points of divergence between the two models involve the degree to which the leader: (1) focuses on the idiosyncratic behavior of each member, as well as on the overall group process, (2) is interested in exploring member-member relationships, as well as member-leader relationships, and (3) is willing to make suggestions, provide positive reinforcement, and serve as a role-model, as well as to make interpretations about the meaning of the group's behavior. The T-group trainer is more willing than is the Tavistock consultant to go in the direction of each of these three variables, and the reason for this difference is directly attributable to the theoretical-philosophic underpinnings of the respective models.

The T-group model, although acknowledging that the trainee needs to become more aware of his underlying feelings, is not nearly as interested in the group's unconscious as is the Tavistock model. Instead it places considerable emphasis on the rational aspects of group life and on certain essential characteristics that are conducive to ideal functioning in the group, i.e., openness and trust, authority based on competence, maximum task involvement, and genuinely democratic values. Embedded within this conceptual framework is an implicit learning-theory model which assumes that identification with an appropriate role-model is a very significant element in learning; therefore the trainer accepts role-modeling as one of his functions, and hopes that members will begin to imitate his straightforwardness, spontaneity, and self-acceptance. The egalitarian emphasis is such that participants are encouraged to gradually accept the leader as another member of the group and one another as potential sources of competence and expertise. The trainer is aware that the typical member has irrational expectations of him, but rather than investigate them in detail, he prefers to circumvent them through his own behavior, which will make clear to the participant that they are in fact only fantasies. In psychoanalytic terms the trainer, rather than nurturing and examining the group's "transference-resistance," attempts to demonstrate by his behavior its inappropriateness.

Once the problem of irrational dependence on the trainer is worked through, it is expected that members will become concerned with one another and will begin to give and receive feedback. During this peer-focused, or interpersonal, phase of training there is as much emphasis on specific individuals and their characteristic ways of relating as on the group process. Underlying this philosophy is the expectation that once people are made less anxious and their defenses less necessary, they will begin to change and to learn more productive ways of adapting. In listening to the interaction, the leader assumes that each participant is speaking for himself; it is only when he begins to hear several members expressing the same thing that he begins to respond to group themes and group conflicts.

The Tavistock model, on the other hand, is directly descended from psychoanalysis. The leader places a strong emphasis on continually interpreting for the group the most unconscious and regressive fantasies that it has about itself in relationship to him; he believes that any gratification of these fantasies will only cause them to be held on to all the more vigorously. As a result, the Tavistock consultant is more aloof from the group than is the T-trainer, more reluctant to step "out of role," and less likely to be viewed as but another member of the group. Each participant is seen as not speaking for himself so much as for the group, and peer relationships are viewed as derivative of the group's relationship to the authority; consequently the consultant's interpretations are pitched to the group rather than to a single individual, and efforts of members to focus on one another are interpreted as a defense against dealing with the leader. The leader's emphasis is always on insight, and he makes little attempt to actively nurture behaviors—like collaboration, constructive competition, and the exchange of feedback—that might conceivably be appropriate in the work group to which a member will return. Instead the participant is expected to internalize whatever understanding he has gained of unconscious group processes and to use it however he deems fit once back on the job. This is a lonelier, more isolating conception of what a group can give the individual than one finds in the T-group, where group participation is envisaged in more open, gregarious, and optimistic terms.

According to Klein and Astrachan, an adequate training model should provide both an appreciation of the irrational aspects of attitudes toward authority (a task that the Tavistock model is uniquely suited for) and an exploration of the legitimate sources of authority (an activity that is better provided for in the T-group, where the trainer attempts to model the role of a more benign, affectively-oriented, egalitarian, and facilitative authority). Therefore Klein and Astrachan recommend that training groups incorporate the best features of both models. This integrated model (unlike T) will not be overly quick to bypass the authority problem by naively "democratizing" the group; on the other hand (unlike Tavistock) it will not arbitrarily restrict the group from an examination of these interpersonal issues that genuinely emerge among the peer-participants. In this amalgamated model, the emergence of demonstrated competence on the part of at least some members can help to dispel unrealistic leader-dependence. Klein and Astrachan claim that without such access to each other (which is denied to them in the Tavistock model), members cannot form relationships to one another independent of the consultant and therefore will be forced into either disregarding him or overthrowing him if they are to succeed in somehow establishing their own identity vis-a-vis one another. In this sense the Tavistock consultant would seem to "double-bind" the membership, for by forestalling the development of intimacy among its members he covertly blocks the group's ability to comfortably accommodate itself to his authority; yet at the same time he refuses to acknowledge that he has created some of the group's difficulty in coming to terms with him, and implies instead that its problem results solely from irrational transference.

T-Group and Encounter. Starting in the late sixties, the distinction between these two models became gradually less precise. More and more people began to use the terms "T" and "Encounter" interchangeably, and an increasing number of leaders now conduct their groups as "sensitivity-training" groups without any clear decision as to which of the two models they are primarily using. In the presentation below we discuss the T-group as it was originally conceptualized within the NTL residential laboratory and described in Chapter 10, and the Encounter group as it is exemplified in Schutz's Open Encounter model (see Chapter 11).

Despite the absence of an explicit agenda, the T-group model is generally more structured and has a more specified theoretical learning thrust than does the Encounter model, particularly when one keeps in mind its original locus in a larger laboratory design involving fixed schedules and distinctive group events, which were in turn oriented toward the implementation of specific learning goals. These goals were geared to the participant's back-home organizational setting, and while the laboratory's designers could not consciously plan just how he was to apply his laboratory learning to his subsequent job functioning, their conscious intention and clearcut responsibilities lay in enabling him to relate whatever self-knowledge and group-dynamics knowledge he had gained in the small group to his administrative functioning and to his behavior in vocational task groups. Indeed, if a human-relations trainee did not have an occupational situation in which increased interpersonal skill could play a helpful role, the T-model, as it was originally designed, would not have had an obvious purpose or rationale. The conceptual underpinnings of the T-model (extending across several disciplines, which included social psychology, personality theory, and sociology) comprised a reasonably systematic integration of behavioral-science theory with actual data derived from empirical research in small group behavior.

Encounter proponents, on the other hand, tend to minimize the cognitive aspects of experience and have generally discouraged academic or research approaches to Encounter. Indeed, some proponents view its deemphasis of all linguistic abstraction as one of its primary virtues. As a result, no single over-riding conceptual theory yet exists for this model, despite some attempts to create one (Burton, 1969). In parallel fashion, the notion of goals or purpose is not very relevant to a model that tends to value affect for its own sake and group interaction as an important experience in its own right. For some, particularly those in the Esalen-Schutz tradition, the act of assigning a specific purpose or function to the model might throw it back into a rational-empirical and means-vs-ends Western mold that it was intentionally designed to offset.

Another difference between the two models involves their respective norms with regard to how members present their personal reactions to one another. The T-group model gave the term "feedback" to this process, the Encounter leaders "confrontation" (Papell, 1972). The semantic distinctions between these two terms are important, since T-group feedback tended to be stated in reasonably rational, sympathetic, and not-very-impolite terms, while Encounter confrontation was often presented in abrasive and highly emotional terms. T-group leaders emphasized the value of constructive feedback, which should protect the overall self-esteem of the recipient by avoiding any statement that questioned his basic worth as a person, and would instead be directed toward concrete, identifiable behaviors. On the other hand confrontation, particularly as it evolved in the context of Synanon groups, was more of a no-holds-barred, sometimes abusive, tongue-lashing that would mercilessly expose any defensive or face-saving behavior on the part of the person confronted. While attack per se was not specifically endorsed in Schutz's Open Encounter, direct expression of anger, to the point of wrestling and loud screaming, was encouraged.

If we look at the specific content of these two types of small group experience, we find that the T-group holds more consistently to a strict here-and-now focus than does the Encounter group. The main concern is with what is happening in the group itself, and a member's introduction of material related to his outside life is usually interpreted by the trainer as an avoidance of the task; in this way the leader hopes to ensure that the nature of his interventions can be clearly distinguished from those of the group psychotherapist. The Encounter leader also leans toward a here-and-now emphasis in that, like the Psychodrama or Gestalt leader, he encourages the participant to make his discussion of problems and events as experiential and vivid as possible. However, the content of this material need not relate only to the group process, but will hopefully include past experiences and outside problems, for the Encounter leader is not so concerned about his activity's encroaching upon the psychotherapist's domain. Indeed, while he is interested in getting the participants to react to one another (so that each can gain valuable insights into how he is perceived), he also is eager that each try to present, and to break through, whatever impasses he is experiencing in his personal life.

Lastly, group processes receive a somewhat different focus in the two models. In the Encounter group there is less conscious focusing on them by the leader, and consequently less interest in commenting on them on the part of the group members, although the leader does of course try to encourage a strong sense of closeness and cohesion in the group. The T-group trainer, in contrast, fosters an intellectual as well as emotional awareness of group process by encouraging the group to engage in a cognitive investigation of its own dynamics. Hence an interaction pattern frequently found in an Encounter group wherein members succeed one another in taking center stage and telling their life story might, if spontaneously developing in a T-group, be pointed to by the trainer as an unconscious norm; the trainer will usually encourage the group to examine this norm in an attempt to determine whether it is productive and should be retained. According to the T-model this kind of procedure on the part of the trainer not only teaches the group something about its own processes, but also, by granting to the group more genuine responsibility for determining each feature of its plan of operation, reduces the group's dependency on its leader.

Gestalt Therapy and Encounter. While Gestalt Therapy and Encounter consitute essentially distinct models, some fundamental similarities do exist between them: both reject psychoanalytic orthodoxy, particularly as it applies to specific techniques of psychotherapy; both emphasize nonverbal aspects of the participant's behavior; both are emphatic about the degree to which "normal," and even exceptionally successful, people have become alienated from their true potential and from their deeper emotional longings; and both stress the liberating effect of living in the immediate moment. In general, each of these two models has been strongly humanistic in consistently rejecting any kind of rigid authoritarianism, be it in the form of sacrosanct theory or the subtly coercive "shoulds" of conventional social, political, and sexual mores. Added room for confusing the two models came from the fact that many Encounter leaders added Gestalt therapy exercises to their repertoires and from the fact that both models were featured in the publicity and prominence given to Esalen Institute in particular, and to the human potential movement in general, during the mid-sixties.

Despite these similarities, there are a few distinct differences between the two models when it comes to both methodology and philosophy. One dimension of difference involves the extent to which a participant receives direct advice from either the leader or the group. Perls was at pains to protect the participant's autonomy against potential encroachment from any kind of implicit program or secret agenda as to what he "should" experience during the session. He did this through two specific procedures. The first procedure restrained the group from interrupting or making comments while the leader engaged in hot-seat work with a participant. The second procedure restrained the leader from deciding what a patient should experience on the hot-seat; instead his only job was to accentuate, or render "more figure," whatever experiences the patient was having. Sometimes this hot-seat work would result in a carthartic experience for the patient, sometimes it would not.

As Denes-Radomisli (1971) indicates, Encounter provides considerably more opportunity for intrusive directions from both the leader and the other participants. First, because the group often criticizes the participant for various qualities that it deems negative, thereby implying that he should change; second, because the leader sometimes strives to produce or generate within the participant a particular affective experience—e.g. he might encourage him to contact his trusting (or mistrustful) feelings by having him engage in an exercise of falling back while another person catches him. According to Denes-Radomisli, the Encounter atmosphere is in general a subtly totalitarian one in which only he who is warm and loving in the group is approved and in which it gradually becomes clear to all that only the person who achieves a dramatic emotional breakthrough or catharsis will be fully accepted.

Encounter leaders deny such attempts to impose a secret agenda on the participant. Schutz, for example, believes that no one can force a group member to do something that he doesn't really want to. Furthermore, Schutz's model makes clear that while groups are sometimes routinely led through touching or trust-fall exercises as a "warm-up" or as a demonstration of Encounter techniques to professionals and students, the skilled Open

Encounter leader, once the group is under way, will not recommend a particular exercise until he is reasonably sure that it is congruent with—and will help to heighten—whatever a participant is already experiencing. Hence, like the Gestalt therapist, he is trying to follow the participant's experience rather than to lead it. However, what does emerge as a clear and real difference between the two models is that in the less structured format of Encounter many more suggestions are made to the participant, by both the leader and the other participants, than is the case in Gestalt workshops. Moreover, these recommendations may relate to the participant's outside personal life, as well as to what he should do to intensify his emotional experiences within the group. According to Schutz, it is the responsibility of each person to decide whether or not he wants to comply with these directions, and in this sense his autonomy cannot really be violated. We shall return to this issue below (see "The Group's Potential Tyranny").

Denes-Radomisli also believes that Gestalt and Encounter take different positions with respect to the issue of human limitations. According to her, Encounter ideology implies that "paradise is in the human breast, not in the Heavens," whereas "Gestalt therapy doesn't promise an elephant he can become a bird." Perls too, in a paper delivered at the 1968 meetings of the American Psychological Association, wondered whether "joy" was as easily or frequently achieved as Schutz suggested in his book by that name (Schutz, 1967). As we shall see below, psychoanalysts have made a similar criticism of the Encounter model. Encounter does seem to raise some fundamental questions concerning the extent to which, and the ease with which, one can become different from what he was. In addition, it appears to challenge the notion that a painful sense of separation is a necessary feature of living; for example, psychic states bordering on nirvana in which one feels oneself merged with other living beings or forces are likely to be viewed as life-enhancing and healthy, rather than as regressive. One aspect of this philosophy involves Encounter's receptivity to Eastern forms of thought, which challenge traditional Western notions emphasizing the sanctity of the individual ego and its inevitable demise through death (see Watts, 1961). One's convictions in this matter must of course rest upon theoretical or philosophical predilection, since no definitive answers can be given to the question of how much aloneness, deprivation, and suffering are fundamental to the human situation.

Encounter and Theme-centered. Theme-centered groups can embrace a variety of themes, including the kind of sensitivity and personal growth themes embodied in the Encounter groups. What we present below is how a Theme-centered group dealing with an Encounter theme differs from the Encounter group itself; once again we shall think of the latter model as best exemplified by Schutz's Open Encounter group.

Let us suppose that the Theme-centered workshop has as its theme

"Directly Encountering Me, You, and the World." In the language of Theme-centered theory, this group would devote more systematic attention to both the "It" and the "We" of the group interaction than would the Open Encounter group. Attention to the thematic, or "It," aspect of the group might at times take the form of an intellectual approach in which members (particularly if they were professionals) made some relatively abstract statements concerning their ability to be in touch with themselves and with others; they might even discuss their respective experiences in psychotherapy, the comparative effectiveness of Encounter group versus psychotherapy groups versus Theme-centered groups, and so on. Although the leader would eventually want to balance this discussion with more emotional exchanges, perhaps including nonverbal ones, he would see this kind of cognitive focus as a valid aspect of the group interaction. The Encounter leader, on the other hand, would more readily tend to view such a discussion as a manifestation of defensiveness or intellectualization. In the Encounter group, the emphasis would more consistently be on the experience of emotional contact, and where emotional expression is concerned, nonverbal communication is often preferred to purely verbal communication.

Because of the Theme-centered leader's more systematic attention to the "We" point of the Theme-centered triangle, he is more likely than the Encounter leader to openly focus on group-dynamic aspects of the interaction. He might comment on apparent subgroup formations; he might wonder aloud why the group has paid so little attention to its silent members, or inquire into the meaning of an interactional pattern wherein successive participants reduce the group to a passive audience while each recites a lengthy monologue. On the other hand, the Open Encounter leader, because of a marked emphasis on what the Theme-centered model refers to as the "I" aspect of the group process, often likes to focus on a single individual for relatively long periods while the rest of the group watches, and will not encourage the group to either investigate, or take responsibility for, this procedure.

Finally, the Theme-centered leader is less willing than the Encounter leader to include psychotherapy as one of his goals in conducting the group. Consequently, while encouraging a distracted or temporarily upset participant to express his disturbance, such activity is more in the service of enabling the person to return his attention to the theme than it is an effort to help him resolve his conflict. In order to prevent a therapeutic focus, the leader actively attempts to relate any strongly personalized or "I" emphasis to the stated theme, and to bring other participants into the discussion. In contrast, the Encounter leader is quite willing to work with a single individual for a prolonged time during which he tries to redirect and to relieve psychic forces in such a way as to promote the permanent resolution of emotional conflicts.

Theme-centered and Tavistock. Just as a Theme-centered interactional workshop can consider an Encounter theme (as described in the comparison above), there is no reason why such a workshop could not set for itself the group-dynamics theme that is the concern of the Tavistock model; for example, it could adopt "Understanding Group Dynamics" as its theme. The difference between these two models in how they would approach this theme helps to highlight their contrasting positions on two distinct variables: (1) the extent to which gratification is viewed as constituting a healthy, as opposed to regressive, aspect of the group process, and (2) the degree of structure imposed on the group by its leader.

In the Tavistock group, any prolonged member-to-member interchange is likely to be interpreted by the consultant as a resistance to the group's task of understanding group processes. This is especially probable if the members are focusing on one another, (rather than their common relationship to the leader) and if their exchange is oriented toward the expression of affect for its own sake (e.g., humor), rather than toward a conceptual understanding of the group process. In this sense the small study group is entirely consonant with Bion's basis theory, which implies that task-group members have little to give one another apart from the fundamental division-of-labor factors that brought them together in the first place. Since the job cannot be done by one person alone, they need one another; however, any support or gratification that they give one another is regressive and in the service of various basic assumptions, rather than of the work-group and its task.

In contrast, the Theme-centered model has a less ascetic view of peer relations. The "We" aspect of the group, i.e., the participants' emotional involvement with one another, is as genuine a part of the interaction as is the "It," or task, aspect. In other words, if we consider our group with the theme of Understanding Group Dynamics as a case in point, the skilled leader will promote maximum fluidity and attentiveness by balancing a cognitive processing of what is happening in the group (the "It") with moments of spontaneous emotionality in which members interrelate for a while without feeling a need to "process" these interactional data. The Theme-centered framework here implies a view that stands in contradistinction to that of Bion. It suggests that just as there is real work to be done vis-a-vis the theme or task that brought the group together, there is also room for the participants to enjoy one another as people; this enjoyment or gratification need not constitute a threat to task performance, but may indeed enhance it.

Now let us contrast the two models with respect to their leadership styles. The Tavistock consultant is concerned with promoting the potential independence of the group as a whole, by throwing into bold relief its habitual and irrational tendency to rely on authority. As a way of forcing the group to take responsibility for itself, he refuses to impose structure or to provide behavioral guidelines, but instead shares with the group what he understands to be the unconscious meaning of its interactions. The Theme-centered model, on the other hand, makes little of the concept of autonomy as it applies to the group level, and emphasizes instead the personal autonomy of the individual member. In order to facilitate the exercise of this autonomy, the leader is fairly active in introducing specific procedures and groundrules. For instance, he consistently reminds the participant of the rules requiring him to speak for himself and to turn questions into statements, and he will occasionally introduce silences, which are designed to help the participant discover what he is most wanting for himself at that particular moment.

Theme-centered and Gestalt. The parallels existing between these two models, and there are several, are more a matter of philosophy and spirit than of specific techniques or procedures. Indeed, in terms of their overt format and the kinds of themes with which they deal they are very different: the Gestalt workshop involves a quite limited interaction of the group as a whole, and the only theme with which it deals involves the facilitation of a single person's moment-to-moment awareness, whereas the Theme-centered workshop encourages a maximal amount of interaction and is designed to encompass a wide variety of themes.

However, there are some striking theoretical-philosophical parallels between the two:

1. The dynamic balancing of the three arms of the Theme-centered triangle involves the kind of figure-ground relationship emphasized by Gestalt psychology and Gestalt therapy. Once one aspect of the group experience (e.g., the "I") has been so highlighted as "figure" that it becomes saturated, the group is ready to focus on aspects of the group process that had up until that moment been "ground" (the "We" or the "It"). The figure-ground relationships emphasized by the Gestalt leader, of course, have an intrapsychic application only, and refer to an individual's awareness, and avoidance, of particular feeling states.

2. The consistent here-and-now focus, which encourages each participant of the Theme-centered workshop to be as aware as possible of what he is experiencing at each moment and what he is wanting at each moment; the narration of outside or past events, while not taboo or forbidden, is not encouraged except insofar as they are either directly relevant to the theme or important in helping a troubled participant to resolve his disturbance so that he can return his attention to the theme and the group. The Gestalt workshop retains a stricter version of the here-and-now focus in that the person's stream-of-awareness is not so much stated or discussed as it is dramatized, is oriented more toward emotion and sensation than toward thought, and is not interrupted by others.

3. The marked emphasis on an individual's autonomy and on the necessity of his taking responsibility for himself in both models. The Gestalt workshop often encourages this through a quite specific procedure of having the patient introduce each of his statements with "I"; for example, if he says, "I hurt in my head," rather than "My head hurts," he may more and more begin to "own" what happens to him in life. Theme-centered methodology also does this, through groundrules that specifically encourage the participant to make as many "I"

statements as possible, and through the overall groundrule of self-chairmanship, which reminds the participant to consistently pursue his own agenda.

The Theme-centered model can be viewed as an application of Gestalt-therapy philosophy to an interactional and theme-connected setting. In essence, the Gestalt-therapy model is an intrapsychic one: "I do my thing and you do yours (Perls, 1969);" my thing for now might be to "work" on the hot-seat while you watch, later yours might be to work while I observe. In other words, the model has little to say about how the various participants can each "do" their respective "thing" and still cooperate around a single joint effort or task. What the Theme-centered method provides is the opportunity to join the experiential-I, and the autonomy, emphasized by the Gestalt model to some notion of *community*, thereby introducing dimensions that involve interdependence, genuine intellectual issues (as opposed to the kind of defense against feeling that is "intellectualization"), and concrete tasks (in those instances where the theme consists of a specific project). A problem that is posed when a group of autonomous "I's" attempt to cooperate is: How can we work on this task together (or relate to this theme) and still leave room for your doing your thing and my doing mine? The Theme-centered interactional method attempts to provide a constructive answer to this problem, since it protects the individual's autonomy (always leaving room for "I" statements of disturbance, dissent, involvement, or whatever) at the same time that it unites the group around a theme or task.

It is relevant that Perls in the last two years of his life became involved with the concept of community, and established a Gestalt-therapy workshop-in-residence in Vancouver, Canada, so that he could pursue this interest. The residential workshop was to be developed along communal lines, wherein each member would do his share of the practical work that was needed to be done for physical survival. In other words, Perls too began to build some concept of community into the Gestalt therapy model—through a communal milieu in which living conditions were equally shared and worked for by the participants. He claimed that the Gestalt workshop per se would fail to provide a truly therapeutic experience unless it was buttressed by a broader scheme of group living that affirmed Gestalt-therapy philosophy. The Theme-centered model, on the other hand, injects the concept of community into the workshop proper, leaving the participants free to determine their own living conditions outside the workshop setting. In a later section we shall return to this theme of community, and to its possible relevance for all group models (see "The Issue of Encounter groups" below).

Theme-centered and Social Group Work. As indicated at the end of Chapter 1, there are a number of important parallels between the social work group and the Theme-centered interactional model. The similarities in these models can, perhaps, best be discussed in relation to their common task orientation, referred to as theme in the Theme-centered model and as purpose or goal in the social work group, and their dual focus on both group and individual levels of interaction. There are, of course, differences between the social work group and the Theme-centered model; the most significant distinction is found in the relatively greater focus on therapeutic concerns of social group work as opposed to the frequent educational thrust of the Theme-centered model. Despite their divergent orientations, the many parallels between the social work group and the Theme-centered model may result in a very similar group atmosphere.

In the Theme-centered model, interaction begins with the theme which provides direction for the group. The leader may select the overall theme in advance of the first group session or may involve members in its formulation. In either case, careful attention is given to the wording of the theme which will provide the central focus for group interaction. In groups that meet for more than a few sessions, subthemes related to the overall theme may be established for each meeting.

The use of goals or purpose in the social work group follows a very similar pattern. A common group goal is established through the process of contract negotiation to guide the group's efforts together. Typically, this purpose would be mutually decided in the group although social group workers following the Vinter model of social group work might predetermine the purpose. Once established, the group purpose or goal provides the structure for the group's activity in each session, much as the theme is used to direct content in the Theme-centered model. In the Schwartz model, the worker uses the purpose to keep group members focused on their work together. The social worker in the Vinter model is concerned with individual as well as group-level goals, but the common purpose of the group provides direction and continuity for his interventions. As in the Theme-centered model, the Vinter worker may find it necessary to set subgoals as he plans for each meeting. The leader's role in each of these three models is to use the purpose or theme to keep the group efforts focused. While social group workers using the Vinter model may do more structuring and may appear more directive, the group leaders following either the Theme-centered model or the Schwartz model of social group work have a similar responsibility for maintaining the group's direction.

In addition to their common emphasis on goal, purpose, or theme, each of these models stresses the need for simultaneous attention to both individual and group levels of interaction and regard this as essential for service to group members. The concepts of autonomy and interdependence in the Theme-centered approach have much in common with Schwartz's description of individual and societal needs that are reflected in the group as a microcosm of society; and, the distinction between individual and group levels of intervention in the Vinter model points to a similar concern. Parallels to the interrelationships depicted in the Theme-centered I-We-It triangle are also found in the conception of individual and group relationships around a common goal in the social work group. In all of these models, too, current interaction in the group is used whenever possible to highlight the group's theme or purpose.

A further similarity in relation to group interaction is the concept of balance between affect and task demands. This is referred to as "dynamic balancing" between interactional and thematic motifs by the theorists of the Theme-centered model. In the social work group, this principle of balance is represented by the Vinter model concepts of group maintenance and goal achievement and by Schwartz's concern with member feelings as well as group tasks. In a like vein, the groundrules of the Theme-centered model and the attention to group norms in the Vinter model's concept of indirect means of influence both stress the need to structure group interaction if the group is to be effective. Thus, it appears that frequently the group leaders in each of these models strive for very similar interactional patterns.

Psychodrama and Behavior Therapy. Although the Psychodramatic and the Behavioral approaches are almost strikingly opposed in some aspects of their theoretical orientations, particularly in their view of man, there are similarities in their group practices and activities. Most clearly seen are the similarities between what we have referred to as the Behavioral Practice Group and the Psychodrama itself. In both, role-playing plays a prominent part to the point where practitioners of the former model have acknowledged their indebtedness to the Psychodrama model. The Behavioral approach to role-play is organized around practicing assertiveness or affective expression in order for group members to learn how to express themselves more effectively in the future. In essence the aim is for members to learn new behaviors to add to their repertoires. Role-play in Psychodrama, on the other hand, frequently begins by focusing on an actual disturbing past event and striving for a cathartic effect. At times, however, when efforts are made to replay the past event in a more satisfactory fashion, role-play in Psychodrama becomes very similar to that of the Behavioral Practice group.

Another way in which the two approaches may be distinguished is the stylistic context in which the role-play occurs. As we have seen, Psychodrama emphasizes spontaneity, free expression, and a loosely organized format, while structure, specificity, and clearly articulated goals for behavior change are central to the behaviorally oriented conception. Thus, although at times a naive observer might view the ongoing group activities in the two groups as remarkably similar, he would, were he to continue to observe for any length of time, eventually see the structural differences mentioned above come to the surface.

Examination of the role of the leaders in the two approaches highlights the same type of contrast. Both the Behavioral Practice group leader and the Psychodrama director may be categorized as quite active and directive, but within the context of this activity level their manner of approach is dissimilar. The director of a Psychodrama at times may become almost a charismatic leader, whose enthusiasm and excitement are extremely important in getting the group into the spirit of things. The Behavioral leader, on the other hand, is directive in a different way; he is concerned about carefully specifying what activities the group will engage in and how it will go about its work.

Behavior Therapy and Vinter Model of Social Group Work. Behavior therapy and the Vinter model of social group work are similar in a number of important respects. Both suggest a sequence of treatment in which the leader carefully assesses the problems of members, determines goals, plans for treatment sessions, and evaluates the progress of members toward goals. In both models the group leader has a somewhat directive or authoritative role and, in both, the group's activities are frequently predetermined. Because the learning theory base of Behavior therapy is compatible with the philosophical and theoretical stance of the Vinter model of social group work, social workers often draw on learning theory principles and techniques in their attempts to change behavior. Thus, at times, these two models may appear almost synonymous in practice. Social group workers, however, draw on a wider range of theories related to human behavior and tend to be more eclectic in practice than Behavior therapists.

In both models, the careful articulation of goals for individual clients is emphasized. Goals are based on an assessment of each member's current functioning and provide direction for the treatment that follows. Although goals typically relate to member behaviors, the social group worker might also direct treatment efforts toward less clearly defined attitudinal changes. Despite the striking similarity around the formulation of goals for individuals, a key difference lies in the specificity with which these goal-directed activities are conducted. The Behavior therapist ensures that goals refer to observable behavior and are stated in measurable terms which allow for evaluation of goal achievement during and after treatment. While social group workers would concur that such procedures are desirable, they may be less exact in defining goals and are less often engaged in research related to their treatment efforts.

Careful planning of treatment following goal formulation is characteristic of both models. Treatment sessions are pre-structured and the group leaders select from a variety of techniques and activities to plan for achievement of individual goals. For several reasons, however, the means used to facilitate treatment aims may be very different. In Behavior therapy, techniques have developed around particular problems so that, for example, saturation techniques might be the treatment choice for smokers while Behavior practice might be planned for individuals defined as nonassertive. To date, Behavior therapy in groups has most often been directed at a somewhat limited number of specifically defined individual problems although its application is increasingly becoming more diverse. In contrast, social group workers practice in a wide variety of settings and work with a broader range of client problems. Further, the explicit focus in the Vinter model on the group itself as a force for change necessitates attention to group-level goals and to interventions directed at building and maintaining the group as a means of influence. Thus, while social group workers may employ behavioral techniques such as Behavior Rehearsal when these seem appropriate, frequently such techniques have not been developed for the particular situations that confront social group workers. To meet these more diverse needs, social group workers using the Vinter model employ many other techniques, including discussion, activities, and games.

Because of the many similarities between the practice of Behavior therapy with groups and the Vinter model of social group work, it is not surprising to note that recent developments in this goal-oriented approach to social group work have been in the direction of Behavior therapy (see, for example, Garvin and Glasser, 1971; Lawrence and Sundel, 1972; Rose, 1967, 1969, 1972; Thomas, 1971). In fact, some social workers using this model have not only adopted techniques already used by Behavior therapists, but have gone on to develop a behavioral approach to groups. In these recent formulations of behaviorally-oriented social group work, the authors provide a framework for utilizing Behavior modification principles while maintaining the Vinter model's emphasis on the group as a means of treatment. Although most applications of this type of framework relate to treatment efforts with children, a procedure for working with adults has been delineated and tested (Lawrence and Sundel, 1972). The sequence of treatment, like that of the Vinter model, includes study, diagnosis, treatment, and evaluation; behavioral procedures related to both group and individual needs are prescribed within each phase. Most significantly, these recent social work formulations require the specificity in describing problems and treatment plans that is so characteristic of Behavioral therapy, and there is a similar stress on evaluating the outcomes of service. While this trend toward behaviorism certainly is only one of the current uses of the Vinter model of social group work, it does emphasize the compatibility of Behavior therapy and this particular model of social group work.

Psychoanalytic and Group-dynamic Therapy. Although acknowledging that group dynamics is a valid field of investigation in its own right and that training groups can offer a useful means of studying and teaching such dynamics, Wolf and Schwartz (whose psychoanalytic group model we emphasized in Chapter 3) strongly believe that the utilization of a group-dynamics approach in therapy groups constitutes a fundamental misapplication of conceptual frames of reference, since for them the single individual, and his unconscious psychodynamics, have to be the main focus of the therapist's attention. In their view, the use of group dynamics concepts in a therapy group tends to foster a group "mystique" and to minimize individual differences, thereby encouraging tendencies toward mediocrity and conformism and undermining one of the key goals of any form of psychotherapy—the enhancement of personal autonomy (Wolf and Schwartz, 1962, pp. 207-237). We agree with Wolf and Schwartz that the development of subtle collusions and of unexamined norms can at times threaten to encroach upon a participant's autonomy. However, we see this threat as existing in all models of group interaction, including the psychoanalytic one, and therefore will give separate consideration to this problem below (see "The Group's Potential Tyranny").

What we strongly question is Wolf and Schwartz's assumption that a *conceptual* approach emphasizing group processes must necessarily coexist with, or lead to, a favoring of the group over the individual in any ultimate, or metaphysical, sense. Indeed, it could be argued that an appreciation of the kinds of social influence processes that are considered in a group-dynamics framework renders a group leader more—rather than less—wary of the possible effects that the group can have on the individual. A case in point here is Bion, who, as a group-dynamics theorist, expressed strong concern about the regressive and symbiotic forces that are often at work in groups. Obviously no group therapist, whatever his theoretical persuasion, can deny the significance of either the individual or the group. If the individual were not important, then why the psychotherapeutic function of the group? And if the group were not in some way important, then why introduce other people into the therapist-patient relationship? Hence to polarize this issue into a question of which of the two is more fundamental is to introduce a false and essentially misleading dichotomy.

Any group event can be conceptualized in terms of either intrapsychic or group-process constructs, and there are probably no longer very many group psychoanalysts who deny that this is so (Durkin, 1972). For example, A's continual domination of the group can be seen in terms of his strong need for omnipotence and whatever light this need sheds on his earlier psychosexual development. Or it can be seen as a reflection of a general concern in the group over who will control and who will be controlled, with A acting out both the group's fear, and the group's denial of its fear, that it might be annihilated by its leader-therapist Since A's behavior is a function of both sets of factors, the question of which of the two approaches, individual-dynamics or group-process, eventually results in more effective psychotherapy is an empirical one that can only be answered, if ever, by the hard data of future research in group psychotherapy. Given the strong commitment that both the psychoanalytic group therapist and the group-dynamics therapist have to the validity of their respective approaches, and our own belief—in the absence of definitive evidence—that many different approaches to group psychotherapy prove effective in the hands of a sensitive and conscientious practitioner, we have little doubt that both approaches work well with some people some of the time.

Actually, even to dichotomize methodological approaches to group therapy in terms of those focused on the group versus those focused on the individual is to oversimplify the actual state of affairs and to create an overly rigid and somewhat artificial dichotomy. The psychoanalytic group therapist who exposes himself to the group-dynamics literature and who participates in training groups probably finds himself becoming more sensitive to such phenomena as group themes, group atmosphere, and group cohesion. Similarly, group-dynamic therapists like Foulkes, Whitaker, and Lieberman make it clear that they at times find themselves silently conceptualizing the dynamics of an individual's behavior in terms of standard psychoanalytic constructs, and at other times gearing a specific intervention to a particular individual and to its likely effect on him rather than on the overall group process. In fact, Ezriel's group-dynamic approach makes a specific point of having the therapist try to indicate how each patient idiosyncratically contributes to the common group tension (see Chapter 4). Hence, while therapists caught up in this controversy have felt compelled to identify themselves with one of those approaches over the other, in actual clinical situations they doubtless find themselves utilizing various admixtures of both.

Psychoanalytic and Encounter. As we indicated in Chapter 11, these two approaches have considerable areas of overlap in their theoretical approach to emotional difficulties; both emphasize the role played by impulse, defense, and unconscious conflict in the creation of particular symptoms and characterological problems. Their disagreement is to some extent one of method; the group psychoanalyst underscores the long period of time required for working through conflicts and the need to approach defenses gradually and supportively, whereas the Encounter leader believes that major gains can be made in a quite short period of time if the therapist uses nonverbal and Gestalt techniques to mobilize intense affect and to thereby penetrate defenses rather dramatically.

Despite a similarity in their conceptual approach to the diagnosis and understanding of psychopathology, Encounter and psychoanalysis are characterized by strong differences in their philosophic views of man and of what is possible to him. This contrast revolves around the same issue of limitations inherent in man that we noted in our comparison of Encounter with Gestalt (see above). According to the psychoanalytic model, the gains that man makes in his struggle to grow and to individuate himself are always hard-won and never fully secure whereas Encounter, according to the criticisms of some analysts, implicitly promises that the ecstasy of the "group high" will lead to more-than-temporary feelings of rebirth and renewal. In a similar vein some analysts question the role of physical contact in the Encounter group, especially as it applies to the leader-participant relationship (Liff, 1970). For them, physically embracing the leader constitutes an acting out of the participant's transference, and tips the gratification-deprivation balance in such a way that the transference aspects of the relationship can no longer be analyzed since what should remain a fantasy—the patient's incestuous reunion with a parent figure—becomes a reality. According to this view, Encounter supports regressive longings of merging with others, whereas psychoanalysis in the group helps the patient to accept inevitable separation and instinctual renunciation.

An emphasis on the importance of first nurturing and then analyzing the transference relationship is of course another reason that the psychoanalytic group model believes that a long working-through period is necessary in therapy. The analysis of the transference relationship not only helps the patient to give up fantasies of reunion and incest, but also his perception of the analyst as omnipotent. According to Durkin (1964), this is even more facilitated in group therapy since the analyst's face-to-face contact with many people simultaneously forces him to be less remote than in individual analysis. According to the psychoanalytic model, then, Encounter similarly makes difficult a working-through of fantasies about the leader's omnipotence: (1) because it is so brief and (2) because the quite active and catalytic role of the leader, wherein he takes a major responsibility for the therapeutic work of the group and often brings about rather dramatic catharses in one participant after another, causes him to be seen by the participant in a strongly charismatic light. The fact that the Encounter leader often produces these results through techniques that, at least for the uninitiated, must appear both esoteric and extremely powerful, can only increase his charisma. On the other hand, the patient in the psychoanalytic group—in the view of the analytic model—will gradually realize that the powers of the group analyst are on a quite human scale, since whatever change he is able to effect (1) cost a great deal in time and effort, (2) frequently seem as much a result of the collaborative work of the group as of his own interventions, and (3) do not seem to result so much from the use of specific and sometimes obscure techniques as from direct and down-to-earth communications that reflect compassion and understanding.

With regard to this last point—the omnipotent image of the leader—Encounter proponents would of course charge that the group analyst is equally prone toward "dazzling" his patients, via impressive interpretations that somewhat esoterically attempt to reconstruct the patient's past on the basis of frequently vague evidence. They also would wonder if the traditional group analyst (as opposed to his more experiential counterpart) is not more authoritarian and controlling than he realizes. On the more general point of gratification and limits, Encounter questions the psychoanalytic equation of emotional maturity with the ability to renounce pleasure and fantasy. They see this view as reflecting psychoanalysis' highly Puritanical heritage, and as accepting a generally Western ethic that deifies the individuated human ego. Subscribing to a more Eastern vision of man that challenges traditional polarities between self and others, and life and death, Encounter tends to embrace a more mystical view of life wherein man is not necessarily the measure of all things, and may be an embodiment of more fundamental cosmic forces that he has not yet begun to understand.

THE GROUP'S POTENTIAL TYRANNY

An issue that has been touched upon more than once in the comparisons above centers around the individual's relationship to the group. This question has emerged in two distinct forms. The first is more or less procedural and concerns the extent to which the leader or therapist conceives of the group interaction, and of the impact of his own interventions, in terms of group-dynamic variables or individual psychodynamic variables; this aspect of the problem has been discussed above (see "Psychoanalytic and Group Dynamic Therapy.") The second, and broader, context involves the degree to which the individual's interests or welfare might be endangered by the group. It is precisely because of this anxiety about group pressure and possible conformism that Denes-Radomisli discourages the Gestalt group from interrupting while she works with the single patient, that Cohn introduces occasional silences into Theme-centered workshops, that Wolf and Schwartz are adamant about the therapist's dealing with the psychoanalytic group from a conceptual framework emphasizing individual psychodynamics, and that Schutz reminds his Open Encounter group at its outset that each participant is responsible for what happens to him during the subsequent sessions. One prominent psychoanalyst who has practiced group therapy, Edgar Levenson, has been less optimistic about the possibility of offsetting the coercive influence of the group, and as a result has renounced its use altogether, claiming that he finds it impossible to effectively control the secret agendas and the subtle tyrannies of the group.*

Do the potential effects of group pressure constitute a real problem for group methods and group leaders? The reality of group pressures and of how they can cause a person to deny his own experience has already received dramatic empirical demonstration in the psychological literature; for example, Asch's research (1952) showed that normal subjects, when pressed by a unanimously held group norm, would often falsify their perceptions in order to conform to it. The step from the visual perception of lines (which were involved in the original Asch experiments) to the formation of interpersonal

*A statement to this effect was made by Dr. Levenson on NBC-TV's *Not For Women Only,* January 26, 1973

and social judgments is not so very great, and these also have been shown by empirical research to be systematically affected by group norms (Hovland, 1953). Therefore, it follows that all group situations render a person vulnerable to influence via advice and feedback, especially since our culture seems to produce a high degree of susceptibility to the opinion of others (Putney and Putney, 1966). Indeed, it was the very awareness that groups have characteristic and systematic ways of influencing individual behavior and of establishing normative frames of reference that led to an interest in group dynamics and training groups in the first place. Moreover, since in present day Western society many important life experiences occur in group settings, learning how to deal effectively with people in groups, and how to be more aware of and better able to cope with group pressure, must be considered an important task for everyone.

The hope of Lewin and his coworkers as they studied group dynamics was that an understanding of group forces would eventually lead to an efficacious and democratic approach to groups in which all participants would benefit from group experiences without any serious impingement on their autonomy or integrity. Such a viewpoint characterizes all of the models presented in the previous chapters, including those oriented toward psychotherapy, since each rests on the assumption that the group can have a valuable impact on the participant without undermining his individuality. These potentially helpful aspects of the small-group experience include opportunities to learn more collaborative ways of relating to others around a common task, to receive support around efforts at personal change, and to experience the symbolic re-creation of one's original nuclear family.

However, the possiblity remains that the individual, in the face of a real or apparent group consensus, may accept feedback that he has not fully integrated or digested, and may agree to expose himself before he has had a chance to fully assess his willingness to do so. Conflict around exposure becomes particularly accentuated in Encounter and Marathon groups in which there is an emphasis on quick results (since the group will usually disband within a matter of days) and on Gestalt and Psychodrama exercises that tend to compress into a brief time span intense affect and fairly detailed autobiographical material. A participant's submission to communication games that he is not sure he is comfortable with, independent of whether or not they might ultimately prove effective in a technical sense, will probably have a demoralizing effect on his self-esteem and his sense of integrity; hence, their therapeutic value must be questioned even though they may appear to result in a catharsis. Naturally our concern for the participant's autonomy rests on the assumption that there does reside within each individual the germs of a genuine or authentic "self" which has the capacity to formulate opinions and to make decisions congruent with how he truly feels at any particular point in time.

However, there can be no doubt that the opinions of other members will have to have some genuine impact on the person if the group is to realize its maximum potential for him. In conceptualizing this problem we find the Gestalt concept of introjection versus assimilation to be useful, for it carefully distinguishes between an undiscriminating taking-in process in which the beliefs and recommendations of others are swallowed wholesale, and a more selective and testing-out process whereby one eventually internalizes what feels right and discards what feels somehow wrong or "toxic." In this way the inputs of a group can prove helpful to an individual, but they are assimilated in digestible quantities, and at a rate that enable him to "own" them and to make them a part of himself. In some instances, particular viewpoints and suggestions may well have to be rejected *in toto*.

The potentially coercive influence of group pressure is relevant to the everyday lives of many people, particularly those who have administrative functions within large bureaucracies. For this reason, it strikes us that another positive function of small group experiences can be to enable those people who are usually passive in the face of group pressure to become more appropriately resistive. For this reason the potential danger of groups can be converted into an asset, provided that the leader and/or model is sensitive to the pervasive effects of group influence and determined to support the individuality of each participant in coming to terms with it.

What can a leader do to specifically enhance the autonomy of each group member? There are a variety of procedures and interventions that might prove useful. One consists of the kind of reminder that Schutz makes to the participants, emphasizing their responsibility to make sure that what they do is what they really want to do and not what the group wants them to. Another is the silences sometimes used by Theme-centered leaders wherein the group interaction is interrupted and each person is asked to decide where he would most like to see the group discussion go if he could autocratically determine its direction. Still another might be the leader's encouraging a person who has received feedback to state exactly which aspects of the feedback jibe with his self-image and which do not. When it comes to a participant who is being urged to take a risk by engaging in a particular exercise, the leader might conceivably intervene quite actively, asking: Would you go ahead and still do this even though you knew for sure that the group and I would like you just as well if you didn't?

The Encounter model might be especially vulnerable to coercive group pressures, for reasons that have less to do with the inherent nature of this model than with the publicity surrounding it, which has encouraged many participants to enter an Encounter group with somewhat stereotyped and sensationalized expectations that dramatic breakthroughs are likely to occur. These frequently romanticized notions, which often involve anticipations of sensual embracing, violent wrestling, and generalized hysteria, doubtless leave room for an exceptional number of "secret agendas" within the membership as to what "should" happen during the session, and the participant who does not "perform" will doubtless be in some danger of being subtly scapegoated unless the leader is exceptionally alert to this possibility. Consequently a simple statement reminding the participant of his responsibility for himself made at the group's outset does not seem a sufficiently stringent safeguard. It would seem advisable for the leader to continuously remind the members of the possible effects of group pressure, not only through general remarks about self-responsibility, but through questions addressed to participants, checking the extent to which they might be responding more to the group's expectations than to their own inner promptings and wishes.

Some writers have suggested that one particular interaction model is better suited than others for dealing with the problem of conformity. As we have already indicated, Denes-Radomisli claims that limiting the degree of spontaneous interaction within a Gestalt workshop helps to protect a participant from group pressures. However, it is equally possible that some people's fears of being engulfed by the group might well be reinforced by a Gestalt therapist's insistence on isolating them from the intrusions of other participants; for them, the most corrective type of experience might be, as we stated above, one that gives them an opportunity to practice autonomous self-realization in the face of potential group tyranny.

Similarly, Wolf and Schwartz have argued that the psychoanalytic model, because it eschews a group-dynamics orientation and focuses instead on intrapsychic factors, is especially well geared to protect the individual against the mystique of the group. Yet there is no indication that group-dynamic theorists champion the group over the individual in any metaphysical sense. In fact, it was Bion, a group-dynamics therapist, who issue one of the strongest warnings against the potential infantilism and destructiveness of the group.

In essence, then, we believe that it is the skillfulness and integrity of the leader as well his awareness of, and attention to, the issue of group pressure that lies at the heart of the tyranny issue rather than the conceptual or methodological parameters of the various group models. Without the ever-vigilant concern of the leader with respect to this danger, all group models may unwittingly encourage conformity within the group, and with that concern, no model need fall victim to the problem.

THE ISSUE OF ENCOUNTER GROUPS

In this section, we shall focus more specifically on the Encounter model, since it is not only the most controversial of the models that we have presented, but is also the one responsible for the tremendous upsurge of interest in small-group experiences on the part of both professionals and the general public in the late 1960s. In doing so, we hope to raise more fundamental questions concerning the goals of small-group experiences in general and what such experiences can reasonably hope to accomplish. The attempts made by the Encounter model to respond to the increasing alienation within our culture and to exercise a specific psychotherapeutic function are not unique to it alone; what is unique is Encounter's attempt to simultaneously accomplish both purposes over a relatively short period of time. Hence we are able to see within Encounter in bold relief some of the processes and problems confronted by all models of group interaction. Much of our presentation in this section is necessarily speculative, for the issues we raise are thorny ones. Our intention is more to point to relevant questions than to provide definitive answers, and our hope is that the interested reader and student will feel motivated to think further about these problems. In discussing this model, we shall focus on two specific issues: (1) Encounter as a response to alienation, and (2) Encounter as a form of psychotherapy.

Encounter as a Response to Alienation. Many writers have attempted to account for the appeal and the popularity of the Encounter movement (e.g., see Back, 1972). In analyzing the needs to which Encounter is responsive, writers usually cite the phenomenon of alienation, which is in turn attributed to a reduction in opportunities for long-standing intimate relationships and to an increasingly fragmented society. The historical and cultural factors frequently cited as creating this state of affairs are manifold and interrelated. Among them are: an evermore mechanized, bureaucratized, and competitive society; increasing urbanization; geographic mobility; the rise of the corporate state; the divorce of leisure from work; the reduced impact of organized religion; the uncomfortable pressure on marriage as the one source of intimacy and open communication; the weakening of the family by divorce and serial marriage; the decline of the small primary group; and so on.

There can be little doubt that the small-group movement in general, and the Encounter group in particular, represent an effort to meet needs for sustained intimacy, for rootedness, and for a sense of community. The central question hinges on the capacity of Encounter—or of any group model, for that matter—to provide the participant with a feeling of roots and ongoing community. Certainly the Encounter group, for the time that it lasts, is experienced by the involved group member as a kind of primary group or community-in-microcosm. Yet the Encounter workshop is relatively short-lived, and for this reason the crucial issue then becomes the degree to which a participant is enabled to transfer to his outside living whatever sense of community, and of cooperative give-and-take, he has gained from the group experience. As we see it, any kind of genuine community, whether a face-to-face one or not, has to unite its members in some way that goes beyond emotional sharing for its own sake, (although some degree of emotional sharing is doubtless involved in a healthy community—just as emotional relating in marriage is often an accompaniment to, or outgrowth of, joint endeavors involving child-rearing and household management). Therefore, the Encounter group will have some inherent limitations in its ability to symbolize community, since it lacks any kind of reality function or task going beyond the group's existence as a place for emotional release and for intimacy. In this sense, no therapy group is ever really a community, though it may appear to be one and may partially satisfy needs for a sense of community. It is interesting to remember in this regard that Fritz Perls' solution to the problem of building "community" into the Gestalt therapy model was for workshop members to actually live together in a commune that he established on Vancouver Island during the last years of his life. His efforts in this direction would seem to have reflected a similar conclusion on his part—namely that the emotional experience of the therapy group, however powerful, cannot in itself either parallel outside communities or create its own genuine community.

It is hard to imagine that today's society can ever constitute anything resembling a single homogeneous community for its citizens. Whatever decentralization should successfully take place in the larger social system, it seems all too likely that most people will continue to belong to several simultaneously-existing reference groups having little overlap among their respective memberships. What does seem conceivably more remediable is the frequently impersonal and dehumanized tone of such groups; hopefully it is possible for them to more spontaneously meet those participant-needs that go beyond task performance, to enable members to feel a stronger identification with the task that unites them, and to provide more avenues for emotional release as members go about task-performance. Were work and community groups more humanized, the family would perhaps experience some relief from the burden of having to provide an emotional haven from those alienating forces within the larger society that make it difficult for one to "be himself."

In some respects the Tavistock, T-group, Theme-centered, and Social group work models would seem better suited than Encounter for the purposes just cited, because they give more conscious consideration to how a participant's emotional reactions and needs can be integrated with a shared task or theme that goes beyond emotional expression per se. In addition, all four models encourage an analysis of how organizations and groups function in general, and of how the work of the group is related to specific organizational situations. To us, this is the meaning of the Theme-centered motto "Sensitivity is Not Enough," and we find ourselves wondering just how serious Schutz was when he suggested that openness and honesty can in themselves constitute a political program (Schutz, 1971, pp. 157-162).

Now let us turn from the question of community to that of intimacy. Naturally intimacy is an issue for all group models, since each of them is in some way concerned with enabling members to relate with more genuineness and more emotional closeness. However, for many models intimacy is a byproduct of the work of the group; for example, in the four models mentioned above—T-, Tavistock, Theme-centered, and Social work—it is an inextricable part of the group process as the participants unite around their common goal or joint enterprise. Even in psychotherapy groups, intimacy cannot be divorced from the therapeutic goals of the individual members; indeed, in some cases a patient's efforts need to be directed toward relating with less rather than greater intimacy—or at least with a more discriminating style of involvement with others.

What is unique to Encounter, then, is that it (1) makes the creation of intimacy within the group one of its primary goals, and (2) equates intimacy with openness, the assumption being that the more openness there is in the group, the more intimacy. A question must be raised, however, as to whether there is something strangely impersonal—or at least unselective—about this kind of group intimacy, since what one reveals is not necessarily a function of a particular relationship between persons who know and care about one another. Instead the Encounter participant is expected to quickly want to share his confidences with every person within the group and with whatever group he finds himself in. Such a situation, in which each of one's peers becomes "interchangeable" with any other—since each serves as a kind of generalized audience—can easily become conducive to a new and subtle kind of dehumanization (Back, 1972, p. 139).

We question whether intimacy can ever be a worthy end in itself, just as we might question whether a sense of community—or even happiness—can ever constitute meaningful goals in their own right. Instead, it would seem that feelings of closeness, of relatedness, and of satisfaction are inadequate goals in and of themselves because they lack specific content or substance; it is difficult to indicate what activities, or "means," are necessary if they are to be achieved. Hence there is the possibility that the Encounter model, by abandoning the clearer structure and goals of earlier group models, leaves itself with an insufficient context in which to function. It is precisely along this dimension of context that we see the T-, Tavistock, Theme-centered, and Social work groups as having greater leverage, for in these groups whatever sense of community, intimacy, or even joy that develops is in part an outgrowth of the group's working on its task.

What of the role of intimacy in non-Encounter psychotherapy groups, where the tasks are somewhat more individualized? We would expect intimacy to evolve most naturally in therapy groups when (1) it is not made a distinct end in itself, and (2) when the continuity of the group allows members to communicate at a rate with which they feel comfortable, and to experience the relationships within the group as developing over time and as coincident with their everyday lives. The more the therapy group atmosphere generates expectations, however subtle, of instant communication and instant revelation, the more it is in danger of developing a somewhat dehumanized notion of intimacy. We are not, however, suggesting that the therapy group need exist over a long period of time in order to develop a context appropriate for a genuine sense of intimacy. All that might be required is some degree of *continuity* in time, and an opportunity for members to develop genuine interest in and concern about each other.

We also believe that no patient should be expected to be able to relate closely with whatever constellation of group therapy patients he happens to join. To think that he should be able to be equally intimate with *any* group of peers, even over time, is again to impersonalize intimacy. Therefore, while wanting to switch therapy groups *may* constitute a resistance on the patient's part, it may also signify a quite healthy recognition of, and trust in, his own feelings; hence any such request deserves respectful attention from the therapist and from the group.

Encounter as a Form of Psychotherapy. As we tried to make clear in Chapter 11, the Encounter group encompasses many diverse goals. In its attempt to put the person into closer touch with both others and himself, it is comfortable in embracing psychotherapeutic goals and in having the participant introduce into the here-and-now of the group process some of his painful memories and current problems outside the group. The model emphasizes the degree to which even the healthiest people suffer to some extent from a sense of alienation—from their bodies, from their feelings, and from other people.

Although we are not much happier with a sick-well dichotomy, or with the notion of cure, than are Encounter theorists, we still believe that any meaningful definition of psychotherapy that distinguishes it from education in general must contain certain ingredients or parameters that are not included within the Open Encounter group, not so much because of limitations inherent in the model itself but because of the reduced amount of time given to the leader-therapist in which to work. These parameters are: (1) some investigation on the leader's part of what the patient considers his problems to be, and of the relationship between these problems and his life experiences and overt behavior: (2) a concomitant opportunity for the patient to gain knowledge about the meaning of a particular emotional problem, either in terms of its relationship to his past or how it expresses itself in present behavior; (3) the paradoxical necessity for the patient to acknowledge or *accept* (though not necessarily feel comfortable with) these aspects of himself that he wants to change—this is an important principle underlying several schools of psychotherapy, including psychoanalysis, but it has received its most direct statement in Perls' Gestalt Therapy; and (4) a sustained period of time, during which the patient can experiment with new behaviors in outside living and explore in the continued testing-ground of the sessions whatever success and failures he encounters in doing so.

Again, we wish to emphasize that the need for group therapy to take place over a long period of time, and with greater continuity over time, than is provided for by the Encounter format does not lead us to argue for psychodynamic models in particular or for long-term therapy in general. There is no reason why the kinds of goals that we have presented cannot be met, at least for some patients, over a period of a few months. For example, the Behavioral model, while not oriented toward an investigation of the unconscious and while not necessarily long-term, meets the criteria set forth above. Psychodrama and Gestalt therapy workshops, at least in their time-limited formats, do not satisfy them, and therefore can be criticized from a similar vantage point. However, the more structured format of these latter two models enable the leader to regulate the group-member's contact with his fellow members in a relatively controlled and protective fashion. As a result, there seems to be much less danger than in Encounter that a participant will leave the group feeling that he has been "opened up," via intense and often hostile confrontation from other members, without having had sufficient opportunity to work through or, more fully understand this experience.

What does happen to the Encounter participant who leaves the group feeling stripped of his defenses and with a keen sense that his present life structure, including marriage and career, is essentially hollow? The group, which has surrounded him with a warm, sometimes womb-like sense of security and intimacy, now leaves him to his own resources, which may well prove to be inadequate, and he returns to a home that he may now experience as devoid of genuine love. One obvious answer to this problem lies in the availability of psychotherapy, but there is no means of ensuring that he finds his way to this path. Since all therapy groups will at some point confront patients with painful truths about their lives, the difficulty again lies with the uniquely discontinuous and confronting nature of the Open Encounter, which provides no opportunity for a more gradual testing, absorption, and reintegration of insights. Schutz believes that this issue is adequately dealt with at that point where he informs participants that they are to bear the primary responsibility for what happens to them in the group. What he seems to forget is that the ability to act in one's own emotional interest and to make nonmasochistic decisions is typically an *outcome* of, rather than a precurser to, effective psychotherapy. The Encounter participant, who often acknowledges that he is seriously troubled, would seem to require protection from his self-destructiveness, his emotional fragility, or his genuine ignorance as to what Encounter entails. Mintz' week-end Marathons (see Chapter 11) would seem to make the participant somewhat less vulnerable in these respects, since he frequently is in ongoing psychotherapy at the time that he attends the Marathon; should he not be, he typically resides in metropolitan New York and therefore has Mintz available to him for further consultation and/or treatment should he wish to avail himself of such contacts.

In addition to the time factor there is a leadership factor. Can the leader who has not had specific psychotherapy training properly attempt to lead a group that sets for itself psychotherapeutic goals? We think not, but again this problem need not be inherent within the model itself, since there is no reason why Open Encounter groups cannot be led by group therapists. We, of course, realize that there will always be some exceptionally sensitive and gifted people lacking professional credentials who could be trained to lead groups in a reasonably brief period of time, but in view of the kind of harm that can result from psychotherapeutic incompetence, it seems wiser to err on the side of caution and to insist on some type of appropriate professional certification.

THE CONVERGENCE OF THE MODELS

As we indicated in the Foreword and at various points throughout the book, the various models seem more and more interchangeable, as T-groups move toward Encounter, as Encounter groups embrace psychotherapy goals, as N.T.L. sponsors an increasing number of nominal T-groups dealing with a particular theme—like marriage or family relations—and as an increasing number of leaders, independent of any specifically designated model, run groups focusing on their particular area of competence, be it bioenergetics, communication, body movement, dance, and so on.

As we stated at the outset, while it seems inevitable that the skilled group leader, much like the experienced psychotherapist, will invariably arrive at a somewhat eclectic orientation wherein he comfortably and idiosyncratically combines features of the several theoretical traditions to which he has been exposed, the novice is probably best trained by being intensively and systematically exposed to one or more distinctive group models. This way he will come to have a thorough understanding of at least one model, including its avowed purpose, its conceptual background, and the intellectual-historical *zeitgeist* out of which it grew. Once he decides to incorporate innovations into his approach, he will be better informed as to what parameters he is departing from and will hopefully be more specific and disciplined in thinking through his rationale for such deviations.

Each of the models is designed to accomplish some purposes better than others. For example, within the Growth and Development category, T- and Tavistock settings are best suited for systematic learning about group processes, especially as they relate to back-home jobs within complex or organizational structures, whereas the Theme-centered method is more appropriate for leading various task and community groups, such as staff and committee meetings, and for experiential learning in the classroom or seminar. And, as we indicated above, we believe it is important for a model—and, by implication, its leader—to make a clearcut differentiation between psychotherapy goals and growth and development goals.

We began initial planning for this book with the hypothesis that the distinctions among the various group models would become increasingly blurred as time progressed. Nothing that we have witnessed since has convinced us otherwise, and an understanding of the historical, conceptual, and methodological issues underlying the distinctions among the models becomes more essential than ever. Therefore we want to conclude by reiterating the cautionary plea originally offered in our Foreword: let us not permit the vagaries of history, a misguided eclecticism, and the similarities that do genuinely exist among the models, to lead us to a point where their distinctive differences become either neglected or forgotten.

References

Asch, S. 1952. Effects of group pressure upon the modification and distortion of judgments. In G. E. Swanson, T. M. Newcomb, and E. L. Hartley, eds. *Readings in social psychology* (2nd ed.). New York: Holt, Rinehart & Winston. pp. 2-11.

Back, K. 1972. *Beyond words.* New York: Russell Sage Foundation.

Burton, A. 1969. *Encounter.* San Francisco: Jossey-Bass.

Denes-Radomisli, M. 1971. Gestalt group therapy: sense in sensitivity, 1971, Unpublished Paper delivered at a conference on Group Process Today, Adelphi University Postdoctoral Program in Psychotherapy, 1971.

Durkin, H. 1972. Analytic group therapy and general systems theory. In C. J. Sager and H. S. Kaplan, eds. *Progress in group and family therapy.* New York: Brunner/Mazel. pp. 9-17.

Garvin, C. D. and Glasser, P. H. 1971. Social group work: the preventive and rehabilitative approach. *Encyclopedia of social work,* vol. 2. New York: National Association of Social Workers. pp. 1263-1273.

Hovland, C., Janis, I. L., and Kelley, H. H. 1953. *Communication and Persuasion.* New Haven: Yale University Press.

Klein, E. B. and Astrachan, B. M. 1969. Learning in groups, Unpublished paper, 1969.

Lawrence, H. and Sundel, M. 1972. Behavior modification in adult groups. *Social Work,* 1972. *17:* 34-43.

Liff, Z. 1970. The group encounter movement and group psychotherapy. *Newsletter:* Eastern Group Psychotherapy Society, May 1970: 14-16.

Papell, C. 1972. Sensitivity-training: relevance for social work education. *Journal of Education for Social Work,* 1972, *8:* 42-45.

Putney, S. and Putney, G. J. 1966. *The adjusted american.* New York: Harper Colophon.

Rice, A. K. 1965. *Learning for leadership.* London: Tavistock Publications.

Rose, S. D. 1967. A behavioral approach to group treatment of children. In E. J. Thomas, ed. *The socio-behavioral approach and applications to social work.* New York: Council on Social Work Education. pp. 39-54.

———. 1969. A behavioral approach to the group treatment of parents. *Social Work,* 1969. *14:* 21-29.

———. 1972. *Treating children in groups.* San Francisco: Jossey-Bass.

Schutz, W. 1967. *Joy.* New York: Grove Press.

———. 1971. *Here comes everybody.* New York: Harper and Row.

Watts, A. W. 1961. *Psychotherapy east and west.* New York: Pantheon.

Wolf, A. and Schwartz, E. K. 1962. *Psychoanalysis in groups.* New York: Grune and Stratton.

Index